W9-BIL-030

RUN, BULLET, RUN

THE RISE, FALL, AND RECOVERY OF BOB HAYES

HARPER & ROW, PUBLISHERS, NEW YORK
Grand Rapids, Philadelphia, St. Louis, San Francisco
London, Singapore, Sydney, Tokyo, Toronto

1817

RUN, BULLET, RUN

BOB HAYES
with Robert Pack

FIRST EDITION

Designed by Helene Berinsky

Library of Congress Cataloging-in-Publication Data
Hayes, Bob, 1942–
  Run, bullet, run: the rise, fall, and recovery of Bob Hayes/Bob Hayes with Robert Pack.—
1st ed.
    p. cm.
  ISBN 0-06-018200-8
  1. Hayes, Bob, 1942– . 2. Football players—United States—Biography. 3. Athletes—
United States—Drug use. I. Pack, Robert, 1942– . II. Title.
GV939.H34A3 1990
796.332'092—dc20
[B]   89-46096

---

90 91 92 93 94 NK/HC 10 9 8 7 6 5 4 3 2 1

CONTENTS

Illustrations follow page 182.

ACKNOWLEDGMENTS

The authors would like to thank for their help their agents, Mel Berger and Frank Weimann; Jethro Pugh; Judy Eisen; Caleb Mason and Peter Ackroyd of Salem House; Wendy Almeleh, the copyeditor; and most of all, our editor, Daniel Bial.

RUN, BULLET, RUN

1

TOKYO GOLD

All I could think of was the pain. And then a second thought flashed through my mind, "There goes the Olympics."

I had broken world records in almost every sprint there was: 100 yards—the glamour event in the United States—plus the 60, the 70, and the 100 meters; the 200 meters on a straightaway; and as part of a relay team. I had won fifty-three races in a row. I was the latest sprinter to hold the title, "The World's Fastest Human." And I was the odds-on favorite to win the gold medal in the 100 meters at the Olympics in Tokyo. But no, on the hot and steamy day of June 27, 1964, fewer than four months before the Olympics were to begin and a week before the U.S. Olympic trials in New York, I had the feeling that the national championships of the Amateur Athletic Union (AAU) at Rutgers University in New Brunswick, New Jersey, had ended my lifelong Olympic dream.

The track at the Rutgers football stadium was a nightmare. It was made of two-thirds crushed brick and one-third cinder, a composition that was supposed to be the fastest there was at the time. The trouble was that the track had been laid just a few weeks before the AAU meet, and it was still so loose that you felt like you were running on puffs of smoke. Besides that, the curve at the end of the stadium began just past the 100-meter finish line, which left me with two choices:

- I could go around the curve at almost full speed, which would be difficult for me. Sprinters traditionally are small, slender guys (forget any pictures you've seen of Ben Johnson; his body came out of a

1

bottle). But I was a football player who just happened to have world-class speed, and I looked like a football player. Coaches, reporters, and all kinds of track experts commented throughout my track career that I looked out of place on the track because of my muscular build and my big butt, which I carried high coming out of the starting blocks, instead of low, the way sprinters are supposed to. Bud Winter, the famous track coach at San Jose State, who developed sprinters like John Carlos and Tommie Smith, once observed that I ran like I "was pounding grapes into wine," and John Underwood, who covered track for *Sports Illustrated*, wrote that "Hayes does not run a race so much as he appears to beat it to death." My "style," if you want to call it that, was to run knock-kneed and pigeon-toed, just like Jackie Robinson, and I often spiked myself when I ran. As a result of my build and my form, I always had trouble running around curves, and whenever I ran a relay, I would run the leg that was either entirely on the straightaway or had as little curve as possible.

▪ Or I could just keep running straight ahead and plow full force into the wall at the base of the stands where the track ended.

Neither alternative appealed much to me. But I stopped worrying about how to finish the race 60 meters or so down the track, when I went into high gear and felt a twinge behind my left thigh. It hurt enough to let me know that what all runners fear had happened: I had done serious damage to my hamstring muscle. I eased up a little, but I was still far enough ahead of the field to burst through the tape in first place with a clocking of 10.3, three-tenths of a second off the world record. Charlie Greene, a freshman at the University of Nebraska, was about a yard behind me, followed by Bernie Rivers from the University of New Mexico, Gerry Ashworth from Dartmouth, and Paul Drayton and Mel Pender, both formerly of Villanova.

Not wanting to hit the wall, I stumbled around the curve. It was obvious that I was hurt, and Vito Recine, the AAU trainer, helped me into the locker room. Vito made me lie face down on a training table and began to examine the back of my leg with his hands. With every minute that passed, the pain got worse, and I could feel something wet running down the *inside* of my leg. I wasn't a doctor, and I had never had a serious injury before, but I knew enough to worry that blood from a muscle tear was trickling down my leg. As soon as he heard of my injury, George Thompson, the head trainer at my school, Florida A & M University, flew to New York. George, Vito, two trainers at New York University who examined me a few days later, and Dave White, the head trainer at the University of Miami, who was a friend of mine and checked me out when I got back down to Florida, all confirmed my own diagnosis: a torn hamstring. The general consensus was that I should stay off my leg and pray that it would heal as soon as possible. Which is what I did.

The first trials for the 1964 U.S. Olympic team were held over the Fourth of July weekend at Randalls Island in New York. The winners were assured of a place on the American team, and the next five finishers at Randalls Island would compete for the remaining two places in each event at a second set of trials in Los Angeles on September 12 and 13, just a few weeks before the games began. At first, I had hopes of being able to run at Randalls Island, but by the second or third day after my injury, I could hardly get out of bed. My only chance of making the team was for a panel of coaches to give me a waiver to bypass the trials at Randalls Island and go straight to the trials in Los Angeles; without a waiver, I wouldn't be able to compete even in the second trials.

I made a point of going to the meet at Randalls Island—I even wore my sweats and carried a bag with my spikes in it, as if there was a chance in a million that I could run—just to let the coaches, who held my fate in their hands, know how much I cared. But I sat in the stands and watched as Trenton Jackson from the University of Illinois (who later had a short stint as a wide receiver with the Eagles and the Redskins) finished first in the 100 meters to clinch one spot on the Olympic squad. Behind him were Gerry Ashworth and Charlie Greene, who pulled up lame with a hamstring injury like mine. Charlie's injury was so bad that he missed out on the Olympics in 1964, although he came back to make the team and win a bronze medal in Mexico City in 1968.

The trials lasted two days, and it was at the end of the second day that the coaches got together to decide who would get an exemption and be able to try out for the team in Los Angeles. As they went into their meeting, I stood by the door to make my final plea and tell them that I would be in tip-top shape by the time of the second trials two months later. Bob Giegengack of Yale was the head track coach of our Olympic squad that year, with Eddie Hurt of Morgan State as his top assistant. I felt a little better knowing that Eddie would be arguing my case, since he was the black coach of an all-black college team and was a good friend of my football coach at Florida A & M, Jake Gaither. And Eddie whispered to me as he entered the meeting, "Don't worry; you're going to L.A." Still, I thought that meeting would never end. The coaches had several other cases to discuss in addition to mine, but they finally broke up after an hour or so. Giegengack and Hurt came over and took me by the arm, one on each side. As we walked along, they asked me how I felt, made small talk, and drove me crazy. Finally, Giegengack said, "We voted to advance you to Los Angeles, Bob."

So I was still alive.

By mid-July, a couple of weeks or so after my injury, I had improved enough to start jogging a mile or two at a time. The U.S. track team was scheduled for the annual meet against the Russians on July 25 and 26 in Los Angeles, and our coaches sent me an airline ticket, hoping that I would be able to compete. As soon as I got to Los Angeles, a few days before the meet, and tried a few easy starts, I knew there was no way I could run against the Russians. Although I was scratched from the meet, my team-mates voted me the captain, and I carried the American flag into the Los Angeles Memorial Coliseum, which was a tremendous thrill.

Robert F. Kennedy was there that day, and he walked up to me and said, "I'm proud of you." I answered, "Senator Kennedy, I'm proud of being an American and I will carry this flag as tall and proud as you would." That was the only time I ever met Kennedy. Four years later, when he was running for president, Kennedy asked me to campaign for him at a rally in Los Angeles, where he was going to announce, "I've got the fastest man in the world on my team." I got tied up on business in Dallas, so I called Rosey Grier, the former National Football League (NFL) star who was one of Kennedy's aides, and told him I would meet them at their next stop, Chicago. I went home and went to sleep. When I woke up, I turned on the television and saw Rosey and the rest of the entourage at the hospital, where Kennedy had been taken after being shot by Sirhan Sirhan.

At the meet between our team and the Russians, I had to sit once again and watch as others ran in my place. Bernie Rivers, who was supposed to run the 100 with me, was injured, too. So Henry Carr of Arizona State, whose specialty was the 200 meters, and John Moon of Tennessee State replaced Rivers and me. They finished 1–2, and Henry also won the 200 meters the next day. I got more and more frustrated. Would I be ready in time?

. . .

When I arrived in Los Angeles for the final trials in mid-September, I had no idea what to expect. During the summer I had increased my jogging to several miles a day, worked out some with the Florida A & M football team, and run sprints without going all out. But I hadn't tried to go full speed in nearly three months, since I got hurt. And my lack of activity had resulted in my gaining almost ten pounds by the time of the second trials. I was so worried and so excited the night before the trials that I couldn't sleep. The finalists for the U.S. team were staying in dorms at USC, right next to a freeway. There was a lot of noise from all the traffic, but that wasn't keeping me awake. Everyone expected me to bring home a gold medal, and if my leg didn't hold up the next day or if I slipped or if any one of a hundred other things went wrong, I wouldn't even make the team. The thousands of miles I had run in training, all the practice starts, all the other races over the years, the records I had set, and the fame I had achieved—none of them would mean a thing. Those trials were the most pressure I've ever had, more than any football game I ever played in, more than the Olympics themselves.

Ralph Boston, who had won the gold medal in the long jump at the 1960 Olympics in Rome and was favored this year, too, was my best friend on the track circuit. Ralph had gone to Tennessee State, an all-black school that was one of Florida A & M's main rivals in football and track, and we regarded each other as home boys. We had hung out together when we traveled through Europe as part of the American team in 1962 and 1963 and had become very close. He and I were always riding each other, but that night Ralph did everything he could to put me at ease. Instead of going to bed early the way he usually did, he came to my room and stayed up with me when he saw that I couldn't sleep. We talked for a long time with the lights off, just whiling the night away.

Early the next morning we went to the dining hall in the dormitory and had some breakfast. My race wasn't until about 2 P.M., so I put on my sweat suit, went out, and walked a couple of miles to try to loosen up my leg. As the time for my race approached, I came back to the dormitory, put on my running outfit, and packed my shoes and an extra pair of shorts and an extra jockstrap into my gym bag. I always carried an extra pair of shorts after my experience running in the rain in Göteborg, Sweden. While standing at the starting line before that race, I pulled my sweats down, and my shorts came down all the way to my ankles. I stood there in my jockstrap and my jersey—everybody was cracking up—and got all wet and I had to run in the wet shorts. I learned back at Matthew Gilbert High School in Jacksonville, Florida, that you never know when a jockstrap may pop and you may need another one. A basketball player, a high school teammate of mine, had his jockstrap pop and he had to play the whole game with his jockstrap hanging from under his shorts. It was extremely embarrassing to him, and I never wanted that to happen to me.

All set to go to the coliseum, I hopped on an elevator for the first floor. What else could possibly happen to me? Well, the elevator got stuck between floors. Al Oerter and Jay Silvester, two discus throwers, and shot-putter Dallas Long were on it with me. The three of them must have weighed close to 900 pounds, which is probably what caused the elevator to get stuck. We were held up for eight or nine minutes, and I was really panicking. The other guys finally forced the doors open about three feet above one floor. I leaped out of the elevator and hurried downstairs. I had missed my ride, so I started jogging toward the coliseum. My muscles didn't tighten up, but my brain did. I really wanted to get over there; I was one of those guys who liked to be early for my event. I had to cross Figueroa Street, a major highway, to get to the coliseum. The traffic was roaring down Figueroa, and I was ducking and dodging through those cars like I was already playing for the Cowboys and Dick Butkus was chasing me. Folks don't stop in Los Angeles just to let a guy cross the street.

The main thing on my mind, though, was my leg. The leg felt good, but the only way I was going to find out if it would hold up was to run on it. And I hadn't wanted to go all out until then. I figured if there was only one race in my leg at that time, let me use it up in the trials. Then, if I made the team and pulled the muscle again, maybe it would heal in time for the Olympics. If not, someone else could take my place over there.

As I got ready to run, I sized up my opposition. The other guys in the race were Trenton Jackson, Gerry Ashworth, Darel Newman from Fresno State, Mel Pender, and Charlie Greene. I wasn't so worried about any of them; I had beaten them all many times before, and, of course, Greene was running with a bad leg. It wasn't so much me against them as it was me against me—with all the chips on the line.

When the gun sounded, I didn't come off with the full thrust from the starting blocks like I usually did. Instead, I gradually built up my speed and stayed with the pack. After about 40 yards, I pulled away from the other guys. I decided not to use my normal acceleration into super-high, or my "scat-gear," as Jake Gaither called it. Even so, I finished first, beating Trenton Jackson by about 2 yards and running a 10.1-second race, which tied the American record held by me and several others and was only one-tenth of a second off the world record. Pender was the third qualifier, behind Jackson, with Ashworth finishing fourth, to grab a spot on the 400-meter relay team, along with Jackson, Pender, and me. Newman and Greene finished fifth and sixth and were out of luck.

A week before I got hurt in June, I ran in the track championships of the National Collegiate Athletic Association (NCAA) in Eugene, Oregon, where I won the 200-meter race, which qualified me to try out for the Olympic team in that event, too. The 200-meter qualifying event was the day after the 100-meter event, and Bob Giegengack and Eddie Hurt tried to talk me out of running in it, for fear that I would reinjure my leg. But there was just the final in the 200 and no heats—the same as in the 100 at the trials—and my leg felt so good after the 100 it was like I had never been hurt. So I went ahead and ran the 200, finishing third behind Paul Drayton and Richard Stebbins of Grambling and a yard or two ahead of Henry Carr, who was fourth. But since Henry had won at Randalls Island and had shown in this race in Los Angeles that he was still in good form, he retained his place on the team, and I was bumped out of a spot in the 200-meter race. Otherwise, I would have had a shot at three gold medals.

To this day I thank my lucky stars that I made the Olympic team. If they'd had the system then that they have now, in which you get only one chance, I wouldn't have made it. If everything had depended on the Randalls Island trials, I probably would have tried to go that day, but I could hardly walk, much less run, and I doubt that I would have finished at all, much less in the top three. The classic example of what's wrong with holding a single trial occurred in 1988. Greg Foster, the super hurdler, broke his arm two and a half weeks before the 1988 Olympic trials. He tried to run anyway with his arm in a cast—talk about guts—and made it as far as the semifinals. If they had had a second set of trials later, Greg would have had a chance to make the U.S. team, which would have been stronger with him on it. Considering what happened between the second Olympic trials in Los Angeles and the 100-meter finals in Tokyo, we probably would have been shut out in the 100-meter hurdles in 1964 if they hadn't given me a second chance.

After the trials in Los Angeles, our next stop was at California Polytechnic Institute in San Luis Obispo, where the track team stayed while we held our final training before our departure for Tokyo. Aside from conditioning, we had a number of things we had to do before we left, and one of them was to get shots to protect us from various diseases. I had competed abroad many times in the previous two years, primarily in Europe, and I'd had to take shots before each trip, but I had never experienced anything like this. Each member of the Olympic team was required to get about fifteen shots (I was deathly afraid of needles until I got older and had to take shots for pain or have a needle stuck in my knee all the time to drain it so I could play pro football). I told the doctors for the Olympic team that I didn't know we had to take all these shots to go to Tokyo; I thought I was going to Tokyo just to run, not for some kind of medical experiment. But the rule was simple: no shots, no go.

That's when I decided to be smart. Instead of having the doctors stick me fifteen times in one arm, I told them to give me eight shots in one arm and seven in the other arm. Big mistake! Both of my arms were so swollen and sore that I couldn't use my hands and arms to get out of my bed the next morning. Most of the guys took all the shots in one arm, so they could still use the other one. I walked around with both of my arms hanging down by my sides, and I could hardly move, let alone train. It was about three days before I could get a normal arm pump going again in my workouts. And it took me five hours, far longer than anyone else, to get my shots, because I had to work up my nerve before each one. I started at 8 P.M., and the doctors didn't get finished jabbing me until 1 A.M.

We would have plenty of reason to feel the pressure once we reached Tokyo, but while we were in training camp, everyone was real loose. Mel Zahn, a friend who lived in Los Angeles, lent me an old Chevy while I was in California. The car was so run down that it didn't even have a real front seat, just some wooden boards to sit on, and Mel didn't mind if the other guys drove it. Mel Pender always was a cheapskate, went somewhere in the car one day and didn't put any gas in it. That night, a bunch of us went out; as we were driving up the hill toward our dorm, we ran out of gas. We started to jog the rest of the way to our dorm, but we had gone only about 50 yards when we heard a coyote howling. I ran back to the car, got in, locked the doors, rolled the windows up, and stayed in the car for a couple of hours until some officials from the U.S. team came and gave me a ride in another car. I had seen coyotes on television and thought they would eat anything when they were hungry. And I wasn't the only one. Ralph Boston and Mel Pender were right on my tail. Ulis Williams, who ran the 400, and Henry Carr ran up the hill; they were from the West and weren't afraid of coyotes. We were so pissed at Pender that we wouldn't let him have the keys again.

The best thing about the training period was getting our uniforms— white pants for the men and white skirts for the women; red and blue blazers; white buck shoes; and, because the president of the United States, Lyndon B. Johnson, was a Texan and our team had a Western theme, cowboy hats. We also got red, white, and blue sweat suits with "USA" on them; and official team luggage—three-piece sets in dark blue with red trimming printed with our team logo; team watches from Timex; team pens, pencils, and stationery; team pins to wear and to exchange with athletes from other nations; and official team toilet articles, which included our USA Olympic team suntan oil—just what I needed. When I, along with some of my best friends—Ralph Boston, Ulis Williams, and Henry Carr—opened up our packages, we went crazy when we saw the suntan lotion. I asked Ralph what he was going to do with his and he said, "Damned if I'm going to give it to some white boy." Ulis and Henry asked Ralph if he was going to use it himself and he answered, "Shit, yes! I'm gonna go out by the pool and put this here oil on and get me a tan. I bet the chicks'll like that."

During our two weeks of training in southern California, we also played tourist, with team excursions to Disneyland, a UCLA–Penn State football game at the coliseum, and other outings. In those days, the United States was still the dominant nation in sports, and everywhere we went we were treated like about-to-be conquering heroes, with people applauding, bands playing, standing ovations, you name it. When we went to Los Angeles International Airport to catch our flight to Tokyo, the ticket agents, pilots, stewardesses, skycaps, ground crews, and the other passengers cheered us on, shaking our hands, calling out encouragement, and asking for autographs. When we went onto the tarmac to board our flight, we found a marching band and another huge crowd, with signs, American flags, and more cheers. That was one of the many times throughout my Olympic experience that chills ran down my spine. And I mean good chills.

My destination was Tokyo! My mission was Gold!

The flight to Japan, via Anchorage, Alaska, took about twelve hours, and I was so excited that I could hardly sleep. When we finally landed at about 5:30 A.M. Tokyo time, a funny thing happened: none of the American Olympic officials was on hand to greet us. Our own people thought we were coming in several hours later, but the press had the time right; reporters and film crews were everywhere.

Our Japanese hosts didn't miss a trick. You have to remember, this was the first time the Olympic Games had been held in the Orient, and, although 1964 seems long ago, it was only nineteen years after the end of World War II. This was Japan's first chance to show off its recovery to the world, and our Japanese hosts ran everything with military precision, from the moment we landed until the moment we left for home. For openers, they not only had arranged a press conference when we landed, they had also set up directors' chairs for the athletes right on the runway. The stars had their names on the chairs, and when I saw the one with "Hayes" on it, I got another lump in my throat. Not that it kept me from talking; hardly anything ever shut *me* up.

One of the greatest things about the Olympics was that my mom was going to be there. My mom had worked all her life as a maid, and the only places she had been outside Florida were Georgia, South Carolina, and New York. She had never even been on an airplane before. Of course, there was no way that she could afford to travel all the way to Tokyo. I had received under-the-table payments totaling $40,000 or so during my track career, but people would have started asking questions if I, a poor boy from the ghetto, suddenly had enough money to fly my mother halfway around the world and put her up in a nice hotel. Several business and civic leaders in Jacksonville saved the day, though. They started a bank account to pay for her trip. Dozens of people contributed to the "Robert Hayes' Mother's Fund," as did the city of Jacksonville; Matthew Gilbert High School, my old school, and our arch-rival, New Stanton High School, and several other high schools I had competed against; and companies like Coca-Cola and Winn-Dixie supermarkets. The fund raised $1,608, and my mother was on her way for what she later called "the happiest time of my life." There were still a lot of problems between blacks and whites in those days, especially down South, but folks in my hometown put race aside, worked together, and made sure my mother could be with me. That's the kind of thing you never forget.

Like I said, my mother didn't have much experience traveling. The first leg of her flight was from Jacksonville to Los Angeles, and Mary Thompson, Ralph Boston's girlfriend, who taught school in Los Angeles, met my mother at the airport for the stopover. My mother landed in Los Angeles with ten suitcases, and Mary had to take her back to her apartment, unpack everything, and fit what she could into three suitcases. Mary kept the rest of my mother's things at her place until Mom got back from Japan.

My mother told me she was arriving on a Sunday, but it was really a Monday because of the time difference. When I went to the airport Sunday night, my mother wasn't there. All I could think was, "Oh, my

God, this is my mother's first trip in an airplane, she's flying all this distance, and something happened." The next day, a Japanese newspaper reporter named Keiko, who was showing me around and looking out for me in exchange for getting the exclusive Japanese rights to my story, came rushing up to me in the Olympic Village and told me my mother was at the airport. My mother had no idea how to contact me in the Olympic Village, so she just sat at the airport and waited for about three hours until somebody found out who she was and told Keiko, who tracked me down. When I finally got to the airport, there was my mother, sitting in a chair, just as calm as she could be. Nothing fazed her. She knew I'd show up sooner or later.

The Japanese did everything they could to be perfect hosts to the six thousand athletes from nearly one hundred nations who competed in the 1964 Olympics. They told the locals not to urinate in the streets during the Olympics and not to go out in public in their underwear. They kept their "working girls" away from the Olympic Village and warned the more innocent Japanese lovelies that whenever one of us asked them for a date, they should say to themselves, "Is this man actually offering me an honorable proposition or is he only interested in deceiving me so he can enjoy me as his Tokyo wife while he is here?" Not too many of us were interested in "Tokyo wives" anyway, at least not until our events were over.

The opening ceremonies, in front of 76,000 spectators, were every bit as majestic as I had dreamed. The athletes filed into the stadium, with the Greek team first, followed by the other nations in alphabetical order. A twenty-one gun salute was fired when Emperor Hirohito and his wife took their places, and the emperor gave the magical command, "Let the games begin." Then a Japanese torchbearer carried the Olympic torch into the stadium on the last leg of its trip from Greece and lit the Olympic flame at the top of the stadium, and a Japanese athlete stood in front of the imperial box, raised his hand, and took the Olympic oath on behalf of all six thousand of us. The only thing that marred the opening ceremony was the release of eight thousand doves from their cages. It was then that a lot of us on the American team were thankful we had big cowboy hats as part of our uniforms, especially when we saw athletes from many of the other countries running their fingers through their hair in disgust. I think the water pressure in Tokyo's municipal water system must have dropped a ton as soon as all the athletes got back to their rooms.

The Japanese couldn't do anything about the weather—it rained most of the time we were there—but they did pass out free bamboo umbrellas. The trouble was that those umbrellas weren't quite as well made as the Japanese products that have swamped our country in recent years, and they fell apart as soon as heavy rain started hitting them. You would see them lying all over the Olympic Village. The village itself was nice enough, and the food was excellent. We could have anything we wanted to eat, American- or Japanese-style, whenever we wanted it, and as much of it as we wanted. The Japanese even provided hundreds of bicycles that were left throughout the village; whenever we needed to go somewhere within the village, we would grab the nearest bike, ride it wherever we were going, and leave it for someone else. Unfortunately, those bikes were built for the Japanese, who were much smaller than the athletes from the United States and many other nations. A lot of the bikes fell apart under our weight, but Joe Frazier and I (Ralph Boston; Joe; Theron Lewis, a member of our 1,600-meter relay team; and I shared a suite in the Olympic Village) witnessed the best bicycle demolition of all. We were walking through the village one day, when we spotted the Russian basketball center, Yan Kruminsh, trying to ride one of the bikes. Kruminsh was seven feet two and weighed nearly three hundred pounds—about the size of Andre the Giant, the "professional" wrestler that George Allen once tried to sign for the Redskins, and he was just about as coordinated as Andre. When someone cut in front of Kruminsh, he swerved suddenly, losing control of the bike, falling on top of it, and crushing it. Joe and I nearly died laughing. I said to Joe, "You think you can beat that guy in boxing?" And Joe answered, "If he puts on a pair of gloves, Bobby, I'll beat him to death. I can't believe this guy is that awkward. Our basketball team is going to beat the shit out of them if he's on their team."

Joe obviously knew something about basketball because our team won the gold medal from the Russians, beating them in the championship game, 73 to 59. The American fans and the press had been a little worried about how the U.S. basketball team would do that year because it didn't have stars like Oscar Robertson, Jerry West, and Jerry Lucas, who were on the 1960 squad. But Bill Bradley, Walt Hazzard, Jumpin' Joe Caldwell, Lucious Jackson, Larry Brown, and the rest did just fine. I wish I could have seen the final game, but the basketball arena held only four thousand spectators, and tickets were impossible to get. The only one of my friends who saw the game was Paul Drayton, who snuck into the arena using Walt Hazzard's pass and said later that "the Japanese think all us blacks look alike."

In general, though, everyone connected with the games gave special treatment to the American team. Everywhere we went in the Olympic Village, the other athletes watched us and tried to see what we were doing so they could copy us. The first time we practiced, on September 30, the day after we landed in Tokyo, two thousand athletes from other countries were on hand for our workout. They seemed to be awed and intimidated by the U.S. team. On my way to practice, sprinters from all over the world followed me, stared at me, and sized me up, watching me work out step for step, studying my arm pump, my techniques, how I got down in the starting block—everything.

I got an eyeful myself during one of the practice sessions. I noticed a swarthy little guy about five feet seven working on his starts, and he looked real fast. I invited him to try some starts with me, Mel Pender, and Henry Carr. We would start, accelerate, and pull up after about fifty yards, and this guy stayed close to me every time. I had no idea who he was, and even though he looked fast, I was confident I could beat him without too much trouble. I always felt that way about runners who were shorter than me. Well, the next day I picked up the newspaper that was printed daily in the Olympic Village, and I found out real quick who the guy was. The Cuban track coach was accusing me of trying to intimidate his star— Enrique Figuerola—who was considered my main competition for the gold medal. Figuerola had finished fourth in the 100-meter race at the 1960 Olympics, but he was only a yard or so behind Armin Hary, of Germany, who won the gold medal in Rome.*

You have every opportunity to get uptight when you're in the Olympics, especially when everyone expects you to win. Coming into the Olympics, I had finished first in the finals of forty-eight consecutive races at 100 yards or 100 meters. Everyone considered me the fastest sprinter in the world, but that title really wouldn't mean anything until I had the gold medal to prove it. That's why they hold the Olympics every four years, to prove who is the best.

Coach Bob Giegengack did everything he could to ease the pressure. He had the perfect attitude: He was real loose. Dressed in khaki pants, an open-necked shirt, and a cap, he always had a Camel cigarette sticking out the side of his mouth. And he didn't try to mess with our techniques. He knew that at that late date all he could do was screw us up. He told us that his philosophy was, "You guys have your training schedule, you have your starting times; I'm just here to make sure everything goes

---

*East and West Germany fielded a combined Olympic team through 1964. The 1968 games marked the first time each country had its own team.

smoothly. All I am is an overseer." It was nothing like the Russ Rogers–Carl Lewis situation at Seoul in 1988. In Tokyo we didn't have the controversy that the U.S. team experienced in so many other Olympics. I was there for one purpose: to win. We knew that we had our best guys running for us. There wasn't any ego inflation or jealousy or any of that. All we wanted to do was get the best team on the track and run, and that's what we did.

Aside from the Olympics, a lot of things were going on around the world to distract us while we were in Tokyo. The Chinese exploded their first nuclear bomb, the Johnson–Goldwater race was going hot and heavy back home, Martin Luther King, Jr., was awarded the Nobel Peace Prize, and Nikita Khrushchev was kicked out of power in Russia. I was sitting around the Olympic Village with Ralph Boston, Joe Frazier, Al Oerter, and some others when the news about Khrushchev came through. Suddenly, a bunch of reporters saw us and started directing questions at me: "Bob Hayes, Nikita Khrushchev has just been ousted as Soviet premier. What do you think?" I said, "I'm just going to answer your question once. I'm here to win a gold medal and not to talk about politics." I've been exposed to some awfully stupid questions in my time, but that was probably the dumbest. What did a twenty-one-year-old kid who was trying to win a gold medal at the Olympics know about what was happening in the Soviet Union? I mean, if the experts in the CIA couldn't see Khrushchev's downfall coming, what was I supposed to know about it?

In 1964, two German companies, Adidas and Puma, made the best track shoes in the world. Most world-class runners knew the history of the two companies. Before World War II, two brothers, Adolf and Rudolf Dassler, started manufacturing track shoes in a little town in Germany, calling their company Adidas. After the war they had a big argument and never spoke to each other again. Adolf Dassler kept Adidas, and Rudolf started Puma right in the same little town. By 1964 they were fighting a worldwide battle, and just outside the National Stadium in Tokyo, where track and other major events were held, Adidas and Puma had tents, where they displayed their shoes and tried to attract attention. Horst Dassler, Adolf's son, was running the Adidas operation, and Armin Hary, whose track career ended soon after the 1960 Olympics when his knee was badly injured in a car crash, was in charge of the Puma tent.

I won't say that Horst was a jock sniffer, but he was the kind of guy who knew everyone in the world of track and he liked to do favors for all the top athletes. I was browsing through his tent one afternoon, a week or so before I would run the 100-meter race, when he walked over to me.

"You want anything, Bobby, it's yours."

"Thank you, Horst," I answered, "but I have all the shoes I need."

"You can never have too many pairs of running shoes, Bobby. What looks good?"

"No, no, I already have too many shoes."

"Well, Bobby, what kind of shoes are you going to run your race in?"

After my experience with under-the-table payments, I knew when I had a fish on the line, so I told Horst I hadn't decided. The truth was, I thought Adidas made the best shoe and I was planning all along to wear Adidas. The Adidas 100 was a very nice-looking and comfortable shoe, made of blue suede with Adidas in white letters on the side and a plastic sole. I loved the Adidas 100. But, of course, Horst didn't know that.

"You know, Bobby," he continued, "if you run in my shoes, I would be quite grateful."

"If yours are the best for me, Horst, those are the ones I'll be wearing."

"Wear mine, and you'll never have to buy another pair of running shoes as long as you live," he said with a wink.

"Thanks, Horst, I'll think about it," I told him. Then I walked out of his tent and made sure he saw me walking over to the Puma tent. Armin Hary must have seen me coming from the Adidas display because he grabbed me right away and we went through the same act.

"You've come to the right place, Bobby. Run in my shoe, and I'll make it worth your while."

"What do you mean, Armin?"

"I'll pay you two thousand dollars in American money to wear Puma when you run."

"Even if I lose?"

"There's no way you're going to lose, Bobby. I'm not sorry I'm hurt, so I won't have to run against you. Nobody can beat the great Bob Hayes."

"Thank you, Armin. Let me think it over."

Horst made a point of running into me the next day, and he asked me right away how much Armin had offered me. When I told him $2,000, Horst said I should be insulted at such a low offer and raised the ante to $3,000. That went on for several days, with Horst and Armin bumping each other up by $500 or $1,000 at a time. When I finally told Horst that Armin had offered me $6,000 and that I had my eye on some beautiful handmade silk suits that a custom tailor in the Olympic Village was making for the athletes for $100 apiece, Horst agreed to pay me $7,800 cash and another $1,100 cash to buy eleven suits. Horst also promised to give me $400 for each of the four girls on our 400-meter relay team. All that was for wearing the shoes I had been planning to run in all along, so I thought it was a pretty good deal. When I told Armin I was going to wear Adidas, he understood; most of the athletes preferred Adidas, and I think Armin knew he never had much chance of getting me. Even if he had offered me a lot more money than Horst did, I probably would have worn Adidas because I didn't want to blow my chance to win a gold medal because of the shoes I wore.

As my big moment approached, an unknown American long-distance runner gave inspiration to all the Americans. In the 10,000-meter run, Ron Clarke of New Zealand, the world-record holder, and Pyotr Bolotnikov of Russia, who had won the gold medal in 1960, were the favorites. Our best hope was a scrawny eighteen-year-old kid from Spokane, Washington, named Gerry Lindgren. Our second-fastest man in the 10,000, Billy Mills, didn't even have a time fast enough to qualify for the Olympics, so a special race was held for him at our second trials in Los Angeles. A lot of us ran around on the infield, just inside the track at the coliseum, pushing him to run fast enough to go to Tokyo, and he made it. Gerry Lindgren hurt his ankle before the 10,000 meters in Tokyo, and it looked like we had no chance for a medal, but Billy came out of nowhere to beat Mohamed Gammoudi of Tunisia and Clarke in the last few yards. Billy, who was part Sioux Indian and became known as "The Running Brave," not only finished first, but his gold medal was the first the United States had won in a distance event since 1908. I watched Billy win the 10,000, the greatest race I ever saw. After that the rest of us were sky-high, we all felt we could win. Thanks to Billy Mills. Billy and I were inducted together into the National Track and Field Hall of Fame in 1976, and just the sight of him gave me the same thrill I felt when I watched him win the gold medal.

Another teammate I was pulling for was Fred Hansen, a pole vaulter from Rice. Some of the white guys on our team were prejudiced, but not Fred. A bunch of us, both black and white athletes, had been sitting in the stands watching some of the events at the final trials in Los Angeles and Fred was eating a popsicle. He had to go to the bathroom, so he said, "Here, Bob, hold this popsicle. I'll come back for it." The popsicle was melting, so I started to eat some of it. When Fred returned, he took it back, and some of the other white guys started giving him grief: "Man, you eating behind this black guy?" Fred's answer was, "Fuck you guys. What's wrong with you all? This is 1964; this is not 1920." I'll never forget that. He closed me—became my friend—right there. Fred's event in Tokyo went on for hours and hours. It got dark, almost everyone left, but I stayed to cheer him on. That was my payback for his friendship. I wanted him to know that there were people out there supporting him, and I felt great when he won the gold medal.

The 100-meter dash has always been the glamour event in track and field, the one that determines who is "the world's fastest human," the one where they make movies about the winner, like Harold Abrahams of Great Britain, the gold-medal winner in the 1924 Olympics who inspired the film *Chariots of Fire*. A Canadian runner, Percy Williams, won that event in the 1928 Olympics, but then the United States won five straight gold medals: Eddie Tolan in 1932, Jesse Owens in 1936, Harrison Dillard in 1948, Lindy Remigino in 1952, and Bobby Morrow in 1956. Armin Hary of Germany had broken our string of gold medals in 1960 in Rome, edging out Dave Sime of the United States in a photo finish, and now we wanted it back.

At the Olympics the 100-meter race was set up so you had to run four races—three preliminary rounds and the finals. The first two rounds were on Wednesday, October 14, a cool, rainy day. Seventy sprinters ran in ten heats in the opening round, with the first three in each heat advancing to the quarterfinals. I had plenty of time to scope out my opposition, since I didn't run until the eighth heat. The hometown hero, Hideo Iijima, got the crowd going to a fever pitch by winning the first heat in 10.3, which turned out to be the fastest time of the day, as the track got wetter and wetter. Edvin Ozolin of the Soviet Union, whom I had beaten before, finished third in that heat to advance. Trenton Jackson won the next heat in 10.5, just ahead of Peter Radford of Great Britain, who had won the bronze medal in Rome in 1960. My other teammate, Mel Pender, advanced by coming in second behind Gaoussou Kone of the Ivory Coast in the third heat. Harry Jerome of Canada, who was expected to be one of my major competitors for the gold medal, took the fifth heat in 10.5, which saw the only other Russian, Gusman Kosanov, eliminated. Two of the other highly regarded runners, Jan Maniak of Poland and Arquimedes Herrera of Venezuela, advanced by finishing 1–2 in the heat right before mine, and then it was my turn.

My first race in the Olympics was an easy one, once I actually got to run it. There were three false starts, none by me, before we finally ran a race that counted. I took first place with a time of 10.4, coasting in ahead of Tom Robinson of the Bahamas and Robert Lay of Australia by about a yard. Ito Giani of Italy; Rogelio Onofre of the Philippines; and Khudher Zalada of Iraq, who ran an 11.1 (I'm not sure what he was even doing in the field), were eliminated in my heat.

Another of the favorites, Ivan Moreno of Chile, moved on to the next round by finishing second behind Fritz Obersiebrasse of Germany in the ninth heat, which set the stage for the last heat, the one I really wanted to see. That was Enrique Figuerola's race. I had never seen him run in an actual race before because the Cubans never competed in track meets in the West, and we Americans ran against only the Russians and the Poles from the Eastern bloc. Figuerola impressed me, running a 10.5 on the wet track to win his heat by about a yard over Lynworth Headley of Jamaica and the University of Nebraska, with Robert Bambuck of France another yard back.

In the second round, later on Wednesday, I coasted in first again in 10.3, one-tenth of a second faster than I ran in the opening round, even though I finished the race looking back over my shoulder to see how everyone else was doing. Arquimedes Herrera was about three yards back, with Lyn Headley and Heinz Schumann finishing third and fourth to advance to the third round. Peter Radford and Roger Bambuck were eliminated in my heat. Trenton Jackson and Mel Pender finished second in their heats, so all three of us were still alive, although Jackson pulled a muscle in his right thigh and Pender pulled a muscle in his right side, just below the rib cage.

I didn't go all out in either race that day because of the rain and the slippery track; there was no sense taking any unnecessary risks with the semifinals and finals still ahead. Even so, I was satisfied with my times and glad that I had placed first in both rounds. My only worry was Figuerola, who matched my time in the second round with 10.3 and easily beat Maniak, the Pole, without pushing himself.

Thursday, medal day, started off cool and gloomy, but by 10 A.M., when it was time to run the semifinals, the sun had come out and it was breezy and starting to warm up. Four runners from each semifinal would advance to the finals, and I decided to open up and give the competition something to think about. The world record then was 10.0, shared by Armin Hary and Harry Jerome, but I got off the starting blocks in a flash, probably the best start I ever had, and blasted down the track to win by two or three yards over Maniak. A few minutes later, the announcement came over the loudspeakers: "Nine point nine seconds for Robert Hayes of the United States"—which broke the world record. The capacity crowd of over seventy-five thousand went crazy, but then everyone groaned, especially me, when the announcer added that my time didn't count as a world record because the tail wind was almost twelve miles an hour, about twice as high as was allowable for a record. That was the second time I had run a 9.9 that was wiped out as a world record because of the wind. The same thing had happened to me at the Mount San Antonio Relays in California the previous year. Tom Robinson and Heinz Schumann were the other two qualifiers from my heat in the semifinals, with Robert Lay, Pablo McNeil of Jamaica, and Arquimedes Herrera eliminated, along with Trenton Jackson, whose pulled muscle flared up; Jackson finished eighth and last in 10.6.

Harry Jerome won the second heat, but he ran only a 10.3, four-tenths of a second slower than my time, and Gaoussou Kone and Enrique Figuerola also qualified. Among the four who were eliminated in that heat was the Japanese runner Hideo Iijima, who was seventh in 10.6, but he had still done well to get that far.

The big thing in the second heat, though, was more bad luck for us. Mel Pender was the last qualifier, finishing fourth in 10.4, but after leading most of the way, he staggered to the finish line and then fell down. The pulled muscle in his side had torn loose from his ribs, and, unlike me, he wouldn't have four months to heal. Mel was carried off the field on a stretcher, and the doctors told him not to run in the finals an hour and a half later. But he insisted on giving it a try and spent those ninety minutes holding an ice pack against his side and taking shots to kill the pain. It was obvious that he wasn't going to have anything left for the finals, which left all our medal hopes riding on me.

After all my negotiations with Horst Dassler and Armin Hary, I almost didn't get to run the finals in either Adidas or Puma shoes. I had a couple of hours between the semifinal and final rounds, so I went back to my room to try to relax. Ralph Boston was there, lying on his bed, trying not to distract me, and then Joe Frazier walked in. Joe was always a bundle of nerves, but especially that day because he had an important boxing match coming up. He started throwing punches at my head. I asked him to leave me alone, so he went over to Ralph's bed and threw jabs up to within an inch or two of Ralph's head. Ralph just ignored him, and finally Joe lost interest and quieted down. After a few minutes, Joe looked at Ralph and me and said, "Anybody got some gum?" I said there was some in the athletic bag I had carried back from the track and told him to help himself. Joe rummaged through my bag, found a stick of chewing gum, thanked me, and zipped the bag up. "Anything going on today?" he asked. "Nothin' much," Ralph answered, with a wink toward me. "Sounds cool," said Joe, and then he breezed out the door, still shadowboxing as he left.

After I got to the track, I started to put on my racing shoes. I always put on my shoes underneath the stands and left them loose until I got on the track, then I would tie them up. I looked in my bag and saw just my right shoe. I looked deeper in my bag, but I still couldn't find my left shoe. Then I turned the bag upside down, but there was only the one blue shoe, four white shoes, and a brand new pair that wasn't broken in. By then, I was in a state of panic. The biggest race of my life, and I was missing a shoe.

At that moment Tommy Farrell, a half-miler from St. John's University in New York, jogged by. Tommy was an introvert who hardly ever said a word, but he could see that something was bothering me and he asked me what the trouble was.

"Tommy, I don't have one of my shoes."

"What size shoes do you wear, Bobby?"

"I wear size eight."

"Well, I wear size eight."

Despite my husky build, I had real small feet, and Tommy was just about the only other guy on the team whose feet were as small as mine. I borrowed his shoe and it fit perfectly on my left foot. Not that it made any difference by then, but Tommy wore the Adidas 100, too. I just thanked God, put on Tommy's shoe, and got ready to run.

At last it was Thursday afternoon, October 15, the moment I had been waiting for: the finals in the 100-meter dash. I walked out on the track. The rain had stopped, the sun had come out, and it was about 75 degrees, the nicest weather we had during the entire two weeks of the games. The announcer gave the final call for the 100 meters, and the judges announced the lane assignments: "Lane 1, Bob Hayes, United States." I said, "No, no, I just ran a 9.9 100 meters in the semifinals;" I thought the runners with the best times would get their choice of lanes, which is the way it had been in every previous race I had run. I preferred to run in one of the middle lanes, because I could see out of the corner of my eye if any other runner was keeping up with me. But on this day I had a much bigger reason for wanting any lane except the first one: Three dozen entrants in the 20,000-meter walk had just finished using the inside lane for three laps apiece at the start of their race, before they left the stadium to continue their event. The first lane was chopped to bits, and it would have been fairer if none of us in the 100-meter final—let alone the guy whose time should have entitled him to the best lane—had to use it. We protested and held the race up for about 10 minutes, which really upset the Japanese, who liked to be precisely on time for every event. But the judges disallowed our protest, insisting that the lanes be assigned for this race by the luck of the draw—and my name had come up for Lane 1. The grounds crew raked the track as best as they could—they didn't even use a heavy roller, which would have done some good—and then I had to get in there and run in Lane 1. To my right were Schumann in Lane 2, Figuerola in Lane 3, Kone in Lane 4, Jerome in Lane 5, Maniak in Lane 6, Robinson in Lane 7, and Pender in the outside lane. I knew I was getting screwed, but it just made me run harder and concentrate more to make up for my disadvantage. I was thinking to myself, "I didn't come all the way to Tokyo to lose, no matter what lane they give me."

Then we were taking off our sweat suits and preparing to run. Most of the other runners were wishing each other good luck. I walked over the Lane 8, where Mel Pender was undressing, and I said, "Mel, I ain't saying good luck to nobody to beat me, but I hope I finish first and you finish second." Mel turned to me and said, "I'm finishing first, I hope *you* finish second." Mel and I both knew he didn't have a chance because of his injury, and he showed fantastic courage just by running with the pain he had.

As I headed over to my starting blocks, a million things seemed to go through my mind: I thought about starting out as a runner at Matthew Gilbert High School in Jacksonville and how my father had refused to let me run for several years because he thought I could make more money in the future shining shoes and running numbers than going to school and participating in sports. I remembered the first time I practiced running in high school; I got so tired that I passed out, and I could not move and had to lie down in the grass for about an hour. I remembered one of my teammates at Florida A & M, a quarter-miler, telling me, "You know, we are all stupid. We start at a point and all we do is run around in a circle to the same point and try to beat the other guys back to the same point we all started from." Which is true. I thought of my mother sitting in the stands with Jesse Owens, about ten rows up from the starting line, and I looked up and caught her eye.

I got in the starting blocks and I started thinking about how so many people had predicted I would win the gold medal. I thought about John Thomas, who was picked to win the high jump in 1960 and all the turmoil he went through because he lost. I thought about how I couldn't go back to Florida A & M if I lost because the guys would tease me to death; I thought about the Japanese people mobbing us everywhere we went; I thought of Robert (Pete) Griffin and Dick Hill, the Florida A & M track coaches who had trained me so I could become an Olympic candidate; I thought of Willie Galimore, the great Florida A & M runningback who had starred for the Chicago Bears and been killed in a car accident three months earlier because he was rushing to get to a television set in hopes of seeing me run. I dedicated the race to Willie and I prayed that I could equal in track what he had accomplished in football.

Then I came back to my senses and started concentrating on that race and thinking, "All I can do is give my best." I remembered what Jake Gaither used to tell us: "We don't schedule football games to win 'em; we schedule them to play them." And he would add, "If you give your best, that's all we ask for." That's what I said to myself, "I'm just going to give my best."

As a runner, you never worry about a false start. I was totally concentrated; I was totally in control of myself and my destiny; and I was totally intense, the more so because I was angry about having to run in the inside lane. Finally I picked out a spot straight ahead of me down the track and vowed that I was going to get there before anyone else did.

Then the gun sounded and we came off the blocks. I got another good start, although Figuerola was about a half a step ahead of me. All the other runners got off slightly behind the two of us, except for Kone, who was last. After about 10 meters, it was the Big Three—me, Figuerola, and Jerome—neck and neck, but by the 25-meter mark, I had pulled a little ahead of Figuerola, with Jerome third. From then on, the race seemed to go by in a blur, punctuated by the noise of all eight of us grunting with effort and biting the cinders with our spikes. I had the feeling that I was in a four-part play. In the first 25 yards, I came out of the blocks like a shot. By the second 25, when I had gotten into my full stride, I zoomed past Figuerola and started opening ground with every stride. That's when I knew the gold medal was mine. The third 25 was when I always went into my maximum acceleration, and in that race I felt like I was running faster than I ever had before. Even so, the farther I got down that track, the farther it seemed like it was to the finish line. I was saying to myself, "Damn let's get to that finish line!" In those final 25 yards, all kinds of

things were going through my mind: "Don't fall! Don't pull a m̶
Relax! Run as fast as you can!"

And then I was on top of the tape and through it, winning by tw̶
three yards, still the largest margin ever in the finals of the Olympic ̶
The timers had me at 10.0 and this time it counted, equaling the wo̶
record held by Hary and Jerome and breaking by two-tenths of a secon̶
the Olympic record that Hary and Sime set when they finished almost dead
even in 1960. The race came out just the way a lot of the experts, including
those at *Sports Illustrated,* had predicted it several week earlier: Figuerola
won the silver medal and Jerome, the bronze. They were followed by
Maniak, Schumann, Kone, Pender, and Robinson.

I did have two regrets. First, I had dreamed of breaking the world
record at the Olympics. But, considering the condition of my lane and my
missing shoe, I was astonished that I was able to equal the record. My
other regret was that I couldn't see the race as well as run in it. But now,
thanks to the miracle of videotape, I get to watch it on tape, too. I still get
chills, watching myself come down the track and hearing one American
television announcer going wild: "So all eyes will be on the man in Lane
one, Bob Hayes, he's the favorite, the man the Americans are counting on
to reestablish their sprinting supremacy. It's a good start! The Cuban Figuerola in Lane three and Hayes are almost dead even! Now Hayes is
breaking away. He has simply exploded. Bob Hayes is making a mockery
of this race, *way* out in front. Hayes just powering along. He wins by an
incredible seven feet! Oh, what a run!"

After I crossed the finish line and coasted to a stop, I looked up to
where Ralph Boston was sitting in the stands and gave him a secret wave
which meant that now I had a gold medal, just like he did. Mel Pender
came over and congratulated me, and I congratulated him just for having
the guts to finish the race. Mel spent the next three days in the hospital.
Then the officials led Harry Jerome, Enrique Figuerola, and me into a
tunnel, where we waited for the awards ceremony. I put on my sweat suit
with "USA" on it; I had never been as proud to represent my country as
I was at that moment. Then they led us back onto the field for the medal
ceremony, and as I took my place at the top of the podium, with Figuerola
below me and Jerome a little lower than him, I saw Emperor Hirohito
walk toward us, accompanied by three young Japanese women wearing
kimonos. Each of the girls carried a black satin pillow with a medal on it.
I couldn't take my eyes off mine. It truly was gold, hanging from a red-
white-and-blue ribbon. When I bent down to receive it, the emperor, who

half inches tall, had a little trouble getting
ally did, and it was truly mine!
ne moment in my athletic career. Winning the
goal for any athlete, especially in the 100 meters,
ions of people follow the event. So few people win
an event like mine, it's for individual effort. My ring
per Bowl means a lot, too, but it's not the same because
am, not the only guy who came in first. And in the Olym-
esenting the whole country, my state, my school, my people,
and every dream that an athlete has in life. I won my event
d myself in a fantasy world, with the emperor putting the Gold
my neck, everybody in the stands cheering, the national anthem
ng, the American flag rising, and my name on the scoreboard: "Rob-
Hayes, 10 seconds flat, new Olympic record, tying the world record." I had set out to do something, I paid the price, and I reached my goal.

Right after the medals were awarded, the Japanese played the Star
Spangled Banner over the public address system and raised the American,
Cuban, and Canadian flags, with ours the highest. As the Japanese played
the first few stanzas of the national anthem, my eyes started to fill with
tears. The Japanese had done that for each gold medal winner, and now
they were playing it for me. When they stopped playing our anthem, the
most wonderful thing happened. One person from a whole group of Americans who were sitting in a section just below where the Olympic torch
was burning pulled out a trumpet and picked up the national anthem
where the Japanese left off, while the other Americans waved our flag. I
later found out the trumpet player was a track fan from Los Angeles, a
man named Uan Rasey who was the lead horn in the MGM studio or-
chestra. He really helped make my day!

After Rasey finished playing, I made my way up into the stands to
my mother and Jesse Owens. It wasn't easy because people were grabbing
me and shaking my hand and patting me on the back the whole way. I
took off my medal, put it in my mother's hands, and said to her, "Here's
your Gold, mother dear, just like I promised you." She was in tears, and
she kissed me and said, "Thank you, son. I have something that no other
mother has, the world's fastest gold medal." Jesse Owens hugged me and
told me how proud he was of me. You don't often get to hear that from
one of your idols, and I have cherished that moment ever since. Right
there he told me that I should continue to run track instead of play football
because I still hadn't reached my potential. I was the first big sprinter, and

he said I was so strong that I looked like a locomotive going do
track. I answered, "I'll think about it, but I love football, Mr. Owen
there's an opportunity there for me to earn a living in the future." In
there was no future for athletes at that time.

After the race I went back to my room, where most of my close friend
on the team—Ralph Boston, Henry Carr, Joe Frazier, Theron Lewis, and
Willie Davenport, the hurdler—were waiting to share my victory with me.
It was like one of us had gotten married and now all the other fellows had
their weddings to look forward to.

Before I started celebrating, though, I looked around for my missing
track shoe. And I found it, too, right under my bedspread. It had fallen
out of my bag when Joe Frazier was looking for the gum. I told the guys
what had happened and then I looked over at Joe and yelled at him,
"Don't you ever go in my bag again." That was about the only time I ever
saw Joe Frazier apologetic. He and I were reminiscing and laughing about
the missing shoe a couple of years ago at a network superstars competition
in Miami Beach. We were matched against each other in basketball. The
guy who makes the most points wins. And Joe kicked my ball way out
onto the beach—that's the kind of guy he is. He and I laughed so hard
after he kicked my ball that we could barely stand up, but I ran out there
and got the ball, ran back, and still beat him by a point.

A few hours after I won my gold medal, Keiko, the Japanese reporter,
my mother, and I had dinner in the revolving restaurant atop the Hilton
Hotel, where my mother was staying. I was as high as a kite. I couldn't
stop going back over the race, and people kept coming over to our table
and taking pictures of me the whole time. Then the three of us went
downtown to the Ginza, Tokyo's equivalent of Times Square, where there
was a picture of me in red-white-and-blue neon lights with the message,
BOB HAYES, USA, WORLD'S FASTEST HUMAN.

Meanwhile, I was wondering if the boys back at Florida A & M knew
yet, and then I got a telegram from Jake Gaither that said, "I want to know
when you are coming home, so everybody from the governor of the state
on down can congratulate you." I later found out that Earl Kitchings, my
high school coach, had stayed up until 2 A.M. to find out the results of the
100-meter final.

. . .

wn the
s, and
rack

y. I had some important business to attend
Of course, if Horst had refused to pay me,
ave done about it, since I couldn't have com-
ficials or the police. But there was no problem.
vertising its product as "the world's fastest shoe,"
iles. We went to the back of his tent, and he pulled
is and counted out 105 $100 bills—$8,900 for me and
women's relay team, which I gave to one of the team's
e back from the Olympics wearing a beautiful silk suit that
of $100 bills in one of the pockets and carrying ten other suits
equally nice.

y mom made out fine, too. She came back to the United States
ed down with televisions, watches, and all sorts of clothing that people
ve her in Tokyo. When her son won the gold medal, my mother became
the first lady of track and field.

Half my business in Tokyo was finished after I won the gold medal in the 100-meter dash, but I still had the second half to attend to: the 400-meter relay. And if I was going to get my second gold medal, I was going to have to do it with a makeshift and crippled team. The four runners who had qualified in Los Angeles to run the 400-meter relay were Trenton Jackson, Mel Pender, Gerry Ashworth, and me. Unlike the individual events, we were allowed to make substitutions on the relay teams in Tokyo if runners were injured, which was lucky for us. Since Trenton and Mel couldn't run in the relay, we wouldn't have been able to field a team without replacing them. And one of our two substitutes, Paul Drayton, who won the silver medal behind Henry Carr in the 200-meters in Tokyo, had a pulled muscle in his leg, but he had to run anyway, because we didn't have anybody else. The other newcomer to our relay team was Dick Stebbins of Grambling, who also ran the 200. Dick finished out of the money in the 200, but at least he was healthy for the relay.

Of course, fielding a team that was put together at the last minute was a big handicap because most of the other countries had relay teams that had practiced together for months. Handing the baton from one runner to another may look easy, but it isn't. It takes split-second timing to pass the baton in such a way that neither runner has to break stride and cost his team ground, and you have to do it within a 10-meter exchange zone. A bad pass means that you either lose ground, or if the baton is passed outside the zone, you get disqualified, which is what had happened to the U.S. sprint relay team four years earlier in Rome and would occur again in 1988 in Seoul.

Our relay team was under tremendous pressure. The United States had won the 400-meter relay in every Olympics since 1912, except for 1960, and we were one of the favorites for the gold medal in 1964, along with France, Italy, and Poland. But that was before we had to start from scratch with a team that was 50 percent new. There were only five days from the 100-meter final on October 15 to the opening round of the 400-meter relay on October 20, and the four of us spent as much time as we could practicing together. Paul would run the first leg, followed by Gerry and Dick, and then me as the anchor man. We knew we weren't that smooth at passing the baton, but we hoped that whatever ground we lost in the passing zone we could make up with our legs.

Our main rivals, the French, didn't think much of our emergency lineup. While we were practicing in the days before the race, the French team watched us work out, and Jocelyn Delecour, that team's fastest man and anchor, told Paul Drayton, "You Americans don't have a good team this year. The only good man you have is Bob Hayes." He was just harassing and humiliating us. We had never formally voted on who was captain of our relay team, but the other three guys looked up to me as the leader after my performance in the 100. Paul came back and reported to me what Delecour had said, and I told him, Gerry, and Dick, "It's embarrassing for someone to disrespect you as an American, when you're one of our top athletes in the 100 meters and we are the best country. It would embarrass me and hurt me if someone came up to me and said I wasn't good enough. If I was you guys, I would give everything that I have. I want you to prove this guy wrong."

There was a total of three rounds in the relay, one fewer than in the 100-meter dash, and in the opening round we were in second place, about a yard behind the Germans, when Dick handed me the baton. I beat the German anchor man easily, but our time was only 39.8, well off the world record of 39.1 and the Olympic record of 39.5.

The second round was run later on October 20, with eight teams in two heats and the top four in each heat qualifying for the finals the next day. France was in the heat with us, and Delecour was about two yards ahead when I took off. I blew him away, finishing first by several yards in 39.5 seconds to equal the Olympic record. England and Jamaica qualified for the last two spots in our heat, and Australia, Ghana, Hungary, and

Nigeria were eliminated. Italy, Poland, and Venezuela finished almost dead even in the second heat, with Italy awarded first place at 39.6 and Russia the fourth qualifier, setting the stage for the finals the next day.

When we got to the track on October 21, we found out that at least we had gotten a decent lane for the finals. We would be in the seventh lane, with Russia in the outside lane, Poland next to us, and then Venezuela, Jamaica, Italy, France, with the British in Lane 1. The inside lane wasn't in nearly as bad shape as it had been for the 100-meter finals, but I was still delighted that we didn't have to run in it.

Right before we got ready to run, I got down on my knees and led us in a prayer: "God, let it so shine as the golden sun. Give us the necessary endurance to run, give us the speed that we may need so that we may our opponents exceed." I learned that prayer from Earl Kitchings in high school, and it went through my mind again as I walked to my position.

Paul Drayton's leg was hurting him worse than the day before, and as the four of us split up to go to our positions, he told us, "Guys, if my leg holds up, I'll just give you everything I have." I was a positive thinker and thought we had a chance as we went into the race. This was my last race of the Olympics, and I was like a pitcher in the seventh game of the World Series who knew he didn't have to save anything for tomorrow. I was determined to give everything I had, call on every muscle in my body, and then see what happened. I knew that nobody was going to beat me running that anchor leg.

Paul ran the first leg around the curve and did a great job, considering his injury. He was second, about two yards behind the Poles, when he gave the baton to Gerry. Gerry ran a good leg on the straightaway, but he and Dick had trouble on the baton exchange, and by the time Dick started running, we were behind France, Poland, the Russians, and even Jamaica. Dick Stebbins ran a hell of a curve on the third leg. He didn't gain much, but he didn't lose any on his leg.

In the passing zone, you always gave the oncoming runner most of the ten meters to pass the baton. But that day, I took the baton at the very beginning of the passing zone, so I actually ran almost ten meters extra. I wanted the baton in my hands.

It seemed like I would never get the baton, and when I finally did, I saw all the other runners ahead of me, led by the French, who were at least five yards ahead. The runners in front of me were kicking up cinders off their spikes, and the cinders were burning my eyes. I was trying to get out of that traffic just so I could see clearly, which gave me more incentive to run fast. And in a way it was an advantage for me to be behind because

I could see those guys in front of me and I knew what I had to do. Even so, I didn't think we had a chance to win when I got the baton. I thought the best we could do was to qualify for the bronze medal for third place. I had told the other guys just to try to let me be fairly close to the leaders when I got the baton, but I didn't mean for them to give it to me *that* far behind.

Suddenly, I started passing guys like they were standing still. Delecour had been so far ahead, but now it seemed like he was stopping. I could not believe I was running that fast. It seemed like I was picking up speed every five meters. I knew I was moving faster in the first fifty meters than I had ever moved before. I could feel it. How could I be running this fast? I could not believe it myself. After about seventy-five meters, I started to hear the noise from the stands; the crowd was yelling like crazy. All I could see was the finish line and the other guys out of the corner of my eyes. I was picking them off one by one, first the Jamaicans, then the Russians, and the the Poles. I never did see Delecour again because I did not look to the side as Carl Lewis did with Ben Johnson in 1988.

I didn't realize I had won until I got to the tape and I was ahead. I started thinking it was going to be a real close race, a photo finish. When I realized that I had beaten Delecour by a big margin, I made my one mistake of the day—I threw my baton way up in the air in jubilation and I never saw it again. It would have been a lifetime souvenir for me; in my joy, however, I made it a souvenir for someone else. But I wasn't thinking about the baton then. All that was going through my mind was, "How could this have happened? I've been running against the fastest men from all these countries and I caught 'em and beat 'em. How good could I be?"

Bob Giegengack came up to me and said, "Bobby, your time was 8.6; it's just incredible." Eddie Hurt came over and said, "Your time was 8.4." Several other men had timed the race at 8.4 or 8.6, and one had me timed at 8.9. Some of the experts later used a stopwatch to time the film of my anchor leg, and the consensus was that I had run at 8.6. Hurt said to me, "You're the only man who could have done that, and that's why we won the gold medal. Only the world's fastest human could have caught these guys."

If I couldn't believe what I had done, neither could anyone else. In 1984 the *Los Angeles Times* called my anchor leg "the most astonishing sprint of all time." A year earlier, a panel of track experts assembled by the same newspaper had unanimously named me the greatest 100-meter sprinter in history, and a group of British authorities reached the same conclusion just before the 1988 games, commenting on my accomplishments in Tokyo: "His performance has never really been equalled, and the [relay] run also went down in history—just as his 100 metres final did—as one of the landmarks in sprinting."

I guess the remark that meant the most to me came from the runner-up in the 100 meters. Even though the United States and Cuba were enemies, Enrique Figuerola showed what the Olympic spirit was all about. After I beat him, he said, "This is the best race I ran all year. Yet Hayes beat me at my best. He's the greatest."

After a few minutes, it was announced over the loudspeakers in the stadium that we had run a 39-flat, breaking the world record by one-tenth of a second. The crowd went wild for the third time over one of my races. Poland was second and France third, both at 39.3; Jamaica, fourth in 39.4; the Soviet Union, fifth, also in 39.4; Venezuela, sixth in 39.5, the same time as the seventh-place Italians; and England, eighth and last in 39.6. Seven of the eight teams, everyone except the British, had broken or tied the old Olympic record in what the experts called the greatest 400-meter relay ever.

Again, it would have been nice to have been able to watch this race and run in it, too. But I have a tape of this one, just as I do of the 100-meter final, and I love to hear the television announcer calling it: "Bob Hayes is waiting. He told his teammates, just give it to me close, but the U.S. is in fifth place, several yards behind. Can Hayes do it? Here he comes! He's going to do it! Bob Hayes wins it and hurls the baton in the air in jubilation! An unbelievable performance! The U.S. sets a new world record! The race was won and an American Olympic hero was born!"

As soon as the race was over, the Japanese officials, with their split-second timing, started herding us off the field so they could get ready for the next race, but I said, "No way." I turned around and the other anchor runners came running up and put their arms around me and congratulated me. Then I started to run toward Dick Stebbins. Gerry Ashworth was coming around the track, and Paul Drayton was coming from across the infield. We met about fifty meters up the track from the finish line and congratulated each other. Paul said, "Man, you burned them up. That was the fastest hundred meters I have ever seen any man run. I never thought we would win that race." I said another prayer, "Thank God for letting us exploit the maximum of our ability and win the gold medal." We finally let the Japanese escort us through a tunnel and into a waiting area, and when Drayton spotted Delecour, he went over to him and said, "Mr. Delecour, I tried to tell you that Bob Hayes was all we needed." But that was just Paul's sprinter's ego coming through, and Delecour and I were very cordial to each other on the victory stand.

When I finally walked outside the stadium, I got mobbed big time. People started ripping off pieces of my uniform, but no one got his hands near my gold medal, which I was wearing around my neck. I didn't take it off for two whole days.

That night I had a little party of my own. A Canadian girl, a hurdler, had been coming on to me for a while. She was about five feet three, blonde, with a nice body—a real good-looking girl. I told her that since my competition was over I was going to go out that night and have a drink and something to eat. She asked if she could come along. I said fine. We went to a Japanese bar with Keiko, the newspaperwoman, who left after a while. The Canadian girl and I each had a couple of drinks and went back to my room and got it on. I never saw her again.

The 1964 games were one of the last Olympics that the American men dominated in track. We won nine of the thirteen gold medals in track, losing only the 800-meters and 1,500 meters, both of which were won by the great Peter Snell of New Zealand, and the marathon and the steeplechase, which weren't really our strong events.

We did have some disappointments in the field events, especially Ralph Boston, who saw Lynn Davies of Great Britain score a tremendous upset. In the long jump, Davies edged both Ralph, who won the silver medal, and the other favorite, Igor Ter-Ovanesyan of the Soviet Union, who got the bronze medal. Ralph was inconsolable, but at least he had the gold medal from 1960. And John Thomas lost again to the Russian, Valery Brumel, in the high jump. They both jumped seven feet, one and three quarters of an inch, but Brumel won the gold medal because he had fewer misses. Our only gold medals in the eleven field events were won by Fred Hansen in the pole vault, Dallas Long in the shot put, and Al Oerter in the discus (his third in a row). Overall, the United States won the most gold medals in Tokyo, thirty-six, followed by Russia with thirty, and the Japanese with sixteen.

It seems hard to believe, but our Olympics were the last ones without controversy. There was the black power protest at Mexico City in 1968, the massacre of the Israeli athletes at Munich in 1972, the African nations' boycott at Montreal in 1976, the American boycott of the 1980 games in Moscow, the Soviet boycott at Los Angeles in 1984, and the steroid scandal at Seoul in 1988. I don't know if the Olympics will ever again be what they should be—the greatest meet of the greatest athletes in the world— but I'm proud to have starred in the games when they went off as they should have. That makes my medals mean a little more.

I finally returned to Florida A & M in late October. The last leg of my trip was a flight from Atlanta to Tallahassee, which landed about 9:30 P.M. I looked out the window of my plane, and there were the lights of buses and cars as far as I could see. The pilot came on the public-address system and said, "Bob Hayes, please wait until all the other passengers have gotten off." I could see Jake Gaither and the boys on the football team waiting at the foot of the stairs. After the other passengers got off, the first one who came up the stairs and grabbed me and hugged me was Carleton Oats, a defensive end who later played several years with the Oakland Raiders. Cecil Daniels, the student trainer who was one of my closest friends, came up and I passed him the money Horst Dassler had given me, so that nothing would happen to it in that mob. As I walked down the stairs, there was a big cheer and everybody started singing the Florida A & M song; all I could do was cry. The ball players picked me up on their shoulders and carried me around.

Florida A & M had a tradition of loud horns on its buses. When we went to other campuses to play, we would tell Tommy Gaines, our driver, "Blow 'em out," to announce that we had arrived and were going to win big, and he would really lean on the horn. And that's what happened that night. The horns on all the buses and cars were blaring. I was in Jake Gaither's white Lincoln with the buses behind us, followed by everybody else in their cars.

When we got to the campus, it was around 11:30 P.M., and all the students were outside waiting for me (even the girls had been allowed outside their dormitories after their curfew). Before I got out of Coach Gaither's car, he said to me, "Baby [that's what he called me sometimes], wave your hands and say hello." I was wearing one of my new suits, a black silk one; a light blue shirt, a tie, and the cowboy hat from my Olympic uniform. When I stepped out of the car, I waved both hands; one girl reached up and snatched my cowboy hat off, and I never saw it again.

That pissed me off! Some folks told me who it was, but when I went to her dormitory to see her the next day, she was gone. She had quit school and left with my hat.

A few days later, I got back to football practice. I was trying to return punts, but I couldn't catch a single one. My football timing was that far off. I just could not catch a ball. All the media were there watching me practice, and my concentration on football just wasn't there. I said, "Jake, I think I'd just better sit out the rest of the season." But Jake said, "Hell, no, son, you're going to play football." Which is what I did.

Shortly after we got back to the United States, the medal winners were invited to the White House. President Johnson and Senator Hubert Humphrey, his running mate in that year's election, were waiting for us, and I will never forget what President Johnson said to me. After he shook my hand, he said, "Bob, I heard the national anthem so many times, I thought it was the number one hit on radio." Seven years later, when he came into the Cowboy locker room after our first game in the brand-new Texas Stadium, Johnson said, "Bob, I'm still hearing those number one hits." He didn't forget.

The next time I went to the White House was also about the Olympics, but it was a totally different affair. In 1980 President Carter invited a group of black athletes to discuss boycotting the games in Moscow. Ralph Boston, Wilma Rudolph, Hayes Jones, John Thomas, and a number of others were there. When my turn came, I told the president, "I don't think that we can hurt a country by boycotting the Olympics. We have to hurt a country by taking money out of their pocketbooks. These athletes have trained too hard, too long, and I'll tell you the truth, Mr. President, the greatest PR you can get for peace and fellowship is by participating in the Olympics." But at the end of the meeting, Carter declared, "We are not going!" and, of course, we didn't.

I have always been opposed to boycotting the Olympics. As someone who has participated in them, I believe that the Olympics are an athletic event, not a political one. If I had wanted to make the Olympics a political issue, I might have missed the 1964 games and never had my day in the sun. A few hours after I ran a 9.1 to break the world record in the 100-yard dash at the AAU championships in St. Louis in June 1963, Dick Gregory asked several outstanding black athletes to boycott the upcoming United States–Soviet Union meet in Moscow to protest the plight of American blacks, which probably would have led to a boycott of the Olympics the following year. Ralph Boston, John Thomas, Henry Carr, and Paul Drayton were among those there.

I have always had a lot of respect for Dick Gregory. Not only is he committed to the cause of black people, but he was once a great runner himself. Not too many people know it, but Dick was named the outstanding athlete at Southern Illinois University in 1953, and he was the third fastest half-miler in the United States back then. So I could relate to him as both a fellow black man and a fellow athlete. Even so, who was he to expect me to give up my big chance?

I was only twenty years old at the time, an unaware kid, but I still knew better than to let someone talk me into something like that. I told Gregory right to his face, "Hell no, I'm not boycotting nothing." He said to me, "Well, then, you're just going to be a token." I said, "Well, I'll be a fuckin' token; I'd rather be a token than be nothing. I don't have much going for me but being an athlete, there's no sense in my going down the tubes. And why haven't you come to me before? Why now? I don't even know you, mister." I told him, "Give me a concrete reason why I should demonstrate." "Because the blacks are not getting their fair share," was his answer. Then I said, "Well, I can't speak for all blacks, but I feel I'm getting my fair share, getting this opportunity. This could open up the door for my son if I ever have one." If I had refused to go to the Olympics, Gregory would still have been a rich celebrity and I would have had nothing. It's easy for the rich people to ask the poor people to sacrifice. After I had my say, I left the meeting, but none of the guys who stayed agreed to the boycott either.

It seemed that whenever someone wanted to get a boycott going, I was the first one to be asked. Harry Edwards, who's still an activist for the rights of black athletes, approached me before the 1968 Olympics and asked me to support a boycott. When I told him I wouldn't, he called me an Uncle Tom in the press and then turned around and denied he had said it. Later, I came to agree with the black protest gesture that John Carlos and Tommie Smith made that year in Mexico City, but the important thing to me is that they still participated in the Olympics. If Harry Edwards had asked me to support a black power protest instead of a boycott, I might have agreed, but once I told him I was against a boycott, I didn't hear any more from him and I didn't know what John Carlos and the rest of them were going to do until I saw them raise their fists on the victory stand.

I understand that people like Dick Gregory and Harry Edwards expected me to be a symbol because of my fame. But I was really amazed by some of the people who tried to capitalize on my accomplishments over the years. Take Jeffrey Archer, the former member of Parliament and British novelist. Archer apparently was some kind of minor-league British sprinter when he was young, and when a British publication, *TV Times,* asked him to write an article about the 1988 Olympics, he wrote: "I remember being in America with the 1964 Olympic 100m champion Bob Hayes. He was following me down some aircraft steps and said, 'You know, Jeffrey, that's the first time I've ever seen your back.' " He made it sound like he and I were close friends. Well, Archer may have gotten off an airplane in front of me somewhere, but that's as much contact as he ever had with me. I mean, I never even met the man.

In a week's time I earned two gold medals for running a total of 700 meters in approximately 70 seconds in seven races—four 100-meter races and three 400-meter relays. The relay final was the last race that mattered in my track career (I ran on a professional track circuit of sorts here and in Australia during a couple of my off-seasons from the Dallas Cowboys), and I did the 100 meters in 8.6 seconds. Although that time was from a running start, don't forget that I actually ran nearly 110 meters, or 120 yards, in those 8.6 seconds, because I took the baton from Dick Stebbins as early as I could.

All my track coaches—Bob Giegengack and Eddie Hurt of the U.S. Olympic team and Dick Hill and Pete Griffin of Florida A & M—as well as Jesse Owens, wanted me to keep running because I hadn't reached my potential. Today, runners make millions of dollars a year in prizes, appearance fees, and endorsements; it has been estimated that Ben Johnson's disqualification and loss of the gold medal cost him as much as $10 million the next year. If I could have made money running—not millions of dollars, but just enough to have lived comfortably—I would have continued to run. But that wasn't possible in 1964, so after the 400-meter final, I hung up my track shoes, and Tommy Farrell's, too, and turned to football full time.

Ever since October 21, 1964, though, I have wondered what might have been if I had continued to run. There are a number of factors to consider:

- My track career ended two months before my twenty-second birthday, long before sprinters reach their peak.

- For all intents and purposes, I spent only about two years running track seriously. If I ignore my minor-league track experience in high school, when I was playing baseball at the same time, my entire track career consisted of spring 1961; spring and summer 1962 and 1963; and spring and early fall 1964, the year I missed the whole summer season with my hamstring injury. Unlike my world-class competitors, all of whom either were in training or running track year-round on the indoor and outdoor circuits, I spent nearly half the year playing football. Football practice at Florida A & M began in late August, and I didn't even look at a pair of track shoes from then until January. Once football was over and I started running track, I eased into it— I was worn out from football—so I didn't really reach peak form for a couple of months.

▪ I ran on tracks that were far inferior to today's synthetic surfaces and in shoes whose traction and spring didn't compare to today's. Not to mention that none of the sprinters in my day dreamed of shaving his head or wearing a hood to cut down the wind resistance.

▪ I never lifted weights when I was running. Weight training was unheard of for sprinters in those days. My training regimen consisted of running and doing isometric exercises. I can only imagine what a top-notch strength coach, like Bob Ward of the Cowboys, could have done for me.

▪ I never even heard of steroids when I was running, much less took them. Testimony at the Ben Johnson hearings in Canada indicated that steroids could save you one meter—a tenth of a second—in the 100-meters. When you saw Bob Hayes run, it was all Bob Hayes. With Ben Johnson, it's Ben Johnson plus. Next, they'll probably allow a little engine on the back of the shoe. I think Ben Johnson is a great runner, but if we could have raced each other when we were both in our prime, without steroids and with everything else equal, I would have taken him.

Steroids and other performance-enhancing drugs should be banned from track and all other sports. As for Ben Johnson, I don't think he should be banned for life. I think he should be given a second chance now, but he will have to prove that he has rehabilitated himself and agree to frequent, unannounced drug tests for the rest of his career.

When all is said and done, the question comes down to this: How fast could I have run, under perfect conditions? What if I had run into my late twenties, trained year-round, run on the kind of tracks they have today, had today's track shoes, and followed the kind of training program that runners do now?

In my own mind, I have to answer that question with another question: How fast is it humanly possible to run? Twenty-five years have passed since I retired from track with a personal best in the 100 meters (unaided by wind) of 10.0. The two fastest times ever recorded in the 100 meters were by Ben Johnson—9.79 at the 1988 Olympics in Seoul and 9.83 at the 1987 world track and field championships in Rome, but both those times have been thrown out because of Johnson's use of steroids. Today, the world record is the 9.92 Carl Lewis ran at the 1988 Olympics, which is less than one-tenth of a second faster than my fastest time.

My guess is that I could have gotten my time for the 100 meters down to at least 9.5, maybe even lower. But, of course, that's in the realm of what ifs. What if Joe DiMaggio had played in Fenway Park instead of Yankee Stadium? What if Ted Williams had played in Yankee Stadium instead of Fenway Park and hadn't lost four or five of the peak years of his career to military service? What if Mickey Mantle had been born with a healthy body? What if Babe Ruth had kept himself in shape? What if Muhammad Ali hadn't lost several years of his career after he refused to be drafted during the Vietnam War? How many points would Wilt Chamberlain have scored if he could have hit his free throws? What would Jimmy Brown have accomplished if he hadn't retired from the Cleveland Browns before his thirtieth birthday? What if Josh Gibson and Satchel Paige and Jackie Robinson and Willie Mays hadn't had to spend all or most or part of their careers in the Negro League instead of in the major leagues? What if Ben Johnson hadn't used steroids? What if pigs had wings and cows could jump over the moon?

We'll never know.

When I was standing on the victory platform in Tokyo, I had no way of knowing that those would be the two most golden moments of my life. At that time, I was confident that I would go on to star in professional football. I didn't realize that nothing I accomplished in the NFL would match the thrills that winning those two gold medals gave me. While I was at the Olympics, it never crossed my mind that I had peaked at age twenty-one. It wouldn't have mattered anyway. I think back to October 1964, and time stands still for me. Hey, that was me, on top of the world!

2

UP FROM HELL'S HOLE

I was a war baby in every sense of the word. My mother, Mary Hayes, was a domestic in Jacksonville, on Florida's east coast, and was married to a builder named Joseph Hayes. Joseph Hayes was in the navy, off fighting World War II, when my mother met a Jacksonville man named George Sanders and had a romance that resulted in my birth five days before Christmas 1942. When Joseph Hayes came back from the war, he accepted what had happened, and I always went by his name, although he never officially adopted me. George Sanders went off to the war himself and was wounded during the invasion of Saipan in the South Pacific. His wound caused his muscles to deteriorate so that eventually he couldn't walk. He spent the last ten to twelve years of his life in a wheelchair and died in late December 1977, a few days after my thirty-fifth birthday. My wife, Janice, and I were flying to Jacksonville so that my father, George, could see our new baby, Bob Junior. But my father passed away a few hours before we got there. Since he and my mom weren't married, the people in the Veterans Administration hospital where he died wouldn't tell us what killed him, but we think it was liver failure caused by heavy drinking throughout his life.

I grew up on Third Street, in the ghetto on the east side of Jacksonville, about a mile from the Gator Bowl. That area has always been known as both Hell's Hole and The Bottom—it's a low-lying part of town, the bottom of the city of Jacksonville before you get to the St. Johns River. When I was a boy, none of the streets in Hell's Hole was paved, there were no parks, and most of the homes were what they called shotgun houses, laid out in a straight line, so a shot fired through the front window would pass all the way through the house and go out the back window.

Our house had three bedrooms, a kitchen, and a bathroom—no living room, dining room, or anything else. We didn't have air-conditioning and we didn't get central heating until 1960, when I was a freshman in college. Until then, we heated the house with red-hot heaters and a wood stove. Of course, we had to chop our own wood and do all our own chores, and my mother used to call me the slowest woodchopper and dishwasher in northern Florida. I guess I was saving my fast movements for other things.

I was the youngest of my mother's four children. My older brother Nathaniel died as a baby, seven or eight years before I was born. Another brother, Ernest, was five years older than me. Ernest was my general overseer, and he was very aggressive. Boxing was his big thing; we used to get boxing gloves for Christmas presents, and he was always pounding me and trying to get me to fight. I used to do roadwork with him on the hot, dusty roads around Jacksonville when I was a little boy, and that's where I got my start running.

Ernest turned out to be such a great boxer at around 125 or 130 pounds that we almost had two Hayes brothers at the 1964 Olympics. He enlisted in the army in 1955, won the U.S. Army lightweight championship in 1959, and went as far as the finals of the 1964 Olympic boxing trials before he was eliminated. Ernest's nickname as a boxer was "Speedie," and one newspaper article about him said that "Ernest's hands are faster than Bob's feet." Ernest was nearly as fast a runner as I was (he ran 9.5 in the 100-yard dash) and was a great baseball and football player, although he was much too small to play football at the college or professional level. Two years after the Olympics, he won a medal of his own—the Bronze Star for being a hero in Vietnam. Ernest was a platoon sergeant, and five members of his unit were ambushed and wounded by the Vietcong. After he helped rescue the five soldiers, he was ordered to send someone to retrieve their weapons. Instead of making someone else undertake such a dangerous mission, he went back and got the weapons himself, with the Vietcong blasting away at him. Ernest was a military career man and retired a few years ago, and I've looked up to him all my life.

I also have an older sister, Lena, who quit school in the eighth grade (I was the first member of my family to go past the eighth grade) to help my mother earn money and put me through school. Lena and my mom sacrificed a lot to make sure that I would have opportunities they never had. We were a close-knit family; my mother's brother, Horace Green, lived with us for many years, and their sisters, Aunt Betty and Aunt Josephine, lived next door. I had three fathers, too. My mom and Joseph Hayes separated on and off until I was eight years old, when they split up for good. My mom later married John Robinson, who's still her husband. And I was closer to Joseph Hayes and John Robinson than I was to my real father, George Sanders.

Whenever George Sanders's friends would look at me and ask him, "Is that your son?" he would always answer, "That's what his mother says." That really hurt me. I never heard him admit that I was his son until I was in the eleventh grade. At a high school football game, while I was jogging off the field after scoring a touchdown for my team, he was next to the bench saying, "That's my boy." I could not believe it. Most of the time, though, he didn't treat me like his son. The people who paid for my mother to travel to Tokyo for the Olympics would have sent my father, too, but he said to me, "I don't feel like going halfway around the world for the fucking Olympics." And when I played in Super Bowl V against Baltimore in Miami in January 1971, I had a ticket for my father, but he didn't show up. This time he only would have had to go the four hundred miles from Jacksonville to Miami, which he had done many times before, but seeing me play in the Super Bowl wasn't important enough to him. I don't know if he wasn't proud of me or what. But he didn't see me run in the Olympics and he never saw me play a single game of pro football. Maybe it was too much effort for him to see me play anywhere other than Jacksonville.

My father owned a shoeshine parlor on Florida Avenue in East Jacksonville, about a mile from where I lived. Florida Avenue was the center of action in Hell's Hole. All the liquor stores, bars, movie houses barber shops, restaurants, and clothing shops—everything—were on Florida Avenue. And my father was one of the stars on the strip. He was a star because shining shoes wasn't his real business; it was just a front for his numbers operation, which sold ten numbers for a dollar.

My father made a lot of money from the numbers and was always flashing big chunks of cash. All the undesirables—the shoplifters, numbers runners, and the rest of the small-time crooks—hung around him; he was the big shot. And on weekends, when everybody was off work, people would put on clean clothes and come straight to Florida Avenue to shop, eat, drink, and play the numbers.

For years, I had to open up his shop at seven-thirty every morning; close it at seven-thirty or eight at night during the week and ten on weekends; make sure the shop was clean; and make sure the soda pop, the cookies, and the candy were lined up. When I shined shoes, I had to split my money right down the middle with my father, just like all his other employees, but I had all those other responsibilities, too. That wasn't fair and I hated it.

I guess the most love my father showed me was when he taught me to drive when I was eleven years old. My father always had a new car, and I was allowed to drive his car. That lasted until I was fifteen, when he bought a brand-new Dodge. About a week later, while I was driving the new car down the hill near my house, I went over a bump too fast and broke the axle. Can you imagine what was going through my mind when I had to walk back up and tell him, "Your car is down there with a broken axle"? Man, was he mad.

Also when I was about eleven, my father bought me a bicycle for Christmas. A few months later, someone stole it out of my yard. When I told my father about it, he said, "You let someone steal your bike; you won't get nothin' else." He won another bicycle, a red Schwinn, in a raffle, and though I wanted that bicycle so bad, he wouldn't give it to me. My father put it in a restaurant that belonged to a friend of his. I used to go to the restaurant every day just to see the bike. My father kept the bike until he could sell it, but he wouldn't let me have it.

My father may not have had a good influence on me, but our next-door neighbor, W. C. Mitchell, did. Mr. Mitchell was the pastor of the Little Rock Baptist Church where I went to church. His full-time job was as a postman, but he somehow had enough money to buy a new car every year, the only new car in the neighborhood (my father didn't live near us), and he drove me to church in his car every Sunday morning. Every time he ran out of cigarettes, he would call me and I would run to the corner grocery store a few blocks away and get him a pack. He would give me a nickel or a dime for getting his cigarettes, so I had money in my pocket to buy candy, chewing gum, comic books, and other things that boys want.

When I was eleven I got into my first organized sports, Little League baseball. We had to walk to the stadium, which was about four or five miles away, but at least we had uniforms, provided by people in the community. I played shortstop and center field, but I wasn't that good a shortstop; the balls came at me too fast, and one time a ground ball fractured my wrist. But I could really get the ball out in center field. And that was when I was glad my name was Bob Hayes instead of Bob Sanders; I used to tell myself I was Willie Mays out there and rhyme Hayes with Mays.

At that time, I dreamed about being a major league baseball player. Naturally, Jackie Robinson was one of my idols. Not only was he a great athlete and a trailblazer, but all during my childhood, I used to hear stories about how the Jacksonville city officials had prevented Jackie's team, the minor league Montreal Royals, and the Brooklyn Dodgers from playing an exhibition game at Durkee Field in 1946 by locking the two teams out of the stadium. The reason Jacksonville's great white fathers gave was, "It is part of the Rules and Regulations of the Recreation Department that Negroes and whites cannot compete against each other on a city-owned playground." That was the atmosphere I grew up in.

Another of my heroes was Hank Aaron, who made history in April 1953, when I was ten, when the Milwaukee Braves assigned him to the Jacksonville Braves of the Class A South Atlantic League. Hank Aaron was the first black to play in the South Atlantic League and with white ballplayers in Jacksonville, and I used to go over to Durkee Field as often as possible to see him play. So did a lot of other folks; Hank was the league's Most Valuable Player that year, and attendance at Durkee Field more than doubled over the year before. He eventually married the sister of a childhood friend of mine, Robert Lucas. Robert went on to play baseball at Florida A & M while I was there, and he's now the head baseball coach at our alma mater.

I had run track in the seventh and eighth grades, and in a span of two weeks, I entered the 50-, 100-, and 200-yard dashes; the 400- and 880-yard relays; and the high jump, long jump, and pole vault, and won them all. But after those two weeks, my father made me stop. He always thought sports was a waste of time.

Josh Baker, my father's right-hand man in the numbers business, used to organize races for me and the other kids on the sidewalk outside the shoeshine shop so that the grownups could place bets on us. Bill Logan, one of our neighbors, was my brother's age, and after Ernest went into the army, Bill and I became close. He knew that I could run fast—he was the first one who detected that I was real fast—and he always bet on me. When I was in the ninth grade, he bet on me against a twelfth grader, whom I beat. I also earned money by betting on myself. But I ran mainly for pride, so I could have bragging rights the next day.

By that time I was at Matthew Gilbert, a junior–senior high school, and Josh Baker was real big in the school's alumni association. Josh had told the high school coaches and the principal about me, and they started keeping an eye on me. Earl Kitchings, who was then an assistant football coach and later the head coach, used to see me in activity class, wearing street shoes and still outrunning the guys on the track team. And in football games in gym class, I was the leader. Earl Kitchings went to Jimmy Thompson, the head high school football coach, and said, "You come around here and see our future star."

Earl Kitchings and Jimmy Thompson visited my father and asked him to let me play for Matthew Gilbert, but my father said no. When Josh asked him why he had refused, my father said, "I want him to stay here and run this shoeshine parlor and help in my numbers business. I make more money than the principal, the football coach, his teacher, and his counselor all put together, and he can do the same thing." Finally Josh said, "I'll keep this place in the afternoon while he practices football," so my father agreed to let me play. Although Josh Baker left the store after two days, I was already on the football team, so my father had to find someone else to run the shop for him.

I joined the Matthew Gilbert football team in August 1958, just before school opened for my junior year. My sixteenth birthday was still four months away, and I was only about five feet nine and 140 pounds. The coaches didn't know if I would ever be large enough to play big-time football in a place like Florida, which has always been one of the top states for producing high school football players, along with California, Pennsylvania, and Texas. Matthew Gilbert played in what was called the Big Nine Conference, which was made up of the best black teams from all over the state. But after I went out for football, I started growing, and in one year I grew two inches to reach my full height, five feet eleven, and went from 140 pounds to 165 pounds.

It was very hot when we started workouts in August, on a sand practice field. And Jimmy Thompson and Earl Kitchings were yelling, "Keep up! Keep up!" That first day was probably the toughest practice of my life. It was the first time I had ever taken responsibility to do something, and I had to pay the price. I was really drained, just exhausted. Every day, we had to put on our uniforms at the high school and then walk to the Boys' Parental Home, where we practiced. It was a mile each way. So we were in condition, that's for sure.

My junior year, my first year of football, we had a great team. We went 11 and 0 and beat Dillard High School of Fort Lauderdale for the state championship of black schools. I didn't play much, just in spots behind

Willie Haywood, our starting left halfback. I carried the ball only nine times all year, although I did run for a 99-yard touchdown from scrimmage against Booker T. Washington High School of Miami at Durkee Field, which is still a Matthew Gilbert record. That's when my father finally claimed me as his son.

During my senior year, we didn't have such a good team. We had only six lettermen back, and our record was 4 and 5. My best friend, Charles Sutton, played fullback, and he and I carried the team. I scored five touchdowns in one game, carried the ball seventy-eight times for 525 yards and a 6.7 average, and led the team in punt and kickoff returns and scoring. I was first-team all-city and second-team in the Big Nine Conference behind Mack Hill, who later played for the Kansas City Chiefs until he died during what was supposed to have been routine knee surgery. I played both ways, runningback and defensive back, and I punted thirty-two times for a 36.2-yard average and I also kicked off and kicked extra points. I could kick off over the goal line and punt as far as 60 or 70 yards. I didn't come off the field from the time the game started until it was over, except for halftime. I even got to throw a pass, the only one of my entire football career. We were playing Jones High School from Orlando, and late in a close game, with the ball deep in our territory, we called a halfback pass. The quarterback reversed and flipped the ball out to me, and I threw the pass. But one of the Jones High players intercepted my pass and ran it in for a touchdown, so they beat us.

The biggest sporting event for blacks in Jacksonville each year was the grudge match between Matthew Gilbert and New Stanton. It was always the last game of the year and was played in the Gator Bowl. On defense, my responsibility as rover back was to cover the best receiver on the other team. In my senior year, I had to cover New Stanton's Alfred Denson, who was considered the best high school football player in Jacksonville. Alfred was an all-American and he led the Big Nine Conference in receiving. When I shut him out in the big game, it opened a lot of people's eyes about my abilities as a football player.

As soon as the football season ended that year, I turned to the basketball court. I led the city in rebounding with an average of nineteen rebounds a game, including thirty-five in one game (even at five feet eleven, I could dunk the ball). I also averaged nearly eleven points a game, although I was primarily a defensive player, and I was named first-team all-city.

Then came my busiest time of the year, the spring. That spring, we had track meets on Wednesdays and Fridays and baseball games on Tuesdays and Thursdays. At least I had Mondays off.

I played baseball only during my senior year, and although my batting average was just .238, I knocked in ten runs in twenty-one at bats and stole seven bases in eight attempts. Our team hit three home runs all season, and I hit two of them. I was a right-handed hitter with a lot of power. We played some games in Durkee Field (the Jacksonville Braves had moved by then to a new stadium out by the Gator Bowl). I always dreamed of being Hank Aaron, and I hit a home run out of the park over the left-field wall with two runners on base in a game against New Stanton.

But my specialty was defense, and between that and my power, I was the first-team center fielder on the all-city team. *Nothing* in center field got by me. Most of our games were played at the field at Boys' Parental Home on the East Side. The field was all dirt and sand, with clay around the bases, and in the outfield there was a big garden with corn and sugarcane. If a ball was hit hard, you had to run through the sugarcane and across a ditch to try to catch it. Whether the ball was hit deep, short, to left center field, to right center field, into the cornfield at the Boys' Parental Home field, or back against the fence at Durkee Field, when I played center field, the ball was caught.

Because of my father's attitude, I had decided not to play anything except football when I was in eleventh grade. But in the spring of that year, I was fooling around in gym class while we were running outside on a blacktop road. The track team was practicing in a field next to the road, and I found out who their fastest sprinter was. I got next to him and told him, "I can beat you." There was no way he could duck my challenge and keep face, so we got it on right there in the road. And I beat him easily, by about five yards. Frank Cannon, the track coach, came running over and said, "I have to have you on my team. You have 9.6 speed. I've never had a sprinter that fast before."

From that first informal race, no one at Matthew Gilbert could touch me. But Alfred Austin of New Stanton was known as the city's fastest runner. He had been beating everybody in the city since he was in the sixth or seventh grade, and he had run the 100 in 9.9, a Jacksonville record. Alfred was a year ahead of me, had been running track for several years, and had it all over me in terms of form and experience; I had no technique at all. And the first meet after I joined the track team was against New Stanton on a grass track; there weren't any cinder tracks available for blacks that week. Of course, I was used to running on grass because we didn't have a cinder track at Matthew Gilbert, so we trained on grass, sand, or on the streets and highways.

I can still picture that race against Alfred Austin. I had on orange-and-white shorts (his were blue and white). I dug a hole to start from, the way Jesse Owens did in the old days (we couldn't afford starting blocks, which made no difference to me because I didn't know how to use them anyway). Alfred had a great start and got off way in front of me. But by the 60-yard mark I was even with him, and I won in 10.1—not a bad time for my first race and on grass. Nobody could believe that Alfred Austin had been defeated. It was as if Spud Webb had beaten Kareem Abdul-Jabbar in a one-on-one basketball game.

The next time I faced Austin we ran on a cinder track at Wilder Park. My start was still terrible, and I stumbled at the gun, but I came on and we were dead even at the finish line. I was timed in 9.6, Alfred in 9.7, and the judges declared him the winner, although a lot of people thought I had won.

Frank Cannon made me work on my starts after that, and I used to do twenty-five or thirty starts a day. When Alfred and I met for the third time in the Duval County meet for black schools, I was primed. I had a decent start and won by several yards. My official time was 9.6. Although Frank Cannon and Earl Kitchings had clocked me at 9.4, they were afraid to report my time as 9.4 because nobody would have believed that a sixteen-year-old with hardly any experience or training had come within one-tenth of a second of the world record. Frank and Earl and the officials at the race were afraid that the whites who controlled the track world would think it was just a case of some black people trying to cheat, so my time was reported as 9.6.

The same day, in the last meet of my junior year in high school, I also won the 220-yard dash; the high jump, with a city record of 6 feet; and the broad jump. And I ran on our 440- and 880-yard relay teams, which also won, to give me six first places in six tries.

My 9.6 or 9.4 or whatever it was against Alfred Austin was the best time I had in high school. Alfred graduated and went on to Florida A & M, and I didn't have any competition in my senior year. Throughout my track career, I ran primarily to win races, not to set records. Of course, I wanted the records, but usually I couldn't do my best unless someone was pushing me. My fastest time during my senior year was 9.7, although in the high jump I did increase my personal best—and the county record, too—from 6 feet to 6 feet 2. I dominated all my usual events that year—the sprints, the high jump, and the broad jump—and I even threw the shot put in one meet and won first place.

When I was in the eleventh grade, there wasn't enough money in the Matthew Gilbert budget to send the track team to the state high school meet for blacks at Florida A & M. The situation was the same in my senior year, but Earl Kitchings and Frank Cannon thought I deserved a chance to face statewide competition, so they paid, out of their own pockets, for me and several others to travel to Florida A & M, which is in Tallahassee, about 175 miles from Jacksonville. Frank and Earl drove us in their cars, they paid for the gas and our food, and we stayed in dormitories at Florida A & M. We left Jacksonville on Friday, took part in the meet on Saturday, and returned home on Sunday. The meet was a bit of a disappointment for me because on one of my tries in the long jump, I hit the board the wrong way and cut my heel open. That injury hampered me for the rest of the meet, and I didn't win a single event. I had six second-place finishes: in the broad jump, the high jump, the 220, and the 100 and as anchor of our relay team in the 440 and 880. In the 100, I won my heat, but came in second in the final to Jimmy "Peach Head" Douglas, a boy from Miami. That race made Douglas the most sought-after sprinter in the state of Florida by the college recruiters, but he got killed in a shooting accident before he had a chance to show how great he could have been on the college level. My loss to him was the second and last defeat in the 100-yard dash during my high school career.

I wasn't what you would call a scholar-athlete. I never cared much for the academic part of school. My attention span was short, I was always hyperactive, and I had trouble concentrating on my lessons. Matthew Gilbert was a small school—there were only 120 students in my graduating class—and I was playing four sports. The sports were time consuming, but they were what I was interested in. Most classes were boring to me. I liked history and math, but I *hated* biology and science and I hated to go to the library. Because my father was a big shot in that area, and I was the school's star athlete, teachers would not fail me. My homeroom teacher, Mr. Scott, and Earl Kitchings went to every teacher and checked on me every month to see how I was doing and to make sure the teachers knew they had better give me a passing grade.

I spent a lot of time hanging out with my buddies, especially Charles Sutton. Charles and I were really close. I was the fastest guy in the school and he was the strongest. He was so strong that he could stand against a telephone pole, grab the spikes that stuck out, and bend them. We used to chase girls and raise hell—the usual sort of stuff. My father lent me his Dodge the night of my senior prom, and Charles and I and a couple of other guys went to the beach with our dates, stopping every few minutes to take a leak because of all the beer we had drunk. We had a lot of fun, but we were good kids. We never stole anything or hurt anybody or did anything very bad.

A lot of my learning took place outside school. My father had quite a few girlfriends. The one I remember best was Edith. Edith was about five feet nine, slender, gorgeous, and maybe fifteen years older than me. She lived in an eight-dollar-a-night room in a hotel where some of my friends stayed, and one day when I was twelve, I went there to visit someone. Edith heard me coming up the stairs and knew it was me from the way I walked. She opened her door and asked me to come into her room. "Bob, have you ever made love to a lady?" she asked me. I admitted that I hadn't. "Let me teach you how to make love," Edith said. She went and took a shower, came out, took my clothes off, laid me right between her legs, stuck it in her, and screwed me. I stayed in there for a while without ever getting an orgasm.

After that I at least knew what I was doing, and I started getting laid regularly when I was sixteen and in the eleventh grade. My girlfriend during the last two years of high school was a girl who was a year behind me at Matthew Gilbert. I used to take her to movies, parties, speedboat races, and then to bed. I got her pregnant, but she had an abortion; neither of us was ready to be a parent.

By the time I was in college, though, I had produced two daughters. One was with a girlfriend of mine from Jacksonville; the other was with a girl I knew in college. Neither mother asked me for money, although I used to give them some every once in a while. I still see the first girl's mother sometimes when I'm in Jacksonville, but I've lost touch with the other. The last I heard, she was married and living in Virginia. A few years ago, when I was visiting Jacksonville, a girl in her early twenties came up to me and said, "You're my dad." Her grandfather and my father were friends, and I did go out with her mother once. Just once—I can't even remember her name now. We went to bed, but she was having her period at the time. She never told me that I got her pregnant, and I don't believe I did.

■ ■ ■

By my last year of high school, I had a big decision to make. Allen University in Columbia, South Carolina; Morris Brown College in Atlanta; and South Carolina State offered me basketball scholarships; a scout from the Los Angeles Angels, who were joining the American League as an expansion team the next year, wanted to sign me to be the next Willie Mays, and in football, I had scholarship offers from colleges and universities all over the country—the University of Southern California (USC); UCLA; San Jose State; Ohio State; the universities of Nebraska, Oklahoma, and Colorado; Syracuse University; and Penn State. Southern University in Baton Rouge and Tennessee State offered me scholarships in both football and track. The only schools that did not go after me were those in the Southeastern, Southwestern, and Atlantic Coast conferences, which didn't have black players in those days.

My first moves were to reject the basketball scholarships that had been offered to me and to tell the Angels' scout that I wasn't interested. The scout and I never got as far as talking about money because there was no way that I was going to do anything but go to college and play football, which was always my first love. I had grown up following Jim Brown; Lenny Moore of the Colts; and my special favorite, Willie Galimore, the great Galloping Galimore, the star runner for Florida A & M and the Chicago Bears, and my lifelong dream was to be a professional football player. I identified so strongly with Willie Galimore because he went to high school in St. Augustine, which is forty miles from Jacksonville. With all the great athletes the state of Florida has produced, he is still considered one of the best high school runningbacks in Florida history. Willie became Florida A & M's first three-time all-American, and he was the school's first alumnus to star on a pro team after he joined the Chicago Bears in 1957. From the time I started playing touch football with my friends as a little boy, I wanted to be Willie Galimore.

Willie Galimore was one reason I leaned toward Florida A & M from the start. Another reason was the school's legendary coach, Jake Gaither, who was idolized in the black community the same way as coaches like Paul "Bear" Bryant and Knute Rockne were in the white community.

A third point in the school's favor was that nearly every black high school football player in the state wanted to go there. To win a scholarship to Florida A & M meant you were recognized as the cream of the crop. While you were waiting to see if Jake Gaither would offer you a scholarship, everyone would be teasing you, "You're not good enough because Florida

A & M only takes the best." The final attraction of Florida A & M was that it was close enough to home for my family and friends to see me play.

Earl Kitchings later told me that Charles Sutton and Louis Hill, a tackle, were the players from our team that Florida A & M really wanted. The school was going to offer me only a half-scholarship, but then Louis Hill decided to attend Edward Waters College in Jacksonville, along with another pal of mine, Charles Grover. When the waiting ended and the scholarships were handed out, five musketeers from Jacksonville, all in the skill positions, were bound for Florida A & M: Charles Sutton; myself; Alfred Denson; Benny Thomas, a quarterback from Northwestern High School; and Calvin Lang, a halfback from New Stanton.

THE BLACK
BEAR BRYANT

I left Jacksonville for Tallahassee in August 1960, a seventeen-year-old man-child, going away from home for the first time. Packing wasn't much of a problem: I went off to college with three brand-new pairs of pants, one pair of shoes, some underwear, a couple of shirts, and twenty-five dollars, which my uncle, Horace Green, had given me. My father wouldn't give me a dime after I got my scholarship. He still didn't believe in education, still thought college was a waste of time, still thought I could make a lot more money selling numbers for him. I didn't have any money to spend until I was the fastest man on the track team and I learned how to ask one of the coaches for money. Jake Gaither; Robert (Pete) Griffin, an assistant football coach and the head track coach; and the rest of the assistant coaches in football—Robert Mungen, Costa Kittles, Hanson Tookes, and Macon Williams—were always good for a few dollars. Sometimes a bunch of us freshmen would go over to Jake Gaither's house and mow his lawn or line the university track and the tennis courts or do other jobs, and employees of the athletic department would give us a little change out of their pockets. And there were a lot of home boys from Jacksonville there, students who would buy me food and things.

I lived in Gibbs Hall, the newest boys' dormitory. Charles Sutton, Benny Thomas, and I were roommates right from the start. We reported two weeks before the rest of the students. The first rule was don't be late for practice, but the three of us overslept and were almost late for the first one. We hadn't been able to sleep, we were so excited, and then we woke up late. We had won scholarships to Florida A & M, which had the greatest coach in the world and a tradition of always winning—and winning big. The 1959 team had gone 10 and 0, outscored the opposition by 407 to 71, and won games by scores like 74 to 0, 68 to 6, 64 to 0, and 52 to 8.

We had run a lot of sweeps in high school, and the coach, Earl Kitchings, had told me that if I was really going to get nailed, just to run out of bounds, "because we can't stand to lose you." On my first plays in practice in college, I was running sweeps way outside, and Macon Williams told me to cut back inside. I just could not do it. But Williams insisted, "I want you to cut inside. This is big-time football now. You are no longer at Matthew Gilbert High School."

After our first workout that first morning of practice, we had our conditioning sprints, and that's when I started beating guys. We freshmen wore red jerseys with white shorts and football shoes, so we were easy to pick out. We had eight or nine guys on the team who could run one hundred yards in under 9.6, but I kept beating everyone in windsprints. Finally, Bob Paremore, who was a year ahead of me and already a star, came over and said, "I'm going to get next to this rookie and see what he can do." I kicked his ass and I said to him, "You will *never* beat me, in a time trial, in a heat, or in anything else." Some of the veterans started riding Paremore, "How could you let this freshman outrun you?" and he kept challenging me to race, but he never beat me, not on his fastest day and my slowest one. Even though we were rivals, we became close friends. After his NFL career ended, Paremore returned to Tallahassee, where he coaches and teaches high school, and we are still friends.

In spite of my speed, the coaches decided to redshirt me and all the other twenty or so freshman recruits, except for Al Denson, my friend and rival from Jacksonville. Al was the only one who made the varsity team that first year.

Even though I didn't play in 1960, I was considered one of the stars of the future, someone who had a shot at being the next Willie Galimore. Willie came back to Tallahassee after the 1960 NFL season, and he and I were introduced and became close friends. He was like an older brother to me; he would take me for long drives in his car and just give me advice. We got closer every year. In 1963, while he was recovering from operations on both his knees, I invited him to come train with me. We used to go out on back roads of Tallahassee and run one hundred yards at half speed, slow down and walk fast for another fifty yards, and do that over and over until we had done five or ten miles at a time. Willie was in the best shape of his life by the time we finished.

But our friendship ended in tragedy. When the U.S. track team met the Russians at the Los Angeles Coliseum in 1964, it had been announced that my hamstring injury had healed and I was going to run. When I got to Los Angeles and tested my leg, I decided not to run, but Willie didn't know that. On July 26, 1964, the night after the meet ended, one of the guys on our team had a party. I was riding back to my hotel after the party—I will never forget this—and I heard a news bulletin on the radio saying, "Two Chicago Bears have been killed in a car accident. We'll be right back with the details." I started praying, "Please don't let it be Willie, please don't let it be Willie." Then the announcer came back on and said, "Willie Galimore of Florida A & M and John Farrington of Prairie View were killed in a car accident tonight near Rensselaer, Indiana." That's where the Bears held their training camp. Someone had told Willie that my race was going to be on television in a few minutes, and he was rushing to get back to his dorm at St. Joseph's College so he could see me run. Willie was driving about fifty-five miles an hour on a winding country road when he tried to go around a curve. His Volkswagen convertible went off the road, turned over, ejected him and Farrington, and rolled over on top of them. When I found out why Willie was driving so fast, I blamed myself, and it took me a long time to get over his death.

Tallahassee is in the northwest part of Florida—right on the Georgia border. A lot of rednecks used to come down and visit our campus and shout, "Nigger," and things like that. When I was at Florida A & M, the city was totally segregated; we could not even go to a white movie theater. The Tallahassee police force was all white, too. These tough policemen used to come into our area and beat up blacks or take them to jail and work them over, and nobody would ask any questions.

One Saturday night in November of my freshman year I was sitting with some other guys on the porch outside Gibbs Hall. We wanted something to eat, so Charles Sutton, Benny Thomas, and I flipped a coin to see who would go to the store and get some bread, peanut butter, and cold cuts to bring back to the dormitory. I lost. As I left the dormitory, I ran into James Vickers, another freshman. Vickers was the defensive back for Booker T. Washington High School in Miami who chased me the time I ran for a 99-yard touchdown in high school. At Florida A & M, he was a runningback and he and I became good friends.

As I started to walk away from the dorm, Vickers asked me where I was going. I told him I was going to the store. The store was east of the dormitory, and you had to walk on a street that had no streetlights, down a hill, and around a corner. Vickers said, "I'm going across town, Bobby, can I walk with you?" I was glad to have the company, so I said yes. While we were walking down the hill in the dark, this short guy was coming up the hill. He was black, but I couldn't tell if he was a teenager or a grownup who happened to be short. I was walking right behind Vickers, who walked up to the guy. I saw a little motion, and at that moment, a police car with two cops in it turned the corner. The cops put their spotlight on, and I turned and saw Vickers put something inside his pants. The cops got out of their car, and I could see that both of them were big. That was all I needed to see. I was pretty sure they were either going to beat me up or arrest me, so I took off and ran, without knowing what happened to Vickers. I never looked back. You didn't look back in Tallahassee at that time.

The next night, while I was eating dinner in the student union building, Charles Sutton told me the campus police were looking for me. I went to them and they said, "We're sorry, Bob, but we've got to take you down to the jail." "What for?" I asked. One of them said, "They made James Vickers tell that you and he robbed somebody." I said, "What robbery?" The campus policeman said, "Last night, when you guys were going to the store." It turned out that Vickers had pulled out a plastic gun, not even a real one, and made the guy, who was a student at Florida A & M, give him what he had in his pockets. The kid who got robbed was as rich as the rest of us; he had eleven cents and two sticks of chewing gum on him. I never saw Vickers pull any kind of gun and I never heard him say a word to the kid we were supposed to have held up.

So I went downtown and they put me in the city jail.

Meanwhile, the football team went to Miami for the Orange Blossom Classic. A lot of people asked where I was, and some of my friends said I was sick and couldn't make the trip, but the word got out that I had been arrested. After the game, Earl Kitchings drove straight from Miami to Tallahassee to see me. The guards wouldn't let him visit me, so he stood outside the jail, which consisted of two wings, and shouted my name until he found out where I was. He yelled up to me—I was on the second floor and I could look down and see him, but he couldn't see me—and asked if I was okay and if I needed anything.

This was one of the few times in my life that my father helped me. Some of the assistant coaches had told Jake Gaither what happened, but Jake hardly knew me at the time and believed I had embarrassed the team, so I might just as well stay in jail. Jake later said his reaction was, "He's a freshman, let him take the punishment for something like that. I don't have time to fool with him." But then my father came and asked Jake to get me out of jail. So Jake looked into the incident and found out it really wasn't my fault; he got them to release me after a week.

By the time Jake got me out, I was both filthy and starving. I had on an orange-and-white jacket and some brown pants when they arrested me, and I wore those clothes the whole time I was in jail, seven days. And it was so dirty in that jail that I did not bathe the whole time. The food was so terrible that I wouldn't eat it, and I lost a lot of weight. I was just eating candy and snacks with money that Charles Sutton had brought me. I thought I was going to get out any time.

After a few days in jail, I signed a confession in the hopes of getting out, and I pleaded guilty to robbery later in court. I couldn't afford a lawyer, and I didn't have any witnesses to back me up, except James Vickers, who was in big trouble because it turned out he had a previous criminal record.

I came up for sentencing on April 11, 1961. My mother and Jake Gaither were there in the courtroom. Jake had gotten me a lawyer, but Jake himself got up and pleaded with the judge. "If you give me this boy for four years, I guarantee you he won't get in trouble and he'll make you proud of him," Jake told the judge. The judge, who was white, thought for a minute. I was afraid he was going to send me to the pen. Finally he said, "Okay, Jake, I'll give you this boy. But he deserves some time. They robbed this boy, took away his rights, and Bob was involved because he was on the scene. Bob could have gotten the police and pointed out the guy who was robbing this boy. But instead he ran." The judge placed me on probation for ten years. Vickers got six months in jail and, of course, never played football for Florida A & M.

For the remaining four and a half years I was in college, I had to report to a probation officer in Tallahassee once a month, as well as any time I left Tallahassee. Before the team went out of town for football games, the team bus would stop downtown first so I could report to my probation officer, tell him where I was going, and then run back outside to the bus. Or Bob Paremore and I would ride to away games in Jake Gaither's Lincoln, and Jake would stop at the probation office.

That system worked fine for football games, but during the spring and summer of my second, third, and fourth years at Florida A & M, I was traveling all over the United States and the world for track meets and personal appearances. I went to my probation officer and told him when I was traveling I couldn't fly all the way back just to sign a piece of paper and talk to him for a few minutes. He said, "We want you here!" Finally,

I took it on my own not to report when I was away. Then I started getting letters from the parole board, so when I got back from one trip during my last semester of college, I went to the parole office and signed in. The parole officer, a white man, said, "You know, we could easily put your fucking ass in jail. We could have had you picked up when you landed in New York or Los Angeles and put your ass in jail."

The whole affair came to an end several months after I won the Olympics. When I was arrested, the police made a mistake and booked me under the name Haynes. A Tallahassee newspaper had a tiny story about the robbery, but nobody picked up on it because nobody had heard of Robert Haynes, and at that time, few people had heard of Robert Hayes. But in March 1965, someone tipped off the *Miami Herald*, which ran the story under the headline "Gold Medal Winner Bob Hayes Outsprints Court Record." You can imagine how embarrassed I was, five months after signing with the Dallas Cowboys.

Needless to say, I hadn't wanted to do anything that might lead to publicity about my arrest. But after the *Miami Herald* broke the story, I had nothing more to lose, and I was very upset about what the probation officer had said to me. So I went to Jake Gaither and said, "Coach, I'm representing this whole country and I'm getting all this bullshit from the local parole office. It's scaring me, I can't concentrate on my studies. Is there anything you can do?" Jake was friendly with the governor of Florida, Haydon Burns, who had been mayor of Jacksonville, my hometown, and knew all about me, so Jake picked up the phone and called Burns. We made an appointment with Governor Burns and went to his office, where I explained to him exactly what was happening. Governor Burns was so upset that he picked up the phone and called the parole officer and told him to walk across the street and bring all my records. My records showed the months that I did not report, but for every time I did not report, we showed the governor where I was running that month. Governor Burns finally said, "I want this man released from probation immediately." Someone from the parole board replied, "I don't think he should have his probation ended. He hasn't been reporting in. He hasn't been following our guidelines and taking his responsibility." Governor Burns said, "If you don't end his probation, I will pardon him myself and see about getting another parole board." Within about ten days, the parole board voted to release me from probation.

If getting ten years' probation for allegedly stealing two sticks of chewing gum and eleven cents isn't racism, what is? But thanks to Governor Burns, I finally got a pardon.

.   .   .

My reputation as a runner got me in some more trouble a year or two later. There was a rape on campus and the guy who did it ran away so fast that nobody could catch him. Soon the police came to my dorm room, took me downtown, and started questioning me. I said, "Look, I had nothing to do with it," but one cop said, "The only one who could run that fast was Bob Hayes." Because my outfit was different from what the rapist was wearing and the rapist was lighter skinned and taller than me, they finally let me go.

Other than those two incidents, I wasn't involved in anything more serious than the normal college pranks. Once, when a bunch of us football players got hungry, we stole some chickens from a farm and went to where one of our tackles, Peter Livingston, lived. We killed the chickens and Peter cooked them. But the chicken rustling turned out a lot better than the chicken cooking did. Peter thought he was putting flour on the chickens, but he used baking soda by mistake. That was the worst-tasting chicken I ever had. It was the first time I ever saw fried chicken that blacks wouldn't eat. After we threw away the uneaten chicken, Al Denson; Curtis Miranda, our center and one of my best friends; and Charles Sutton showed up. When they found out that we had stolen the chickens, they said, "Man, this is a state university and the FBI is after you guys." I couldn't eat for a week, I just knew I was going back to jail.

In one way, my arrest with James Vickers worked out to my advantage. If it had never happened, I might never have gotten as close as I did to Jake Gaither, who turned out to be the most important man in my life.

Like almost every other black high school football player in the state of Florida, I had grown up dreaming of playing for Jake and for Florida A & M. Jake took over as coach and athletic director at the school in 1945, and in the fifteen seasons before I arrived in 1960, his record was 120 wins, 20 losses, and 4 ties. Since 1945, his team had won the Southern Intercollegiate Athletic Conference (SIAC) championship every year except 1951 and 1952 and was named the National Negro Collegiate Football champion in 1950, 1954, 1957, and 1959.

Jake was so great that he actually put a handicap on himself by refusing to recruit football players from outside Florida. Most coaches recruited players from out of state, but Jake, recognizing that the pool of talent in Florida gave him an advantage over the coaches of teams he played, would not approach a player from another state. Jake knew he could win with just the Florida boys. If a player from out of state wanted to play for Florida A & M, he had to contact Jake first.

Jake had a brilliant football mind, as brilliant as Tom Landry's. Jake invented the split-line T-offense in the mid-1950s, which had our offensive line spread out much wider than the standard split-T to stretch the defense and give us more holes. His teams averaged fifty points a game for many years—more than a lot of college basketball teams did in those days—and Jake was known as one of the top coaches in the country, black or white. Jake was the coach who first said he liked his players "a-gile, mo-bile, and hos-tile," which has become the favorite expression of many coaches, and he was involved in another innovation that came out of Florida A & M—spiking the ball after a touchdown. Willie Galimore was the first player to spike the ball in the end zone. Jake never stopped his players from spiking; in his words, "When we score at A & M, I'm happy and the boys are happy. What does it hurt to fling the ball to the ground? We've never ruined a football yet." I think a lot of people don't understand that spiking the ball isn't meant to show up the opposition; it's just a celebration of self-satisfaction for the athlete who has scored.

In addition to the best players and the best system, Florida A & M also had the best facilities. Even our bus, which we called "The Snake" because we were the Rattlers, was famous because we were the only black school with a new, air-conditioned bus to use on road trips. We even had the best band, the Marching 100, which was invited to appear at numerous NFL games and made many appearances on national television. With everything added together, Florida A & M had a fabulous tradition.

Jake retired at the end of the 1969 season, after twenty-five seasons and a record of 203 wins, 36 losses, and 4 ties. Of course, all Jake's records were made in games against other black schools. The team never played any of the white schools, which had everything to lose and nothing to gain by scheduling us. The coaches of the major colleges were afraid of us, but they respected Jake as their equal. Jake held an annual coaching clinic at Florida A & M that attracted white coaches like Bear Bryant, Woody Hayes, and Ara Parseghian. I remember when Jake Gaither and Bear Bryant started joking with each other at one of Jake's clinics. Jake had just finished writing a book on the split-line T and he was explaining, "I can either have my linemen tight and run a counter or I can have them open and run off the tackle or off the guard." I remember Bear Bryant saying, "I got some guys like Lee Roy Jordan and I'll put them in the gaps and we'll just shoot those gaps and beat you all day." And Jake said, "Yes, and if you do, I'll put the fastest man in the world going around those ends on you, buddy, and you'll never catch us.''

There's no doubt in my mind that Jake would have coached a major college or professional team if not for racism. When I joined the Dallas Cowboys, Jake Gaither had prepared me so well that I was primed to play pro football. As a matter of fact, we were using exactly the same terminology for audibles at the line of scrimmage in college that the Cowboys used, so I had no trouble picking up the Cowboy system.

Since our team couldn't play in the Rose Bowl, Orange Bowl, Sugar Bowl, or any other big bowl game, Florida A & M had started the Orange Blossom Classic in the 1930s, with the team playing the other top black school from around the country at the Orange Bowl in the final game of the year. Jake knew that black teams didn't have the opportunity to live it up first class the way the white powerhouses did, so he arranged with the sponsors of the Orange Blossom Classic and businessmen from all over Florida to make everything about the game high style. The visiting teams flew into Miami, instead of traveling by bus, and both Florida A & M and our opponents lived and trained at Miami Beach and got exposed to the better things in life. A lot of guys from opposing teams have since told me what a privilege it was for them to be a part of the game. Thanks to Jake, the Orange Blossom Classic became one of the biggest athletic events for blacks each year. Blacks from all over the country would go to it, and whites enjoyed it, too. The crowd was usually about half black and half white, and George Mira and the rest of the University of Miami squad came to see us every year I played in it.

Even Jake's physical presence was commanding. He was only about five feet ten, but he weighed 200 pounds, had a barrel chest, a deep, powerful voice, and the thickest legs I ever saw. He was fifty-seven when I entered Florida A & M in 1960, but he still looked like he could kick any butt on the team. On top of everything else, Jake was the son of a minister and was a deeply religious man. To say that I was totally in awe of him, just like every other kid who ever played for him, would be an understatement. And then I got arrested and got to know him.

Jake knew my background. My mother worked, my father took off, and I didn't have much parental guidance as a kid. I was emotionally immature; I took care of whatever responsibilities I felt like doing. I never had to come home and study my lessons after school (I never did study much; I just got by on natural ability), I always got help because I was the fastest guy around, and I always got pats on the back no matter what

I did. And then, right after I got to Florida A & M, I found myself in serious trouble.

After Jake got me out of jail, I started spending a lot of time at his house. Jake and his wife, Sadie, never had kids of their own. Willie Galimore and I became their kids, and Jake and Sadie treated us like their own flesh and blood. I spent many a night at their house, where I had a little room to myself. Jake and Sadie trusted me with everything, including the key to their home. After Jake got me out of jail, he said, "I want you to promise me one thing, son, you are *not* going to get in trouble again." I promised, "I am not going to get in trouble again." So the day of my drug trial in Dallas nearly twenty years later, I could not say a word to him. All I could do was cry because I knew I had disappointed him. He asked me if I was guilty in the drug case. And I told him I knew that I was legally wrong but morally right because I did not sell any cocaine or take any of the money. He agreed with me after he saw the circumstances.

Jake is still like a father to me. He has always been there when I needed someone to talk to, and I guess he has been my number-one fan. Sadie tells a story about the time when they were on vacation in the summer of 1970, after he had retired. The Cowboys were playing an exhibition game against the Packers, and Jake was listening to it on the radio of his Lincoln Continental. This was one of those see-saw games that the Packers wound up winning, 35 to 34, but I caught a touchdown pass from Craig Morton that put us ahead, 34 to 28, in the fourth quarter. Right about then, smoke started coming out from the hood of Jake's car. Sadie jumped out and yelled, "Jake, Jake, the motor's on fire!" But Jake wouldn't turn off the radio and leave the car. "Wait a minute, Sadie," was all he would say. "Bob just scored a touchdown."

In addition to Jake and Sadie, Pete Griffin, the track coach, and his wife, Charlotte, were another couple who treated me like a son. So when I was at Florida A & M I was surrounded by love. Until then, the only persons who had told me they loved me were my mother, my Aunt Betty, my sister Lena, and my brother Ernest. Otherwise, I didn't know what love was.

I guess what really impressed me about Jake was something that happened in 1961, my first year on the varsity. We were 7 and 0 and getting ready to play Southern University, which had a great team and had handed us our only defeat the year before. Before the game, Jake started praying in that religious voice he had, which he must have inherited from his father. He had each of us stand up by position and tell him, "I'm going to give you everything I've got today." Curtis Miranda, our center, and our right guard, Charley Hobbs, got up, started crying, and said, "Coach, I'm going to give you everything I've got today." That closed me right there with Jake. For some reason it has stuck in my mind ever since. I had never seen anything like that before, and I haven't since. And we went out and pounded Southern, 46 to 0.

I finally got to play a little during that 1961 season. We were famous for our three teams that wore down the opposition—the blood unit, the sweat unit, and the tears unit. Curtis Miranda was the captain of the blood unit, which was the number-one unit. If you made one of those three units, it was like making a professional team. I played some with the blood unit, especially on kickoffs. where I showed my speed, averaging 34 yards on 10 returns, and on punts. But on offense I played behind Bob Paremore and several others at halfback. I carried the ball just fifteen times (for 171 yards and a 10.7 yard average) and caught five passes for 75 yards. We were a dominant team, a lot like Oklahoma is today, except that we could pass as well as run when we needed to. We went 10 and 0 in 1961 and beat Bethune-Cookman College, 76 to 0; Allen University 71 to 0; South Carolina State, 60 to 0; Morris Brown College, 56 to 0; and Benedict College, 52 to 0. Jake Gaither was named the best small college coach of the year. We were so good that halfway through the season, when we were 5 and 0 and had outscored our opposition by 293 to 6, Jake called the team together and warned us not to get cocky. "Beware, there is a law of averages," he lectured us. And then one of our players yelled out, "No, sir, we repealed that law."

I scored three touchdowns that year. My first college touchdown came in the 76 to 0 rout over Bethune-Cookman, which was a private school and wasn't getting the best athletes. I also scored a touchdown in our 34 to 12 victory over North Carolina A & T, in Greensboro. Jesse Jackson, who had transferred from Illinois to North Carolina A & T, was a quarterback on that team, although he didn't play much. Black schools didn't have the best facilities, and A & T's field, which was also used for baseball, still had the pitcher's mound in it. My touchdown was on a long run, and I almost tripped over the pitcher's mound. I was going full speed and didn't see it, but kept my balance and went all the way.

I came into my own as a college football player in 1962, my second season. I started at left halfback and was the second leading rusher on the team behind Bob Paremore, with sixty-six carries for 532 yards and an 8.1 average, the highest on the team. I caught only six passes, the third highest number on the team (we didn't throw the ball that much), but I showed how explosive I could be as a receiver by averaging 26 yards a catch, and I led the Rattlers in both kickoff returns and punt returns, for which I had a phenomenal 30-yard average on seven punts. We went 9 and 1, losing only our final game, 22 to 6 to Jackson State in the Orange Blossom Classic, which broke our 21-game winning streak.

Carrying the ball sixty-six times and catching just six passes was significant for me. Being a runningback helped me a great deal when I went to the pros because running with the ball was natural to me, unlike the other track stars who tried professional football. I didn't have to overcome contact shyness or learn how to run with the ball after I caught it once the Cowboys converted me into a full-time receiver.

I had several big games during 1962: In a 52 to 6 win over Bethune-Cookman, when I gained 121 yards on eight carries; in our 20 to 0 defeat of Tennessee State, when I scored our first touchdown on an 18-yard run; and when I gained 98 yards on just six carries, in our 67 to 0 rout of Allen University.

But I saved my best for our final game of the regular season, when we went home to Jacksonville to play Texas Southern University (TSU) in what was called the Gateway Classic, held at the Gator Bowl. Haydon Burns, who was mayor of Jacksonville then, declared it Bob Hayes Day and gave me a plaque at halftime, and I was all fired up. I opened the scoring with a 90-yard punt return down the left side for a touchdown to give us a 7 to 0 lead in the first quarter. But TSU had a good team, which scored right away, although our team kept the lead at 7 to 6 because Walter Highsmith (whose son, Alonzo, was the Houston Oilers' first-round draft choice several years ago) blocked TSU's extra-point attempt. TSU scored twice more on touchdown passes to Warren Wells, who went on to star for the Oakland Raiders, and they had us down, 18 to 7, going into the fourth quarter. That was the only time I saw Jake get emotional in my five years at Florida A & M. He thought our guys were lying down, and he exploded. All the players were looking at him, and I went over and told him, "Jake, you're our leader and you just can't get that emotionally upset." He looked at me and he said, "You're right." And I said, "Don't worry about it, we're going to get ourselves together and whip them." And we did.

Bob Paremore got us back in the game early in the fourth period with an 85-yard run that cut TSU's lead to 18 to 14. Right after that, we recovered a fumble on the TSU 45; on the first play, I ran up the middle all the way for a touchdown that put us ahead 21 to 18. I scored on a 9-yard run later in the fourth quarter and wound up with 100 yards on eight carries, and we won, 28 to 18.

I didn't do that much in our third game, a 36 to 12 win over Morris Brown, but I'll never forget the trip to Atlanta, the biggest city I had ever been in. I was amazed at the size of the city and the amount of traffic. A friend of my father's always used to say, "You country boys come to the big city wearing taps on your tennis shoes," and that's how I felt in Atlanta.

I also remember a game near the end of the season in Baton Rouge, where we beat Southern University, 25 to 0. I caught a long pass, and one of the Southern players knocked me out of bounds and shoved me into Mrs. Gaither and Conchita Clark, Miss Florida A & M, and I got up fighting.

At the end of the 1962 season, I won my first collegiate football honor, when I was named to the SIAC all-star team, along with Alfred Denson; Bob Paremore; and our fullback, Hewritt Dixon, another future Raider.

My best year on the football field for Florida A & M was 1963, when we went 8 and 2. In our opening game, at home, against Lincoln University, our quarterback, Jim Tullis, threw me touchdown passes of 72 and 76 yards, and we won big, 44 to 6. I scored three touchdowns—two receiving and one running—a couple of weeks later when we won 66 to 0 against Morris Brown. After three wins, we went to Nashville and lost our first game, 14 to 12, to Tennessee State, when Tullis's long pass to me at the end of the game was intercepted. Tullis threw four touchdown passes— one to me, one to Carleton Oats, and two to Al Denson—when we beat North Carolina A & T 32 to 0 in Greensboro. None of us felt much like playing football on November 23, the day after President Kennedy was assassinated, but our home game against Bethune-Cookman went ahead as scheduled, and I scored three touchdowns, two on passes from Tullis and one on a 50-yard punt return, to lead us to a 37 to 14 victory.

Our final regular-season game was again in Jacksonville against TSU. Warren Wells caught passes for TSU's first two touchdowns, and we were behind, 14 to 8, when I tied the game with an 85-yard punt return late in the fourth quarter. But TSU controlled the ball for the rest of the game and scored with nine seconds left to hand us our second loss, 20 to 14. We ended the season as usual in the Orange Blossom Classic, beating

Morgan State 30 to 7. Leroy Kelly, the future Browns star, opened the scoring with a 3-yard run in the second quarter, but after that they couldn't stop us.

Jake Gaither tried to use me sparingly in 1963 because he was worried about my getting hurt with the Olympics coming up the following year. Even so, I was our second leading rusher behind Bobby Felts, although I carried only 55 times for 260 yards and a 4.7 average. I also finished as our second leading receiver, behind Al Denson, with fifteen catches for 401 yards—an average of almost 27 yards a catch—and six touchdowns (I scored 11 altogether, to tie Bobby Felts for the team lead). And I led the team on both punt and kickoff returns. I made the SIAC all-star team for the second year in a row and was named the conference's outstanding athlete.

One of the highlights of my 1963 football season occurred off the field. When we went to Greensboro to play North Carolina A & T, a number of other Florida A & M players joined with a lot of the North Carolina A & T players at a rally where we campaigned for Jesse Jackson, who was running for president of the A & T student body. Jesse played a little against us as a substitute quarterback in that game, but the big thing was that he was elected president, which was his first important office. It was also the start of my lifelong friendship with Jesse.

I learned that Jesse loved to talk, so when I got into the computer-calling business years later, I called him and told him how he could use this machine to talk to people even while he was asleep. I flew to Chicago with the machine and showed him he could use it for dial-a-prayer, fund-raising, or talking to teenagers about teenage pregnancy and drugs. Jesse liked it, and we recorded his message and started calling people from criss-cross directories. He was so pleased with it that when I went to a church service with him one Sunday, he introduced me and told the congregation, "You know, this Bob Hayes here has got me to where I can talk to folks even when I'm asleep."

Jesse and I formed a great relationship over the years. He truly is a great man, even if he does have about the biggest feet I have ever seen for someone his size (he wears size 13 or 14 shoes). He and I used to travel together all over the country, especially while he was leasing our computer. Jesse wanted me to head a fund-raising department for his Operation PUSH, but I would have had to move to Chicago, which I didn't want to do; it's too cold there. I also became close to Andy Thomas, Jesse's personal physician and one of his best friends. The day I got out of jail in 1980, Andy Thomas called me and said, "I want you to come to Chicago and work on this computer. I want you to get out of that redneck state." I still didn't want to move to Chicago. But I did go to Chicago for a few weeks at a time to work on fund-raising with the organization.

One of my best memories of Jesse goes back to 1979. Jesse's youngest son, Yusef, was playing a peewee football game against a team from the West Side for the championship of Chicago. Jesse could not be there, so he called me. Jane Byrne was running for mayor, and to get the black vote, she had bought fancy uniforms for the teams of deprived black kids from Chicago's West Side and for the cheerleaders, but Jesse was worried about how his son's team would play. He asked me to come to Chicago and talk to Yusef's team. Andy Thomas picked me up at the airport. I went out to the football field and told the kids that I didn't come all the way from Dallas to Chicago to see them lose. Jesse's wife, Jackie, and everybody were there on the sidelines. And Yusef's team won the game by several touchdowns.

Looking at Jesse's kids tells a lot about him. You might think they would be spoiled because of their father, but they are not. When they were younger and came home from school, they were not allowed to watch television, talk on the telephone, or listen to the radio for two hours; they had to study.

With my arrest record, I thought I had to stay away from Jesse's presidential campaigns, but I did everything I could behind the scenes. My former Cowboys teammate, Pettis Norman, was Jesse's campaign manager in the Dallas area in 1988, and I worked to get out the vote for Jesse.

When I'm in Chicago, Jesse and I often jog or play basketball. He was a damn good basketball player and still is a fine athlete. He's always pulling off pranks, too. A few years ago, there was a guy in his PUSH organization who thought he could run. One day, Jesse introduced me to this guy as "Bob" and told him, "My friend here will race you in the quarter mile and beat you." The guy wanted to bet twenty dollars that he could beat me in the race. When we got out to the track and he found out who I was, he backed out. Jesse had set him up big time.

By the time I returned from the Olympics in 1964, it was late October, the football season was half over, and we had a problem that divided our team—me. I had never dreamed that my friends or teammates would be jealous of me for achieving the most that an amateur athlete could by winning the Olympics. I was getting all the praise, from the president to the governor, to the president of the university, plus all the press coverage, worldwide, national, and local. But Bobby Felts, Paul Washington, an end (he and I used to date the same girl at times), and a few others were very jealous. They didn't want to be around me, and if I walked up, they would walk away. If I walked into the dining area, they would turn their heads and get into a conversation with someone else. I asked the student trainer, Cecil Daniels, who was one of my best friends, what was going on. He said, "Bob, they're jealous and envious." And I said, "Well, Cecil, this is going to create a lot of dissension on the team. What shall we do?" We decided that Cecil should tell Jake about the situation. I wanted to win football games, that's all I cared about, but we sure couldn't win games if the other players were envious of me.

One day, I walked up to practice, and Jake Gaither pulled me aside and said, "Bobby, I want you to go inside. I don't want you to practice today." That was the first time I had ever heard of a coach telling an athlete who was healthy not to come to practice. I wondered what was going on. As I walked up the hill toward the gym, I saw the whole team huddle around Jake. Instead of going to the gym, I peeked around the ROTC building. Jake Gaither told them, "I think you boys should be proud to have Bob Hayes as a member of your team. I heard that some of you call him 'Hollywood' because he gets so much exposure. All the writers are around him. I know that when we go out of town, the local papers say, 'Bob Hayes and the Florida A & M Rattlers Are Coming to Town.' If you guys are so jealous of Bobby Hayes, I know how every one of you can get just as much publicity as Bob does. Now raise your hand if you want as much publicity as Bob gets." They all raised their hands. "You want the exposure Bob Hayes gets?" "Yes!" they all yelled. "Well, you only have to do one thing." And they all yelled out, "What, coach?" And Jake said, "Outrun him." And everyone of them put their necks down on their shoulders and that was the end of the business. Jake never heard anything else about it.

After that we got back to the business of winning football games. The team had already played and won four games without me, and I didn't have my timing down enough to help much in my first few games. But I did remind them that I was still a football player in our final game of the regular season, when we made our annual trip to Jacksonville to play TSU. My hometown called it Bob Hayes Night, and I made it my night on the field, too, scoring all three of our touchdowns—on passes of 43 and 19 yards and a 58-yard run—as we beat TSU 24 to 14, for our eighth win in nine games. I thought the touchdown run was one of the best plays of my college career. I went around left end on a halfback sweep. The middle line backer blitzed right at me but I saw him coming; after he missed me, nobody else had a chance.

My last game as a Rattler was against Grambling State University in the Orange Blossom Classic in the Orange Bowl. Grambling's Tigers had a great team, and we were underdogs for the first time in years. The Tigers were led by several future pros, including Frank Kornish, Al Dotson, and the quarterback, Mike Howell. Coaches didn't give blacks the opportunity to play quarterback in pro football in those days, so the Browns converted Mike into a defensive back, and he covered me many times. In that Orange Blossom Classic, we went in at halftime with a 14 to 7 lead after I was used strictly as a decoy in the first half; I didn't carry the ball or have a single pass thrown my way. But in the second half, I caught a 30-yard touchdown pass and ran for a 20-yard touchdown and two 2-point conversions, and we shocked the oddsmakers and blew Grambling out, 42 to 15. In spite of missing half the season, I led the team in kickoff returns and was among our leaders in rushing, receiving, scoring, and punt returns.

The only disappointment of my college career was that I never earned my degree. Several people, including Sadie Gaither, who was an English instructor, and James Eton, who taught history, spent countless hours tutoring me and never asked for a dime. If there had been more instructors like that and if I had applied myself harder, I would have been a better person and learned a lot more. But Florida A & M wasn't quite Harvard, especially back then, and I still wasn't much of a student. Because I was traveling all over the place for football games and track meets while I was in college, I missed a lot of classes. And I was an education major, which meant that I had to student teach. Being the fastest man in the world, I couldn't just go in and teach elementary school kids like a normal teacher. Whenever I tried, it was a circus, so I just gave up. I still love working with kids, particularly those with learning disabilities.

Although I didn't graduate, after five years at Florida A & M, I was ready to do what I loved best—play football—and get paid for it. My days of being a poor boy in Hell's Hole were a world behind me.

THE WORLD'S
FASTEST HUMAN

4

If it hadn't been for Robert (Pete) Griffin, I would have been strictly a football player. No world's fastest human, no Olympics, no gold medals.

Although I was redshirted from football in 1960, I practiced with the team every day until the season ended in December. After that, I was looking forward to some time off until spring football practice began a few months later. Jacksonville was just a three-hour drive from Tallahassee, most of my friends were going home nearly every weekend, and I was planning to go home with them and have some of my mom's cooking. I had liked track when I was in high school, but football was always the big thing in Florida, and football was all I really wanted to play in college. I still have a copy of my application to Florida A & M, which I sent in on July 2, 1960, and in answer to the question of what my goal in life was, I wrote: "I would like to be a professional football player and better the conditions of my family."

Running track meant that I would have to stay in Tallahassee every weekend until school was over in June because the track team had time trials or a meet every Saturday. And I already had a scholarship for football, so I didn't have to run track to pay the tuition.

But Pete Griffin was a hard man to say no to. He had been an all-American center for Florida A & M in 1938 and then became the line coach in football and the head track coach. As soon as football ended, Pete started telling me he wanted me to run track. When I kept saying no, he got my best friends on my case—football teammates like Curtis Miranda,

Charles Sutton, and Al Denson. After about three weeks, I finally agreed to go out for track, and I always wondered if Pete Griffin had regrets after he saw me in my first time trials in the 100 yards in track practice. I came in third, behind Paul Denson, a quarter-miler from Hackensack, New Jersey, and Bob Harris, another sprinter who was also sports editor of the student newspaper. By the next time trials, I was in better track shape and I beat everybody. From that day on, nobody at Florida A & M ever beat me in a time trial or a race. As a matter of fact, I chased our best sprinter, Eugene White, right off the track team. Eugene, who was two years ahead of me and was also a star halfback on the football team (he later played briefly for the Oakland Raiders), had won the SIAC championship in the 100-yard dash the previous spring with a time of 9.4. I beat him regularly during windsprints in football practice, and I kept on beating him after I joined the track team. After losing to me for several weeks in a row, he quit the track team.

Pete Griffin saw right away how unorthodox my style was, but he had sense enough not to mess with it. My style was just natural for me. All runners go about 70 or 80 percent on natural ability; the rest is training. You can teach a guy to run faster than he has before, but you can't make a slow guy run fast. You either have that natural speed or you don't. You can work on your concentration, your arm pumps, your conditioning, and your starts; that's all you can learn from a coach. Everything else comes from you.

One thing Pete did teach me was how to break the 100 yards down into four segments. The first 25 yards, you concentrated on your starts; the second 25 yards, you tried to accelerate; the third 25 yards, you were into your ultimate acceleration; and the final 25, you tried to hold your top speed. But I've never seen a sprinter who could run the last 25 yards as fast as the next-to-last 25. Someone timed my 25-yard splits at the SIAC meet in Atlanta in May 1964, and that race will show you what I mean. I got off to a slow start, running third for the first 20 yards and doing the opening 25 yards in 3 seconds flat—which would have worked out to a 12.0 for the race if I had run the entire 100 yards at that speed. I started moving and pulling away from the rest of the field in the second 25, which I ran in 2.2, and I really turned it on in the third 25 with a time of 1.9, which John Underwood of *Sports Illustrated* said equaled 26.9 miles an hour, "probably the highest speed ever attained in the 100." I did the final 25 in 2.1, but even though I slowed down slightly, my competition fell even farther behind in the last quarter of the race, which I won with a time of 9.2. The only time I ever ran a perfect race was in the 400-meter relay final in Tokyo. In every 100-meter race I ever ran, even the ones in which I set records and won the gold medal, I always thought that my last 25 yards were slower than the third 25.

The most important thing that Pete taught me was conditioning. He used to take us out in the country and make us run ten miles. The first day I couldn't do it; I ran, stopped, ran, stopped, the whole way. Bob Harris was a sophomore, so he had already been through this ordeal for a year. I asked him, "How the hell do you guys run so far?" But every day I got better—it was the first time I had ever trained this hard—and finally I could run the entire way without stopping.

Coach Pete did have one idiosyncrasy: He would never tell us what times we ran in practice. He would time us with his stopwatch and hit the stop button at the end of the race, just like any other coach. All the guys would hang around to see the time, but he would cover the watch and put it in his pocket and walk away. Then he would go off by himself and look at it, but the time was a big secret. You would say, "Coach, what time did I run?" "Don't worry, son. You're doing good." The only times we knew how fast we were running was in meets and time trials.

In my junior year, Dick Hill replaced Pete as the track coach. Dick was a good-looking, well-dressed guy, and all the girls liked him. The first time I met him, I was sitting at a restaurant drinking beer and he told me he was coming to Florida A & M to teach, so I offered him a beer. I didn't know that he was going to be the new track coach. I was pretty embarrassed when I found out that he was going to be my coach. But Dick was a real character, and a beer from one of his athletes didn't bother him. I'll never forget the time he and I were in New York for a meet at Madison Square Garden and we stayed at his parents' home in Yonkers. We got off the bus at Thirty-ninth street and First Avenue and were walking across the street, when Dick jumped up in the street, made a forward roll in the air, and came back down on his feet—right on the sidewalk.

Dick was the kind of guy who made our workouts fun, or at least as much fun as possible. We used to run behind his car listening to Ray Charles, Aretha Franklin, and Gladys Knight and the Pips, my favorite group. All the sprinters on the team, ten or fifteen of us, would get behind Dick's green Plymouth, and Dick would turn on the stereo real loud. Then we had to fulfill certain responsibilities: run 150 yards, jog, and walk fast, until we completed five or ten miles on the dirt roads outside Tallahassee between Florida A & M University and the airport. Dick would adjust the speed he was driving to the speed we were supposed to be running.

Dick brought a lot of innovations to track at Florida A & M—isometric contractions and other exercises we had never done, which would make us use muscles that we had never used before, and putting a harness around us that we would drive off of to get the fullest extension of our arm pump and legs. He had been a high jumper, a great one, and he knew a lot about track techniques. Dick really helped me improve my speed. He kept me running more and he had me run the quarter-mile for the first time. After I ran a 46.4, I told him I was never going to run that again, although, of course, I did. After a quarter-mile, every muscle in my body was tight and I had cramps all over. I was just a big piece of muscle and I never could run distance races, but running the quarter-mile gave me more stamina for the 100-yard or 100-meter races.

Another guy who helped me was Alfred Austin, my high school opponent from Jacksonville. Alfred turned down a football scholarship to Florida A & M to go to the the school on a track scholarship. In college, we outgrew our high school rivalry, became good friends, and teamed with Bob Harris and Bob Paremore to form a record-setting relay team. Alfred, who was a great starter, worked a lot with me on improving my starts. Great as he was in high school, Alfred never ran better than a 9.6 at Florida A & M because he was hurt most of the time. If he wasn't pulling one muscle, he was pulling another one. He used what they called Atomic Balm, a hot salve that was good for strained muscles. Atomic Balm had a minty smell, and because Alfred's muscle problems were so bad, he would smear huge amounts of Atomic Balm all over his legs. When he walked around the campus, you could smell him coming from miles away.

I got off to a blazing start in my first college track meet, running a 9.4 to win the 100-yard dash at the Florida A & M Relays in March 1961. My time equaled the record for college freshmen that Jesse Owens had set in 1934 when he was at Ohio State.

A few weeks later, I ran a 9.5 to win the Tuskegee Relays, and considering the condition of the Tuskegee track, that was one of my best races of the year. Tuskegee Institute, the Harvard of the black colleges, is one of the oldest black colleges in the country, and the track was old and poorly taken care of. It was called a cinder track, but I would say that nearly half the track was plain dirt.

My next big meet was the SIAC championship in Atlanta, in which I ran another 9.5 to win the 100. But my big race that day was the 220. I ran a 20.1 on a wet track, the fastest time in the world in 1961, only one-tenth of a second slower than the world record set by Dave Sime of Duke

University a few years earlier, and four-tenths of a second better than the old record for a college freshman.

A few weeks later, not quite six months past my eighteenth-birthday, I achieved two firsts in my life:

- I took my first airplaine ride, to Sioux Falls, South Dakota, for the annual track and field championships of the National Association of Intercollegiate Athletics (NAIA), the schools that were too small to compete in the Championships of the National Collegiate Athletic Association (NCAA). Pete Griffin and I flew from Tallahassee to Atlanta to Chicago to Minneapolis to Sioux Falls. It was scary being up that high, moving so fast. Until then, the highest altitude for me had been up in a tree or on top of a house.

- My plane finally landed in Sioux Falls, but I stayed high. On June 2, 1961, I tied the world record in the 100-yard dash for the first time with a clocking of 9.3 in a qualifying heat. Mel Patton had set the record in 1948, and several runners, including Dave Sime, Ray Norton, and Bobby Morrow, had tied it during the thirteen years in between. My time also broke the NAIA record of 9.4 that Morrow, running for Abilene Christian College, had set in 1955. I followed up the next day by winning the finals in the 100 in 9.5 and the 220 in 21-flat.

It was in Sioux Falls that I made one of my best lifelong friends, Ralph Boston, who had won the gold medal in the broad jump at the Olympics in Rome the year before. Ralph was at the NAIA meet with his Tennessee State team, and he had seen me run before. Pete Griffin and I were staying in a dormitory room on the campus of the University of South Dakota. I could hear Ralph and Stone Johnson, a sprinter from Grambling who had been on the 1960 Olympic team with Ralph, talking loudly in the next room. Stone was arrogant, saying how ugly Ralph was and how he was lazy, just like everybody from Tennessee State. And Ralph said, "Let me tell you something, Stone. There's a guy here named Robert Hayes from Florida A & M, who's going to kick your butt." I could hear all these guys talking like that. They finally knocked on the door. "Who is it?" I called. "Is Robert Hayes here?" "No, he's gone outside," I said. They had been to the Olympics, and I was just awed by them. I finally came out of hiding and got to know several of the other athletes, and Ralph became my best pal.

The NAIA meet in Sioux Falls was my last one of the 1961 season.

Because I was still relatively unknown, I didn't get invited to run in any of the international competitions that were held during the summer after the college track season ended. But my 9.3 made me think for the first time that I had a shot at the 1964 Olympics. After not even wanting to run track at all a few months earlier, I now had my eye on the pinnacle for a track athlete.

By the end of 1961, Ralph Boston wasn't the only one who had heard about me. *Track and Field News*, reviewing the 1961 season, named me champion freshman athlete of the year. And I had only just begun.

"Unknown Runs 100 Yds. in 9.2" read the headline in the *Philadelphia Bulletin* on February 18, 1962. This was the second time—and my second race in a row—that I had tied the world record in the 100. When I ran my 9.3 the previous June 2, I was the last athlete to equal the 9.3 record. But I was still pretty much a secret then, and a lot of people may have dismissed my 9.3 in Sioux Falls as a fluke. Anyway, my 9.3 was pretty much forgotten—in fact, it was never even submitted to the AAU for certification as a world record—because just three weeks later, Frank Budd lowered the record to 9.2 at the AAU championships in New York, a meet I didn't run in. Ironically, Budd's 9.2 wasn't approved as a world record until just a week before I tied it.

After playing football for Florida A & M in fall 1961, I took a few weeks off and then started training for my second season of track. My first race of the 1962 season was on February 17 at the Florida Athletic Club's invitational meet at the University of Miami. That was the first time a black school had ever competed against white schools in the state of Florida. The competition that day was hardly world class; aside from our Florida A & M team, there were teams from such schools as the University of Miami and Dade County Junior College. But having Florida A & M in the meet was all I needed because my teammate, friend, and rival, Bob Paremore, was the one who pushed me to the 9.2 time. Actually, I almost had the world record all to myself that day, because two of the five timers clocked me at 9.1, while three clocked me at 9.2.

I ran that 9.2—as well as 20.7 in the 220, seven-tenths of a second off the world record—in spite of several handicaps. The Miami track was cinder and clay, and Bob Downes, the University of Miami track coach, said it was "slow to very slow" that day because it hadn't been cared for properly. (I still hadn't run on the new asphalt composition tracks, which were faster.) And I had to run *into* a 4 1/2-mile-an-hour headwind. A couple of other amazing things about that race were that I didn't feel all that sharp because I wasn't yet in top shape and I got off to a bad start. I came out of the starting blocks with my head high, instead of low, the way you're supposed to, and Paremore was ahead of me for about the first thirty yards. I still didn't have that much experience with starting blocks at that point in my career.

I did have something to fire me up for that meet: Jackie Robinson, who was playing in a golf tournament in Miami, was staying at the hotel where we stayed, the Hampton House, and I met him for the first time. He took me to dinner so the two of us could get to know each other and talk privately. During dinner, he put his arms around me and told me he liked me because I was just like him. I asked, "How's that?" and he answered, "Because you're pigeon-toed and you've got a big butt that sticks up in the air." I said, "I'd love to be like Jackie Robinson because when I was a little kid everyone used to say I reminded them of you." I told Jackie how much it meant to me to have him there when my school and I ran for the first time in an integrated meet in the state of Florida, that I knew we wouldn't be doing it except for him—his guts, his heart, his desire, and the shit he had taken for all black people.

Ironically, my 9.2 was never accepted for a share of the world record, one of several races I ran that were disqualified for record purposes on technicalities. Vin Lally, head of the host Florida Athletic Club, declared right after the meet, "There's no doubt of the record's validity. This is an AAU-sanctioned meet, the track meets all specifications, and the gauge recorded a 4 1/2-mile-an-hour wind against Hayes." What Lally didn't know at the time was that the starter had used a .22-caliber pistol instead of a .32-caliber, which gives off a more visible puff of smoke for the timers to start their watches by, and my 9.2 was disallowed a few months after the race. Unbelievable!

I was invited to another meet at the University of Miami a month later, and a huge crowd turned out in hopes of seeing me break 9.2. A University of Miami football player tried to give me some extra incentive in that race. While I was standing in the infield before the race, this guy came walking up to me and said, "Bob Hayes, you all from Florida A & M are the Rattlers, aren't you? Well, I got something for you that will make you run faster today." Then he grabbed a big black snake that he had wrapped around his shoulders and held it out toward me. I moved away as fast as I could and said, "Man, you might be right, but get that thing away from me." Everybody was laughing, including me—once I got out of the snake's range. Unfortunately, I stumbled about fifteen yards into the race and ran only 9.4 against a 7-mile-an-hour crosswind, although I still took first place ahead of Paremore. At least 9.4 was my official time. Pete Griffin clocked me at 9.15, which would have been a world record, and two other backup timers had me at 9.1 and 9.2. But the three official timers clocked me at 9.3, 9.4, and 9.5. Pete Griffin was really upset because one of the official timers dropped his sunglasses and had to grab for them just as the race was starting, which distracted him and probably messed up his time. I also won the 220-yard dash that day and anchored our 440-yard relay team to a victory.

A week later, on March 24, 1962, I scored a rare double, winning the 100-yard dash twice in two different locations. First, about 1 P.M., I ran a 9.3 at the Florida A & M relays in Tallahassee, with Bob Harris second. Then Bob Paremore and I took a shower, put on some clothes, hopped over to the Tallahassee airport, and flew to Miami. A private plane met us at the Miami airport and flew us to Hollywood, where there was another meet that evening. We got off the plane in Hollywood, rushed out to the stadium, changed clothes, warmed up, and ran the 100 meters. I ran only 9.4 in Hollywood, but it was still good for first place ahead of Paremore and Bob Sher of the University of Miami, who tied for second.

Two of the top events in the track session each spring were the Drake Relays in Des Moines, Iowa, and the Penn Relays in Philadelphia, which were held the same weekend in late April. Pete Griffin had contacted the organizers of the two meets in the past about inviting us, but they had never shown any interest until 1962, when both meets wanted me. We chose the Drake Relays, and I have to say one thing about Iowa at the end of April: It wasn't like Florida in April, and it wasn't even like Florida in January. The temperature was about 42 degrees, the coldest weather I had ever run in. Maybe that's why I did so well—I was in a hurry to finish my races, leave the track, and get back to the dressing room, where it was warm. The Drake organizers said they had assembled their finest 100-yard-dash field ever, including Nate Adams of Purdue, who had recently run a wind-aided 9.3, and Roger Sayers of Omaha University—Gale Sayers's brother—but I won my preliminary heat by five yards in 9.4 on Friday and came back the next day to run a 9.5 on a wet track and easily win the finals over Adams.

I also anchored our 440- and 880-yard relay teams to victories over TSU, which had won thirty-seven races in a row. The TSU runners messed up their baton passes in the 880 and were disqualified, although we would have won anyway, but I had to catch their anchor man in the 440. Bob Harris, who ran the third leg for us, thought I wasn't moving my legs fast enough, and I can still hear him yelling, "Run! Run! Run! Get out! Get out!" After the race, Bob asked me why I didn't get out faster and I said to him, "Bob, did it occur to you that you may have been running faster than you ever ran before, which made you think I was running slower?" The sportswriters and broadcasters who covered the meet were a little more impressed by my performance than Bob Harris was; they named me the outstanding athlete in the meet by a vote of 22 to 2.

My next stop was the SIAC meet in Atlanta on May 11 and 12, where I ran 9.3s in the two preliminary rounds of the 100 and then won the final in one of my greatest races ever, although it didn't go down in the books that way. Here's how *Sports Illustrated* described it: "[Hayes] ran 100 yards with more impatience than usual. Among the judges, presumably atremble at the sight, there were watches stopped at 8.9 and 9.0 seconds. This was impossible, of course. Nobody would ever believe such a thing. Hayes's time [was] rounded off to a sensational but uninflammatory 9.3 seconds."

All the coaches and timers, including Pete Griffin, huddled before they announced my time at 9.3, and Pete told me later that because all the coaches, timers, and athletes were black, nobody would have believed my time and it would have made them all look like fools. All I could think after that race was that maybe, someday, I would run a 9-flat or better under circumstances that would force everyone to believe it.

I also won the 220 in the SIAC meet with my fastest time of the year, 20.4. Coach Griffin asked me if I would run the 220 to give us another chance at a medal. Bob Harris was our best hope in the 220. In practice, I used to ask him to wait for me at 180 yards so we could cross the finish line together because I was dying; the 220 was too long for me. When we got to Atlanta, I said, "Bob, when you get down about 125 to 130 yards, wait for me." He told me he would; there wasn't that much competition, and we knew we would win. Well, I jumped out of those starting blocks and when I got down about 120 yards, I was just relaxing and running, waiting for Bob, but Bob never showed up. I broke the tape, and Bob came running up to me real angry: "Yeah, you told me to wait for you, but you wouldn't wait for me." I said, "I waited for you." He said, "You call that waiting for me? You ran a 20.1, fool!"

The time had come for my first big showdown at the O.K. Corral. The two main contenders for the title of fastest man in the world then were Frank Budd from Villanova and me. Our first meeting was set for the Coliseum Relays in Los Angeles on May 19, 1962, in what was being called "the battle of the century." Budd had finished fifth in the 100 meters at the Olympics in Rome, but he was almost dead even with Enrique Figuerola and four or five feet behind Armin Hary. He had laid claim to being the world's fastest sprinter by being the first man to run 100 yards in 9.2 seconds, but by the time we got ready to face each other, *Track and Field News* had ranked me number one in the world at 100 yards, with Budd second.

Budd had run 9.2 eight months before I did, and he didn't like having to share the record and the spotlight with me. He was the one who kept building up our rivalry, making comments like "I know I can beat Hayes's time" after I matched his 9.2 in February. He also claimed I was ducking him because I had turned down invitations to run against him in 60-yard indoor races at two big meets in Madison Square Garden in March. Of course, I wasn't afraid to face him, but I had never run indoors. We didn't have an indoor track at Florida A & M, so I had never even trained indoors; with the warm weather in Florida, we ran outdoors from the time we started training in January each year. I though that when Budd and I did meet, it should be outdoors, where each of us had plenty of experience.

Our race in Los Angeles was going to be at 100 meters to get us ready for upcoming international events, and it was an open final: no heats— one race for all the glory. When I arrived in Los Angeles, Ralph Boston was waiting for me. He took care of me as always, instructing me, "Home boy, just take your time, relax, and forget about the bright lights and the big city." But there was no way I could forget about the bright lights and the big city because the meet was at night, and when they introduced us for the 100-meter race, they cut off all the lights in the coliseum and focused the big spotlight on each one of us. Henry Carr, Richard Stebbins, Bob Hayes, Frank Budd. I said to myself, "Shit! Damn! This is the greatest competition I've ever faced." I started praying.

The starter was getting ready, and I could hear everybody going, "OOOOOUUUP, this is the race of the century." I got down in the starting blocks. The starter fired his gun, but I was already several yards down the track. That was the first time I had ever jumped the gun. I said to myself, "Did I fly all the way from Tallahassee, Florida, to L.A. to get disqualified?" So now I had to stay in the blocks; a second false start and I would be out. The next time, Frank Budd jumped the gun. I thought to myself, "Frank Budd is just as nervous as I am." The race finally got off, and I ran a 10.2 and beat Budd by about two yards. Nobody called Frank Budd the world's fastest human again.

Pete Griffin was a real dapper dresser, and he had brought all his

Hickey-Freeman suits and his straw hat so he could look just right for our first meet in southern California. Although Pete didn't want us to know it, he was also superstitious; he always carried a rabbit's foot in his pocket for good luck. Right after I beat Budd, Pete came running up and grabbed me, and the rabbit's foot fell out of his pocket. Cecil Daniels, our student trainer, picked it up and said, "Coach, here's your rabbit's foot." Pete Griffin said, "No, that's not my rabbit's foot. Where you get that shit from? That's not mine." The coach did not want us to know that he was so superstitious that he carried a rabbit's foot from Tallahassee to Los Angeles to bring me luck to beat Frank Budd. We teased Pete for a long time, but he never would admit it was his.

From Los Angeles, I moved the next week to central California for the California Relays in Modesto, one of my most controversial races. The organizers of the Modesto relays had assembled a great field for the 100-yard race, including Harry Jerome, who had been one of the favorites at Rome in 1960 but had become lame in one of the heats there, Henry Carr, and Dennis Johnson of San Jose State, another world-class runner. I beat Johnson in my heat in 9.3, tying the meet record, and Carr and Jerome finished 1–2 in theirs, setting the stage for the finals.

Jerome got off to a great start and was a step ahead of me all the way until I caught him about eighty yards down the track. For the final twenty yards, we ran stride for stride together, until I broke the tape across my mustache. The cord actually cut my mustache and ripped into my skin. After the race, I was jogging back down the track to put on my sweats when I heard the track announcer say, "First-place judges, Harry Jerome. Second-place judges, Harry Jerome." Harry and I were so close together that the first-place judges thought he had finished first and the second-place judges had him second. The judges got together and gave him first place at 9.3, claiming that I was second at 9.4, the same time as Johnson, who was third.

I couldn't believe I had lost the first race of my college career, and neither could the local newspaper, the *Modesto Bee*, which said that Harry's "victory" was "the greatest robbery in history since the Brinks holdup. . . . Most everybody in the pressbox . . . as well as those seated in the stands along the finish line, had declared Hayes . . . the winner. The official announcement of Jerome, the Canadian sprinter, as the winner, stunned the crowd. . . . At the finish line it looked like Hayes was the winner by a nose."

The Modesto officials tried later to make up for the judges' mistake by sending me a Longines watch, which was the prize for finishing first. In spite of that race, Harry and I became good friends. After he died serveral years ago in a car accident, I was asked to speak at a dinner to raise funds for a statue of him in Vancouver.

Harry did beat me legitimately on the anchor leg of the 440-yard relay at Modesto (two of my future Cowboy teammates, Mel Renfro and Mike Gaechter, were part of Harry's University of Oregon relay team), but by then, I was coming down with the flu. Despite a fever of 102 degrees, I had agreed to run in the NAIA championships the following week in Sioux Falls, the meet in which I had first run a 9.3 the year before, and I felt I had to keep my commitment. By the time I got to Sioux Falls, I was as sick as a dog. In addition to the fever, I was sick to my stomach and throwing up constantly. I never should have run. I didn't have any acceleration that day, and Roger Sayers handed me my second consecutive defeat in the 100-yard dash, with Homer Jones of TSU, the future New York Giants star, coming in third. Among the also-rans was Leroy Jackson of Western Illinois, who was the Redskins' first-round draft choice in the big trade that year that sent Bobby Mitchell from Cleveland to Washington and the rights to Ernie Davis of Syracuse from Washington to Cleveland. (Davis, the Heisman Trophy winner in 1961, developed leukemia and died a year or so later without every playing professional football.) Later in the NAIA meet, Homer won the 220, with me second, and Roger third. But the 100 was my specialty, and Roger's victory over me was a big thing. A teammate of his, a light-skinned black guy, kept yelling, "You beat him! You beat him! You finally beat him!" Three years later, after Gale Sayers won the NFL Rookie of the Year award over me, I told Gale, "If it isn't one Sayers, it's another. First your brother beat me in the 100, and now you beat me for Rookie of the Year."

I took three weeks off after the NAIA meet to recover from the flu and then I faced Frank Budd for the second time at the national AAU championships in Walnut, California. I got to run in that meet only because Governor Farris Bryant of Florida paid $500 out of his pocket to send me back to California, since there wasn't enough money in the Florida A & M budget to pay my way and the AAU people didn't provide transportation.

This AAU meet had one of the best fields I had ever run in other than the Olympics'. In addition to Frank Budd and me, there were Harry Jerome,

Roger Sayers, Paul Drayton, and several other top-notch sprinters. I won my first two heats to qualify for the final, along with Budd, Jerome, Sayers, Drayton, and two others. Budd got off to a good start in the finals, with a lead of about two yards over me. But about fifty yards down the track, I drew up alongside him, and at that instant he pulled a muscle in his leg. He lunged off the track without finishing the race, and I went on to win in 9.3, a yard or so ahead of Jerome and Sayers.

Frank Budd never ran the 100 again, leaving me two-for-two against him. He signed a contract with the Philadelphia Eagles, and spent a season with the Eagles and one with the Redskins as a wide receiver, and that was the end of his pro football career. Frank hadn't played football since high school, and he wasn't a true professional football prospect as I was. Even though we were rivals, there wasn't any bad feeling between us, and I felt kind of sorry for him. He'd had polio when he was growing up, and his right calf was a couple of inches smaller than his left, but he overcame that. Then he reached his peak between two Olympic cycles and never won the gold medal. He was one of the best sprinters I ever ran against. I wish he had stayed around for the Tokyo Olympics—no telling the time the two of us might have run with each other for competition.

As the top two American finishers in the AAU meet, Roger Sayers and I qualified to represent our country in dual meets later that summer against Poland and Russia. The first meet, against Poland, was held in Chicago during the weekend of June 30–July 1, and I was first in the 100 meters in 10.3, with Roger second in 10.4 and the two Polish runners, Marian Foik and Andrzej Zielinski, trailing us. I also ran on the U.S. 400-meter relay team, which won in 40-flat, one-tenth of a second slower than the world record that one of the American relay teams had set a year earlier. We beat the Polish team by 131 to 81 in that meet, my first in an international competition, but it was actually kind of a letdown for me. The only reason the meet was held in Chicago was that there was a large Polish community in the city. However, the track was bad, the city didn't impress me, the fans didn't seem to have a lot of enthusiasm, and I was glad to get it over with.

I didn't have any trouble getting up to run against the Russians, though. The meet was July 21 and 22 at Stanford University, and I worked myself into top shape. I trained harder for that meet than for any other meet except the Olympics. And I'll never forget several things about it.

First, the Russian coach, Gabriel Khorobkov, called one of his own sprinters a coward. He was probably just trying to psyche up his runner, but I didn't think a coach should say something like that publicly. His sprinters had to be good; they had qualified in Russia to run against us.

Second, Wilma Rudolph, who won the 100-meters and anchored our 400-meter relay team to victory, came out of the stands before my 100-meter race to say hello to me. While I was helping her climb over a fence onto the track, she put her weight on me, and we both fell to the ground. I said, "Wilma, I didn't know you were that heavy," and from that day on, we were good friends. Wilma also figured in some controversy at that meet; she showed one of the Russian female athletes how to apply makeup, and when the Soviet officials got a look at the girl, they put her on the first plane to Moscow.

Third, Paul Warfield from Ohio State, who became one of the leading receivers in the NFL at the same time I was, was one of our two broad-jumpers. Paul finished third, behind Ralph Boston and the Russian star, Igor Ter-Ovanesyan.

In the men's 100 meters, Roger jumped out ahead of me, but I edged him at the tape, with both of us timed at 10.2. Amin Tuyakov was third and the other Russian, Edvin Ozolin, was last. I ran the second leg in the 400-meter relay because it was on a straightaway, and Hayes Jones, our leadoff runner, was about two yards behind the Russians when he handed me the baton. Ozolin ran the second leg for the Russians, and I caught him and passed him by a couple of yards, and then Homer Jones and Paul Drayton took care of the last two legs as we set a world record of 39.6.

My 1963 track season opened with another record-tying performance that didn't make it into the record books. On February 3, 1963, running on a grass track at the AAU-Southern Games in Port of Spain, Trinidad, I blazed 200 meters around a curved track in 20.5, tying the world record held by Paul Drayton, Ray Norton, Stone Johnson, and an Italian runner, Livo Bertuti. One remarkable thing about this race was that I had no competition; I beat the second- and third-place finishers—a couple of local runners from Trinidad, Irving Joseph, and Cirpriani Phillip—by about 12 yards. But the most astonishing thing about this race is that it didn't qualify for record purposes. What was the excuse this time? I entered the meet at the last minute, and my name wasn't published in advance in the program for the race. I mean, is that chickenshit or not?

Thirteen days later, though, I finally set a world record that no nit-picking rules could take away from me. Racing indoors for the first time on February 16, 1963, at the Mason-Dixon games at Freedom Hall in Louisville, I ran seventy yards in 6.9, to break the old record of 7.0 first set by a runner named Loren Murchison in 1926. (After I joined the Cowboys, the team's owner, Clint Murchison, teased me that Loren was a relative of his, but I don't think Clint had heard of Loren any more than I had.) The gun was the right size; I was listed in the program; the hot dogs had mustard on them; there were separate bathrooms for men and women; and the starter had two eyes, two ears, ten fingers and ten toes, and was wearing clean underwear, so they decided that my record could count this time. Just for good measure, I ran 6.9 twice—once in a heat and once in the final. I set this record, too, without the best competition; two guys named Scott Tyler and Roosevelt Smith finished second and third, several yards behind me. I had never met either of them before, but Scott Tyler and his friends were betting that he would beat me because I had never run indoors; the best part of my race was the finish, not the start; and seventy yards was at least thirty yards less than I was used to running outdoors. After the race, one of the guys who had bet on Tyler walked up to him and slapped him in the face, saying, "I knew that Hayes would beat you!" But I didn't care who I ran against. All I could think of was, "At last, a record is mine."

I had a third straight brush with a world record two weeks later in the Florida Athletic Club's annual meet at the University of Miami, where I had run 9.2 a year earlier. I was hoping to do at least as well in the 100 this year, but there was an eight-mile-an-hour headwind, and although I won, I ran only a 9.5. By the time I ran the 220 a little while later, I was angry at myself for my time in the 100, and I let it all out. Once again, I tied the world record of 20.5, the same time I had made in Trinidad a month earlier—even though I made a mistake this time and slowed up long before the finish. I slowed up because the 220 started on the back-stretch just before the curve, and when I rounded the curve and got to the straightaway, there were two finish lines—the first for the 100, and the second, about thirty yards down the track, for the 220. When I crossed the 100 finish line, I thought for a moment that the race was over, so I eased up. As soon as I realized my mistake, I started sprinting again until I crossed the correct finish line, about ten yards ahead of Bob Harris, who was second. I could only think that my legs that day were faster than Drayton's, Norton's, Stone Johnson's, and the Italian's had been when they ran their 20.5s, but my bulb was a little dim on that particular day. Average out my legs and their brains, and we all had a 20.5.

Then came still another brush with a record on April 27 at the Mount

San Antonio Relays in Walnut, California. This time I ran the 100 meters in 9.9—the fastest in history—but, just as in the Olympics, it was disallowed for record purposes because I had an eleven-mile-an-hour tailwind. By now *Track and Field News* was predicting that I would become "the greatest sprinter who ever breasted a tape."

Henry Carr thought otherwise. He and I ran in the Coliseum Relays in Los Angeles on May 17, 1963. The promoters of the meet wanted us to race each other in the 220, which was Henry's specialty. I was willing, but I thought it was only fair that Henry should enter the 100, my best distance, especially since the finals in the two events were only about twenty minutes apart. But Henry knew he didn't have a chance against me in the 100, so he refused to run, and I won in 9.3.

The final in the 100 was the third race I had run that night, including heats, so I told Dick Hill to scratch me from the 220. Why should I run against Henry at his best distance, when he was fresh and I had just run three tough 100-yard races? "Okay," Dick said, "pull on your sweat suit and relax. I'll get you scratched." But Dick came back a couple of minutes later with some new information: "Hey, Bob, I just saw Henry talking to his coach. They looked worried. I don't think he wants to run against you." I didn't realize that Dick was just trying to do a snow job on me and get me to run, and I fell for it. I finally asked him, "Do you think you can get me back in the race?" Of course, he had never scratched me to begin with, and I took off my sweat suit, took my place at the starting line, and came out of the blocks like a shot. I surprised myself, maintaining my speed most of the way over that longer distance and beating Henry with a good time of 20.8.

The races between Henry and me were summit meetings like the ones between Carl Lewis and Ben Johnson in the past few years, except that we didn't hate each other. In fact, we were good frinds. I was traveling around the country so much that I usually couldn't get in as much training as I wanted to. To run better in the 100, I often ran the 220, not because of Henry Carr, but to see what I could do and to condition myself. Of course, I wanted to do my best and to win, but I was just trying to stay in shape. I had lots of success in the 220, but Henry certainly was a better 220 runner than I was.

I continued winning that spring, taking first place in the 100 in the Tuskgee Relays, the NAIA meet in Sioux Falls, the California Relays in Modesto, the Compton Relays near Los Angeles, and other events. But my main focus was on the AAU championships, which were held at the old Public Schools Stadium in St. Louis on June 21, 1963. The stadium was in terrible shape, but there was a new rubberized macadam track, a mixture of rubber, crushed rock, and asphalt, that was state-of-the-art at the time, and I had my mind set on a record. Frank Budd had lowered the record for 100 yards to 9.2 two years earlier, and Harry Jerome had matched his time since then. I had tied it, too, in February 1962, but, of course, that didn't count because of the .22-caliber pistol. Now I wanted the record, and I wanted it all to myself.

I coasted to a 9.3, several yards ahead of John Moon of the U.S. Army, in the opening round of the AAU 100, and found that the track truly was the fastest I had ever run on. I figured I had two more chances, in the semifinals and in the finals, and I decided to go all out in both of them and give myself two shots at a record. We had two false starts in my heat of the semifinals, and then I stumbled a bit on our third try, which counted. But by the midway point, I was really motoring, and I was five yards ahead of the runner-up, John Gilbert of the Southern California Striders, when I broke through the tape at the end. I held my breath until the official announcement was made: "The time in the last heat was 9.1 seconds, a new world's record, for Robert Hayes of Florida A & M." As always when a record was set, the crowd of four thousand went wild, and this time there were no foul-ups. The wind was light, just 2.2 miles an hour; the right kind of starter's pistol was used; and the most glamorous record in track and field was mine. I came back to win the final the next day over Gilbert and Paul Drayton with another clocking of 9.1, which didn't count as a record because the wind was blowing at nearly 8 miles an hour. But who cared? Not me—now that I was officially the world's fastest human, with a record that lasted until 1974, when Ivory Crockett, who, ironically, was from St. Louis, ran a 9.0.

I accomplished everything I had hoped to in that 1963 race. *Track and Field News* observed that "Hayes, with a perfect 1963 season in the 100, is well on his way to establishing himself as the greatest 100 man of all time. He ran fast times consistently and spread-eagled fast fields with monotonous ease." *Track and Field News* named me the U.S. Athlete of the Year and coholder of the award for best track and field athlete in the world, along with C. K. Yang of Formosa, the world decathlon champion, and Valery Brumel, the Russian high jumper. I came in third in voting for the Sullivan Award, which is given to the outstanding amateur athlete of the year, and I was the first black athlete to be elected to the Florida Sports Hall of Fame—even though my athletic career had hardly begun.

And I was in the perfect position for a great 1964—the year of the Olympics.

I had been cooling out at home in Jacksonville after the American team beat the Russians at Stanford in July 1962, when all of a sudden I found myself a wanted man. I'm not kidding. There had been talk about AAU officials sending me as part of a U.S. team to tour Europe, but I hadn't heard anything for a month or so, and I was just enjoying my summer.

Then, on August 2, 1962, the *Jacksonville Times-Union* had a headline that said "WANTED" in huge letters, and underneath: "Hayes for Travel." The article began, "Where, oh, where is the world's fastest human? . . . He is wanted for a month-long track trip through the Scandinavian countries. But he must be in New York tomorrow." The story ended with the words, "If Hayes should read this, he is to call the New York AAU office collect immediately. The number is Courtland 7-6876."

I didn't see that article myself, but my high school coach, Earl Kitchings, did, and he had also been contacted by Jake Gaither after the AAU people called Jake from New York. Between Jake and Earl, half the population of Jacksonville and Tallahassee must have been looking for me.

Meanwhile, my mother, my stepfather, and my sister had gone to Georgia on vacation; my older brother was in the service; and I was staying with my aunt and uncle, Verdell and Horace Green. My aunt and uncle went out one night, so I spent the night at the home of another woman who was a family friend. The people who were looking for me had no idea where I was, and I had no clue that I was "WANTED."

The morning after the *Times-Union* ran its story, Earl ran into me by accident at a laundromat, where I was washing some clothes. By then, he even had the police looking for me, television stations running announcements, you name it. When Earl found me, he got all excited and asked me where I had been and then told me there was an AAU dragnet out for me. Jimmy Thompson, the principal at Matthew Gilbert High, joined up with us, and the two of them wouldn't let me out of their sight while I showered, packed, and locked up my mother's house. Since I was broke, they gave me several hundred dollars for personal use and emergencies and then took me to the airport and put me on a plane for New York. When I got to New York, I took a taxi to the hotel where Chuck Coker of the Southern California Striders, the head coach for the trip, and the rest of the team were staying. The AAU people issued me my uniform and my passport, and I was ready to go.

Our first meet in 1962 was in Kouvola, Finland, and most of the people who lived there had never seen a black before. One day, Ulis Williams, Paul Drayton, Jim Dupree, an 880 runner from Southern Illinois University who was originally from Florida, and I were walking to a department store. (Department stores were one of the places where we met girls.) A little girl walked up to Ulis, put her finger to her mouth, and wiped his skin to see if the black would come off. Ulis got all upset, yelling, "They're prejudiced over here, too!" but I told him to calm down. I knew the people in Finland weren't prejudiced; they just didn't know what to make of us.

Most of the guys on the Finnish team spoke perfect English, and they all wanted to show us around. Some of them took us to a sauna, where the attendants beat us with reeds and gave us the whole treatment. That was great, but then the Finnish runners asked us if we could swim. We had big egos, so we all said we could, but we didn't know what we were letting ourselves in for. We found that what they had in mind was a race about forty yards across a pond. I dove into the water, which was so cold it just about froze my teeth. Talk about being miserable! At least I didn't come in last. I beat Ulis and one of the Finnish athletes. The main thing on our minds was to finish the race as fast as we could and get back to the sauna.

For the two tours I made of Europe, in 1962 and 1963, our headquarters were in Göteborg, Sweden. One of the highlights of each trip was that Count Basie, who celebrated his birthday every year in Göteborg, gave a concert, and the members of the American track team sat in the front row. Count Basie introduced us to the audience, which didn't hurt at all with the local girls.

In Malmö, Sweden, three girls were after Ralph Boston, John Thomas, and me. The best-looking one, a blonde named Lilli, liked me. While I was in the bathroom, John started talking to my date, and when I came back, he wanted me to take his date. "You take her, Bobby. You'll like her better than I would." I said, "No way, Jose." He got stuck with the least attractive one, and we teased him for weeks.

Actually, the most beautiful woman I met during the two summers I was in Europe was an American who was born in England. When I ran at White City Stadium in London in 1963, I went to a banquet, where I met Elizabeth Taylor, who was sitting next to Richard Burton. Elizabeth Taylor was the most gorgeous woman I had ever laid eyes on. Someone introduced us, and she said she was going to have a party and invite me when I got to Los Angeles, but we never connected. I sure wish we had, especially if it had been a party for just the two of us.

On my first European tour, I was innocent about how the business of track and field operated. But, as usual, Ralph Boston took me under his wing and taught me the ropes. He taught me to go to the meet promoters and say, "I can't run for you because I have to go back home and work. If you have a hundred yards or a hundred meters, you won't have the best field in the world without me in it."

A Swedish businessman promoted all our meets in Scandinavia, and he used to take Wilma Rudolph shopping and buy her anything she wanted—suede and leather skirts and jackets, you name it. Ulis Williams, Henry Carr, John Thomas, Mike Larrabee, Wilma Rudolph, Joanne Terry, Vivian Brown, Edith McGuire, and Wyomia Tyus—all the top American athletes—got payoffs for running in Scandinavia. The European athletes did, too. But the promoters mainly wanted Americans. We were the best. We drew the crowds. Our team was so good, in fact, that we dominated our host countries. After a few meets, we got the idea of running three of our guys in the relay and having Wilma Rudolph run the anchor leg, but the promoters wouldn't let us do it; they said it was too embarrassing.

During a stop in Malmö, Sweden, on my first tour in 1962, I told the promoter I had to go back home and work so I could earn money for college. He asked me how much I made on my summer job. I told him I made $10,000, which was high by about $10,000. The promoter believed me, or at least he considered $10,000 a fair price to have me run. He came to my hotel room, where we could be alone, and gave me $10,000 in cash for the whole tour. I knew he could afford it; we had about ten meets over there, and this guy was making a fortune off us.

In my second year on the European circuit, 1963, I got paid $25,000 for the Scandinavian part of the trip. By then, I had broken the record in the 100-yard dash, and the promoter, the same guy as the year before, would have paid me just about anything I asked for. He visited my room, just like he had in 1962, and gave me 250 $100 bills.

It was much harder getting under-the-table payments in the United States. At most track meets in the United States in those days, all we received were our expenses—airfare, hotel room, meals, and a per diem, which was ten or twenty dollars a day. For first place, we'd get watches or television sets and plaques. I gave away most of the prizes to my family and friends.

From the athletes' standpoint, the two most lucrative U.S. meets were the Long Beach Relays and the Coliseum Relays in Los Angeles. One year Mal Whitfield, the gold-medal winner in the 800-meter races in the 1948 and 1952 Olympics who was meet director at Long Beach, gave me $1,000 in cash. And the top officials of both the Long Beach and the Coliseum Relays would send me four or five round-trip airline tickets from Tallahassee or Jacksonville to California. One ticket would have my itinerary to California, and the others would be open tickets. The airlines would give me cash for the extra tickets, no questions asked. Or I could exchange the ticket to California for a trip to somewhere else. A few of the other meets gave out an extra airline ticket or two, but the Penn Relays in Philadelphia and the Millrose Games in Madison Square Garden were strictly for prestige; they didn't pay anything.

The money, the women, and the scenery—everything was great in the Western European countries. And then, on the 1963 tour, we went to Russia. Talk about a major letdown!

At our meet in Moscow on July 20 and 21, I won the 100-meter race in 10.2, ahead of Edvin Ozolin. Our 400-meter relay team also finished ahead of the Russians, but Paul Drayton and I, running the third and last legs, messed up in passing the baton and got us disqualified; the same thing had happened to the American 440 team at the 1960 Olympics. Losing the race almost cost us the meet, since we edged the Russians 119 to 114.

That meet was held in Lenin Stadium in front of about 70,000 people, and it was strange because we couldn't see a single black face in the stands. Even in the Western European cities, there had been a few blacks in the crowd, but in Moscow there were none. Moscow was also the first place I had run where you couldn't understand your own name until it was translated into English. There is no "h" in the Russian alphabet, so the Russian pronunciation of my name was "Gaze."

But the worst thing about Russia was Russia. All the cities were big and cold looking, and we never saw a single-family home. Everyone seemed to live in government housing projects. If you saw an American and a Russian walking down the street in Moscow, you would know who was from the West by the outfit, the makeup, the perfume, the shape of the body, and the look in the eyes. You could see it; you just knew it. I went to Russia once, and that was more than enough. One thing my foreign travels did for me was give me an appreciation of the United States—no matter how bad things were for blacks there.

Come to think of it, maybe the worst thing about Russia wasn't Russia, after all; it could have been the girls. Let's face it, when you're a healthy, single twenty-year-old male traveling around the world, one of your main interests is women. When the Russians ran against us in the United States the year before, we had taken them on a tour, so their athletes took us on a tour of the free and democratic people's socialist republic. One day, while on a boat trip to the Black Sea, we saw women on the beach in two-piece bathing suits, not as skimpy as American bikinis, and every one of them was fat. I said to myself, "So this is the Soviet Union. Let me out of here!"

Back in Moscow, I saw a woman bus driver who had a flat tire right in the middle of Red Square. It was a city bus, and she got out and lifted this great big tire off, jacked up the bus, and changed the tire, all by herself. She was probably retired from the "girls'" track team or something like that. None of the women we met in Russia wore makeup. That was one place the coaches didn't have to worry too much about what we were doing with the girls.

Then again, maybe the worst thing about Russia was the food. Being an athlete, I worked up an appetite, and I usually wanted to sample the local food. Not in Russia. The first meal in the hotel where we were staying in Moscow was a buffet that featured a big animal with a head like a dog. Whatever it was, it had been fried. I said right then, "I'm not eating here." I don't know for sure what kind of animal it was, but I didn't see any stray dogs running around Moscow, I'll guarantee that. I think I lost about ten pounds in one week. The Olympic committee had warned us not to eat outside the western area of Moscow, because the farm products were not the same as ours and the food was prepared differently from what we were used to. I finally got smart. I went to the American Embassy and gave a couple of the guards tickets to the meet, so when I got hungry, they let me eat at the embassy. The United States had shipped American food over for us, but the Russians wouldn't let it in. Our food finally caught up with us when we left Moscow and went to Warsaw for a meet, and we really piled into it to make up for the food in Russia. Luckily the Poles weren't better athletes, or they might have been able to beat us, what with all we were eating.

Having our own food was the only good thing about being in Poland. In all my travels abroad, Poland is the country where I was treated the worst. Right after we got to Warsaw and moved into our hotel, Henry Carr, Hayes Jones, Ulis Williams, Ralph Boston, and I were waiting outside the hotel for some food the U.S. track officials had told us was about to arrive from home. About twenty-five Polish hookers were out there, and they started to follow us, offering their services. We weren't sure what they were saying—they spoke only Polish and we didn't speak any. We saw photographers everywhere taking pictures of us. Unfortunately, they took a picture of one of the girls walking up to Henry Carr and talking to him. The next day the Associated Press ran the photo in the United States, with a caption about American athletes talking to Polish girls. It was untrue; Henry Carr never attempted to talk to them—just the opposite. But Henry's wife saw the picture back home, and she wasn't too happy about it, so Henry had to do a lot of explaining by telephone.

Also, there were demonstrators surrounding our hotel, people with signs saying, "Go home, Yanks; we don't want you here." All the adverse publicity pissed us off so much that when we got those Polish athletes out on the track, we taught 'em a lesson, routing them 125 to 86 as I again won the 100 in 10.2 and anchored our relay team to a victory that counted. Marian Foik, a sprinter who was near the end of his career, was one of the few Poles who was nice to us. Marian showed us around and told us through an interpreter that the protesters represented only a small portion of the Polish people, that they were just a handful, like the Ku Klux Klansmen in the United States. But Marian Foik was the exception among the Poles we met, and we all celebrated when the Polish leg of our trip came to an end.

One of the best things about the 1962 and 1963 international tours was the lifelong friends I made. Ulis Williams was one of them. Ulis, whose specialty was the 400-meter race, wore the thickest eyeglasses I have ever seen. He was blind without them, and he didn't see so great with them. Once, when we were in Kuvola, Finland, for a meet, he had to run the 400 meters in the rain. His glasses fogged up, and he couldn't see where he was going, so he ran around a curve, followed the steeplechase route, and went full speed over a steeplechase bar and into a pit of ice-cold water. The paramedics had to come and pull him out of the pit. I asked him what had happened, and he said, "Why, man, I thought I was following the line for my lane." We teased him about that for days.

Then we went to Hamburg, to run against the German team. The 1,600-meter relay was the last event, the big race of the day, and right before it, the grounds crew raked and went over the track with a hard roller. The first lane was a little bit shinier then the remaining lanes; it looked just a little different. Ulis ran his whole lap in the second lane instead of the inside lane, and we missed the world record by one-tenth of a second. After the race, Dick Banks, a track-and-field expert who was traveling with us, told Ulis we would have had a world record if he had run in the inside lane, and we all asked him why he had run in the second lane. His answer was, "Man, I thought that was the infield there. I thought that was grass. You mean that was the inside lane?"

During training for the Olympics, we were playing volleyball, and Ulis jumped up real high and his eyeglasses fell off his head. While he was down on the ground looking for them, I snatched them up and put them in my pocket without him seeing me do it. When we asked him if he was ready to play some more, he said, "Oh, sure, I'm ready, I can see, I can see." So somebody hit the ball to him, but it bounced right by him and kept going. After a while, I gave him back his glasses and he muttered, "You son of a bitch, you know I can't see."

Because of his poor vision, Ulis was at his most dangerous behind the wheel of a car. Ralph Boston once bought a new Oldsmobile in Los Angeles and asked Ulis and me to help him drive it across country. I told Ralph I wouldn't go if Ulis was going to do any of the driving. Henry Carr, who was a teammate of Ulis's at Arizona State, had warned me about Ulis's driving. Ulis had a green-and-white 1955 Chevy convertible, and he liked to take Henry when he drove to Los Angeles to visit his family in Compton. Henry said Ulis's eyesight was so bad that he would swerve from lane to lane, scaring Henry to death.

Ulis and I remain friends to this day. He was living in Los Angeles, and I hadn't heard from him for several years before I got arrested in 1978. But when I got in trouble, he flew to Dallas, stayed with me during my trial, and testified for me. That's what I call friendship.

Ralph Boston was another close friend on the track circuit. I always used to call Ralph "Poodle" because he liked to say that in his next life he wanted to come back as a poodle. When I asked him why, he answered, "Because poodles get treated better in America than we blacks do."

Ralph thought he could have been a sprinter. He had always wanted to run in the relays, and we finally let Ralph run the anchor leg in the 400-meter relay against the Swedish national team. We won, too, and the organizers of the meet gave us some beautiful sweaters as our award. When Ralph bent over to receive his sweater, he slipped and fell off the stand, right onto his head. His legs went into a split and he pulled a muscle. Was he mad!

Still another close friend I made when I was running in Europe was another sprinter, Paul Drayton. Paul, who was from Cleveland, was a teammate of Frank Budd's at Villanova. I assume they didn't have too many dogs around the track at Villanova because Paul was terrified of dogs. On a cool, overcast Sunday afternoon, while he and I were jogging through a park in Germany, we saw two big German shepherds. When Paul wasn't looking at me, I came up behind him and grabbed his ankle like a dog was biting him. He was so frightened that he kicked me in the head, leaving me with a big knot over my left eye. He ran off and got hives all over him and even came down with a fever. I didn't even know he was afraid of dogs; I was just playing with him. I'm glad I wasn't racing against him that day because I know I would have lost.

Unlike most of the other guys on the track-and-field circuit, John Thomas was a spoiled brat who thought he should have anything he wanted. Being from the Northeast, he also thought that southern blacks were not good enough for him. In the 1960 Olympics in Rome, John was expected to win the gold medal for the running high jump, but the Russian Valery Brumel beat him, and the United States never accepted him after that. He walked around with a chip on his shoulder for a long time.

Black magazines used to carry advertisements for great Italian-style shoes that were made in Boston, and I'd always wanted a pair. John went to Boston University, so I gave him $25 and asked him to bring a pair to me in Los Angeles the following week. When I saw him in Los Angeles, he said he hadn't had time to buy the shoes. After three months, he still hadn't brought the shoes or repaid my money, even though we saw each other every week or every other week. This was before I started getting paid to run, and $25 was a lot of money to me then. Finally, when we were in Los Angeles again, I said to him, "Well, John, since you didn't bring the shoes, give me back my $25." He said, "Oh, I've only got $125 in my pocket." I said, "If you don't give me the $25, I'm going to take it, John." You have to understand, John was about six feet five, but he was a wimp. He kept refusing to give me back my money, so I picked him up in the lobby of the Sheraton West Hotel in Los Angeles, with Ralph Boston standing right there, dumped him on the floor, went into his pocket, got out my $25, and gave the other $100 back to him. John got up, put the rest of the money back in his pocket, and forgot about it immediately. In spite of run-ins like that, John and I got along, although I wasn't as close to him as I was to Ralph Boston, Ulis Williams, and some of the others.

The Russians always knew how to psyche John out. One day, I got to see for myself how they did it because Valery Brumel and I were close friends. Every time Valery and I attended a function, they sat us together as world record holders and our friendship just grew. We used to play back and forth with our flags. I would say, "My flag is better than yours," and he would slap mine aside with his Soviet flag, and then I would do the same with my flag.

Anyway, we were getting ready to run against the Russians at Stanford, and Valery Brumel and I were outside playing basketball while John was watching us. Brumel started pointing at the hoop and yelling, "Jump, Bob, jump!" I jumped up and grabbed the rim with my two hands and hung there, but Valery said, "No, foot, with foot." I jumped up and tried to touch the rim with my foot, but I couldn't quite reach the net. Then Valery walked toward the basket, took a couple of steps like he was going into a high jump, jumped up, touched the rim with his foot, and landed with perfect balance. I couldn't believe it. I was leaping up and I could just barely touch it with my hand, and Valery Brumel came along and touched the hoop with his foot. John was watching and I said, "Okay, Big John, it's your turn. You've been saying you're going to beat Valery, so you got your chance right here." I was really egging him on. John attempted to do it, and the highest he could touch with his foot was the net, even though he was several inches taller than Brumel. I ridiculed him so bad. I said, "Now I know why the Russians can beat you. They train harder and you just bullshit around. Here's the Russian come all the way over here. He's much shorter than you. You're a world record holder and he's a world record holder. And you let this man play with you. He's not even serious about this. How do you think you can get out there at a track meet and beat him?" John never could beat Brumel, he was totally psyched out. He never won again after the Russians beat him in Rome, and Americans started looking down on him. He just couldn't handle the pressure.

My 1964 track season was nothing more than preparation for the Olympics—a plan that was ruined when I got hurt in New Brunswick and had to start from scratch. But in the first six months of 1964, I continued to run in a number of meets, looking to win, set records if I could, and get myself in tip-top shape for what lay ahead.

I started the New Year with a bang, tying my world record with a 9.1 in the 100 at the Orange Bowl Invitational in Miami. This was another meet in which my time was wasted, in this case because I had a tail wind of about ten miles an hour. In some races when the times were nullified because of the wind, I felt that the wind hadn't really helped me, but in this race, I could feel the breeze on my back, pushing me to a faster time. On the other hand, it had been pouring for two days in Miami, and the cinder track was wet and soggy (a fact that track officials have never taken into consideration when deciding whether a time qualifies for a record). Just for good measure, I threw in a couple more 9.1s later in the season, one on April 18 at a meet for black schools in Orangeburg, South Carolina, and another on May 2, at the Volunteer Games in Nashville. Meanwhile, in the Orange Bowl meet on January 1 on that same slow track, I also ran a 20.1 in the 220, one-tenth of a second slower than Dave Sime's world record, even though I had to slow up near the finish to avoid a crowd of fans who had gathered a few yards down the track. Sime, who was then a surgeon in Miami and was there that day, called my race "fantastic" under the circumstances.

I spent the next couple of months concentrating on the indoor circuit and serving notice that my world record in the 70 a year earlier was no fluke. On January 25 in Albuquerque, I won the 60 by a yard over Bernie Rivers of the University of New Mexico, tying the world record at 6.0. Adolph Plummer, a quarter-miler for the Southern California Striders who was from New Mexico, was a friend of mine, and he asked me to run the race as a favor to him. Ralph Boston was representing the Striders then, and he and I knew that Adolph wasn't in the best of shape for that meet, in which he was to run the 300. We kidded Adolph that he was going to run the first lap real hard, run out of gas, and collapse into the long-jump pit. I'll be damned if that's not exactly what happened. Adolph came off the curve running full speed, tripped, and fell right into the pit. Everyone in the stands was upset because he was their God and he was lying there like he was really hurt. Ralph and I really rode him for that; we told him he was an actor and should be in Hollywood.

I made my Madison Square Garden debut the following week in the Millrose Games, where I won the 60 in 6.1. I continued tying records, with a 6.0 in the 60 in Los Angeles on February 8 and an identical performance in Madison Square Garden five days later. Then I returned to Louisville two nights after that to run the 70 and match my 6.9 from the year before. But I wanted to break more records, not keep tying them. Meanwhile, something happened that made me feel that I really had to run a spectacular race. While I was visiting Miami, my aunt Frankie and my uncle Billy took me to a famous nightclub for blacks called the Nightbeat to hear Baby Washington and the Impressions. Muhammad Ali (who was then called Cassius Clay) was training for his upcoming world championship fight in Miami with Sonny Liston, and Jim Brown was in town, too. As my uncle and aunt and I entered the club, Jim Brown and Cassius Clay were standing by the door—two great athletes. My uncle introduced us; I hardly knew Jim and I didn't know Cassius at all. Then Jim said to

Clay, "Cassius, here's the world's fastest human right here. He's a Florida boy." Clay shook my hand; grabbed me; hugged me; and, as the three of us stood there with me in the middle, he told everyone who walked by, "This is three bad niggers. This is the three baddest niggers in the world here. The best boxer, the best football player, and the fastest runner."

Clay's fight with Liston, who was the defending heavyweight champion, was on February 25, and Liston was the overwhelming favorite. One reason I looked up to Cassius then was that he had won a gold medal at the 1960 Olympics, and I wanted to do something to let him know that he was special to me. And I had an opportunity coming up: Three nights before the big fight, I was scheduled to run the 60 in front of a capacity crowd of over fifteen thousand at the AAU indoor championships in Madison Square Garden. Before the race, I was walking around the track with Ralph Boston, John Thomas, and Jesse Owens, when this little guy with great big glasses walked up and interrupted our conversation.

"Are you Bob Hayes?" he asked.

"Yeah, I am."

"Well, I'm Charlie Greene from the University of Nebraska, and if you beat me tonight, you're going to have to break the world record."

"Okay, Charlie, okay."

Charlie was right, too. He ran a 6-flat to tie the world record held by Frank Budd, among others, and I ran a 5.9, finishing two feet ahead of him. We got to be good friends after that and we still talk back and forth all the time and tease each other about that night. After the race, I flew to Miami to see the Clay-Liston fight. When I got there, I told Cassius I had done something for him and I wanted him to do something for me. Not that it really had anything to do with me, but Cassius beat Liston so badly that Liston refused to answer the bell for the seventh round, saying his shoulder hurt him. It was one of the biggest upsets of all time.

By the end of March, I was running outdoors again—and it looked like I had set yet another record, an incredible 8.7 in the 100-yard dash at the Florida A & M Relays. The trouble was that my mark that day really was incredible. The meet officials measured the track after the race to certify the record and discovered that someone had made a mistake in laying out the course, which was 6 yards short. At least I could say I was the world record holder at 94 yards.

During the next three months, I kept on winning the 100 all over the country. And then came the AAU outdoor championships at Rutgers. And near disaster.

5

WELCOME TO
THE NFL

After the 1963 football season at Florida A & M, I had one more year of eligibility in college football, but since I had been at A & M for four years and had been redshirted, I was available for the pro football draft as a future choice. A number of teams had contacted me before the draft, including the Green Bay Packers (who sent me a telegram signed by Vince Lombardi saying they were interested in me), the Los Angeles Rams, the Pittsburgh Steelers, and the Cleveland Browns. But the Dallas Cowboys had shown the most interest. For several years, they had been sending me and my mother material that pushed all the things the Cowboys did for their players and the opportunities for housing, jobs, and so forth in Dallas. Even so, going into draft day, you never knew. I mean, I had established my reputation as a football player and was already known as the world's fastest human, although the Olympics were still ahead of me, but there was always doubt in the back of my mind: Does any team really want me?

On the NFL's draft day, December 2, 1963, I spent the morning in Jake Gaither's office, waiting to see if I would get drafted. The first round alone lasted eight hours, and after the fifth round, when it was late at night and I still hadn't gotten picked, I left and went to get a snack. When I got back, everybody was running around yelling, "You got drafted! You got drafted!" Jake Gaither shouted louder than the others, "Shut up! I will tell him." I asked, "Who did I get drafted by, Jake?" He answered, "You got drafted by two teams. First, you got drafted in the seventh round by the Dallas Cowboys." "The Dallas Cowboys," I said to myself. In the back of my mind, I thought about the assassination of President Kennedy in Dallas. But I knew I wanted to play pro football, and the Dallas Cowboys didn't kill him. And I said, "Who else?" And he answered, "The Denver Broncos." I said, "Well, damn, two Cowboy teams." The Broncos were in cowboy country, and they had a horse on their helmets.

I found out later that the Cowboys had selected Mel Renfro, the player they really wanted, with their top selection, which was in the second round, and had gotten Perry Lee Dunn, a runningback from Ole Miss, in the fourth round and Billy Lothridge, a quarterback from Georgia Tech, in the sixth round. Tex Schramm, Tom Landry, and Gil Brandt decided together on who the Cowboys would draft, but by the time the sixth round ended, Tom and Gil stepped outside the Cowboy's draft headquarters because they weren't that interested in the lower-round choices. That left Tex Schramm to decide by himself. The Cowboys had a list of prospects in the order they planned to draft them, but Tex decided to ignore the list when he had a choice in the seventh round and picked me because of my speed.

A few minutes after Jake Gaither told me the Cowboys had drafted me, Gil Brandt called and passed on the same information. "Now you're a Dallas Cowboy," Gil added. Of course, it wasn't quite as simple as that. First, I couldn't sign until after the Olympics the following October, and even then, I still had that year of college eligibility remaining in both football and track. Also, this was at the height of the battle between the NFL and the American Football League (AFL), and there was a bidding war going on. I probably would have gone with whichever team offered me the most money, but, assuming the offers were pretty equal, I was leaning toward the Cowboys all along for three reasons:

- The NFL was the more established league. It had been in business for forty years or so, while the AFL had been in operation only since 1960. The AFL at that time was an inferior league without the great players the NFL had.

- I was a warm-weather boy, and the idea of living and playing in all that snow up in Denver didn't appeal to me. The climate in Dallas, though, was a lot more like that in Florida, where I had lived all my life.

- Tom Landry. After we played Southern University in Baton Rouge when I was a senior, Jake Gaither and I flew to Dallas in a private plane as Landry's guests to see the Cowboys play, and Landry impressed me. When it came time for me to decide which team to go with, and Jake and I were talking it over, Jake said, "Let me tell you something, Bobby. This Tom Landry is a religious man like I am. He's a family man, too, and a smart coach. Everything I've heard about this man is good." Jake was negotiating my contract—he was more than my coach, he was my friend and like a father to me, and I trusted him—and Jake had known Landry for a long time and loved him.

Once the 1964 football season at Florida A & M ended, I sat down with Jake Gaither and Dick Hill, the track coach. I told them I owed everything to Florida A & M and I would be glad to run track in the spring. But they both insisted I had done plenty for the school, and since there was nothing left for me to prove in track, I should sign a pro football contract and not risk getting hurt and blowing the whole deal.

After that, Jake and I had an easy decision. True, the Broncos had shown a lot of interest in me; they had somebody calling me all the time. When I pulled a muscle running at Rutgers in June 1964, the injury that almost forced me to miss the Olympics, the Broncos had somebody there and they wanted me to sign with them right away, even though I was hurt. But the bottom line was that the Cowboys offered me $100,000 in a three-year deal, about $30,000 more than Denver offered. If it had been the other way around, I might have had trouble making up my mind, but this way, there was no question that I was going with the Cowboys. Ironically, the Broncos later traded my rights to the Jets, and the Jets offered me double the money that the Cowboys had offered me. But no one knew I had already promised the Cowboys I would sign with them. Just think, I could have played with Joe Namath, too. Imagine what Joe and I could have done together! If I hadn't already signed with Dallas, I would have gone with the money and Namath. And the Jets didn't have a bad coach, a guy named Weeb Ewbank.

Jake and I flew to Dallas, and at a team luncheon on December 8, 1964, I signed my contract and officially became a Cowboy and an NFL player, fulfilling one of my lifelong dreams. The Cowboys also gave me a six-thousand-dollar Buick Riviera as part of my signing bonus. That car caused me a little trouble when I got back to school. You see, there weren't many black kids my age (I turned twenty-two less than two weeks after I signed with the Cowboys) driving cars like that in good old Tallahassee. About once a week or so, some of Tallahassee's finest would stop me and ask, "Boy, whose car is that?" I would tell them it was my car, and they would give me a ticket for anything they felt like—speeding, running a stop sign, driving on white folks' streets—you name it. I finally got smart. I went downtown and bought a chauffeur's black cap and put it in the back seat. Every time the police pulled me over after that and asked me whose car I was driving, I would say, "It's my boss man's car," and they would let me go. This was the era when, while driving from Dallas back to Florida, I would pass restaurants all over Louisiana, Mississippi, and Alabama with signs that read, "No colored" or "Colored around back." I was good enough to represent their country in the Olympics, but not good enough to eat with them.

My first order of business after I signed with the Cowboys was the North-South All-Star game in the Orange Bowl on Christmas Day. After playing for and against segregated black teams throughout my high school and college careers, this was the first time that I had ever played football with white guys. My South team lost 37 to 30, but I scored a touchdown on a 39-yard end around, caught several passes, and was named the South squad's most valuable player. On my touchdown, even Roger Staubach threw a good block to help me go all the way.

My next stop was the sixteenth annual Senior Bowl in Mobile, Alabama, where my college teammate, Bobby Felts, Dick Gordon and Jerry Rush of Michigan State, and I were the first blacks to play in the game. Joe Namath used to spend a lot of time in Miami when he was at Alabama. I hung out there too, and he and I had become friendly. His Alabama team played Texas in the Orange Bowl on New Year's Day, and afterwards he and I were booked on the same flight to Mobile. But we didn't reconfirm our reservations and got bumped off the flight. So we got in Joe's green Lincoln with the white top—New York Jets colors (he had just signed his huge contract with the Jets)—and we drove from the Miami Airport to Mobile. We spent ten or eleven hours on the road, including a stop in Tallahassee, where I showed him around the Florida A & M campus and the Florida State Campus, where Fred Biletnikoff was getting married under the goal posts. Freddie used to come to Florida A & M to watch me run track, and we were friends even though the newspapers tried to create a rivalry between us, with stories like "Bob Hayes is a good football player, but he's not a Fred Biletnikoff."

Joe and I were on the South team in the Senior Bowl, and our head coach was Tom Landry. At our first practice, Namath said, "Let me see how fast you can run, Mr. World's Fastest Human. Go deep down the right side." "Joe," I answered, "by the time you get your snap from center, drop back your ten yards, and throw the ball as far as you can, I'll be down the field." All the guys stopped to watch us. The center snapped the ball to Namath, who dropped back the ten yards and zoomed the ball about seventy yards down the field, but the pass was behind me a bit. That made me a little cocky, so I ran the ball back to the center real fast and said, "Well, look, Mr. Namath, since you can't throw so accurate on the right side, I'm going to give you another chance. Let's try the left side." This time he hit me perfectly about seventy yards down the field. I jogged back to the huddle, and Landry said, "Okay, my starting quarterback is Joe Namath and one of my starting wide receivers is Bob Hayes."

Joe, of course, was just about the biggest hero in Alabama at that time, and knowing that I was one of the four players integrating the Senior Bowl, he told me, "Bobby, if you have any trouble with any of these rednecks, don't worry, I'll take care of you." The people of Mobile treated me fine, though, certainly better than I was used to being treated in my home state. The only problem I had was with some of the players on the North team. The word "nigger" popped up several times during the game, although I never knew which players said it because it happened when my back was turned. It just made me want to get out there and kick their ass on the football field—that would pay them back more than my trying to retaliate. I've been called that all my life and it hurts, but what can you say when it comes from ignorant people?

One of the players for the North was Lance Rentzel. He had to play defensive back, and when he saw that he was covering me, his eyes got as big as half dollars. But Lance wasn't covering me on the play that counted: Late in the game, with the South trailing 7 to 0, Namath threw a short pass to me with guys from the North all around me. I shook them off, turned on my own jets, and went 53 yards for our only touchdown in a 7–7 tie.

My visit to Rutgers for the National AAU meet in June 1964—the one in which I hurt my leg and that almost made me miss the Olympics—left me with a lot of scars. I had noticed Altamease Martin, a girl from New Brunswick who went to Florida A & M, around the school, but I was a big man on campus. I was surrounded by girls and living in the fast lane, while she was being raised by an uncle who worked in the orange groves. Also, I thought she was married, but she wasn't.

When I got to New Brunswick for the AAU meet, Altamease started phoning me at the Rutgers dorm where I was staying. She called me again and again, and I finally agreed to have lunch with her at her parents' house. Our relationship just took off from there, and then when we got back to campus in the fall, we started to date. We were both due to graduate from Florida A & M in June 1965. A couple of months before graduation, I took her out to our track, which was the most significant place on campus for me. The track was where my success began—the symbol of my achievements. One of my buddies, Owens "Butch" McKay, drove his car around the track, with Butch and me in the front seat and Altamease sitting in the back. Altamease had asked me to bring her a pearl from Sydney, Australia, where I had recently run in a track meet. I brought her a diamond ring instead and proposed to her in the car, circling the track.

By then, I had signed with the Cowboys and I was spending a lot of time in Dallas, working out, learning the Cowboy system, and getting ready for my first pro football training camp. Three months after I gave Altamease the ring, I asked her to come to Dallas and help me decorate my apartment. When she got there, I told her we were getting married, and we did. We went to city hall on July 9, 1965, and a judge married us, with Gil Brandt, the team's chief talent scout, and another Cowboys executive as our only witnesses.

But Altamease and I didn't live happily ever after. When I found that we couldn't have our own children, it was the beginning of the end of our relationship. We stayed together long enough to adopt a beautiful five-week-old daughter, Rori, in 1968, but that was mostly Altamease's doing in hopes of holding onto me and saving our marriage. By then, I had already stopped loving Altamease. Sometimes I would go to the oyster bar at a restaurant in downtown Dallas called Buddy's—one of the hangouts for the black guys who played for the Cowboys—and pick up women. We would go to a hotel, their house, my car. Anywhere.

Like me, Altamease had left Florida A & M without graduating. I paid to send her to Bishop College in Dallas to get her degree, but she didn't study and failed her courses. That made me angry; it was just like throwing my money in the trash can or flushing it down the toilet. I asked her to work, but she didn't want to. We hired a nurse to look after the baby and a housekeeper, so everything was taken care of; but Altamease still wouldn't work. She spent a lot of time shopping; she always wore nice clothes, expensive jewelry, and fur coats and drove Lincolns. She really got into playing the role of Mrs. Bob Hayes around Dallas. But the truth is that I was just as frivolous as Altamease, and I believe she was taking her lead from me. I also spent a lot of money on material things like clothes and automobiles (and hotel rooms where I took other women).

I blame myself for a lot of our problems because I traveled without Altamease a great deal in the off-season, doing public relations for Royal Crown Cola and Braniff Airlines. I was always gone. I didn't have time for my wife or, rather, I didn't make time. I thought only about football and making money. I was afraid of being broke and I thought I was meeting Altamease's needs by providing money. Money meant success to me, and I wanted to be a success and I wanted my wife to have a successful husband. I never stopped to realize that I was neglecting my wife and my home life. I thought then that I was doing the right thing, but now I see that I was not fulfilling my wife's needs.

Altamease was an extremely good mother, but not a good wife, any more than I was a good husband. Several years after we got married, I sat down one day in the off-season and started going over my accounts; I was staggered when I saw how much Altamease had spent in the last three months. I suspected she was also giving money to her mother without my knowledge. We finally split up in 1972.

She and I were on bad terms until a year or so ago. As a result, I've been pretty much estranged from Rori, too. Rori is now a social work student at Prairie View A & M University. She has told me that I wasn't a good father while she was growing up, which is true, but I think she and I are straightening out our problems now that Altamease and I have worked things out.

The 1965 College All-Star game, matching the cream of that year's rookie crop against the defending NFL champions, the Cleveland Browns, was more like the future Dallas Cowboys against the Browns. Thanks to two great drafts by the Cowboys, the All-Stars were loaded with the Cowboys' draft choices: me and Roger Staubach, who had been drafted three rounds after me, in the tenth round, as a future in the 1964 draft; and several 1965 choices, including number one, Craig Morton; number two, Malcom Walker, a center from Rice; number eight, Russell Wayt, a linebacker from Rice; and Ralph Neely, who had been drafted by Baltimore but traded to Dallas for a draft choice after the Cowboys signed him for the NFL in the war with the AFL. We had a great All-Star team that year. Some of the other players on our team were Gale Sayers; Dick Butkus; Fred Biletnikoff; Verlon Biggs, a defensive end from Jackson State who was later a star with the Jets and the Washington Redskins; Marty Schottenheimer of the University of Pittsburgh, now the head coach of the Kansas City Chiefs and former coach of the Cleveland Browns; Lance Rentzel; Tucker Frederickson from Auburn University, who was a star with the Giants; Roy Jefferson, who was a defensive back for the All-Stars but was a great wide receiver for the Pittsburgh Steelers, the Baltimore Colts, and the Redskins; and John Huarte, the quarterback from Notre Dame who had won the Heisman Trophy in 1964.

Even so, Cleveland beat us, 24 to 16. It must have been the coaching. Cleveland's head coach was Blanton Collier, and ours was the incomparable Otto Graham, the former star quarterback of the Browns. I would say that Otto threw the game to his old team, except that he wasn't that smart. To give you an idea of what kind of judge of talent Otto was, he had badmouthed Jim Brown's abilities; he had said the year before that Charley Taylor was lazy and predicted he wouldn't make it with the Redskins; and he didn't think much of Gale Sayers, whom he kept on the bench for the entire All-Star game. Other All-Stars Graham didn't like over the years included Bob Lilly; Duane Thomas; and, from the 1965 team, Clancy Williams and me. Clancy, a defensive back from Washington State, got so pissed off that he left camp for a few days. When Clancy returned to practice, Otto gave him a hard time, and Clancy finally told him, "Screw you. I'm the number-one draft choice of the Rams, I don't care what you think of me." Clancy started for us against the Browns and went on to have a fine career, even though Graham didn't think he would make it in pro football.

Graham didn't think I was a football player. He dismissed me as just another track star trying to learn how to play football and, as a result, he wouldn't let me return punts. What's strange about that is that Graham himself had been a two-sport star at Northwestern in football and basketball and went on to have an outstanding career with the Browns. But he didn't think I could become a star in the NFL like he had. He was afraid I wasn't enough of a football player to catch a punt and return it, too—sort of like not being able to chew gum and walk at the same time—so he didn't use me on punt returns. Funny thing, though, I went on to be one of the best punt returners in the NFL for the next few years.

What happened during practice for the All-Star game confirmed Otto's opinion of me. Our other wide receivers—Rentzel, Biletnikoff, and Jack Snow of Notre Dame—got hurt in training camp and couldn't practice for a while. Since I was the only healthy wide receiver, I had to catch most of the passes in practice, and Craig Morton, who threw the ball harder than any other quarterback I ever played with, split open several of my fingers with his passes. With all the catching I was doing, my fingers never got a chance to heal and I started dropping a lot of balls. A few days before we played Cleveland, we had a scrimmage against the Chicago Bears, and I dropped a sure touchdown pass. I beat Benny McRae on the play, and Roger Staubach threw a bomb that was slightly too long. My hands were extended all the way, and the ball hit my fingertips and bounced off. That gave Otto an excuse to comment that I had "9-flat speed and 12-flat hands," which the press picked up.

But what goes around comes around, and after Graham was named coach of Washington the next year, I always tried my hardest to beat the Redskins because of him. The Redskins fired Graham after three seasons for not winning enough games, and he hasn't been heard from since. Graham just didn't prepare his teams well enough, he relied too much on the athletes' natural ability, he wasn't well organized, and he didn't seem to have a real game plan the way Tom Landry did, with plays for first and 10, second and 15, third and 8, and so forth. Every time we played the Redskins while Graham was their coach, Graham would run across the field to shake my hand, and being a gentleman, I shook his hand. A lot of Cowboys respected me and were watching me, and I didn't want them to think I was angry about what had happened with the All-Stars. The truth is, though, that I was bitter. And every time I caught a pass against the Redskins, I thought about what Otto Graham had said about my having 9-flat speed and 12-flat hands and I knew that every single catch I made against the Redskins hurt him and his team.

A couple of assistant coaches with the All-Stars—Marion Motley and "Hopalong" Cassady—taught me a lot. I was one of Cassady's favorites, and he didn't like what Otto Graham had said about me. He taught me how to control my speed and how to plant my cutting foot, not my inside foot, so I could keep my balance. I used to try to get Hopalong to race me. I kept telling him, "I heard you were one of the fastest guys in the league when you played. Let's you and I and Lance [who was another of his pets] get down and race; I guarantee you you'll be second and Rentzel third." He said, "I'll beat Lance but I won't run against you, Bob. I have a reputation to protect, too."

Another good thing about being a College All-Star was that I made several lifelong friends—guys like Al Nelson, a defensive back from Cincinnati who played for the Eagles; Lance Rentzel; and Roger Staubach.

I reported to the Cowboys' training camp at California Lutheran College in Thousand Oaks on Saturday, August 7, 1965, the day after the College All-Star game. I arrived with mixed emotions: both excitement and disappointment. Charles Sutton, my lifelong friend and teammate in high school and college, had signed with the Cowboys as a free agent, but he failed his physical and was released before I got to Thousand Oaks. The doctors discovered during Charles's physical that he had a heart problem and couldn't play football anymore.

I had Sunday, a day off, to get my head together, and on Monday, I went to work in the profession of my choice. That first day we were working over and over on a play in which I lined up next to the tackle and was then supposed to cut across the middle of the field. Bill Van Burkleo, a defensive back from Tulsa, was supposed to cover me, and if I released on the outside, Van Burkleo would flow with me and wind up in the area where a runningback was supposed to catch the ball. If I went inside, Van Burkleo had to follow me, and the runningback could slip into the outside and Don Meredith could dump the ball off to him. We ran the play over and over, and Van Burkleo kept cheating to the inside, preventing me from cutting across and knocking me into the tackle every time.

The receivers' coach was Howard Hickey, but everyone called him "Red" because any time he got angry or excited, he would turn all red. I told Hickey, "Coach, I can't get by this guy unless he stops playing so strong to the inside, but I can just go right by him to the outside and he'll never touch me." Well, this was one of those times that Hickey turned bright red. He yelled, "I want you to go to the inside and you're going to do it. If you don't do it, I'll send your butt home!" I'm thinking, "Is this the way it goes here?" But we got back in the huddle and Don Meredith, the quarterback, said, "We'll get him off you." So Meredith told me to go outside, Van Burkleo played me strong to the inside, and I escaped to the outside and caught a quick out. We had changed the play on our own, and Red Hickey got real mad and started yelling at Meredith. I waited for Don after practice and thanked him as we walked off the field. I should have spoken up for him when Red Hickey chewed him out, but I was a scared rookie at the time and didn't have the nerve to defend him when one of the coaches was angry. At least Don knew I was on his side.

After Billy Van Burkleo started playing me normal again, I was able to make my move to the inside and open up the outside for one of the runningbacks. But I was still more than a little worried about Hickey's threat to cut me and send me home. The Cowboys invited college coaches to attend training camp every year, and that year they had invited Jake and Sadie Gaither. I told Jake and Sadie that night what Hickey had said to me at practice, and Sadie gave me a piece of her mind. "Coach Hickey knows what he's doing," she said. "He's just trying to make you a better football player. You're a professional now and you'd better do what he says." Jake was a lot more worried about what had happened than Sadie was, and he went to talk to Red the next day. Red told him not to worry, that there was no way they were going to cut me and that he was just trying to get my attention. He certainly succeeded in doing that.

From then on, Hickey took me under his wing and would come out twenty or thirty minutes before practice to throw balls to me and work with me on my pass catching. I had a bad habit of jumping for the ball even when I didn't have to, which made me break my stride and lose ground to the defenders. Red taught me to catch the ball with my feet on the ground, how to hold my hands so I could catch better, how to judge the defensive coverage and linebackers and adjust accordingly, and always to watch the ball all the way into my hands instead of taking my eye off it and looking at the defensive back. He threw me hundreds of passes in his spare time, which he didn't have to do, and he's the one who really made me a professional football player. Red noticed my improvement from the start, and several years later he told the press what I meant to the Cowboys: "Bobby's arrival coincided with the beginning of the rise of the Cowboys. He became a star and he lifted the ball club. If ever any one man came in who started a team on the road to being exciting, he was the one."

As the days went by in my first Cowboy training camp, I started to make an impression on the veteran players. Meredith and I became friends when he learned that I could catch the ball and I discovered that when he went back and cocked his arm and threw, the ball would be where it was supposed to be. He had a knack of getting that ball there, and I was fortunate to be able to play with a quarterback like him.

Some of the veterans asked Don, "What do you think of this guy

Hayes?" And Don said, "He can catch. He's going to be great." I was practicing against outstanding defensive backs—Mike Gaechter, Cornell Green, and Mel Renfro—and I could hear Gaechter saying, "This guy can play." With guys like Hickey, Meredith, and Gaechter in my corner, I felt like I was going to make it.

6

YOU CALL THESE GUYS AMERICA'S TEAM?

Anyone who wasn't part of Tom Landry's Dallas Cowboys had a false picture of the team: a computerized, colorless collection of robots who were assembled out of a data bank, ran plays called by some unknown electronic gadget, and fed to a coach who stood there on the sidelines with his stone-faced look, not capable of human emotion.

Well, I'm here to tell you that that image is untrue. During my ten years with the Cowboys, we had more than our share of wild and crazy characters—guys who wanted to win just as much as the next player, but who were fun to be around, too.

It all started with our coach. Standing on the sidelines, always wearing a hat to cover his bald head, hardly ever changing expression, Tom Landry did give people the idea that he was lacking in emotion. It's true that for many years Landry has been one of the leaders of the Fellowship of Christian Athletes and he's not a hell-raiser like a lot of athletes (don't forget he was an outstanding defensive back at the University of Texas and with the Giants). Still, even though he's not a Mike Ditka or a Vince Lombardi, Tom is not without his human side.

I discovered one of Tom's vices my first day with the Cowboys. After I signed with Dallas in December 1964, I rode from my press conference at the downtown Sheraton to the Cowboys' headquarters on Central Expressway with Coach Landry and his wife, Alicia. Coach Landry was driving a Pontiac Grand Prix and he was going about one hundred miles an hour.

I said, "Coach, please slow down, I know I'm the fastest man in the world, but are we at the Daytona 500 or what?" I mean, he does not drive slow. He said, "Bobby, I'm in a hurry, I have to get back to my office." As for Alicia, she didn't say a word, she was used to it. She just sat there, as comfortable and beautiful as ever.

Tom truly is devoted to Alicia. I can't imagine him playing around with women; in fact, I'm not even sure he played around with Alicia during the season. Like Joe Gibbs of the Redskins and Dick Vermeil, the former coach of UCLA and the Eagles, Tom lived football, twenty-four hours a day, seven days a week, during the season. I always thought it was bullshit. I never thought it did a damn thing for these coaches to watch the same films over and over. How many times do you have to watch a play before you can figure it out? I told Landry once he reminded me of the time Bill Cosby was on the Johnny Carson show and Bill's wife had just given birth to another girl. Bill wanted a son, and Carson asked him what he was going to do. Bill lit up a big cigar and said, "Well, Johnny, I'm just going to keep at it until I get it right." And Landry said, "That sounds to me like a good theory, Bob. And I'm going to just keep on watching these films so I can get the plays run right."

When Landry got really emotional during a team meeting over a mistake someone had made in a game he would say "Hell!" or "Damn!" That was the strongest language he ever used. But he was a lot more emotional behind closed doors than he appeared on the field over game plans, mistakes you had made, or assignments you had failed to carry out. He would turn bright red when he got angry.

There were times when I wished Tom would have a little more fun out on the field, like Don Shula, for instance. In one game against the Baltimore Colts, Lance Rentzel and I lined up on the same side and we both ran deep patterns. After the play was over, we were heading back to the huddle and we jogged right past the Colts' bench. Shula yelled, "Fuck you, Rentzel! And that goes for you, too, Hayes." I called over, "Hi, Coach Shula. How are you doing?" And he called back, "Get back in your huddle! Get your ass away from over here on our sideline!" Lance, Shula, and I were all laughing. That's my kind of coach. If I had played for another team, I would have wanted to play for Shula. He's a great coach and a great guy.

The only time I saw Landry take a drink was after we lost the 1970 Super Bowl to Baltimore in Miami. I got along great with Alicia, who always said I was one of her favorite Cowboys players. For some reason, Tom was delayed getting to our team party at our hotel in Fort Lauderdale after the game. Since I had a personal relationship with Mrs. Landry, she asked me to walk her around the room in Tom's absence. I took her by the arm, and we went to every table and she congratulated every single member of the team on a great year. She has a certain grace and charm about her. Landry finally walked in, and I said, "Coach Landry, here's your wife." He thanked me for looking after her, they kissed, and each one picked up a glass of champagne. And that was the one drink of his life, at least the only one I ever saw him take.

Landry ran a tight ship on the sidelines, but he didn't mind having ballplayers tell him when we thought a play might work. He didn't like us bothering the quarterbacks while he was talking to them when our defensive unit was in the game, but we could go up to Landry and say, "Coach, I can do this, I can get open on this type of route." I didn't do that too often because there's only one ball and everybody wants it, but when I did tell him a play that I thought would work, he always appreciated it.

All the Cowboys' assistant coaches tried to imitate Landry, and it got to be a standing joke within the team. After team meetings in training camp, Landry would go into the dining hall and have an ice cream cone. So, naturally, all the other coaches would have an ice cream cone. I can still see Ditka and some of the other hell-raisers licking their cones, trying to be like Tom.

When Coach Landry talked, the assistant coaches hung on his every word. I mean, E. F. Hutton didn't have anything on him. Once, while Landry was at the blackboard diagramming a play, he started coughing, really choking, hard. All the coaches jumped up, and Dan Reeves and Ernie Stautner ran to get water for him. They both hit the door at the same time and got stuck in the doorway. It was one of the funniest sights I ever saw, and all the players were trying to keep a straight face.

The players didn't take everything Landry said quite as seriously as the assistant coaches did. Guys liked to sit in the back row during skull sessions, so they could lean their heads against the wall and sleep. But Jethro Pugh was just the opposite. He would sit up straight, right in front of Landry, and cross his big feet (about a size sixteen shoe), and Coach Landry never knew that Jethro was asleep. Coach Landry would walk back and forth in front of the board and stumble over Jethro's feet, and old Jethro would sleep through it all.

Since the Cowboys started going bad in 1986, people have been asking me if I think pro football passed Tom Landry by. He was sixty-four and had been head coach of the Cowboys for twenty-nine years—the only coach Dallas had ever had—when Jerry Jones bought the team in early 1989, fired Tom, and brought in Jimmy Johnson from the University of Miami. In Tom's last three seasons, the team seemed to be getting worse, not better. My answer always was, I knew Landry was still a good coach, but he needed help from his staff. Losing wasn't Tom's fault. The only players who were worth a damn by the time the Landry era ended were Herschel Walker, Michael Irvin, Eugene Lockhart (a linebacker), maybe Steve Pelluer, Ed "Too-Tall" Jones, Nate Newton, Crawford Kerr, and two or three others. The Cowboys *have* had some tough luck. For example, Billy Cannon, Jr., the linebacker who was their number-one draft choice in 1984, broke his neck, which ended his career after just one season. And Mike Sherrard, the wide receiver from UCLA who was the number-one choice in 1986 and caught forty-one passes—the most for a Cowboys rookie since I caught forty-six in 1965—broke his leg twice and never played for Dallas again. (Talk about making a guy feel old: Mike's mother, Cherie, was a hurdler on the U.S. Olympic team with me in 1964.)

It's the ownership and the front office that really let the team fall apart. Bum Bright, the principal owner before Jerry Jones, got into so much financial trouble after the collapse of the oil and banking industries in Texas that a few months before he sold his interest to Jones, he defaulted on a loan, which made the Federal Deposit Insurance Corporation owner of 10 percent of the Cowboys. So the Cowboys really were America's team. At the same time, Gil Brandt and the scouting staff didn't do their jobs well, so the team kept losing and Landry looked bad. If Landry had had some players, then we would have known whether he could still coach. The problem is that it takes years to rebuild a team that is as bad as the Cowboys have become, and now Tom won't have a chance to show if he could still win when he had winning talent. It's a shame.

The whole time Landry was head coach, there never was any question that he was the boss, but players used to talk back to him occasionally. I'll always remember the time Mike Gaechter challenged his authority in training camp. Each year when we reported, we had to run what was known as the Landry mile, in which players had to run a certain time, depending on our position, to prove we were in shape. In 1966, my second season, we were warming up for the Landry Mile, when Landry told Gaechter he wouldn't have to run for at least ten minutes. So Mike, who had been an outstanding sprinter at the Unviersity of Oregon, ran a quarter mile at half speed. As soon as he was finished, though, one of the coaches said, "Okay, you defensive backs, your turn to run the mile." Mike's tongue was hanging out, and he looked toward Landry and said, "I thought you said we weren't going for at least ten minutes. What's wrong with you all around here I thought you were supposed to be a smart coaching staff. A man has an IQ of a hundred fifty and he can't even give me the right time." Everybody got real quiet, and Landry just stared at Mike, as if to say, "Are you crazy? You don't talk to me like this." Mike finally ran and made his time, and nothing more was said about what had happened.

Everyone looked up to Landry, but I certainly don't want to give the impression that he's perfect. One of the worst things he ever did was let Don Meredith take the blame for a call that cost us a chance to tie Cleveland in a big game during my rookie year, 1965. With Jim Brown as their leader, the Browns usually beat us in those years, and we had had a close loss to them, 23 to 17 in Cleveland, earlier in the season. After losing five games in a row, we had won our last two and were hoping to beat the Browns when they came to Dallas in late November.

Studying films all week before the game, we had seen that Cleveland always used a seven- or eight-man front near their goal line, so we knew that if we got down there, we would probably have to pass. With the score 24 to 17 in favor of Cleveland late in the fourth quarter, we moved down the field and had first and goal at the Cleveland 1. There was plenty of time left to try a running play or two, but Landry called the offensive unit to the sidelines and reminded Meredith, "The only way we can score on these guys is to pass on them." So on first down, Don threw a pass for Frank Clarke in the end zone, but the ball was a little behind Frank, hit him on the shoulder pad, bounced into the air, and was intercepted by Bernie Parrish for a touchback. The biggest crowd in the Cowboys' history to that time, over seventy-six thousand, had come to see us try to beat the Browns, and the fans practically booed Don out of the Cotton Bowl after that interception. It wasn't just that the pass had been intercepted; it seemed like a dumb call. We wound up losing, 24 to 17. After the game, the media humiliated Don, and Landry would not admit that he was the one who had called that play. The whole offensive team knew that Landry had called the play, but he wouldn't own up to it publicly and back up his quarterback. Landry's behavior really hurt Meredith's feelings, and I think it was one of the things on Don's mind when he retired before the 1969 season, even though he could have played another five years or so.

Landry did something to me that really upset me: When I was traded to San Francisco in the summer of 1975, he never called to let me know. It hurt me to my heart that Coach Landry didn't pick up the phone and say, "You've been traded. " When Pettis Norman was sent to San Diego in the Lance Alworth trade in 1971, Coach Landry drove to the bank where Pettis worked and sat down and talked to him. After what I had given to the Dallas Cowboys on the field and to the whole organization off the field—not just all the touchdowns, but the fame that the Cowboys got through my name around the world—I wasn't worthy of a personal call from Tom when they traded me. I was in Dallas at the time—most of the team had already reported to training camp—and Gil Brandt called me from Thousand Oaks and said, "Bob, I apologize for Coach Landry, but he wanted me to let you know that you're traded to San Francisco and wish you good luck." Landry got a glorified scout to call me and give me the word. I can forgive that, but I can't forget it.

I think Tom resented that I was outspoken, especially about black-white relationships on the Cowboys, because he saw it as a challenge to his authority. We had our ups and downs the whole time I was with the Cowboys. At times, he would treat me great, put his arm around me at practice, walk with me, ask me how I felt, and tell me that his whole game plan depended on me. But at the start of nearly every season, he would go to the press and complain about my blocking, my concentration, my weight, what have you. I guess he did that to motivate me, but I would have felt a lot better if he had spoken to me in private.

Landry was so used to my speed that he took if for granted. Sometimes I would run through the middle in practice and the safety wouldn't react because he knew I was a decoy. Landry would get pissed off with *me*, even though the safety was the one who was loafing. He would yell, "Bobby Hayes, you're going to run that route until you get it right!" But I couldn't make the safety move. If he already recognized the play because of his experience, what the shit could I do? I would yell back, "Well, why don't you get your safety to react and follow me? Here I am twenty yards behind him, and he's still standing back there."

Today Tom Landry and I have a great relationship. After my season with the 49ers, I came back to Dallas and, like many former players, I have spent a lot of time at the Cowboys' headquarters ever since. We never spoke about the trade or his failure to call me; we just swept it under the rug as if it had never happened and went on from there. I hope that someday I'll get elected to the Pro Football Hall of Fame, and I'll tell you this: If and when that day comes, I'll have to have someone stand with me and introduce me at the induction ceremony, and I will be proud if it's Tom Landry.

■　■　■

Until they were sold in 1989, the Cowboys had the same three men running the team throughout their existence: Tex Schramm, the president and general manger; Gil Brandt, the vice president and chief talent scout; and Landry. Nearly everybody in the Dallas area who I talk to makes negative comments about Tex. Either you like Tex Schramm or you hate him. A few years ago, I had to take my money out of the deferred payments the Cowboys owed me to try to keep myself above water. That should have been my business and should have remained private between me and the Dallas Cowboys, but Tex went to the media and told them I'd taken my money out of deferred payments and that all my deferred money had gone to waste. My money went to pay bills and to take care of my kids; I needed the money to live on. Tex had no right to talk about it with anyone but me.

Tex often criticized the team, the players, the coaching staff, and scouts. He's the kind of person who thinks everything is always someone else's fault, and people in the Cowboys organization didn't like it.

Gil Brandt is like a Dr. Jekyll and Mr. Hyde; one day he'll speak to you, and one day he won't. I was not one of Gil Brandt's favorites, and he usually omits my name when he mentions the great Cowboys from the glory days—Meredith, Staubach, Calvin Hill, and Walt Garrison, to name a few. At one time Gil was dating a nurse who was, in turn, dating a black Dallas Cowboy. Gil thought it was me, but it was Les Shy, who was a runningback for the Cowboys in the late 1960s. Maybe that's the reason, or at least a reason, why Gil started to dislike me. Too bad I wasn't going out with his girlfriend—I had to pay and didn't get to play.

Gil also may have suspected I was having a romance with Joan, who was among the first of his several wives. A big Cowboys contingent was in Los Angeles for the Pro Bowl in January 1967, and a bunch of us were at a cocktail party hosted by the Cowboys. Somebody asked me where I was going after the party, and I said I was going to the coliseum to see a track meet and be introduced to the crowd. Joan asked, "Can I go?" I said, "You want to come? Sure, you're welcome to come if you want to. But you'd better check it out with Gil." Although my wife was in Los Angeles for the game, she got sick, and I was going to have to go to the coliseum by myself. I left the party and was walking down the hall when Joan came up to me and said, "I'm going to the track meet with you." I saw Gil following her and Mrs. Landry say to her, "Please stay; don't leave,

Joan, don't leave." But Joan just didn't want to be there. Gil had no choice, so he finally said, "Yes, Bobby, it's fine if she goes to the track meet with you." We drove to the meet in my rental car and then came back to the hotel. That was the whole deal, but I honestly believe Gil Brandt held that against me for a long time.

Also, Joan was a little too friendly with the black players, as far as some of the white players and team officials were concerned. Once when Gil and Joan were first married and the team was flying home from a game, all the black players were sitting in the front and all the white guys were sitting in the middle of the plane. Joan came to the front and started talking to the black guys and sat on the arm of my chair. After she left, Rocky Colvin, a white defensive tackle, said, "If that was my wife I would kick the shit out of her." I asked, "Why?" "For talking to the niggers," he said. That incident made Gil lose face with the team, and I had the feeling he blamed me for that, too.

Another incident wasn't as serious, but it still annoyed Gil. One night, early in my career, Jethro Pugh and I decided to have dinner at Campisi's Egyptian Room, which is the best Italian restaurant I have ever eaten in. Each year the NFL security people would tell us which restaurants and bars were off-limits, and Campisi's was always at the top of their list. They thought that Joe Campisi had ties to the Mafia, and there was a rumor around Dallas that Jack Ruby's first phone call after he got arrested for shooting Lee Harvey Oswald was to Joe Campisi. Well, football players love to eat, and all we cared about was that Campisi's had great food.

When Jethro and I entered the restaurant that night, we found Gil Brandt and Lamar Hunt, who is from Dallas and was one of the founders of the AFL, eating dinner. (Hunt started the Dallas Texans of the AFL but lost the battle for Dallas to the Cowboys and moved his team to Kansas City and renamed the team the Chiefs.) I said, "Gil, this place is off-limits. What are you doing here?" Gil just gave us a little brook-trout look. But he was a lot more embarrassed at us seeing him than we were at having him see us. I've seen all the top Cowboys players and officials, the executives of the Dallas Mavericks basketball team—you name it—in that restaurant. It's a great restaurant, and no one has ever come up to me there and suggested anything illegal. I still go to Campisi's all the time, and when it's real busy, they let me in the back door to avoid waiting in line. I sure never thought I would brag about getting into a restaurant through the back door, not after my experiences growing up in racist Florida.

Gil Brandt used to call Jake Gaither every Sunday after our games when I was young and say, "This guy here is going to be great for the Dallas Cowboys." But by the fifth year or so, I started getting bad vibes from Gil, especially after I had contract disputes with the team in 1970 and 1971.

I was the first Dallas Cowboy who ever played out his option. My lawyer, Steve Falk, a friend of mine from Miami, was tough, but he was obnoxious, too. Of course, he had to be. Steve told the press during our negotiations, "Not only am I going to get Bob a big raise, but I'm going to make them pay for my trip from Miami to Dallas." That wasn't fair to the Cowboys, and Gil Brandt couldn't handle it. After that, a lot of the white guys on the team said, "This nigger should go back to the farm," and I always suspected that Gil felt the same way.

So much for the brain trust. Now let me introduce some of my fellow Dallas Cowboys, position by position:

At tight end, number 84, was Pettis Norman, who had joined the team in 1962 from J. C. Smith College, a small school in North Carolina. He lasted until 1970. Pettis used to have cotton in his mouth instead of his teeth during games, and he didn't want people to know that he played without his teeth. Every time he scored or made a long gain, he would pull the cotton out so he could breathe properly. We used to tease him all the time: "Pettis, put your teeth in, please. I can't understand what you're saying." He used to leave his teeth in a glass in his locker. If I had it to do over, I would steal his teeth at least once. Pettis was real goosey. At practice, while he was down in a set position, whoever would go in motion would touch Pettis's butt as he ran by, and Pettis would jump offside every time. Coach Landry would yell, "Would you guys please get serious?"

Pettis was a very emotional player, just like Ralph Neely, who usually lined up at tackle next to him. The two of them would argue from the huddle to the line of scrimmage over who they should block. While the play was being called, you could still hear them arguing. The coaches would change the scheme of blocking from week to week, and Pettis and Ralph would forget. Sometimes even the coaches would forget and tell one guy to block someone and tell another guy to block the same man. So Pettis would tell Ralph who to block, and Ralph would tell Pettis who to block. "No, man, I block the inside man, you block the outside man." And they would go back and forth, back and forth until the ball was snapped. No jumping offsides, no missed assignments, but they sure had the guys on the other team trying to figure out what was going on out there. By the time we ran our play, though, the two of them always made their blocks and got the right man.

Old number 89 from Pitt, Mike Ditka, played tight end for us from 1969 to 1972. Mike is legendary for his fire, his desire to win, and his dirty play, all of which were true. Mike wanted to win at everything, even at a dollar-a-pot poker games in training camp and on trips. I once saw him rip a telephone book apart and throw a chair against a wall in the dormitory because he lost a poker hand. He could lose five dollars and be upset.

Ditka was always gritting his teeth, chomping on his tongue or on chewing gun (one of hs nicknames was "Chipmunk"), and snarling at the line of scrimmage like an animal. He wanted to attack somebody, kill them. If he wasn't upset with the opposition, he was upset with himself. He was never satisfied.

Phil Villapiano of the Raiders was one of the dirtiest linebackers I ever played against. He would beat you into the ground, kick you while you were lying on the ground, fall on you, stomp you—anything. When we played our annual exhibition game against the Raiders in 1972, Mike's last season as a player, Ermal Allen, one of our assistant coaches, said it would be interesting to see what Villapiano would do against Mike Ditka. Well, Phil didn't do one single dirty thing to Mike. Phil may have been a vicious ballplayer, but it depended on the opposition; he wasn't crazy.

One time Ditka snuck out after curfew the night before a home game to have some fun. On the way back, he ran a yellow light, and a car ran into him and almost knocked his teeth out. He called Dan Reeves, and Dan picked him up and got his teeth and his mouth wired up before the following day's game. The next day, while we were getting ready for the game, everybody saw these braces on Mike's teeth. He hadn't had them on Saturday afternoon when we praticed or on Saturday night at our team meeting. All the players asked him, "Mike, what happened between curfew and this meeting?" Mike could hardly talk; he just mumbled something, but nobody could understand him.

Ditka became an assistant coach in 1973 after he retired as a player. In one of Mike's first seasons as an assistant coach, we played Houston, and a referee made a bad call that went against us. Ditka started yelling at the referee, "You called a bad play! You called a bad play! You referees aren't worth a damn!" The referee walked over to Ditka to discuss the call, and Ditka asked him, "Are you in the FCA?" That was the Fellowship of

Christian Athletes, Landry's favorite organization. "FCA?" the referee asked. "What does that mean?" Ditka answered, "The Fellowship of Christian Athletes." The official said no, he wasn't. So Ditka said, "Well, fuck you, fuck you, fuck you, you son of a bitch!" Coach Landry looked at Ditka and said, "Ditka, go down to the other end of the bench and stay *down* there! Ditka, go! Ditka, go! Ditka, go!" And Ditka finally walked away.

The referees talked like that, too. And they let us say almost anything. Most of the referees treated the players as men, not as college students. We weren't supposed to curse them, but they let a lot of it go by instead of calling it unsportsmanlike conduct and penalizing us fifteen yards.

Maybe the referees let us get away with things because they loved doing games in Texas Stadium. At least, that's what Tommy Bell, one of the veteran referees in the NFL, told me when I met him at banquet near the end of my career. "What teams do you all like to call?" I asked him. "The Dallas Cowboys," was his answer. I thought, "I know why he likes the Dallas Cowboys. We have a tradition of winning, we've been in a lot of big games, we look good in our uniforms." My ego was all inflated and I said to him, "Well, why the Cowboys? Because of the star on the side of the helmet? Tom Landry? Roger Staubach? Me?" "Hell, no," Bell answered. "Man, when we have a time-out, we're all over there checking out the cheerleaders."

Also at tight end we had number 84, Jean Fugett, who played from 1972 until 1975, when he became a free agent and jumped to the Redskins. Jean was like Calvin Hill, an intellectual; Jean had gone to Amherst. Maybe it was because of his background, but Jean was one of the only two guys I knew on the Cowboys who used marijuana regularly. The other was Steve Kiner.

Whenever we traveled, we used to carry attaché cases packed with our toilet articles and personal belongings. Once, when I went to the bathroom on a flight home from a game, Jean was in there—he always carried his bag into the bathroom—and I told him I smelled something funny. He had a pipe with some marijuana in it, and he took a few puffs and then stayed in the bathroom until the scent was gone.

A lot of us tried to use marijuana, but we didn't know how to use it and we didn't get any kick from it. It was like when Walt Garrison tried to teach us how to use chewing tobacco, that Skoal stuff. A bunch of us went into the team meeting room one night—me, Roger Staubach, Bob

Lilly, Cornell Green, and Jethro Pugh—to dip some snuff. You're supposed to spit it out, but I swallowed mine, and I got sick as a dog and so did some of the others. Roger wanted to do it right, so he was holding it in and turning red in the face because he didn't want to admit there was something he couldn't do.

Billy Joe DuPree, a tight end from Michigan State, came in as our number-one draft choice in 1973 and succeeded Ditka as number 89. Billy Joe was a very awkward player when he joined the Cowboys, and I worked a lot with him on the field. Later, he became successful in the construction business and he forgot his roots; several years ago, he told the media I was a nobody, which really hurt my feelings and showed how ungrateful he was.

At wide receiver, number 19 from the University of Oklahoma, Lance Rentzel was one of my best friends and favorite people. Lance played for the Cowboys from 1967 to 1970, and he and I have been friends ever since. Lance was a momma's boy—his mother always used to refer to him as her "blue-eyed baby boy." One year I won a lot of Oak Farm Dairy awards for Player of the Week. At the end of the year, the fans would vote on their favorite players from among the Oak Farm winners, and the player with the most votes would win a trip to Hawaii. Lance's mother went to the Oak Farm headquarters and got lots of ballots and had many of her friends and kids in her neighborhood send in votes in his name. (Her efforts were successful; Lance won the trip.)

Being momma's boy, Lance was naive and was always the butt of jokes and pranks. One year, while we were in training camp at Thousand Oaks, some of the guys got Lance in the locker room, put tape over his whole body except his eyes and mouth, and taped him to the bench like a mummy. Dave Manders, Walt Garrison, Mike Gaechter, and most of the linebackers were the ringleaders. Lance struggled, but if he moved too much, he would pull the whole bench over onto the floor. All his pubic hairs, the hair around his eyebrows, his mustache, and his sideburns were being pulled out and he was yelling, "Ow! Ow! Ow!" Then we went out to practice and Landry asked, "Where's Lance? Where's Rentzel?" Lance finally came out on the field (the trainers had cut him loose), and all his skin was bleeding and red and full of welts.

Lance treated himself to a Mercedes with the license plate, "DC-19," and everybody used to ask him, "Lance, what does that mean? Dumb Chit?" And he would take the bait every time and say, "No, that's Dallas Cowboys number 19, " as if we didn't know.

We were practicing one time at Forest Field in Dallas while some work was being done at our regular practice facility. Lance was one of the foremost ladies' men on the team, and a beautiful girl, Miss Atlanta, Georgia, was coming to visit him. As we were putting on our uniforms, Lance started to pick little things off himself that were itchy. He didn't have lice or crabs or anything, but he wondered if he did. Craig Morton said to him, "Man, those are crabs on you, Lance." Then Craig and Dave Manders and some of the others wrote all over the blackboards, "Lance has got crabs." Lance got all upset, and when practice was over, he was the first one in the locker room. He rushed to the phone and called the girl in Atlanta to tell her not to come, that he wasn't feeling well. And there wasn't one thing wrong with him. He was just gullible.

Lance used to keep a list of women in a little black book and grade them A, B, or C. If he was in a town and thinking about calling a chick, he'd look at her grade and say, "Maybe so." He used to take out people like Barbara McNair, the beautiful black singer and actress, and some of the white players didn't like the idea of Lance dating a black woman. A lot of guys, both married and single, would ask Lance for names. Of course, the wives did not want their husbands hanging out with the single guys like Lance because the single guys drew girls. I don't think the Cowboys' wives were ever as delighted as they were in 1969 when Lance finally married Joey Heatherton, the beautiful blond dancer, singer, and actress, which took him out of circulation.

Joey and Lance made a great couple. They were so much in love and a lot of fun to be with, even though she was real shy offstage. Joey was laid back, kind of spaced out, very casual, and very nice. When I separated my shoulder during the 1969 exhibition season, Lance and Joey went to Trader Vic's and brought some ribs and food to my hospital room, and a stereo, too. None of my other teammates thought to do anything like that.

When Lance got arrested in November 1970 for exposing himself to a ten-year-old girl, he called Cornell Green and me at home. Cornell was team captain and I was one of Lance's best friends. We were having a regular team meeting that day, but Cornell and I left early to talk to Lance. Lance said, "I'm getting indicted for indecent exposure with this girl. What should I do?" I said, "Well, Lance, I think you should be a man and tell the team before everybody hears about it." But it was too late. Bobby Franklin, one of the assistant coaches, told Cornell and me that he had already heard the news on the radio. By the time Cornell and I got to the meeting, most of the players knew about it. Lance came in and told the team what had happened and asked whether he should play in our next game. I said, "Lance, I never heard of anybody booing you if you score a touchdown. I think you should play."

The squad finally voted unanimously that Lance should continue playing, but it didn't make any difference. Management had its own ideas. The team officials didn't want Lance around, and he never played another game for the Cowboys. He sat out the rest of the season and then was traded to the Rams. I would later learn that lesson myself: The Cowboys were with you all the way if you won or tied. But once you screwed up, it was, "Lance Rentzel? Bob Hayes? Not sure we remember them. What were those names again?"

When Lance went to the office of his lawyer, Phil Burleson (who was my lawyer when I got arrested eight years later) and then to the jail to turn himself in, I went with him. I didn't know all the camera crews and reporters were going to be there, but I would have gone anyway. As a friend first and as a teammate second, I wanted to be with him. All the news media reported, "Bob Hayes, Rentzel's teammate, was with him." Some of the players got upset with me, saying, "You shouldn't have gone with that asshole," because they did not like Lance getting charged with indecent exposure in front of a little girl. But I did it out of the grace of my heart just to help a friend. It was my personal decision. I thought that when a guy has his back against the wall, his friends should help. I didn't think Lance was a bad guy; I thought he was a sick person who needed to get well. (Lance was sentenced to five years' probation.)

I'm still proud that I was with Lance when he needed me. And I know he appreciated it. He wrote in his book, "Hayes was a good friend, and what were good friends for but to go to jail with you when you had to post bond . . . [At the jail] a hand on my arm guided me to the elevator. It was Phil Burleson and Bob Hayes . . . 'Easy, man . . . easy,' said Bob, his hand squeezing my arm."

It's funny, the guys who were most upset about my accompanying Lance were the less established players, like Claxton Welch, a reserve runningback. The team leaders—Cornell Green, Rayfield Wirght, Jethro Pugh, and guys like that—understood. They weren't close enough to Lance to go to jail with him, but they didn't criticize me for doing it. Another strange thing: Craig Morton, who was Lance's best friend, even closer to Lance than I was, was nowhere to be found. That's what kind of guy Craig was.

■   ■   ■

Another wide receiver was number 88, Drew Pearson, who joined the Cowboys as a free agent out of Tulsa in 1973 and eventually broke my Cowboy career records for passes caught and yards receiving. Drew used to get excited all the time, to put it mildly. Roger would look Drew in the eyes and say, "Okay, Drew, be looking out, this pass is coming to you," and Drew would start throwing up. If Drew would miss a pass, he would throw up in the huddle. If Drew would score a touchdown, he would throw up jogging back to the bench. He had the weakest stomach I have ever seen in a man. And I'll tell you, when you play in Texas Stadium on artificial turf, a guy who is throwing up in the huddle is not a pleasant smell or sight. I'm just glad that Drew and I weren't playing together on a basketball team.

Ralph Neely, number 73 from Oklahoma, was one of the best offensive linemen who played for the Cowboys in my time with them. Ralph joined the team the same year I did, and right from the start he and I used to talk about race. Ralph considered himself a liberal on racial matters because, as he put it, "You know, Bob, I've come a long way, because my grandfather was a Ku Klux Klansman, and now here I am, sitting here and talking to you." I said, "Ralph, do you know what, I can tell you that my grandfather hated whites. So what does that have to do with you and me? Speak for yourself and not for your grandfather." He and I became good friends, and whenever I scored a touchdown, Ralph Neely was always the first guy down the field, real excited, picking me up in his arms and hugging me. That's one thing about football; with a few exceptions, it helps break down racial prejudices on both sides, and a lot of guys learn how to relate to each other as human beings, not as blacks and whites.

Despite our friendship, Ralph had a reputation among some of the black players for being a racist. One year, when we played the Colts, Bubba Smith told me he had heard that Ralph was a racist and said he was going to kill Ralph out there. I told Bubba that it wasn't true and that Ralph was one of the first guys who would help me out and take care of any defensive back or linebacker who took a cheap shot at me.

So Bubba didn't go after Ralph that day, any more than he would have gone after any offensive lineman, which was more than enough for Ralph. Every time I ran by Bubba, I slapped him on the butt. When Ralph saw me do it, he came running over to me as we went back into the huddle, grabbed me, and started shaking me. I said, "What's wrong, Ralph?" He said, "Let him alone, Bob. Don't piss him off!" I said, "Ralph, he's a friend of mine, I'm not making him angry." He said, "Well, don't piss him off, he's tough enough as it is." I said, "I'm sorry, Ralph, I made a mistake and I apologize."

I could joke around with Bubba and explain to him that Ralph wasn't a racist because Bubba and I had become friends on the banquet circuit between seasons. Then in 1971, the Cowboys' first draft choice was Bubba's younger brother, Tody, a defensive end from USC. Bubba asked me to look out for Tody, which made Bubba and me even closer. And, believe me, Tody took a lot of looking out for. In midseason of one of the two years Tody played for us, either 1971 or 1972, we were practicing kickoff returns, and Dave Manders came down the field and blocked Tody, number 85, on his sore knee. Tody thought Dave did it on purpose, so he got up and hit Dave across the helmet, and they started to fight. Jim Myers, the offensive line coach, came running up after Tody to protect his man, Manders. Tody hated Myers because he thought Jim was a racist. After Tody and Dave finished their little struggle, Jim Myers started to walk off the field. Tody snatched off his helmet and ran up behind Myers and was about to hit Myers on the head with his helmet when some of the guys grabbed him and stopped him. Tody was so much taller than Myers, and he could have swung his helmet down on Myers's head hard enough to kill him. A lot of us held him back—me, Jean Fugett, and several others. Tody was one of the meanest guys I ever saw on the football field. He would fight anybody. He was much meaner than Bubba, but he didn't have Bubba's talent. The Cowboys finally traded him and Billy Parks, a wide receiver, to Houston and got the number-one choice in the 1974 draft, which turned out to be Too-Tall Jones.

Jim Myers seemed to have a problem with blacks. He didn't want blacks on his offensive line. He only put Rayfield Wright in as offensive tackle after Ralph Neely got hurt in 1969 and he didn't have anyone else to face Deacon Jones the following week. Rayfield, number 70, was the Cowboys' seventh-round choice out of Fort Valley State College in Georgia in 1967. He spent thirteen seasons with the Cowboys and turned out to be our best offensive lineman, but that never would have been detected if Neely hadn't gotten hurt, because Myers wouldn't have given Rayfield a chance. Myers had the idea that blacks couldn't think that fast.

The time that Rayfield Wright had to replace Ralph Neely against Deacon Jones, we were walking through the tunnel going off the field at halftime and Deacon Jones, looking all beat up, came up to me and said, "Hey, Bob, where did you all get this guy Wright from?" I said, "Well, shit, Deacon, we got him from the same place you're from, the South. We got another Deacon Jones, but he's an offensive ballplayer." He said, "Well, I sure wish Ralph Neely was playing." When I told Rayfield what Jones said, Rayfield asked, "Did he say that? Are you sure? Stop lying to me, Speedo." That really built up Rayfield's confidence, and Deacon got near our quarterback only once. We were double teaming him a lot, too, and whenever Deacon would use his hand swat, Pettis Norman would cut his legs from under him. Deacon was the best of the Fearsome Foursome, even better than Merlin Olsen, Lamar Lundy, and Roger Brown, and we were very concerned about an inexperienced player like Rayfield having to go up against him. But Rayfield more than held his own that day and went on to be a star.

Also on the offensive line was number 65, John Wilbur. John was from Stanford, and he was highly intelligent, had long hair, and was considered one of the original hippies on the Cowboys. All the guys from the South used to tease him, although the truth is that he was out of our league intellectually.

John played for us from 1966 to 1969, but my best memory of him was after we traded him to St. Louis and then he got sent to Washington. John used to do everything he could to get an advantage, like sew up his jersey around his biceps so defensive linemen couldn't grab his jersey and sling him around, and put a lot of grease on his pads so that when they grabbed him, their hands would slip off. The first time we played the Redskins after John joined them in 1971, Jethro, who was a close friend of Wilbur's, noticed all this grease and all this blood on his hands, and he wondered where it came from. A couple of plays later Lee Roy Jordan noticed blood all over his hands. He had gotten blocked by no one but Wilbur. Lee Roy looked around and said, "Man, that's got to be Wilbur." So they examined Wilbur and found razor blades in his shoulder pads. Jethor laughed so hard that all he could say was, "Vaseline is one thing, but razor blades?" Razor blades sounds bad, but on the field it was just something we got a kick out of, that Wilbur would do something like that to get an edge, as it were.

■ ■ ■

Another of the intellectuals was number 35 from Yale, Calvin Hill. Our number-one pick in 1969, Calvin was a great runner, but he had this attitude that because he had gone to Yale, was studying theology at Southern Methodist University (SMU)—which earned him the nickname "Elmer Gantry"—and was a middle-class black from Baltimore, guys like me were just poor niggers from small schools. Calvin liked guys like Otto Brown, a defensive back from Prairie View, who looked up to him as a mentor. My accomplishments were much greater than Calvin's, so I never treated him with the respect he thought he deserved, and he and I weren't close. We weren't enemies; we just weren't the best of friends; he resented people who treated him as an equal instead of saying, "Oh, my God, Calvin Hill from Yale, you're my idol!"

When we ran twenty-yard windsprints, Calvin always wanted to beat me. He was real serious about it. He and I would take the same number of steps, but I would always beat him. He was six feet three—four inches taller than I was; his legs were longer; and he and I took the same number of steps, so he couldn't understand how I could beat him. He tried to intellectualize it, but he couldn't figure it out, and it bugged him for a long time. What he couldn't admit to himself was that my legs were a lot more powerful than his and that I could come down and touch the ground faster than he could.

Calvin was so thorough about learning things that he used to hold us all up when we were going over plays, even the most simple, basic plays. He had to know exactly what everybody was doing on each play—which actually made him a better football player—but the rest of us wanted to get the lesson over with. Landry would go over each individual position and tell everyone his assignment. Once all the players grasped their assignments, we would go on to the next play. After we had gone to the next play, Calvin would say, "Coach, just a minute. Can we go back over that play again." It would be a simple toss play to the right side off an I formation. Landry would explain it to him very patiently. Calvin would say, "But I still don't understand this play." And I would say to him, "Calvin, are you sure you went to Yale? I'm from Florida A & M and I didn't have any trouble picking up this play." He would just stare at me like I was crazy.

Calvin was a real straight arrow, like Roger Staubach, and he hardly ever used foul language. But in one game, somebody slapped Calvin hard.

Calvin got up off the ground, all the guys around him, and he yelled, "Shit! Let's play! I want to kick ass!" All the players looked at Calvin and said, "Calvin, is that you?" Even the official asked, "Is that Calvin Hill?" Calvin hunched his head into his shoulder pads and walked away, but there was a big number 35 on his back and the word "Hill," so it was him all right.

Calvin and Jerry Rhome were probably the worst dressers on the team. Another of Calvin's nicknames was Rueben James, as if he were a real fancy gentleman. Calvin got hurt against the Rams in the 1973 playoffs, and when the Cowboys lost to Minnesota in the National Football Conference final, he was standing on the sidelines with his elbow in a sling, wearing an old gray sweater, old brown slacks, and some old yellow tennis shoes. Janet, his wife, said, "Bob, please, tell Calvin not to be out on the field with that outfit on," but there was nothing I could do. Calvin had different values, and things like clothes, that were important to most of us, were not important to him.

In 1970, the year after the Cowboys picked Calvin Hill as number one, they took another runningback in the first round: Duane Thomas, a Dallas boy who had gone to West Texas State University. When Duane reported to training camp at Thousand Oaks and put on jersey number 33, he was wide eyed and rarin' to go, just like any other rookie. Rookies had to run errands and do things for the veterans as part of the hazing process, so one night I told Duane I wanted him to go to the store for me. My friend Mel Zahn had lent me a Lincoln Continental, and I gave Duane the keys and told him to pick up some stuff for me. When he saw that car, Duane's eyes lit up and he asked, "Wow, man, am I going to drive a Lincoln Continental to the store?" I said, "Yes." Duane said, "Shit, I'll go to the store for you anytime; you just let me know."

I think the beginning of Duane's problems with the Cowboys was his rookie year, when Coach Landry kept moving him back and forth from halfback to fullback. When Calvin Hill got hurt, Landry wanted Duane to move from fullback to halfback and let Walt Garrison, who was much slower than Duane, play fullback. Duane got real angry and said he wasn't going to do it, that he couldn't get his timing down playing more than one position. Not only was Duane angry at the coaches after that, the coaches were angry at him. And Duane could have picked up both positions easily; he was intelligent, a great runner, a great blocker, and had great instincts.

But Duane never developed a sense of teamwork and never lived up to his potential as a professional football player.

After his rookie season, Duane spent the summer in Los Angeles, fell under Jim Brown's control, and came back a different person. Until then, he had spent his whole life in Texas, but the bright lights of Los Angeles changed him entirely. He had different priorities; he just didn't seem to care that much about football. And, of course, he was bitter because of his differences with the coaches over the position he was going to play and with the front office over his salary. Once he called Tom Landry a "plastic" man and said that Tex Schramm was "sick, demented, and a complete liar," his days with the Cowboys were numbered.

By 1971, his second and last season with the Cowboys, Duane had established himself as a different kind of football player. Unlike most of us, he read all the time. One day I asked him, "Duane, what's the deal?" He said, "I want to be an author one day." I said, "You want to be an author? Would you have a pen name?" Duane said, "Yes, I want to be called 'Othello.'" I said, "I guess you know that Othello was a character, not an author," and he said he did. Then I told him a guy in my high school class was named Othello. "Was he an author?" Duane asked me. "No, he was a dummy." From then on I always called him Othello.

Duane was a strange bird, all right. Unlike most other football players, he ate a lot of fruit and hardly ever ate meat. Today we know that he was right, that he knew more about proper diet than the rest of us. Another image I have of Duane was the time the team was staying in Fort Lauderdale, practicing for the 1970 Super Bowl against Baltimore, when I was awakened about 6:30 A.M. by a commotion outside my window. My room was on the second floor, and when I looked out the window, I saw Duane out on the ocean in a little rowboat, with a lot of reporters standing on the beach yelling out to him, "Duane, Duane, where are you going?" Duane never had much use for the press, but he broke his silence long enough to shout back, "Australia."

During training camp in 1972, the year after Duane led us to our first Super Bowl victory, things were really breaking down between him and the team. Ray Renfro, one of the assistant coaches in charge of the offense, knew what a great player Duane was and didn't want to lose him. Ray came to my room and told me that Landry was on the phone talking to San Diego about trading Duane. He asked me if I could persuade Duane to go to Landry and say that he wanted to stay with the Cowboys. I went looking for Duane and found him in the university library, sitting at a table reading a newspaper. In fact, he and the librarian were the only people in the library. I tried to talk to him, but Duane wouldn't talk much; he was irritated that night. So Landry went ahead and traded him to the Chargers.

Renfro told me that after Landry closed the deal, Landry told Ray and Dan Reeves, "One of you guys go tell Duane he's been traded." The two of them looked at each other and simultaneously said, "I ain't going!" One of them had to go, so they flipped a coin, and Ray lost.

Cornell Green and I shared the room next door to Duane's, with only a bathroom in between. Our door was open, and I could see Ray walking down the hall trying to figure out what the hell he was going to say to Duane because Duane was moody and wouldn't talk to anybody—nobody could get to him. Normally a coach would knock real loud when he was coming to tell you you had been traded or cut, and yell, "Okay, guys, are you in the room?" But when Ray came around, he tiptoed up, knocked on the door softly, and said real low, "Du-ane, Du-ane, are you in there?" Jethro was visiting in our room, and he, Cornell, and I stood there laughing. Duane winked at us and motioned to us to be quiet and not let on that he was there. Duane wouldn't answer, so Ray knocked and called real softly again. "Duane, are you there? Duane, please answer." Knock, knock, knock. "Duane, please answer." Duane finally answered real loud and tough, "What? What do you want?" Ray asked, "Can I come in?" "No!" Duane yelled. Ray said, "But Duane, I have to come in there. Coach Landry sent me around here." "I don't want to talk!" Duane said. Finally Ray just opened the door and said, "Duane, you need to talk to Coach Landry and take your playbook with you." It was probably the longest charade in history over telling a player he was no longer with the team.

Meanwhile, Reeves was lurking around. He couldn't wait to ask Renfro, "How did you tell him? What did he say?"

When I look back at Duane's two years with the Cowboys, I think what a waste it was. I said at the time that if I had been him, I would have done things differently, that if you're part of a team, you have to act like it. Some of the players got angry with me and said I was taking the management's view instead of Duane's. But that's the way I felt. Duane was emotionally immature and made a lot of mistakes, just like I did. I didn't have a problem with a player trying to renegotiate his contract, but I did have a problem with a player letting down the ten other guys on the field.

The bottom line is that Duane wasted his talent. He could have been one of the greatest players of all time, but he blew it. Jim Brown had a lot of influence over Duane, but Jim used his influence the wrong way, and Duane was too immature to see what was going on. Jim told Duane how the Cowboys and the press and everyone were screwing him, and Duane believed him. I hate to say it, because Jim Brown means as much to me as he does to anyone, but Jim is the one who screwed up Duane's head. The best example of Jim's influence over Duane was when Jim set Duane up to insult Tom Brookshier of CBS in a famous locker-room exchange after we won the Super Bowl. Duane hadn't talked to the press all season, and after the Super Bowl, with Brown beside him, Duane gave an "interview" to Brookshier that had Brookshier asking Duane, "Are you fast?" and Duane answering, "Evidently," before Jim cut in and asked Brookshier, whom Jim had played against many times, "Are you nervous, Tom?" Duane idolized Jim Brown, just like we all did, and Duane tried to be bad like Jim. But Duane forgot one thing: Jim Brown was a great ballplayer first, and after that he was bad. Duane tried to be bad like Jim was without being a superstar first.

One of the more typical football players at runningback was old number 32, Walt Garrison, who came in as number-5 draft choice from Oklahoma State in 1966. One night in Pittsburgh during Walt's rookie year, Don Meredith and some of the other guys took Walt out for dinner the night before the game. Walt was second string behind Don Perkins then and he wasn't expecting to play much, so he had quite a few drinks. The next day he was really hung over. We were way ahead of Pittsburgh, so Meredith asked Coach Landry to put Walt in the game. Meredith ran Walt about ten straight times. Walt was out there dying: He was tired, had a hangover, and wasn't used to playing. But Meredith kept running him. That's when we knew Walt was tough.

After Walt cut himself whittling with his knife and had a number of stitches in his hand, he refused to let Landry take him out of the lineup and played against Philadelphia. The only time I ever saw Walt get hurt one-on-one was when we played our last exhibition game against Oakland in 1972, which we won, 16 to 10. At one point, Walt ran around right end, and Jack Tatum got a good running start, hit Walt, and hurt him.

. . .

Then there was number 30, Dan Reeves, a runningback and sometime quarterback from South Carolina who was one of our mainstays from 1965 to 1972. We had played the Bears a couple of times in exhibition games, but in 1968 we played them in the regular season for the first time since Dan and I had joined the team. The game was at Wrigley Field, and as both teams came out of our dressing rooms for the introduction of the players, Dick Butkus looked over at Dan and yelled, "Hey, Reeves, I'm going to kick your ass today! I'm going to kill you out there, you son of a bitch!" We had been watching films of Butkus all week; he was every bit as vicious as his reputation, just awesome. Reeves had a crewcut like he had just gotten out of basic training, he looked like a choir boy, and spoke in a soft voice. He wouldn't hurt anyone and he looked it. Dan walked out behind Bob Lilly, Jethro, and George Andrie and said in that little voice of his, "You know, I have never even met the guy. I don't even know him. I wonder what he's got against me." It was all he could do to keep from crying, and all the rest of us could do to keep from laughing. Fortunately, Butkus didn't do much damage that day; we were the ones who killed the Bears, 34 to 3.

Don Perkins, a runningback from New Mexico who wore number 43, was one of the black leaders on the Cowboys from his first year, 1961, until he retired after the 1968 season. Everybody called him "Perk" and he, Cornell Green, Pettis Norman, Frank Clarke, Warren Livingston, and I used to ride to practice together every day. Dallas wasn't integrated in those days. We couldn't live in North Dallas, so we all lived near each other in an apartment development in Oak Cliff near the Cedar Crest golf course.

Perk was an instigator. He gave everyone nicknames. He christened Jethro "Buzz," which stood for Buzzard, because Jethro was bad luck, although Don never told Jethro why he called him that. He called Cornell Green "Sweet Lips," Rayfield Wright, "Big Tom Cat," and me "Speedo." And it was Perk who stole Willie Townes's car keys to make Willie get some exercise one year in training camp when Willie was trying to lose weight.

Another runningback was number 44, Robert Newhouse, a short, chubby guy who was our second-round choice from the University of Houston in 1972. Newhouse was better known as "Shithouse," "Outhouse," or just plain "House." He was also extremely well known for his appetite. For his size, he could outeat anyone, even Willie Townes.

Before every home game, we would have a team meeting on Saturday afternoon and then a team dinner at which there was a big buffet with all the food we could eat. After dinner, we had a lot of free time from 7 P.M. until curfew at 11:30 P.M. We would stay around the hotel, play cards, talk, tell jokes, watch television, and visit each other's rooms. Newhouse used to go back to his room and get a big trash can, go in the shower and wash it out real good, line it with cloth napkins, and come back down to the dining room and fill up the can with fried chicken, all the way to the top. Then he'd smile while he carried the can back to his room. Between 7 and 11:30, the chicken was eaten. The next morning, we would go into Newhouse's room and find the trash can full of chicken bones. Newhouse had eaten thirty to forty pieces of chicken. He roomed with Calvin Hill, who was a tall and slim guy, and they really made an odd couple.

Curtis was the night manager at the Holiday Inn Regal Row on I-35 in Dallas, where we used to stay the night before home games. After the coaches checked the rooms, at curfew, Curtis would hook the phones back up so everybody could make or receive phone calls. That way the women could get in touch with us.

The kitchen was closed by then and we would get hungry, so Curtis would go out and get hamburgers for us. One of Curtis's special jobs was to make sure that Newhouse was well fed. At our Saturday-night buffet, there were all kinds of pies—apple, cherry, potato, pumpkin pie, you name it. Newhouse would take a whole apple pie, get Curtis to go to the kitchen and warm it up and get him a half gallon of ice cream, and then he would eat the whole damn thing. With a smile. You know the way a dog protects his food? That's the way Newhouse was, with his hands and arms around that food. If you got between Newhouse and his food, you were in trouble.

In spite of Newhouse's appetite, he lasted twelve years with the Cowboys. And when he left, he did what every ballplayer dreams of doing. When the Cowboys told him his career was over at the end of the 1983 season, Newhouse, instead of going in and taking a shower and changing his clothes, kept his uniform on—his shoulder pads, his helmet, and everything—and drove home.

The loosest guy on the team, as you might imagine, was old number 17, Don Meredith. Don had signed a personal services contract with the

Cowboys right after his senior year at SMU in 1959 and he became the Cowboys' property without going through the 1960 draft. He had already been with the team for five years when I came in, and he was a well-known character. He lived up to his reputation in the four seasons I played with him.

Dandy, as he was called, used to hum country-and-western songs in the huddle, just like he did in the broadcast booth on Monday Night Football. Nothing ever got him upset—not even Coach Landry. Our opening game in 1966, we were playing the Giants in the Cotton Bowl, and, as usual, pounding the shit out of them. The final score was 52 to 7. There was a striptease dancer in Dallas at the time named Bubbles Cash, a blond with huge tits. For some reason, I looked over toward the bench and saw Bubbles Cash walking down the stairs, wearing a tight sweater and a miniskirt. From every section she passed, everybody applauded her. I nudged Don and said, "Dandy, looka there." Don looked over at her and immediately called timeout. Landry was on the sideline, looking at us, and Meredith was looking right over Landry's head, so Landry thought Meredith was looking at him. But the quarterback did not jog over to the coach during the timeout to get his instructions. All of a sudden Landry turned around and saw Bubbles. Then he turned back to Meredith, who had wasted one of the three timeouts we got in each half, and shouted, "What did you call timeout for?" "Bubbles Cash, Coach," Meredith called back. Landry was so shocked he was speechless.

Don Perkins was great at running the delay trap. Once, when we were playing the Rams, Rosey Grier was waiting for us to run it because Tom Landry had used the same terminology when he was an assistant coach in New York and Rosey played for him. After every play was over and I was on my way back to the huddle, Rosey would say to me, "Hey, Bob, when are you guys going to run that delay trap?" Meredith got tired of it, so he called the delay trap and Don Perkins ran it right by Rosey Grier and scored a touchdown. I walked back by him and said, "Rosey, what happened? You been waiting for the delay trap all day. What happened?" And Rosey said, "I lost my head on this one." As long as Meredith was our quarterback, we had a lot of fun.

But Meredith was much more than just a free spirit. He was, and is, one of the greatest guys I have ever met. A year or so after I got out of prison, when I was broke and needed help, Don Meredith was in Dallas at a Cowboys' reunion. I needed $3,000 to pay some bills and I asked him if he could help me. Don said, "I'll give you some money." The reunion ended, everybody went home, and I hadn't heard from him. Two days later, I received a cashier's check from him in the mail for $3,000. I still owe him that money, and every time I've seen him since then, Dandy Don says, "Don't worry about it, when you can pay it, you will." I've always appreciated Don's concern for me. He and his wife Susan have been good to me. That's one debt I hope to repay.

Behind Meredith at quarterback my first few seasons was Craig Morton, number 14. Craig and I came in as rookies together—he was our number-one draft choice from the University of California in 1965—starting off with the College All-Stars. I talk a lot about him in other parts of the book, but I think that the following few incidents say more about Craig than anything else.

In 1968 or 1969, Altamease had a surprise birthday party for me at our house in South Oak Cliff, which was a predominantly black neighborhood. Most of my teammates, black and white, came. Craig parked his car three or four doors from my house and left the keys in the ignition and the windows down. When he and his date walked outside to leave, the car was gone. He came back in and said, "You live in a bad neighborhood. I got my car stolen from Bob Hayes's house." There was definitely a racist tone to Craig's remark: I lived in a black neighborhood, and my neighbors had stolen his car. But he was the one who had left his keys in the ignition—not me or my neighbors. It was Craig's fault; he just didn't want to admit it.

Since I was the host and I had two cars, I told him he could use one of my cars until he found his or got another one and he could return my car at practice the next day. The car I gave him was a Firebird convertible with a 450-horsepower engine. Craig fell in love with my convertible and wouldn't give it back. He must have had it for six to eight weeks. I kept asking him, "Craig, are you ever going to give me my car back?" Finally he returned the car. While I was driving it home, I noticed he had left a tape in the tapedeck. I put the tapedeck on to see what kind of music Craig liked and I heard his voice saying over and over, "I will not throw an interception! I will not throw an interception! I will not throw an interception!" I think he was going to a hypnotist and nobody knew it. I talked to Dan Reeves about it and he said he had borrowed Craig's car one day to run an errand right before practice and heard the same tape.

Memo to Craig: You always threw too many interceptions. That tape didn't do you any good.

Craig, along with Lance, who followed Craig a lot, once got the whole team in trouble and cost us our four-day Thanksgiving vacation. After we played on Thanksgiving Day, Landry used to give us the next four days off. We didn't have to be back at practice until Monday. I used to go back to Florida and spend Thanksgiving with my mother and Jake Gaither and come back Sunday night or Monday morning. I think it was in 1970 that Craig and Lance flew to Las Vegas after our Thanksgiving game and didn't get back until Tuesday. After that, Landry made us come in every year on Saturday, just to show up. The team didn't like that at all.

And then there was another quarterback, number 12 from the U.S. Naval Academy. Roger Staubach was drafted in the tenth round as a future in 1964, the same year the Cowboys drafted me in the seventh round as a future. He practiced with us in summer camp, but he wasn't able to join the team full time until he finished his obligation to the U.S. Navy in 1969.

Roger and I first met and got to know each other well when we played together for the College All-Stars in 1965. He hurt his shoulder scrambling against the Cleveland Browns. Most of the guys were rejoicing in the locker room after the game because we had come close to winning, but Roger sat in front of his locker with his head down. I went over to him and said, "Roger, do you have to go to the hospital? I'll be more than happy to go with you." He said, "No, thanks, Bob." But he has never forgotten my concern, and from that day on, when I needed help, he was there, just as I was for him. Of course, he's done a lot more for me than I could ever do for him.

I enjoyed knowing Roger in the All-Star camp for three weeks, and then after he joined the Cowboys. He was not only a great quarterback, he had a presence about him. He's a real gentleman—even more of a straight arrow than his public image. Roger often wore a Fellowship of Christian Athletes T-shirt and he always had a sense of pride and dignity about him in the way he walked and practiced. At first I didn't like the way he would always try to win a game by himself without the other players, but I later came to appreciate his burning desire to win. He and Dan Reeves were just alike—if they lost, you didn't want to be around them.

As I think back over my ten years with the Cowboys, one thing about the quarterback situation strikes me as really strange. Don Meredith was a good ole boy from east Texas and SMU; Roger Staubach was a real conservative religious guy from the navy; and Jerry Rhome, the third stringer for several years, was another southern type who had gone to Tulsa. But all three of them got along fine with blacks, and Craig Morton, who had gone to school at Berkeley, the center of liberalism, seemed to have black-white problems.

Roger went out of his way to relate to the black players, and sometimes it was comical. Once, we were playing cards in training camp and Roger walked into Jethro's room when we were listening to a Temptations record. Roger said, "Oh, yeah, man, the Four Tops sure sound good." He wanted us to know that he was hip. I said, "Roger, that's not the Four Tops; that's the Temptations." "Oh, sure, Bob," he answered, "it does sound like the Temps." Like I say, it was funny, but it also made us black players feel good because (at least) Roger was trying.

Walt Garrison's birthday was on July 23, early in training camp, and one year he and Craig Morton bought a case of Wild Turkey and started celebrating. After a while, they decided to have some fun at Roger's expense. Walt and Craig found a couple of gorgeous blondes, probably college girls, slim with nice breasts—about 8 on a scale of 1 to 10—and brought the girls to the dormitory, paid them a hundred dollars each, pointed them toward Roger's room, and said, "Go down there and get Mr. Straight Arrow."

I was standing in the hallway, watching along with most of my teammates—Rayfield Wright, Jethro, Dan Reeves, Dave Manders, and Calvin Hill, to name a few, plus, of course, Garrison and Morton. Roger's door was open, and the girls walked in and started taking off their clothes. He asked them to get out, but they sat down on his bed and continued to unbutton their blouses (they were also wearing slacks). Roger got up while they were undressing, I'll never forget it, he was wearing green-and-white boxer shorts and a white V-neck T-shirt and had a Bible on the table and a playbook in his hand. He looked real serious and he said to the girls, "If I do something like this, what can I tell my wife and daughters when I get home?" With that, the girls got up, buttoned up their blouses, and left. They came back out in the hall and said, "We can't do that to this man." And the two of them left with Walt and Craig and went out drinking. Roger really impressed me that day. I don't know any other guy who would have turned down a couple of honeys like that, especially after two weeks in training camp with a hundred football players.

After the girls left, we went back to our normal activities, which was a good thing, because Coach Landry had heard about what was going on and was on his way to our rooms. We had been going through practice twice a day (what we called "two-a-days"), and everybody was getting crazy. We were tired of the two-a-days, tired of each other, and tired of being away from our families.

Jerry Rhome, a thirteenth-round pick in 1964, was one of the few ballplayers who wore number 13 (most of the guys were too superstitious to pick 13). Jerry was a little different in many ways. He was the cheapest player I ever saw; he wouldn't spend a dime. He had a nice Buick convertible, but it was always filthy because Jerry wouldn't pay to have it washed. And Jerry wouldn't buy any clothes. He always wore the same jersey, an old pair of pants, tennis shoes, and no socks to practice every day. He hated to change clothes, much less wear a coat and tie. I'm not sure he even owned a coat and tie, but he definitely had something going for him—he married a beautiful model. Models and other gorgeous women around town liked guys who spent money on them, but this one must have been different because Jerry Rhome was so tight that he squeaked when he walked. More to the point, he rattled; he always was rattling a lot of change in his pockets. After his playing days were over, Jerry became an assistant coach in the NFL, and he's probably one of the few assistant coaches who is a millionaire. I'll bet he has the first dime he ever made—and the last one, too. But, then again, I think I know what Jerry's wife saw in him. Jerry was one of the nicest guys on the team, and I was proud to have him as a friend.

One of the all-time Cowboy characters was another Tulsa boy, number 71 at defensive end, Willie Townes. Willie joined the Cowboys as our second-round draft choice in 1966. He came in weighing 265 and had a weight problem for the three years he was a Cowboy, which was the main reason he got traded to New Orleans.

Cornell Green, Frank Clarke, and I and our wives used to get together on Friday nights during the season. One Friday night, Willie dropped by my home on King Cole Drive in Oak Cliff. I had these tall iced-tea glasses. Willie was drinking rum and coke at the time and he poured about three-quarters of the glass full of rum and ate a giant-size bag of potato chips. The next day at practice someone said to Willie, "What did you do last night, Willie?" And Willie said, "Oh, I was over at Bob's house and I had one drink." It was one drink, all right, but it was a giant one. That was the kind of appetite he had.

One year everyone was drinking Boone Farm wine. A few of the Cowboys were holding unsupervised workouts without the coaches during the off-season. Willie used to leave his bottle of wine on a table as we were jogging around the track and as he would pass by, the way distance runners do, he would grab his cup full of Boone Farm and drink from it and just keep going. Every day I used to ask him, "Willie, how much you weigh?" And he would say, "Speedo, I'm just one over, just one over."

Before training camp in 1967, Willie had a thigh operation in Dallas, which meant he wasn't going to be able to work out for a while and would probably gain more weight. Coach Landry got all the black leaders to-gether—Cornell, Jethro, Mel Renfro, Perk, and me—and said, "Look, men, Willie has always had problems with weight. I want you to check him every day and make sure he isn't overeating." Landry would not tolerate a defensive lineman coming into camp at over 255 pounds, although he let Willie come in at 265 pounds since Willie was susceptible to gaining weight.

The first night at training camp, all of us took our physicals, which included weigh-ins. Everybody was in perfect health, but Willie was stand-ing in a corner, and we were all waiting for Willie to get on the scale. So Willie took his clothes off and got on the scale, and the pointer went all the way around to 290. Willie jumped off the scale, kicked it, and yelled, "This darned scale is wrong!" Everybody was wrong except Willie. He had gotten out of the hospital at 250 pounds after his operation and just con-tinued to gain weight.

Then we had a meeting and Landry welcomed us to training camp and congratulated us for being there and for being the right weight. He said it signified that we wanted the team to be a contender that year. He said, "There is one man on this team who is so independent I just don't know. Normally I would fine someone for being overweight, but I'm not going to fine Willie. What I'm going to do is to put him at the Fat Man's Table." All there was to eat at the Fat Man's Table was Jell-O, lettuce and tomatoes and other vegetables, and water. Someone did a drawing of a black face wearing a number 71 with his big stomach hanging out of his jersey and sitting at the Fat Man's Table. The rest of us sat at the other tables and called out, "Willie! Look at these steaks! They're just great!"

After two weeks of two-a-days, we had a terrible practice; we fumbled, we got all the plays wrong, we dropped passes, we jumped offsides, we were in motion. And Landry said, "You all don't want to make the sacrifice to be champions. There is only one man on this team who exemplifies that he wants to be world champion, and that is Willie Townes. He's not eating what you guys are getting to eat, he's weak out there, and this man is continuing to drive every day, wearing those sweats under his uniform and losing weight, but he still has the desire to get out there and play football. And I admire Willie Townes for that.''

The next day, Landry called a weigh-in. And at the weigh-in Willie was 300 pounds. The day after Landry had bragged about Willie exemplifying the desire it took to be a world champion and how much he admired him, he found that Willie had *gained* ten pounds. All Coach Landry could say was, ''Good God! What's happening?'' We went out to practice and Landry sent the trainers to Willie's room to see if he was sneaking food. They found cases of beer under the bed and jars of mayonnaise and stacks of cold cuts in the shower. About the same time, some of the players found out where Willie was getting some of his food late at night when the pizza delivery boy got the rooms mixed up one night. The delivery boy knocked on a door, calling, ''Mr. Townes, your pizzas are here.'' The trouble was, the pizza boy had knocked at Dave Manders's door. And Willie wasn't ordering one pizza or two; he was ordering three. Landry finally had no choice but to fine Willie, although he later gave the money to his charity of choice.

We all used to get tired of the dormitory food in training camp and would order cheeseburgers and hamburgers at night. While playing cards, we'd order ten hamburgers and cheeseburgers and four or five big pizzas. I saw Willie eat a cheeseburger and ball up the yellow wrapper and throw it under the bed. But the rest of us didn't eat our burgers until we finished playing cards. Then everybody dug in, and Willie had a second one. So we were one burger short and Mel Renfro was left out. Mel said, ''Where's my burger?'' I said, ''Well, Willie just ate a burger.'' ''I didn't eat no burger, man!'' Willie insisted. I looked under Willie's bed later, and there was a pile of hamburger wrappers.

Willie was always dieting, right? The kickers didn't have to attend all the team meetings, so they used to have a lot of spare time, and we would send Toni Fritsch out for some pizzas—after we ate the burgers. Willie would have a big giant pizza or two or three with everything on top except anchovies, which was about the only kind of food Willie didn't like. During the night, he would put away at least a six-pack of beer. After the hamburgers, the pizza, and the beer, he would finish his evening snack with a Diet Pepsi. That was his way of dieting, after two cheeseburgers, several pizzas, and a six-pack of beer. And he was always complaining, "I'm drinking diet soda and I don't know why I can't lose weight."

We had to walk only a block and a half from the dormitory to the field house. Although Willie was trying to lose weight, he rented a car; he did not want to walk that distance. He was just LAAZEE! Don Perkins, Cornell Green, and I stole Willie's car keys, so he would have to walk. We kept the keys for two weeks, and Willie was really upset. Willie knew we had the keys and that we were even driving the car. We had the keys hidden in an attic of our room where he would never find them. Right before we were ready to leave camp for Dallas, we gave Willie the keys, and he called us every kind of name in the book. But he finally admitted, "Okay, you guys did a good job."

Willie had the same attitude on the field. We were coming out for a game with the Eagles, and Willie was going up against Bob Brown, who was probably the best offensive lineman in the league. Bob Brown looked at Willie and said, "Home boy, you're going to be great one day, but you ain't going to be great this day." Willie loved to talk and he mumbled, "I don't know, I can beat you, I can beat you, just like you think you can beat me." During the game, Bob Brown played Willie real tough. Willie and Jethro not only played next to each other on the defensive line, they were roommates and best friends; they even had the same kind of car, Pontiacs, both blue. After one play Willie walked up to Jethro and said, "Hey, Jethro, are you beating your man good? Are you beating your man?" Jethro said, "I'm doing all right." So Willie said, "Well, look, Jethro, let's limbo this time. [Limbo meant the defensive tackle and defensive end would do a stunt, crisscross.] And you go first and make sure you hold Bob Brown." Jethro said, "You crazy? I got me an offensive guard who ain't all pro, and you got the best offensive tackle in the league and you're telling me to go first? You think I'm crazy? My mother didn't raise no foolish kids. You going to have to have this battle all by yourself today."

Willie had a jazz show on a little radio station near Fort Worth, and he made the mistake of calling Jethro late one night. He woke Jethro up and said, "Jethro, I want to interview you and have you say hello to my audience." Normally when a disc jockey makes a phone call, the radio station sets it up and makes sure the other person is on the line and prepared to go on the air, but Willie just picked up the phone while he was on the air and called Jethro. Jethro didn't realize Willie was on the air, and he yelled, "Why the hell are you calling me at this time of night, you dumb son of a bitch? You done woke me up and I don't like it." Willie got all kinds of letters from his listeners saying, "Willie, will you please front the calls to your teammates next time because you sure didn't do it right this time."

Willie and Jethro probably shouldn't have been rooming together because there was only one toilet in their room, and during training camp, they both liked to spend half an hour or so in the morning sitting there, reading the sports pages. Willie would take two or three cans of beer and some cigarettes and just hang out in the bathroom. And every day he and Jethro would race back to their room to see who could get to the toilet first. Willie was real quick when he wanted to be, and Jethro would usually arrive to find the bathroom occupied. At least the locker room had more than one toilet. During halftime, while Landry was at the blackboard, Willie and Jethro would both spend the whole fifteen minutes in the bathroom. They didn't care what Landry had to say—we'd all heard it a million times before—and Landry couldn't order them not to go to the bathroom, so the coach would go ahead and talk for the benefit of whoever couldn't find a stall.

Willie was one of those guys like Lance Rentzel who was always the butt of jokes and never seemed to catch on. Linemen were supposed to be tall, but Cornell Green was about the same height as Willie—about six feet four. Cornell used to tease Willie, "You know, Willie, everyone thinks that I'm the defensive lineman and you're the cornerback. They're all wondering, what is that fat guy out there doing playing cornerback?" He used to tell Willie he really was only six feet two. And Willie used to fall for it every time and get real angry and tell Cornell to shut up.

Also at defensive end was number 79, our third-round draft choice from East Texas State in 1973, Harvey Martin. Pat Toomay was three years older than Harvey, but along about 1974, Harvey's second season, Harvey started coming on strong. Landry was really looking closely at the two of them, trying to decide who would start at right defensive end. Pat had been our leading pass rusher the year before and he started in our opening exhibition game against the Raiders. At halftime, Landry announced, "We're going to make a change; Harvey Martin will start the second half at right defensive end."

Pat Toomay, as a teammate, was trying to give Harvey advice on how to play the Raiders, even though Pat and Harvey were competing for the same position. Oakland had a left offensive tackle named Art Shell, who was one of the best linemen in the league, went on to the Pro Football Hall of Fame, and became the first black head coach in modern pro football when Al Davis picked Art to coach the Raiders in 1989. When we were playing, it was legal for a defensive lineman to head slap an offensive lineman, which the offensive players hated because it made their ears ring and gave them a headache. And Art Shell hated it worse than anyone. We were in the tunnel going back to the field for the second half, and Pat Toomay was saying, "Now, Harvey, whatever you do, don't head slap him. He's too good; you have to use your speed and techniques to go around him, and he hates to be head slapped. Don't head slap him 'cause he'll kill you out there." Harvey was so excited about starting that what Pat said went in one ear and out the other—"Yeah, yeah, okay, man, I understand, I understand, I'm going to get out there and I'm going to get him, I'm going to get him, Pat, I'm going to get him."

Kenny Stabler was the quarterback, and on his first pass attempt Harvey went up to Art Shell and slapped him across the head. Pat Toomay was on the sideline standing next to me, and he said, "Hey, Bobby, look." What we saw was Harvey about ten yards off the line of scrimmage; his chin strap was near the sideline and he was on his hands and knees, trying to get up. He was having trouble seeing, too, because his helmet had been twisted so violently that he was peeping through his ear hole. Harvey had made the mistake of head slapping Art Shell, and Art had really nailed him. From that play on, Harvey always listened to Pat.

I played only one season with Too-Tall Jones, number 72 from Tennessee State. In 1974 he was a rookie defensive end and I was in my last year with the Cowboys. Too-Tall was a hell of a nice guy, but he was best known for being the black version of Long John Holmes. I mean, the guy was hung like a horse. I walked into the shower one time, and Too-Tall was the only other guy in there. I made a U-turn and walked out before someone else walked in and saw just the two of us in there. If they had looked at him and then looked at me, and compared us it would have been kind of embarrassing for me. I wasn't the only ballplayer who felt that way; no one wanted to stand up to Too-Tall, if you know what I mean.

One of our defensive tackles was number 75, Jethro Pugh, better known as Buzz, the nickname Don Perkins had given him. Jethro was the one who had everyone on the team start calling each other "Turkey," which is what his college coach used to call all his players.

The Cowboys used to bring in all these obscure players from schools no one had ever heard of, like Jethro, who was from Elizabeth City State in North Carolina. They also used to draft or sign as free agents athletes who had made reputations in sports other than football—like me and Mike Gaechter, who was also a world-class sprinter at Oregon; Cornell Green and Pete Gent, who had been basketball players at Utah State and Michigan State; Merv Rettenmund, our nineteenth choice out of Ball State in 1965, a baseball player who went on to be a star with the Baltimore Orioles and Cincinnati Reds; Lou Hudson, a basketball player from Minnesota who was our twentieth-round selection in 1966 and became a basketball star; and even Pat Riley, the Cowboys' fourteenth choice as an "end" from Kentucky in 1967. Yes, *that* Pat Riley—the same guy who is now coach of the Lakers.

In our rookie season, a bunch of us, mostly from Division 2A schools, got close—Jethro; me; Brig Owens, a quarterback from the University of Cincinnati whom the Cowboys drafted as number 7 and converted to defensive back; Mitch Johnson, an offensive tackle who was our seventeenth choice from UCLA; and A. D. Whitfield, a free-agent runningback from North Texas State. Ironically, three of the five of us—Brig, Mitch, and A. D.—wound up with our archrivals, the Redskins, after spending a short time with the Cowboys.

Whenever we played in Washington, Brig and A. D. used to pick me up at our hotel and take me out to dinner the night before the game. Then on the day of the game, they would give me a ride to the stadium. There was no team rule about how you got to the stadium, just as long as you got there on time. Once when we played in Washington, Brig and A. D. were tied up, so an ex-classmate of mine from Florida A & M, Chauncey Ford, who was a high school track coach in the Washington area, picked Cornell Green and me up at our hotel and took us to his house for dinner. We were staying at the Marriott Hotel at the Fourteenth Street Bridge, right beside the Potomac River. After dinner, Chauncey lent us his car to drive back to the hotel, saying he would pick it up the next day. We were staying in Room 232, and when we got to the hotel, our room key didn't fit in the lock. Well, there is another Marriott at Key Bridge, which is also on the river, and, of course, we were in the wrong one. By the time we got to the right hotel, we had missed curfew by a few minutes and the coaches were sitting in the dining area watching us come in. I explained what had happened, but we got fined fifty bucks anyway.

A. D. Whitfield's real name was A. D., just like Harry Truman's middle name was S, and Jethro, who had grown up in a small town in North Carolina and never left there until he signed with the Cowboys, just couldn't understand it. The first time Jethro and A. D. met when we were all rookies, A. D. introduced himself as A. D., and Jethro asked him, "What does A. D. stand for?"

Whitfield: "That's my name, A. D."

Jethro: "Right, but what does it stand for?"

Whitfield: "It doesn't stand for anything. My name is A. D."

Jethro: "I know that, but what do the initials A. D. stand for?"

Whitfield finally lost his patience and snarled, "They stand for Ass Dumper, you dumb motherfucker," and stalked away. Before long, though, Jethro and A. D. became the best of friends.

Another incident that shows what a hick Jethro was occurred in 1969 or 1970, when Rayfield Wright bought a big, new, white, four-door Cadillac. It was one of the first cars with delay-action windshield wipers. A bunch of us were driving home from the airport after a road game on a dark, drizzling night. We had had some beers on the plane and had stopped off at a store and gotten some more beer on the way home, which was a thirty- or forty-minute ride from the airport. All of a sudden, Rayfield put the windshield wipers on delay. The wipers went across the windshield and then stopped. Jethro jumped up in his seat and started staring and looking around. He asked, "Am I seeing things? Did you just see that, Bob? Cornell, did you see that? Something just went across the windshield." Rayfield, knowing exactly what Jethro was talking about, started to laugh. Then the wipers went back across again. So Jethro said to Rayfield, "You spent all that money for this car? And the windshield wipers don't even work." Cat, as we called Rayfield, said, "No, man, these are delay windshield wipers."

Jethro said, "Man, don't ever do me like that again. First of all, those things scared the hell out of me. And now you guys pulled these delay windshield wipers on me. I got to get me some of these!"

I guess the best linebacker Dallas had while I played on the team was number 55 out of Alabama, Lee Roy Jordan. Lee Roy started a couple of years before I came in, and he lasted a couple of years after I was gone, probably because he was not only talented, but he would do anything to win. Linebackers are supposed to be crazy on the field, and that's the way Lee Roy was. My best memory of Lee Roy was during one game against the Cardinals. Dan Dierdorf, the great St. Louis lineman who is now on "Monday Night Football," made the mistake of putting his hand in Lee Roy's mouth. Lee Roy bit down on Dierdorf's fingers. After that, Dierdorf always made sure he knew where his hand was when he was around Lee Roy.

One of our linebackers, Harold Hays, number 56 from Southern Mississippi, was a racist, just like Rocky Colvin, the defensive tackle who made the comment about Gil Brandt's wife being too friendly with the black players. Rocky was also upset when a black player, Jethro Pugh, took his job, but Rocky has since cooled out, matured, and turned into a nice guy. I can't say the same for Harold Hays, who had his nose out of joint before I ever reported to the Cowboys from the College All-Star camp because he kept getting a lot of mail addressed to me—and I was getting mail by the sack that soon after the Olympics. We had one party, which all the wives attended, and Mel Renfro, who'd had a couple of drinks, asked Harold's wife, Lillian, to dance. Harold said, "I don't like this, I never will like it, I don't enjoy this black dancing with my wife." And he made her stop. The rest of us felt, if you don't want anybody to dance with your wife, leave her home, pal.

Harold Hays was a real conservative, but another of our linebackers, Steve Kiner, was just the opposite. Steve was number 60, a third-round choice in 1970 from Tennessee. He lasted only one season with us and then got traded to New England, but what a season it was. For one thing, Steve smoked marijuana when he was with us, one of the first players I knew who did that. He was a wild man, and one of the incidents that contributed to his departure was when he hit an off-duty policeman with a folding chair at a rock concert during the 1970–71 off-season.

But the biggest impression Steve made during his year with the Cowboys was when he parked in Tom Landry's personal parking space at our practice field. It was raining hard that day, and Steve pulled into Landry's space, which was clearly marked, in his old beat-up Volkswagen Beetle that was painted about four different colors. When Landry pulled up to park in his parking space and found it was taken, he had to park somewhere else. He came into our meeting room, wet as a dog and madder than hell, and said real loud, "Who's parked in my parking space? There's an old beat-up Volkswagen out there!" Everybody on the team looked at Kiner, who was sitting in the corner in the back of the room. Kiner finally said real softly, "Coach, it's my car." Landry turned real red like he did whenever he got mad and shouted, "Get out there and get that car out of my parking space! It says, 'No parking.' Some of you guys on this team just don't understand." Kiner got a mark against his name that day, as well as a fine. He just didn't belong on a team with an authoritarian coach like Landry.

Another guy who played with us for only about one year but was unforgettable was number 31, Otto Brown, a defensive back from Prairie View, Kenny Houston's school. I had known Otto for years because when I was at Florida A & M, his brother was there on a golf scholarship, and Otto was going to Florida A & M High School, which was right on the college campus.

In 1969, the full year Otto played for the Cowboys, our third regular-season game was in Philadelphia. This was our ninth game of the year, counting the six exhibition games. Jack Eskridge, our equipment manager, used to come in before each game and ask all the guys, "Do you have any tickets for Will Call?" Dan Reeves and I were sitting next to each other getting dressed for our pregame warmup in Philadelphia, and suddenly Otto looked over at us after Frank Eskridge asked us about tickets and said, "Hey, man, who is this guy, 'Will Call'? He must be rich. That son of a bitch be everywhere. Every time we go to a game, all I hear is this guy saying, 'Will Call. Will Call. Will Call.' Who is he? Is he from Dallas?"

Dan Reeves got all weak with laughter, his shoes fell out of his hands, and he slipped off the bench and banged his knee on the floor and almost couldn't play in the game. I was laughing so hard I couldn't talk. Everybody was staring at Otto, and I finally said to Otto, "When you were playing in college, didn't you give folks tickets?" He says, "Yes." I said, "Well, didn't you guys have a Will Call gate?" "No," he says. I said. "Well, how did they get the tickets?" And he said, "They used to walk up there while we were warming up and we would have the tickets on the bench, and when a friend of mine walked up, I would give them to the water boy or someone and he would stick the tickets through the fence and give them to my friend." From that day on, Otto wasn't Otto any more. For the rest of his time with the Cowboys, he answered to the name, "Will Call."

• ■ •

One of the nicest guys on the team, Cornell Green, a defensive back, number 34 from Utah State. Cornell was better known as "Sweet Lips," the name Jethro had given him because Cornell always licked his lips when he talked. I was Cornell's walking telephone book. I have a photographic memory, and Cornell never could remember his home phone number, so he always asked me for it. I would ask him why he couldn't remember his own phone number, and he would say, "I never call myself."

Among the great defensive backs who played for the Cowboys when I was there was number 20, Mel Renfro from Oregon. Mel and I had known each other as rivals on the track circuit when we were in college, and he and I often were the deep men on punts and kickoffs for the Cowboys, but we weren't the best of friends. Although the Cowboys selected both of us in the 1964 draft, I still had another year of college, so Mel joined the team a year before I did. He received a lot of publicity that year and was disappointed when I came in in 1965 and received more publicity than he was getting, especially since I was from a smaller school. And when he did get attention after that, it wasn't as much for him alone as it was for him and me as the two members of the Cowboys' "Jet Set." He used to go around saying I wasn't as good a punt returner as he was, I didn't run pass routes that well, I loafed, and things like that. He had his own circle of friends, guys like Dickie Daniels, a defensive back who is now assistant general manager of the Chargers; Les Shy; and Phil Clark, another defensive back. I was never part of Mel's clique.

Among the punters, there was number 88, Colin Ridgway. Colin had been an Olympic high jumper in Australia before he came to Lamar Tech in east Texas. He was a rookie the same year I was, and I used to love to watch him kick. He really had strong legs and used to punt the ball 60 or 70 yards every day in practice. In an exhibition game at Kezar Stadium against the San Francisco 49ers in 1966, the wind was terrible. We had to punt from our own 14 in the third quarter. When Ridgway got back to punt, he hit a good one. The trouble was, the wind blew the ball back in his face and it landed at the 19 for a net of 5 yards. Poor Colin just couldn't believe it. He used to play with these Australian boomerangs at practice, and after that punt everyone took to calling him "Boomerang." His nickname didn't last long, though, because Danny Villaneuva beat him out, in large part because of the 5-yard punt, and Colin got cut a few weeks later.

I had a real appreciation for the punters because I was the backup punter for four or five years in case of emergency, just as Tom Matte had to play quarterback in Baltimore when Johnny Unitas and Gary Cuozzo got hurt. I punted every day in practice. But I never had to punt in a game.

One of our placekickers, Toni Fritsch, number 15, was an Austrian soccer player who had not attended college in the United States. When he arrived at training camp in 1971, he spoke hardly a word of English. In training camp, naturally, we used every kind of cussword you can think of, and Toni thought these words we used, "you asshole, you dumb motherfucker," and so forth, were nice words and that we were calling each other these names as a compliment.

Toni was used to driving in Europe, where there were no speed limits, and after we broke camp and went back to Dallas, Toni got stopped for driving about a hundred miles an hour on Central Expressway. He told the policeman, "Toni Fritsch, kick, kick, Dallas Cowboys." The policeman said, "Okay, Toni, I understand what you're saying. You're a Dallas Cowboy, and we really love you around here. I'm not going to give you a ticket this time, but please slow down before you have an accident." As the policeman was walking back to his car, Toni said, "Thank you, you dumb motherfucker." Toni thought he was saying, "Thank you, officer, I really appreciate you letting me off the hook." Well, the police officer got furious and gave Toni a ticket.

Toni used to get all decked out in fancy clothes and he had plenty of women, but the way he was built (he was real bowlegged), he looked like an egg with legs. But he was a damn good kicker.

We did have some American kickers, and one of them was number 17 and 83 (he wore both jerseys), Mike Clark from Texas A & M. Mike, who kicked for us for several years in the late sixties and early seventies, was best known as "Onside" because he flat missed an onside kickoff attempt in a 1969 playoff game against the Browns in the Cotton Bowl. When Mike missed the ball, we got penalized 5 yards for being offside. He tried another onside kick, but it didn't go 10 yards, and we got penalized another 5 yards. He finally kicked the third one deep down the field, and

Leroy Kelly ran it back 18 yards to the Cleveland 39. It didn't matter much because the Browns beat the hell out of us that day anyway, 38 to 14; Mike's ill-fated onside kick attempt came after the last score of the game, with just four minutes to play. Who knows—if his kick had worked, we might have recovered it and scored a touchdown, which would have made the final score 38 to 21.

Training camp was always a grind, but now that it's been fifteen years since I was in camp, I remember all the fun times we had. We had to study our plays in camp over and over and we would get bored. So one day we all got big cigars and puffed away. Coach Landry started coughing, so we had to open the windows and pull up all the shades.

We were just like little boys, and a lot of wild things used to happen in training camp. If you have several dozen grown men living together in a college dormitory for weeks at a time in California, with all their wives and girlfriends back in Dallas, they get out of control after a while. Bob Lilly and George Andrie used to buy dart guns that shot rubber darts and they would shoot dozens of them and wake guys up in their rooms before practice. Walt Garrison used to put charcoal fluid in his mouth, light up a lighter, and blow the fluid out, so there would be this huge ball of fire. He used to go up to the rookies' rooms about 2 A.M. and yell, "Fire! Fire!" One rookie actually jumped out the window and broke an ankle.

Football players never had any trouble finding women, especially during training camp. John Wooden, the wizard of Westwood, hosted a basketball camp at California Lutheran College, where we held our training camp, at the same time we were there. Girls in bikinis would watch us and Wooden's players practice, and afterwards they would screw the ballplayers from their favorite sport.

At least 75 percent of the guys on the team were fooling around. Walt Garrison had a girlfriend with long black hair, who was stacked. She used to come around all the time. But she wasn't just in Garrison's room; she was in a bunch of rooms. Nevertheless, she was in love with Walt, even though she slept with some of the other guys. A lot of these girls came to town just for the games, stayed in the same hotel we did, and supported the Dallas Cowboys in every area that we wanted them to. The ones who didn't play around were Roger Staubach, Don Meredith, Cornell Green, Calvin Hill, Mark Washington, and Jethro Pugh. The coaches used to check the rooms, but the girls would hide in closets. All the coaches would do is open the door, look in, and make sure the guys were in their beds. They weren't looking for anything else, and they didn't find it. A lot of us, including me, used to sneak out after curfew and visit each other's rooms or the rooms where the girls were staying. Girls would knock on your door and give you their room key or give you their room number. You would go to their rooms and they would have on negligees or sexy nightgowns with slits cut in the sides, or have nothing on. They excited you. So you'd stay in their room for an hour or so and then go back to your own room. I can't even remember their names, and I often didn't bother to learn their names. I was fulfilling my fantasies. Sometimes I would even slip and call the girl I was with by the name of the one I was fantasizing about while we were in bed. The girls never complained; shit, they just wanted to be with an athlete. It was all fly by night. I was married at the time, and these girls didn't really mean anything to me, but neither did my wife. Now I know that what I did was wrong, for the girls and because of Altamease, but I was too young and involved with myself and took advantage of my situation.

A lot of times in training camp I was so worn out after practice that I had trouble staying awake. The year Mel Zahn lent me his Lincoln Continental to use in camp, I picked up a girl who was helping out at practice and gave her a ride from the field house to the student union building. While she went into the student union to buy us a couple of ice cream cones, I stayed in the car with the engine running and soon fell asleep. I had a dream that I put the car into gear, backed it out while I was asleep, and then pressed down on the accelerator, started the car up, and went straight through some hedges at about forty miles an hour. Suddenly, it dawned on me that it had actually happened, and I panicked in my sleep and woke up. I had dreamed exactly what happened. It scared the hell out of me. I got out of the car, my heart pumping like crazy, went up to my room and stayed there for about an hour until I was sure I was awake, and then went out and parked the car. The next morning when the players were going to breakfast, they saw where my car had gone through the hedges and torn up the lawn and they all teased me about it. They thought I drove the car like that to be crazy; none of them could believe that I had really done it in my sleep while I dreamed about it. I finally told Coach Landry that I had done it before he found out from someone else. I don't know what the girl did when she came out with the ice cream cones; I never saw her again.

Back then everything seemed funny. We laughed a lot, but we don't laugh so much any more. I guess that's what age does to you. We also used to bitch and moan a lot about how tough all the practices were, but if I could give advice to today's players, I'd tell them to enjoy it while they can. Being at training camp is a thousand times better than *not* being at training camp. But they'll learn that soon enough. I'd give my left nut to be back at training camp this minute, working out until I couldn't keep my eyes open, laughing and cursing and complaining all the way. Thanks for the memories, Tom.

(ALMOST) ROOKIE
OF THE YEAR

I made my debut with the Cowboys on August 17, 1965, against the Rams in one of my favorite stadiums, the Los Angeles Memorial Coliseum. Being in the coliseum again brought back a lot of memories of when I had run against the Russians and of my first race on the national scene—the big race against Frank Budd.

The Rams had Roman Gabriel at quarterback and their famous defensive team led by Rosey Grier, Merlin Olsen, and Deacon Jones. George Allen, who had coached the Bears' defense two years earlier when the Bears beat the Giants for the world championship, was the Rams' head coach. I will never forget how Deacon Jones and Merlin Olsen came up to me as we were walking through the tunnel from our dressing rooms and congratulated me on winning the gold medal in Tokyo. They were really nice guys. Deacon and I talked about our being home boys from Florida for a minute and then we went out on the field.

I had come to training camp from the College All-Star camp only a few days before and I hadn't had much chance to practice and familiarize myself with the Cowboys' plays, so I wasn't really expecting to play. But I did get in on our last offensive series. With the Cowboys trailing 9 to 0, my first catch in professional football was on a pass from Jerry Rhome on second down and 10 from our own 25-yard line. I gained just inches less than ten yards, but Amos March picked up the first down on fourth and 1. My catch was on a zoom route, where I went two yards out and cut right in front of their middle linebacker. He was all over me, but I still caught the ball. After Marsh got the first down, I caught another pass on

151

the same route for 3 yards out to our 39-yard line, but that's as far as we got before we gave up the ball on downs and the Rams ran out the clock and shut us out. Still, it felt great to know that some of the pressure of coming into pro football as the world's fastest human and not being taken seriously as a football player was taken off me. I was getting more exposure than any of the other Cowboys rookies, and everybody was focusing on my speed, not on my ability to play football. A lot of people had been making jokes about me and treating me like a freak. Now at least they knew I could catch the ball, too.

I played only a little in our second exhibition game against the 49ers in Portland, Oregon, a 27 to 7 loss, but the flight to Dallas was a lot more interesting than the game itself. First, when the plane was taxiing out to the runway, the pilot got a call, "Hey, you're leaving two ballplayers here." We had to taxi back and pick up Don Meredith and Buddy Dial. We were a high-spirited bunch, finally going back to Dallas with training camp behind us. Shortly before we landed, Mike Gaechter, who used to keep everybody loose, went into the cockpit, grabbed the microphone from the pilot, and started giving orders: "Okay, you married guys, you can put your wedding bands back on now; we're landing in Dallas!" Coach and Mrs. Landry, Tex and Mrs. Schramm, and all the assistant coaches were trying to act dignified, and all the players were going crazy.

Then Gaechter said, "All you guys, when you get home, you got to take the floating test." I turned to Jethro and asked, "What is the floating test?" "Don't ask me," he answered. Then I asked Cornell. Cornell explained, "Okay, Speedo, a floating test is this: When you get home, your wife will fill up the bathtub with water and she'll have you take your clothes off and lie on your back. If your nuts float on the top, that means they're empty and that you've been doing something in camp. But if they sink with you, that means you've passed the test at home."

After a 21 to 12 victory over Vince Lombardi's Green Bay Packers in the Cotton Bowl, in front of sixty-eight thousand fans, the largest crowd ever to see a Cowboys home game, we played the Minnesota Vikings in Birmingham. I was really looking forward to my first trip to my home territory as a professional football player, and some of my friends came from Florida. Unfortunately, we returned to our pre-Packers form. Actually, we were even worse than that. Minnesota stomped us, 57 to 17, although

I caught my first long pass as a Cowboy, a 42-yarder in the second quarter from Don Meredith as I beat the Vikings' safety, Ed Sharockman.

What I really remember about that trip, though, are things that happened off the field. This was the height of the Martin Luther King era, when blacks were fighting for civil rights in the South. One of the big movie theaters in Birmingham would not admit blacks, but Coach Landry arranged for us to get in anyway. It wasn't optional; the whole team had to attend. The entire upstairs was roped off for us; nobody but the Cowboys, who were integrated, of course, sat up there. I said to myself, "If I go in here and somebody throws a bomb at me, they're going to get some white boys, too." I walked between Bob Lilly and George Andrie, who were both about six feet six. That's what you call a reverse Oreo. I sat between those two guys, hunched down in my seat. I didn't know what movie was on, and I didn't care; I spent the whole night looking around to see what was going on in the theater.

In those days, racial incidents were hard to avoid. During my rookie season, we were at Love Field in Dallas, getting ready to catch a plane for an away game. I was wearing a dark suit and tie, which our dress code required on road trips. A well-dressed white woman came running up to me with her suitcases and said, "Skycap, skycap, would you please take my luggage to the counter?" I had to set her straight: "Ma'am, I have a ticket like yours. I don't work here, I work for the Dallas Cowboys—not for Love Field or for American Airlines or Braniff." I guess we all looked alike to her.

Out last exhibition game was against the Bears in Tulsa, where Jerry Rhome had been a big star. Jerry never was one of those three yards-and-a-cloud-of-dust, ball-control types of quarterback. He loved to trick the defense. With two minutes left in the game, several plays after I had returned a kickoff 45 yards to our 49, we were ahead by 27 to 21. We had the ball second and 8 at the Chicago 26. Jerry called for me to run a hook and go, and the weak safety went for my fake. I took off again at full speed, and Jerry laid the ball out toward the rear of the end zone. He actually threw it too far, but I was able to catch it just before I ran over the end line for my first touchdown in an NFL game, which clinched the win for us.

In addition to the touchdown catch, I had my first big game as a Cowboy, gaining 53 yards on 3 catches, 88 yards on 4 kickoff returns, and 16 yards on 1 punt return, for a total of 157 yards. On one of those kickoff returns, I got my bell rung when I was blindsided. The shock of getting hit that hard made me bite my tongue, and I couldn't eat for a couple of days. That was the worst pain I had ever felt in my life. I don't know who hit me and I didn't want to watch it on film because watching it would have made me start hurting all over again. Coach Landry took one look at me and yelled, "Off the kickoff team!" (He was afraid I would get seriously hurt returning kickoffs and would not be able to play.) He kept me from returning kickoffs in our next two games, but I was back under kickoffs in our third regular season game and went on to finish among the league's leaders.

Tom Landry said later that that game, particularly my touchdown catch, convinced him to change the offense and make me one of our main weapons. He left Buddy Dial at flanker, moved me from flanker to split end, and converted Frank Clarke from split end to tight end. "That long one was a startling revelation," Landry said. "It looked like Rhome had thrown the ball out of sight, but Hayes went after it and suddenly he was under it. You see plays like that and don't know what he may do." With praise like that from The Boss, I was all set to start playing in games that counted.

We opened the regular season against the New York Giants in the Cotton Bowl on September 19 in front of 59,366 fans, the largest crowd for a regular season home game in the Cowboys' history. It was perfect weather for a Florida boy—hot (nearly 90 degrees) and humid. And you couldn't ask for a better opponent than the Giants. Although they had lost to the Bears in the title game in 1963 and they still had Del Shofner, Jim Katcavage, Joe Morrison, and a few of their other great players, the Giants had gone from the top to the bottom in one year, finishing 2–10–2 and last in the Eastern Division in 1964.

Midway through the first quarter, I caught my first official NFL pass. We had the ball second and 6 at our own 41, and Don Meredith called the quick screen to the wide receiver that Landry had installed in our offense to take advantage of my speed. I was split out to the right, and the Giants linebacker on my side made it even easier for us by blitzing. Dandy hit me in the flat and I took off—a little too soon, in fact. I went 37 yards to the Giants' 22 before Olen Underwood, a Giants linebacker, tackled me, but I probably would have gone all the way if I had waited for my blockers to set up a wall. Also, I had run straight down the field instead of cutting back to my left, where I had open field. When I got back to the bench, my roommate, J. D. Smith, one of our runningbacks, came over to me and yelled, "Roomie, you got to wait on your blockers!" "Roomie," I answered, "I ain't got time back there to wait on no blockers with the pursuit coming after me." J. D. started laughing, but he told me, "If you see the pursuit coming, don't worry about it, just do what you're supposed to do."

Three plays after my first catch, we were still at the Giants' 22 with third down and 10. Meredith hit me over the middle to the Giants' 10, but the play was called back because Ralph Neely was holding. Ralph was one of the best offensive linemen in the league throughout my ten seasons with the Cowboys, but he had one weakness: getting caught by the referees for holding. His sin wasn't holding, it was getting called for it. After a few years, it got to the point that anytime they threw a flag against us, Ralph would turn around, walk back to the huddle, and signal to the rest of us, "It was me. It was me." When we had our twentieth anniversary reunion in 1979, they introduced the Cowboys' greats one by one, and as Ralph ran through the goal posts and onto the field, he threw a huge yellow flag up in the air. The crowd went bananas.

The holding call messed up our drive against the Giants, and Danny Villaneuva kicked a 41-yard field goal to put us ahead, 3 to 0. So my first catch had led to a score, the game-winning score that day, as it turned out.

The highlight of the day for me, though, came with four and a half minutes left in the game when we were ahead 24 to 2. We had stopped the Giants at their 40, and I bobbled Ernie Koy's punt and then fell on it at our 16. From there, we marched downfield to the Giants' 45. With second and 4, Dandy threw me the same pass in the right flat that I had made a big gain on in the first quarter. The pass was a little wobbly, but I caught it and this time I let Ralph Neely and Dave Manders set up to block for me. Ralph nailed a Giants defensive back and almost knocked him into the stands, and I headed for the goal post. Jim Patton and my old track pal, Henry Carr, had an angle on me, but I outran them and went all the way for the last score of the game. Tom Landry was really impressed; he said that Patton and Carr figured to converge on me at the Giants' 25, but when they reached that point, I was already 5 yards past them. "I've never seen this in the NFL, where defensive backs judge the angle and then get there and are lost," Landry said.

I also made my mark that day as a blocker. I really nailed Dick Lynch, a veteran cornerback for the Giants. After the play was over, he looked up at me and said, "I didn't know you could hit that hard." "Well, you're lyin' on the ground, ain't you?" I answered. It was all in good fun; Dick wasn't a dirty player, and I hadn't tried to hurt him; I had just tried to make a good, hard block.

I didn't go away empty handed after the game. I was named the first winner of the new Dallas Cowboys Player-of-the-Week Award, which earned me a month's supply of milk and a set of luggage. I won prizes like that ten times during the next two seasons. I gave most of the milk to guys who had kids, like Don Perkins, Cornell Green, and Frank Clarke. Some of the luggage I kept for myself—I traveled so much that I was always wearing out my suitcases—but I gave away a lot of luggage, too.

Our second game was at home against the Redskins. When the Cowboys entered the NFL as an expansion team in 1960, the Redskins were just about as bad. Both teams improved during the next four years, and by my rookie year, both teams thought they had a shot at winning the Eastern Division championship and our rivalry was starting to heat up. Unlike the Giants, whose cornerbacks, Jim Patton and Dick Lynch, were hard-hitting but clean, the Redskins would be covering me with Johnny Sample, a bigmouthed cheap-shot artist who was probably the dirtiest player I ever played against. And Sample didn't need to play that way; he was a good ballplayer who hadn't been beaten for a touchdown the entire 1964 season.

We took the opening kickoff and moved to the Washington 45, where we had a first down. When we lined up, we could see the blitz coming, and our line picked it up perfectly. I was split out to the right, so I faked to the outside, looked back and saw that Meredith was still waiting for me, and cut to my left, going diagonally toward the middle of the field. Don hit me right in stride, and I ran between Sample and Rickie Harris, another Redskins defensive back, for a quick touchdown.

I scored another touchdown in the second quarter on an 11-yard end around, to put us ahead 14 to 0. Leon Donohue and Ralph Neely were blocking for me, when all of a sudden I saw big Sam Huff coming after me. I ran right between Leon and Ralph, and the next thing I knew, I was in the end zone. Fear makes everybody run faster, and if you weren't afraid when Sam Huff was headed your way, your head must not have been screwed on right. Even Johnny Sample was impressed; when I reached the end zone, I looked back and Sample, who was lying on the ground by then, told me, "Good move."

Just before the end of the half, I scored another touchdown, the kind I still refer to as a Ralph Neely touchdown. We had third down and 11 at the Redskins' 23, and Meredith hit me perfectly on a corner route for an easy touchdown. Unfortunately, Ralph was holding, and the play was called back.

Johnny Sample kept cursing me, elbowing me in the chin, and slapping me on the helmet with his palm for most of the day. I waited until the fourth quarter, and when none of the officials was looking, I caught him in the jaw with my elbow. From then on, he just played football against me. Of course, Sample was a little discouraged by the fourth quarter. We were ahead 27 to 0 by then, on our way to a 27 to 7 victory. Sample was supposed to be covering me. He must not have done a very good job because I had touched the ball three times and scored three touchdowns, although one of them was called back. After that game, I figured that at least one NFL defensive back must know that I was a football player as well as a track star. And that defensive back was Johnny Sample.

We had played two games and won them by a total score of 58 to 9. This was the way it had been at Florida A & M, and I was thinking, another 12 games like this, and we'll be 14 and 0 and playing for the championship.

Then we played our first road game, in St. Louis. The Cardinals not only ended our winning streak at two, 20 to 13, they shut me down with two catches for 21 yards. I returned one kickoff for 21 yards and one punt for 5, but I didn't do anything notable, and, for the first time in a game that counted, I failed to get into the end zone. The Cardinals' defensive backfield—Pat Fischer, Jim Burson, Larry Wilson, and Jerry Stovall—was by far the best I had ever played against, and it had us covered all day. Our only touchdown, as a matter of fact, was by Mel Renfro, who intercepted one of Charley Johnson's passes and returned it 90 yards with twenty seconds left in the first half.

I did have one shot at a touchdown, at the end of the first quarter after Bill Triplett, a Cardinals runningback, fumbled, and one of our defensive backs, Warren Livingston, recovered at the Cardinals' 37. We were behind 14 to 0 at the time, and a score would have put us back in the game. On first down, Meredith threw incomplete to me, and on the next play I got open in the end zone, but Meredith's pass was short and Burson intercepted it on the Cardinals' 2 and ran it back 23 yards to end our threat.

■   ■   ■

My "slump" ended at a game in Week 4 against Philadelphia, in the Cotton Bowl, but it didn't do any good, since the Eagles beat us, 35 to 24. Don Meredith had had a terrible game against the Cardinals, with only 9 completions in 23 attempts for 108 yards and no interceptions, plus he had been intercepted twice and sacked twice, and Landry benched him against Philadelphia. Dandy got in the game only to hold on place kicks, Craig Morton and Jerry Rhome shuttled at quarterback, and I had fun playing with both of them.

The game started off as an offensive duel—the Eagles received the opening kickoff and marched 75 yards for a touchdown, and then Mel Renfro returned the Eagles' kickoff 30 yards out to our 43. Two plays later, we had second and 2 at the Eagles' 49, and Craig hit me on a slant-in over the middle at about the Eagles' 30. I caught the ball in full stride and ran right between Eagles' defensive backs Nate Ramsey and Joe Scarpati into the end zone to tie the game. Ramsey had the primary coverage of me, and a few plays later, when I tried to block him on a run, he pushed me and we got into a shoving match. But he became one of my best buddies. Wide receivers and defensive backs probably have the biggest egos in football, and though Nate used to take it personally whenever I beat him, he would forget it when the game was over.

Just before halftime, I had a very embarrassing experience, if you can call a 47-yard punt return embarrassing. It wasn't the punt return itself that was the problem, it was the way it ended, with King Hill, the Eagles quarterback and punter, getting in my way, which allowed the great Ollie Matson, who was finishing out his career with the Eagles, to tackle me at the Philadelphia 21. We did get a field goal out of it, to leave us behind, 14 to 10 at halftime. But King Hill wasn't exactly the world's second fastest human, and there's no way I should have let him slow me up, especially with the fine blocking I had on that play.

I got a chance to redeem myself on a lucky break about five minutes into the third quarter. We started off at our own 35 after an Eagles punt, but on the next two plays, Rhome got sacked for a 10-yard loss, and a Morton screen pass to Don Perkins lost another 17, leaving us with third down and 27 at our own 18. Jerry faded back near our goal line from the shotgun formation and aimed the ball at me, more than 50 yards downfield. Irv Cross was covering me, and he tried to knock the pass down, but he barely got a finger on it and the ball stayed in the air and fell into my hands at the Eagles' 40. No one was close to me, and I coasted the rest of the way for an 82-yard touchdown, the second longest in our history, which gave us the lead, 17 to 14.

Things went downhill from there, though. The Eagles came back with a 78-yard drive to go ahead, but we started driving to take the lead again. After Ralph Neely, of all people, returned a short kickoff 13 yards to our 32, we had a long march that included a couple of short passes to me and got us down to the Eagles' 21. That's when Morton got chased back almost to the Eagles' 40, fumbled, and had George Tarasovic, a big, slow Philadelphia lineman, pick up the ball and somehow run it 62 yards for a touchdown to put them ahead, 28 to 17, early in the fourth quarter.

We still had plenty of time to score two touchdowns and win, but a Jerry Rhome bomb intended for me was intercepted by Irv Cross at our 41-yard line. The ball was a little behind me, and Irv caught it, but he had only returned it 1 yard when I grabbed him around the waist and slung him down as hard as I could, right in front of the Eagles bench. He got up and gave me a dirty look, but he and I never had any problems; he was another one of those great ballplayers who played hard but clean. After Irv's interception, the Eagles went 40 yards and clinched the game on a 3-yard run by Timmy Brown.

Even though we lost, this was the first of my truly outstanding games for the Cowboys. We gained a total of 250 yards passing, and I accounted for 177 of those yards on eight catches. My yardage was the third highest for one game in the history of the Cowboys, and I had the two touchdowns. I also had that 47-yard punt return (which should have been for 68 yards and my third touchdown) and returned two kickoffs for 29 yards, so my total offense for the day was 253 yards, which won me a sport coat and a pair of slacks as the outstanding Cowboy.

I had made a hell of an impact in the NFL. In my first four games, I had handled the ball 14 times and gained 336 yards and scored 5 touchdowns, 4 on passes and 1 on a run. "Talk about all your great rookies, guys like Bobby Mitchell and Lenny Moore," Red Hickey told the press, "and Hayes is way ahead of them at the same stage. If nothing happens to him physically, he'll have to be one of the all-time greats—just because there has never been another man with his possibilities. He has the most amazing speed in history, he has moves, he's tough, he's durable, he's teachable. What else can you ask?" Red also compared me to Babe Ruth, saying that people used to get excited just watching the

Babe strike out and that I was just as exciting missing a long pass as Ruth was when he fanned.

I twisted my ankle when Bernie Parrish of the Cleveland Browns stepped on my foot during our third loss in a row. I didn't think too much of it at the time, but my ankle hurt more and more as the week went by. We were facing the Packers in Milwaukee, and I didn't know until game time if I would be able to play.

Right before we took the field, Coach Landry was all set to lead our team prayer. I was in the trainers' room next to the locker room, looking at the biggest needle I had ever seen, which was in the hands of Dr. Marvin Knight, our team physician. When Dr. Knight stuck the needle into my bone, trying to kill the pain, I used a lot of words that are not in the Bible. Landry turned to the rest of the team and said, "Just a minute, guys. Let's wait on Bobby Hayes, because we can't pray with the words he's using in there."

Worst of all, the shot didn't kill the pain, I couldn't play, and the Packers shut down our passing attack—Meredith completed 10 of 20 passes for 61 yards, but he was sacked nine times for minus 62 yards to leave us with minus 1 yard passing. We actually did better passing than the Packers did, since Bart Starr completed only four passes for 42 yards and lost 52 yards on sacks for a net of minus 10 passing, but we turned the ball over five times and lost, 13 to 3.

We lost our fifth straight game in Pittsburgh, 22 to 13. Anyone who thinks Tom Landry is cold and uncaring should have seen him in our dressing room after the game. Tom blamed himself for our defeat, and he was in tears. "I thought my game plan would work, but it didn't," he told us. "I should have prepared you guys better than I did." None of the rest of us felt much better.

After such a promising start, we found ourselves 2 and 5 halfway through the season. We opened the second half at home against San Francisco, and it was just like pre-Bob Hayes times in the Cotton Bowl: Only thirty-nine thousand fans showed up. Those people who stayed away missed a great game.

Mel Renfro set the tone on the opening kickoff. He fielded Tommy Davis's kick on our goal line, headed up the middle, cut to his left, and ran 100 yards for a touchdown. As he ran by our bench with about 30 yards to go, it looked like Mel was running with a piano on his back. His days as a sprinter were behind him, but so were the 49ers, and even though it looked like he would never reach the goal line, he did so before any of them could catch him. While he was trying to catch his breath, I asked him if he wanted to go one on one with me for old times' sake, but he didn't even answer.

George Mira, my home boy from the University of Miami, went all the way at quarterback for San Francisco, with John Brodie and Billy Kilmer watching from the bench; George threw a 4-yard pass to Bernie Casey that put the 49ers ahead, 10 to 7, late in the first quarter. But on our next drive, which started with me returning the kickoff 22 yards out to our 24-yard line, Meredith threw me a quick screen, and I ran 24 yards, right between two San Francisco defensive backs, for a touchdown that gave us the lead again, 14 to 10.

We had opened our lead to 27 to 10 by halftime, but then it got hairy. The 49ers drove 77 yards off the second half kickoff to cut our lead to 27 to 17, and then Tommy Davis kicked off to me. I fielded the ball at our 4, got some great blocks, and went 66 yards down the right sideline before Jimmy Johnson, the 49ers defensive back who was the brother of Rafer Johnson, the 1960 Olympic decathalon champion, ran me down at the San Francisco 30. Jimmy was almost as fast as I was, and with the angle he had on me, I just couldn't get by him. A couple of plays later, Don threw me a 13-yard pass to the San Francisco 11, but the 49ers held, and Danny Villaneuva kicked a short field goal that made the score Dallas 30, San Francisco 17.

The 49ers didn't seem to know when they were beaten. They came back with a 73-yard drive that ended with Dave Kopay, who later made headlines by revealing that he was gay, scoring from the 3. That left us with just a 6-point lead, but I had visions of glory. I returned the 49ers kickoff 18 yards to our 25, and on the next play, Dandy got the ball to me for a 37-yard gain to the San Francisco 38-yard line, where Wayne Swinford ran me out of bounds. The 49ers stopped us again, so Danny Villaneuva tried a 37-yard field goal that would have given us a 9-point lead at the end of the third quarter. But Charlie Kreuger blocked it, Jimmy Johnson picked up the ball and ran it down to our 39, and we started getting real nervous. I stopped feeling neighborly toward George Mira on the second play of the fourth quarter, when he passed over the middle to Dave Parks for a touchdown that put us behind, 31 to 30.

We traded punts with San Francisco and then got a blocked field goal of our own by Larry Stephens, one of our defensive linemen. Obert Logan, a reserve defensive back, recovered the kick and ran it to our 47, and we were in business. Three plays later, we had a first and 10 at the San Francisco 34, and I ran a fly route, got past two defensive backs, and looked up; Don Meredith had the ball right there for me at the 4-yard line. One more stride, and I was in the end zone and with four minutes to play, we were back ahead, 36 to 31, after Don fumbled the snap on the point after and Danny Villaneuva couldn't get the kick off.

Villaneuva kicked his second field goal with less than a minute left, to make the final score 39 to 31. It was nice to be back in the victory column and even nicer to be named the Associated Press Offensive Player of the Week in the NFL. I felt I deserved the award after scoring two touchdowns, including the one that won the game, and gaining a total of 236 yards, 108 on four pass receptions and 128 on four kickoff returns.

I scored the game-winning touchdown for the second week in a row when we got even with the Steelers for beating us two weeks earlier. I was happy to help pull this game out because I had made a couple of big mistakes earlier that day and lost a touchdown on a referee's call.

My first controversial play was early in the second quarter. The score was tied, 7 to 7, and we had second down and 10 at our own 46. Don Meredith threw me a short pass on the left side. I caught it at our 49, slipped to one knee without any of the Steelers touching me, got up, and ran 51 yards into the end zone. But as I was getting up, Brady Keys, the Steelers cornerback who covered me most of the day, ran by and touched me, and the officials called it a tackle and only a 3-yard gain. That ruling cost us four points because we had to settle for a field goal at the end of that drive.

Brady Keys was a guy I really enjoyed playing against. He was the only defensive back who made a point of congratulating me for a nice play. Brady was very emotional, and the way he got himself jacked up was to talk a lot. If you beat him, he hated it, but he would congratulate you. In turn, when he broke up a play, he wanted you to give him that respect. "Didn't I do good this time, Bob? You didn't catch it this time."

Pittsburgh tied the game early in the second half, and then I made two big mistakes. The second one gave the Steelers the lead. Midway through the third period, the Steelers punter, Frank Lambert, got off a 53-yard kick that I fielded at our 3-yard line. I should have let it go into the end zone for a touchback, which would have given us the ball on the 20, but I made a real rookie's mental error and caught the ball. Two of the Steelers downed me on our 8. We could gain only 5 yards on three plays, but Colin Ridgway got us out of the hole I had put us in by punting 48 yards to the Steelers' 39, where Roy Jefferson caught the ball and was tackled in his tracks. Bill Nelsen threw three incomplete passes and then Lambert punted to me again. This time, I did even worse than on the last punt. I caught the ball on the 15, returned it 3 yards, and lost it when one of the Steelers hit me. The ball bounced back to our 15, and another Steeler, Lee Folkins, picked it up and ran into the end zone to give Pittsburgh the lead, 17 to 10.

Worse than that, Folkins, who had played for Dallas the three previous years and had then been traded to Pittsburgh, celebrated his touchdown by running over to our sideline and throwing the ball at our bench. Folkins apologized after the game, claiming he respected Landry, had a lot of friends on our team, and threw the ball at us as a joke, but he had shown us up—because of me. Landry didn't show his anger, but Folkins had made fools of us, and I was furious.

We tied the game early in the fourth quarter on a 2-yard run by Danny Reeves after Cornell Green intercepted one of Nelsen's passes at midfield. Then, with two and a half minutes left and the game tied, a new Steelers quarterback, Ed Brown, threw a pass to Roy Jefferson. Chuck Howley hit Roy as the pass arrived, and the ball bounded into the air, got batted around a few times, and landed in Dave Edwards's hands at the Pittsburgh 31. After Perry Lee Dunn ran for 3 yards on first down, Don found me wide open behind Brady Keys on the left side for a 28-yard touchdown that won the game, 24 to 17. To be fair to Brady, he was playing with a broken hand that day, which gave me a tremendous advantage.

What Folkins had done taught me a lesson: Don't make the other team mad. Folkins really did me a favor because throughout my athletic career, when I got pissed off, I got even. Getting screwed with Lane 1 in the 100-meter finals in Tokyo, having a coach get on my case, having another ballplayer show me up—every time it happened, it made me do even better than I might have otherwise. I guess because I was so much faster than almost everyone else, I subconsciously may not have done my best at times. Not that I was loafing, but I could have done better. A lot of athletes do better when they're angry, and that's the way I was. Maybe the coaches should have singled me out for criticism every week, but they didn't know it.

All in all, I had had another good day, with 5 catches for 95 yards and the winning touchdown, and another 67 yards on kick returns. Even when I wasn't catching the ball, I had helped open up the field for my teammates. After the game, Dandy Don noted, "They were afraid of Hayes deep. They kept giving us the square out and we kept taking it." And Mike Nixon, the Steelers' head coach, said Pittsburgh had to change its entire defensive scheme because of me. Nixon said the Steelers had to give me double coverage most of the game because I was too fast for anyone in the league to cover me one on one. It was the first of many compliments from opposing coaches, and I never got tired of hearing them.

A 24 to 17 loss to Cleveland left us with a 4 and 6 record and eliminated us from the race, but we still had our pride to play for in the last four games. In our next-to-last game of the season, a 27 to 13 win over St. Louis, I had a big day, scoring one touchdown and setting up the other two. After a pass from Charley Johnson to Sonny Randle put the Cardinals ahead, 10 to 3, late in the first period, we started driving. On first down from our 30, Meredith completed a pass to me for 11 and another first down, and four plays later from the St. Louis 46, we called a bomb even though Pat Fischer, who was covering me, was playing me so deep that he didn't think we would go deep. We decided to go for it anyway, and I used a stutter step to freeze Pat for an instant, ran by him to the outside, and Meredith hit me in stride at the 5. I cruised on into the end zone to tie the game. Fischer said later that he thought he was running right beside me, but when the ball came down, I was way behind him. Pat was a real tough little guy and a real smart defensive back, but he didn't have the speed to stay with someone like me.

The game was tied again, 13 all, early in the fourth quarter, when the Cardinals stopped us on downs after a long drive to their 1-yard line. We had them backed up so far that we decided not to go for the field goal, knowing they would be in a hole if we didn't get the touchdown. We didn't let them gain a yard, and on fourth down Jim Bakken, their punter, outkicked his coverage with a 51-yard punt that I caught on the Dallas 48. I picked up a wall down the right side and returned it 24 yards to the

St. Louis 28, and we scored the go-ahead touchdown three plays later on a 23-yard pass from Meredith to Reeves.

I wasn't finished yet, however. With about six minutes left in the game, we had a second and 10 at our 41. Meredith threw a bomb to me, and I caught it and went 47 yards to the St. Louis 12, where Fischer ran me out of bounds. We scored our final touchdown four plays after that on a 3-yard pass from Meredith to Pettis Norman. Everyone knew that Pettis was a great blocker, but other teams often underestimated his catching ability. They often tried to cover him with just the strong safety and didn't realize that he had 9.7 speed, which was really fast for a tight end. As the season went on, we started taking advantage of the coverage on me and going to our tight ends, and this time Don hit Pettis for a touchdown.

This was another good game for me. I caught 3 passes for 103 yards and 1 touchdown and had another 48 yards on kick returns, a total of 151 yards gained.

I'll never forget walking into Yankee Stadium for our final game of the regular season and looking at all the monuments to the great New York Yankees players, like Babe Ruth and Lou Gehrig. I just got chills. There had been some great ball played on this field, both football and baseball. All the veterans were upfield working out before the game, and I had Meredith throw the ball as far as he could so I couldn't get to it, to give me an excuse to go over and look at the statues quickly before Landry could come over and jump on us for not putting out.

Landry had no cause to worry that we wouldn't take the game seriously. We and the Giants were the only two teams that still had a chance to finish second and go to the Runnerup Bowl, which matched the second-place teams from the East and the West. New York was 7 and 6, one game better than us, but if we beat them, we would finish 7 and 7 and we would win second place because we would have beaten them twice. We thought we had the edge going in because we had had an easy time defeating them in the opening game of the season. We remembered it well, and we assumed they did, too.

We were leading 3 to 0 late in the first quarter when Meredith called for me to run a streak down the left sideline on second and 10 from our 35. The play worked just like they diagrammed it—no Giants defender was near me, Don put the ball right in my hands, and I breezed in for a 65-yard score.

The Giants scored a few minutes later as Earl Morrall kept hitting passes, the last one to Aaron Thomas for a 30-yard touchdown, but then I took things into my own hands. First, I returned the kickoff by Bob Timberlake, my College All-Star teammate, 31 yards to our 34. A few plays later we had third and 6 at the New York 33, and I took a short pass in the left flat all the way for my second touchdown, making it 17 to 7 at the half.

I had another long kickoff return, for 30 yards out to our 43, in the fourth quarter, after the Giants had scored a touchdown to close to within 24 to 20. Then Meredith took over, scrambling 14 yards to the Giants' 33 after it looked like he was going to be sacked, and finally hitting Buddy Dial for a 29-yard score with five minutes to play. We got another late touchdown to make the final score 38 to 20, and for the first time in the Cowboys' history, we had qualified for postseason play.

I wound up the season the same way I had started it, with a big game against the Giants. With 3 catches for 94 yards and 2 touchdowns, I accounted for almost half our passing yardage, and I gained another 88 yards on 3 kickoffs, for a total of 182 yards in the game.

On the flight home from New York, I had a couple of glasses of champagne and started feeling real good. The season had ended, we had finished at .500 for the first time and had won the game in New York in front of the most prestigious press in the world. We were going to Miami to play in the Runnerup Bowl in front of my home folks, the first playoff game in the Cowboys' history. (And not a very good one, either—the Baltimore Colts killed us, 35 to 3.) But on that flight from New York to Dallas, I was so full of champagne and gratitude for all the help Red Hickey had given me that I walked back to where the coaches were sitting and offered Red a can of beer. At Florida A & M, you had better not offer a coach a can of beer, and the Cowboys were the same way then. But Red saw that my offering him the beer was my way of expressing appreciation for all he had done for me, and he understood and accepted it, muttering, "Thank you, Bobby, thank you very much." Being a rookie, I was normally quiet, and I could hear the other coaches saying, "That Bobby Hayes sure is in a good mood tonight, isn't he?" I certainly was, especially when I heard Red tell someone else, "It's times like this, when you see a kid come through, that make coaching worth it all."

I made the Pro Bowl team as a reserve—Sonny Randle of the Cardinals, Pete Retzlaff of Philadelphia, and Gary Collins of Cleveland were our starting receivers—and I caught only one pass for three yards, but it was a tremendous honor to have the other players throughout the NFL vote me into the Pro Bowl as a rookie. It made me feel accepted as a football player, like the other players in the league knew I was on my way to being a star in the NFL.

A lot of players don't take all-star games seriously, but Blanton Collier, the Cleveland coach who was the head coach of the Eastern Division that day (Vince Lombardi coached the Western Division), fired us up. He told us he was tired of hearing how the Western Division had the best players and the best teams; the Western Division had won most of the NFL championships and the Pro Bowls in the past few years. We went out and kicked their butts, 36 to 7, and Jim Brown scored 3 touchdowns in what turned out to be the last game of his career.

I had a whole season of professional football behind me, but I was still the wide-eyed rookie. Before the game in the Los Angeles Memorial Coliseum, I saw Jim warming up by himself and I ran over to our bench to get my camera and take some pictures of him. Who was on the sideline, taking pictures of me? Bill Cosby. I said to myself, "Man, I have to come to Los Angeles more often."

I was very satisfied with what I had achieved as a rookie. I caught 46 passes (the thirteenth highest in the league). With 1,003 yards (the most in the Cowboys' history and the fourth highest in the NFL in 1965, behind Dave Parks of San Francisco, Pete Retzlaff, and Tommy McDonald of the Rams), I became only the second rookie in the history of the NFL to go over 1,000 yards receiving (the first was Mike Ditka in 1961). My average gain per catch, 21.8, led the league. My 12 touchdowns receiving tied Dave Parks for the league lead, were 2 more than the Cowboys' total passing in 1964, accounted for almost half the Cowboys' 25 touchdown passes in 1965, and were only 1 less than Bill Howton's 1952 record for an NFL rookie. With the touchdown I scored rushing, I was the eleventh-highest scorer in the NFL and the second best on the Cowboys; I had 78 points to 85 for Danny Villaneuva. I also tied Irv Cross for sixth place in the NFL on kickoff returns, with a 26.5 average on 17 returns for 450 yards, and I had the third best average on punt returns, 12.8. I gained nearly 1,600 yards overall and had the winning touchdown in two of our last five victories.

It wasn't quite the same as winning the gold medal, but my accomplishments during my first year earned me several awards: I was selected to the *Sporting News* All-NFL team as well as the Pro Bowl, and I not only made the all-rookie team, I was runnerup for Rookie of the Year behind my old friend, Gale Sayers, who scored a record twenty-two touchdowns for the Bears. The first thing I did after I heard that we had finished one–two for Rookie of the Year was call Gale to congratulate him, remind him of what Otto Graham had said about the two of us, and ask him why the Sayers brothers kept beating me in both track and football.

8

WHO'S AFRAID OF THE SOPHOMORE JINX?

When your specialty is the 100-yard dash and every-thing depends on what you do in 9 or 10 seconds, you have to be able to handle pressure. Before my second season began, Tom Landry gave me all the pressure I needed. He went to the reporters who covered the team and told them, "We need a more consistent week-in, week-out effort from Hayes. With his great potential, there's just no way to predict how well he may do. If he does the job, we'll have more consistency throughout our offense."

I thought I had been pretty consistent in my rookie year—becoming the first Cowboy to have more than 1,000 yards receiving, scoring touch-downs in 9 of my 13 games, gaining over 100 yards on pass catches in four games and coming close in four more, and leading the team in re-ceiving in 8 of 13 games. I understood what Landry was doing, trying to make sure that I wouldn't come in overconfident and be a victim of what is known in sports as the "sophomore jinx." A lot of players have out-standing rookie seasons, start thinking it's too easy, and bomb out in their second year. But I didn't want that to happen to me. I approached football the same way I had approached track: In track you're only as good as your last race. As the years went by, though, I came to see that Tom regarded me as almost superhuman because of my speed and that his expectations for me were so unrealistically high that I found it impossible to live up to them.

In our final exhibition game of 1966, we showed how much we had improved from the year before, beating Minnesota 28 to 24. Again, it was just an exhibition, but it had only been an exhibition in 1965 when they beat us 57 to 17. This time I scored two touchdowns, but, maybe just as significant, I picked up 40 yards on a penalty when George Rose interfered with me in the third quarter. Norman Van Brocklin, the Vikings' coach, said after the game, "We don't have anyone with 9.1 speed. He's always going to get one on you. Tonight he made the two big plays and that was the game." That was for publication. I also heard that privately, Van Brocklin was all hot and bothered because I, a mere track star and nonfootball player, at least in his opinion, had humiliated his team. He planned to get even when we played the Vikings again in three weeks—no matter what they had to do to stop me. One of the writers also told me that Van Brocklin, who was legendary for his bad temper, had referred to me as "that little roadrunner." For all I know, Van Brocklin meant that as a compliment, but I didn't take it as one. I had a name: Bob Hayes. I wanted to make sure Van Brocklin kept it in mind.

Our favorite team, the Giants, visited the Cotton Bowl to open the 1966 regular season, as they had done the year before, and we served notice to the league that we were about two touchdowns better than last year. In 1965 we had opened with a 31 to 2 rout of the Giants; this time, in the Bubbles Cash game, it was 52 to 7. Too bad we could play them only twice a season.

Dandy and I barely missed connections on a bomb late in the first quarter, but it gave the Giants something to think about, in case my three touchdowns against them in two games in 1965 weren't on their minds.

Spider Lockhart, a friend of mine, was playing weak safety for the Giants. He was from Dallas, and he and I worked out together in the off-season. Spider was a skinny guy (that's how he got his nickname), but he was a hell of a football player. Still, I had him beaten on this particular play. Meredith called a fly pattern to me and when I raced downfield, past Lockhart, and looked back, the ball was in the air. I thought I was going to get it, but just before it came down in my hands, a gust of wind in the Cotton Bowl blew the ball farther and it went straight over my head. When I got back to the huddle, Dandy said to me, "Bobby, I cannot believe it. I must have taken some extra vitamins this morning." I said, "I don't know what you took, Dandy. But you sure threw that ball. Maybe your wife has been good to you."

Dandy Don and I got our act together a few minutes later. It was early in the second quarter, the Giants had tied the game at 7 on a 20-yard touchdown pass from Earl Morrall to my old track rival, Homer Jones, and we had the ball second and 4 at our 26 after the Giants kickoff. Clarence Childs, my former teammate at Florida A & M, normally played on the outside of the wide receiver, but on this play with me on the left side, he lined up inside of me, knowing that we ran a lot of inside routes by the wide receiver. Ordinarily if he lined up inside, I would run a fly pattern straight down the field and if he lined up outside, I would break across the middle. But this time, although he lined up inside, I ran an inside route. Meredith was patient, even though Clarence bumped me on the shoulder pad and threw me offstride a bit as I went by him, but as I broke by Clarence, Dandy drilled the ball to me. I caught the pass just across our 40-yard line, about a step ahead of Clarence, and then he and I ran down the middle of the field, stride for stride for stride. At about the Giants 20-yard line, I could sense that he was going to take a dive at me and I could see his shadow. When I saw his shadow move, I leapt a bit and he just grazed my heel with his fingers, right before he landed face down in the grass. I stumbled slightly, but then regained my balance and ran the rest of the way untouched for a 74-yard touchdown.

When I got to the sidelines, one of our trainers, Larry Gardner, asked me if I was worried that Clarence might catch me. "Well, you know, Clarence only ran a 9.4," I answered. Larry looked at me like I was crazy— "*Only* a 9.4?" I said, "We're both Florida boys. We can run down there." Larry just shook his head and said, "Bobby, if there's any more of those guys like you and Clarence Childs down at Florida A & M, let us know, we'll go down and sign them."

Clarence had been a senior at Florida A & M when I was a freshman. The upperclassmen did all kinds of things to haze us. They made us crawl through the dining hall and wear beanie caps all the time; at team meetings, they made us wear the jock straps that we had worn to practice that day around our necks. We were the last to eat in the dining hall and after we ate, the upperclassmen made us do push-ups. I have to admit that Clarence wasn't one of the worst at hazing us, but even so, he had to pay for what some of the others did. We met after the game, and I told him my touchdown was a payback. "Clarence," I told him, "I have a reputation as the fastest man in the world and here you are, a fellow alum. Don't you know you almost, *almost* ruined my reputation? Do you know how much exposure you would have gotten if you had run me down?" He said, "Bob, just look at it this way: It just would have been that two guys from Florida A & M are that fast instead of one."

I have that play on videotape, and every time I roll it, I think it's one of the greatest races I've ever seen. You have to remember, carrying a football will slow you down by 10 to 20 yards in the 100-yard dash, because you can't pump your arms properly, and there I was, football under my arm, and still not losing an inch to a 9.4 guy. Clarence is now dean of men at Bethune Cookman College in Daytona Beach, Florida, and he and I have kept in touch over the years. Whenever we run into each other, we discuss everything under the sun—everything except that play, which we have never mentioned since September 18, 1966.

With just over two minutes left in the half, we were ahead 17 to 7. I beat Spider again for 42 yards to the Giants' 2, and Dan Reeves scored on the next play to make it 24 to 7. After catching the pass from Dandy inside the 20, I had to zigzag all over the field to try to get away from several Giants defenders. When Spider pulled me down at the 2 and kept me from getting into the end zone, he said to me, "Well, I finally caught the fastest man in the world. Now maybe I won't get bitched at by the coaches, because I'm the one who should have stopped the play."

Two minutes can seem like forever, especially for as bad a team as the Giants. Less than a minute before halftime, Mike Gaechter intercepted a pass by Earl Morrall and was tackled at the Giants' 40. With twenty-three seconds left in the half, Dandy aimed a pass at me in the end zone, and Clarence ran up my back for pass interference. Clarence was understandably upset because of my earlier touchdown over him, and this time he played me a little too tight. The officials gave us the ball on the 1, and Meredith passed to Reeves for another touchdown that increased our lead to 31 to 7 with only ten seconds left in the half.

Even with a lead like that, we came out smoking in the second half. The Giants kicked off to us, and a few plays after that I ran a crossing route over the middle and beat Clarence and Henry Carr for a 39-yard touchdown. There was still almost half the game to play, and we were ahead, 38 to 7.

We stopped the Giants' next drive and took over at our 20. On this possession, they held me to "only" 50 yards on two catches, and Meredith threw 19 yards to Reeves for another touchdown and a 45 to 7 lead, late in the third quarter.

I had earned my paycheck that week. Two touchdowns on six receptions for 195 yards, the second best game in the Cowboys' history, behind only the 241 yards Frank Clarke had gained receiving against the Redskins in 1962. One of the local sportswriters called this game, "Dallas in Wonderland." How true.

. . .

A few days before our rematch with Minnesota the next week, Van Brocklin told the press, "Hayes is no superman. I only hope some of our players give him a rap in the mouth and we'll see how well he does." His strategy was to have one of his cornerbacks, Earsell Mackbee, work me over on nearly every play. Mackbee lined up right on my nose at the line of scrimmage and kept blocking me, hitting me with his elbow, doing everything he could to hold me up. If I got by him, the free safety would pick me up. One of the Vikings whispered to me that Van Brocklin had told Mackbee before the game, "If Hayes beats you for a touchdown I'm going to fine you because you don't have any other responsibilities today."

Their plan worked, to some extent. I caught only 2 passes for 52 yards, but one of them was a 37-yard touchdown on a post route over Mackbee that put us on the board and cut Minnesota's lead to 10 to 7, three minutes before halftime. I lined up in the slot position just behind the line of scrimmage on that play, and that gave me enough room to get downfield and into full stride. Van Brocklin said later that their secondary had made a "mistake" on the play. Good thinking, coach. I guess you could say that some defensive back makes a "mistake" on every touchdown pass.

Van Brocklin's focus on me opened up other things for our offense, and we overpowered them in the second half. Buddy Dial had a good day catching the ball, and Dan Reeves chewed up yardage on the ground. Each of us scored a touchdown, and Meredith rolled around left end for one of his own. Van Brocklin may have won, or tied, the battle with me, but the final score was 28 to 17, Dallas.

After the game I went over to Van Brocklin and said, "Coach, con-gratulations, your team played a good game today." He winced and I could tell that I had made him feel bad and let him know that I was a bigger man than he was, which was what I wanted to do. But he regained his composure and told me, "I have never before defensed a player the way I defensed you today. You have proved to me that you are a real football player." I thanked him, but then reminded him that he had called me a roadrunner and that my name was Bob Hayes. From then on, he and I had no more problems, and his remark to me about putting in a special defense for me reemphasized to me that speed was what a rival coach or player fears the most.

After a 47 to 14 rout of the Falcons, we went after our fourth win in a row against Philadelphia. Joe Kuharich, the Eagles' head coach, marched to a different drummer. I think his drummer had a mighty slow beat because

Joe was ten years or so behind the rest of the league. Instead of covering me tightly, the way Minnesota and Atlanta had, Kuharich stationed Joe Scarpati, his weak safety, way the hell downfield, kind of like a goaltender in hockey or soccer. That left the rest of the Eagles playing us 10 on 11. It didn't work.

Early in the game, with us ahead 7 to 0, we moved the ball down to the Philadelphia 24. The Eagles somehow left me wide open down the left side for a touchdown to make it 14 to 0. Three offensive plays by the Eagles, and a Sam Baker punt rolled out of bounds on our 31. It took us four plays to move to the Philadelphia 36. On the next play, Scarpati lined up about 40 yards off the line of scrimmage—it seemed like he was standing deep in the end zone when the ball was snapped. That defense wasn't working because if you look at the films of the game, you will see that after running a crossing pattern and beating Aaron Martin and Scarpati, I was all by myself in the end zone when Dandy's pass landed in my hands. I was so wide open that when we looked at the films, there were no Eagles in the picture, and you couldn't tell which team we were playing against. The score was now 21 to 0 with only forty-seven minutes left in the game.

I was pretty quiet from then until late in the third quarter, when Dandy hit me for a 15-yard gain over Jim Nettles; then came my way again with a pass that caused an interference call on Philadelphia, giving us 20 yards and a first down at the Eagles' 26; and, finally, on second and 9 from the Eagles' 12, hit me with a third pass in, or at least partially in, the end zone. Some people said I had one foot inbounds and one foot out, but none of those people were wearing striped shirts, and we didn't have the benefit of instant replay, either. The touchdown counted; the score was now 42 to 0, with four minutes to play in the third quarter.

That was the end of my day's work, and perhaps without me to inspire them, the guys on our defense let down and allowed Philadelphia to score in the fourth quarter. The final count was 56 to 7, and we set team records for most points, the biggest margin of victory, the most first downs (32), the most total offense (652 yards), and the most net yards passing (440). With three touchdown catches out of a total of 6 receptions for 107 yards, I tied a club record held by Frank Clarke, as well as the record for most touchdowns running and receiving in a single game, held by Clarke and L. G. Dupre. Dandy also tied a club record with 5 touchdowns passing. We didn't expect to see Joe Kuharich's 10-on-11 defense again.

■   ■   ■

Just looking over at the Redskins bench before a game in mid-November in Robert F. Kennedy Stadium, I knew I was going to have a great day. Who did I see there but Washington's new coach—my dear friend, Otto Graham.

Charley Taylor, a home boy from Dallas, had a sensational game. Charley caught 11 of Sonny Jurgensen's passes for 199 yards and 2 touchdowns. But Charley was only the second best receiver on the field that day; it turned out that Dallas had a wide-out who had 9-flat speed but did not have 12-flat hands!

I got going late in the second quarter, with us ahead, 7 to 6. On first and 10 from our 26, following a Redskins punt, I went 10 yards with a pass from Don Meredith before Jim Shorter ran me out of bounds. Two more plays got us to our 48, and Don's first-down pass for me was incomplete. On the next play, though, the Redskins blew their coverage, and I was all alone for a 52-yard touchdown.

The best was yet to come. The Redskins couldn't go anywhere with the second half kickoff and they had to punt. I fielded the kick and got tackled at our 10, but clipping was called against us, and we were penalized back to our 5. Because of Jethro Pugh, Don and I used to call each other "Turkey" sometimes, and in the huddle he looked at me and said, "Turkey, what do you think?" "The same thing you do, Turkey. The bomb?" "Who do you want to run it on, Bobby? Lonnie Sanders?" "Yeah," I said, "Let's run it on Sanders," and I lined up on his side of the field, the right. The chances were that the Redskins would be expecting us to run that deep in our own territory and would leave their cornerbacks to cover our wide receivers one on one. Sanders was a tall, slender back, a pretty good ballplayer, but nowhere near fast enough to stay with me, and those long legs of his made it hard for him to recover as fast as most cornerbacks. If anything, he was too tall to play the corner.

As we started to break the huddle, Don said, "Everybody else block, and I'm going to need a little more protection. I'll be throwing from the end zone, and we don't need for those guys to come in and tackle me for two points." When the ball was snapped I broke off the line, watching what Sanders would do. He didn't want to commit himself and kept waiting for me to make my move. I ran right up to him, accelerating when I was on top of him and it was too late for him to recover, and went by him at full speed, just like I was sprinting straight down a track. Don threw the ball about 50 yards, right on the money, and I was already 5 yards past Sanders when I grabbed it at midfield; Sanders didn't have a chance to catch me. When I reached the end zone and looked back upfield, though, I saw a penalty flag and thought to myself, "Oh, shit!" But the call was on the Redskins for a personal foul and the play counted, a 95-yard touchdown—to this day the longest ever for the Cowboys. Just recently, in fact, the *Dallas Times Herald* named that touchdown one of the ten greatest moments in Cowboys history.

The 95-yard play put us ahead, 21 to 6, but then the game developed into one of the most exciting we ever played. The Redskins came back to take the lead at 23 to 21 on a 4-yard pass from Jurgensen to Jerry Smith, a 78-yard Jurgensen-to-Charley Taylor touchdown, and a field goal by Charlie Gogolak. We went in front, 28 to 23, on a 1-yard run by Dan Reeves early in the fourth quarter, right after I caught a pass on a corner route for 27 yards to the Washington 3, but the Redskins refused to die. They drove 69 yards after our touchdown and regained the lead at 30 to 28 on an 18-yard pass from Sonny to Charley Taylor.

Washington stopped our next drive and took over the ball at midfield, but we forced them to punt and got the ball back on our 3-yard line, with a minute and a half left to play, no timeouts, and us two points down. I was able to distract the Redskins enough for Pete Gent to get open for receptions of 26 and 25 yards, and the Redskins helped us with a personal foul that cost them another 15. We made it to the Washington 12 with fifteen seconds left, and Danny Villaneuva stepped back to the 20 and kicked a field goal that won the game, 31 to 30.

Beating the Redskins that day was especially nice because Sam Huff and some of the other Washington defenders kept trying to make us jump offsides by calling out "hut, hut, hut" in cadence with our snap counts. That was illegal, and we complained to the referees, but they wouldn't do anything about it.

I wound up with 246 yards, which is still a Cowboys record, on 9 catches. Plus, I had the 2 touchdowns. The Associated Press named me Offensive Player of the Week in the NFL, and you didn't hear anyone saying I didn't deserve it.

The Redskins came to the Cotton Bowl for a rematch four weeks later, and Sam Huff had blood in his eye. A few days before the game, a Washington sportswriter asked Pete Gent what he thought of Sam. Pete answered, "Oh, Huff, he's old, he's fat, he's finished." During pregame warmups, all Huff would say was "Meredith! You run Gent across the middle one time for me! I'm going to kill him, and if you don't run Gent across the middle for me, I'm going to kill you!" Pete heard Huff and said, "No way am I going across the middle."

On one play in the first half, Washington lined up with a gap between our right tackle and right guard. Don Meredith called an audible for Dan Reeves or Don Perkins to run through the gap. As Meredith was calling signals, Huff stepped right into the gap. Meredith stopped his snap count and said, "Sam, would you get out of the way so we can run the play we're supposed to run." Huff said, "You go ahead and run it. I'm going to get you until you run Gent across the middle with his big mouth." Well, Meredith wouldn't give Sam a shot at Gent, and Sam was good to his word—he creamed Dandy on a blitz late in the second quarter and knocked him out. Dandy had to sit out the second half, and Craig Morton and Jerry Rhome alternated in his place.

The first half was a defensive struggle that ended with the Redskins leading, 10 to 7, but both teams opened up in the second half. Danny Villaneuva tied the score with a field goal early in the third quarter, and then we stopped the Redskins and Pat Richter punted to our 14, where I called a fair catch. We got going—I caught a 17-yard pass from Morton to the Washington 44—and then Craig threw me a quick pass in the right flat. Ralph Neely made a great block, and I went in for a 23-yard touchdown to put us ahead, 17 to 10.

When I got back to the bench, Don Perkins and J. D. Smith were standing there. J. D. was saying, "Hey, Perk, is my roommate bad? Is my roommate bad? Ain't he a bad bitch?" And Perk answered in that heavy voice of his, "Yeah, the young guy is great." I think J. D. was more excited about the touchdown than I was.

After that we started exchanging scores, and in less than one quarter, Sonny Jurgensen threw touchdowns to his three great receivers—Bobby Mitchell, Jerry Smith, and finally Charley Taylor—to tie the game, 31 to 31, with three minutes to play. Charlie Gogolak kicked off into the end zone for a touchback, and Craig Morton threw toward me on two of our next three plays. The first one was too low and the second one was too high, although it didn't matter, because Craig had already crossed the line of scrimmage and we got penalized 5 yards and the loss of a down. Danny Villaneuva punted to Rickie Harris at the Washington 46 right at the two-minute warning, and the Redskins stayed on the ground and ran the ball down to our 22. With four seconds left, Gogolak kicked a field goal to win the game for Washington.

Aside from my one touchdown, I hadn't done that much. I caught 3 passes for 52 yards and returned 1 punt for 17. At least I had my health: On one play, Rickie Harris could have smeared me when I had my head turned and didn't see him, but instead he ran up to me and went, "Boo!" Luckily for me, Rickie was a clean player; a lot of other players would have really belted me.

The most important news of the day was from the scoreboard. St. Louis and Cleveland both lost, which clinched first place for us. St. Louis could have tied us at 9–4–1 if they beat Cleveland the following week and we lost our final game to the Giants, but we would have won the division anyway, because we had beaten the Cardinals once and tied them once. Even though I hadn't had a great day and we had backed into the title, only one thing mattered: We were champions of the Eastern Division!

And so it came down to us versus the Packers for the NFL championship on New Year's Day in the Cotton Bowl. The winner would play in Super Bowl I. Vince Lombardi had said the week before the game: "We will not allow Bob Hayes to distort our defense. We have the speed and the ability in Bob Jeter and Herb Adderly to cover Hayes man to man most of the time, and we will."

Much as I respected Lombardi and the Packers, I thought the man was blowing smoke. I had beaten Adderly for two touchdowns a few months earlier in our exhibition game, and he was their best defensive back, so I went into the championship game feeling pretty confident. What I didn't know until later was that Adderley had lost ten pounds after I beat him in the exhibition game, to give himself extra speed so he could cover me.

It seemed like everything went wrong that day, right from the start. The Packers scored 2 touchdowns in twelve seconds, before our offensive unit ever got on the field. First they took the opening kickoff and drove 76 yards in 8 plays, with Bart Starr passing 17 yards to Elijah Pitts for the touchdown. Mel Renfro fielded Don Chandler's kickoff at the goal line, returned it to our 18 and fumbled. And Jim Grabowski scooped up the ball and ran in to make it 14 to 0.

Even though we were in a state of shock, we still thought we could beat the Packers. Mel held onto the next kickoff and ran off a nice return, to our 35. We got to their 34, third and 1, and instead of trying to pick up the first down, Meredith went for 6 on a bomb to me. But this was a lot different from the exhibition season. Adderley and Tom Brown were right with me, and they knocked the ball away. We decided against going for the field goal on fourth down, and Reeves picked up 4 yards over left tackle before Ray Nitschke tackled him at the 30. That put us in business with a first down, and Meredith came right to me with a quick pass in the flat. I caught the ball, but I tried to run with it before I tucked it in and the ball bounced out of my hands. I fell on it, but what should have been a big play, maybe a touchdown, gained us only 1 yard. Little did I know that that was going to be my only catch of the day.

We scored a few plays later on a 3-yard run over right tackle by Reeves, and then we came right back on our next possession and went 59 yards for another touchdown on a 23-yard run by Perk. After the way the game had started, we were all fired up, now that we had fought back into a 14–14 tie at the end of the first quarter.

But then the Packers started showing us why they were champions. They held us to two field goals, and Bart Starr threw for 2 more touchdowns to give Green Bay an 8-point lead by the time the third quarter was over.

We still might have won, except for me. The score was 28 to 20 Green Bay when Chandler got off a 54-yard punt to our goal line early in the fourth quarter. Mel Renfro was back there with me and he was yelling for me to let the ball go into the end zone, which is what I should have done. But I hadn't done anything catching passes and I knew that whenever I made a big play, it fired up the rest of the guys. I thought I could get some good yardage on the return, so I fielded the ball at our goal line, but my momentum carried me back into our end zone and I got only 1 yard out before the Packers smothered me. It was a gigantic mistake, and it cost us six points. We had to punt from our 7, and Danny Villaneuva got off a nice kick, 41 yards, but Donny Anderson called a fair catch at our 48, so Green Bay had great field position. And the Packers scored again on a 28-yard pass from Starr to Max McGee, Starr's fourth touchdown pass. The only blessing was that Bob Lilly blocked Chandler's point after, so the score was 34 to 20 Green Bay instead of 35 to 20. There were still nine minutes, forty seconds to play, and two touchdowns would tie it for us.

We had a hairy moment on our next drive when Reeves caught a pass from Meredith and fumbled it, but Meredith recovered it for a 10-yard loss to our 32. On the next play, Reeves went in motion to the right, taking Dave Robinson with him, and I took Willie Wood and Bob Jeter with me, deep down the left sideline. That left Frank Clarke open over the middle, and Meredith hit him for a 68-yard touchdown, which left us down only 34 to 27, with four minutes to play.

While the Packers had the ball, Meredith gathered the offense around him on the sideline and told us he would call two plays in every huddle.

He also told me to look for an opportunity to run an out and go; either I would be open for the tying touchdown—assuming Green Bay didn't score while we were talking—or I would take a couple of their defenders with me and someone else would be open.

The Packers picked up one first down, but then Dave Edwards sacked Bart Starr for an 8-yard loss, Willie Towns batted down one of Starr's passes, and Lee Roy Jordan made a sensational play, bringing down Jim Taylor for a loss of 7 on a swing pass. Don Chandler had to punt and he did us a big favor; the ball wobbled off his foot for only 16 yards before it went out of bounds at the Green Bay 47.

On first down, I cleared out the secondary for Frank Clarke, and he caught a pass for 21 yards to the Green Bay 26. Perk went up the middle for 4, and they stopped the clock for the two-minute warning. With second and 6 from the 22, Clarke got open again, this time in the end zone, and Dave Robinson had no choice but to interfere with Clarke.

First and goal for us at the 2, and still one minute, fifty-two seconds to play. Reeves gained a yard, but then Meredith's pass for Pettis Norman was incomplete. Worse than that, the referees said that someone on our offensive line moved before the snap; to this day, we think that if anybody jumped, it was one of the Packers. Anyway, we got penalized back to the 6. Don Meredith threw to Norman, but Tom Brown tackled him at the 2, and the whole season came down to one play.

Now it was fourth and goal at the 2, forty-five seconds left, and, for the first time all season on a goal-line play, I found myself in the lineup. Ordinarily in this situation, we would go to a two-tight end alignment, with both Frank Clarke and Pettis Norman playing instead of me. But when Pettis replaced Frank at tight end, Frank left the field instead of taking my place, and I had to stay in. I knew I wasn't supposed to be there, but if I had left the field, we would have had only ten men and would have drawn a penalty. Meredith called a rollout to his right, where he had the option of running it in or passing for a touchdown if someone was open. We had scored three touchdowns on that play during the regular season, and the Packers were ready for it. My assignment was to try to block Dave Robinson, an All-Pro who outweighed me by sixty pounds, and then drift into the end zone. I blew the block, not that I had much of a chance; Robinson just grabbed me and tossed me aside like a sack of feathers. Then he went for Meredith and got a hand on him. All Meredith could do was throw a desperation pass toward me in the end zone. For a moment, I thought I was going to catch it, but Tom Brown beat me to the ball and intercepted it in the end zone for a touchback, giving the Packers the ball on their 20. There were only twenty-eight seconds left, and all Bart Starr had to do was fall on the ball twice and the Packers won, 34 to 27.

This was the toughest loss of my life, the more so because I blamed myself. I had caught just the 1 pass for 1 yard; screwed up by catching the punt at our goal line, and then seen everything go wrong on our last play— I wasn't supposed to be on the field at all, I didn't block Robinson, and I couldn't get to Meredith's pass.

The Pro Bowl was another downer for me, even though we beat the Western Division for the second straight year, 20 to 10. Altamease went out to Los Angeles with me for the game, but she got sick and spent several days in the hospital. The game was played in a downpour; the weather was so bad, in fact, that only fifteen thousand people showed up and the coliseum seemed empty. The field was in terrible shape, I was worried about Altamease, and I just couldn't get going. Don Meredith and Frank Ryan, the Eastern Division quarterbacks, must have thrown five balls toward me that might have been touchdowns, but I couldn't catch up to them. Don kept calling plays for me; he said he wanted me to be the Most Valuable Player. But even though I started and played a good bit of the game, I didn't catch a single pass. Tom Landry, who was the Eastern Division coach, even asked me what was wrong. My mind just wasn't on the game; I couldn't stop thinking about Altamease. Here I was, a young guy, away from home, my wife in the hospital. A lot of my teammates were out there with me—nine of the twenty-two starters for the Eastern Division (nearly half the starting team) were Cowboys—and I should have shared my problems with some of them, but they were on vacation and I didn't want to mess up their fun, so I kept my thoughts to myself. Especially after my screwups against the Packers, my second Pro Bowl was one of the worst experiences of my life.

In spite of the way it ended, 1966 was a great year for the Cowboys and for me, particularly when you consider that opposing teams started double teaming me, holding me up at the line of scrimmage, fouling me, and doing everything they could to keep me from catching the ball. I made every All-Pro team, and my 64 catches were one less than the club record and fourth in the NFL that year, behind only Charley Taylor of the Redskins, Pat Studstill of Detroit, and Dave Parks of the 49ers. My 1,232 yards gained receiving set a Cowboys record and were second in the league to Studstill's 1,266, and my average gain per catch, 19.3, was second behind Homer Jones, who averaged 21.8, but had only 48 receptions and 1,044 yards. My 246-yard record in one day against the Redskins was the best any receiver in the NFL had that year. I also scored touchdowns in nine of our thirteen games; led the league in touchdowns receiving with 13, and was fourth overall in touchdowns. The Cowboys had two of the top four touchdown scorers in me and Dan Reeves; Leroy Kelly and Dan tied for the most with 16, and Charley Taylor had 15 (of which 3 were rushing). The amazing thing about Reeves was that he must have gotten run down from behind a dozen or more times. If he had had any speed, he would have easily broken the all-time record for touchdowns that Gale Sayers had set the previous year with 22. I also had a good year returning punts, 17 for 106 yards and a 6.2 average, seventh best in the league.

As for the Cowboys, not only did we win the Eastern Division with a 10–3–1 record and almost beat the Packers and nearly make it to the Super Bowl, we scored 445 points in the regular season, a team record that stood until the 1980 team, which played two more games than we did, scored 9 more points. We averaged nearly 68,000 fans a game in the Cotton Bowl during the regular season, twice as many as the team had drawn two years earlier without me, and drew another 75,000 for the championship against the Packers. We were so successful in 1966 that Clint Murchison announced during the off-season that he was going to build a brand-new stadium, just for us. So we had something else to look forward to: a great new stadium for a great young team.

When the U.S. national team, ready to leave on an international tour, couldn't find me, the *Florida Times Union* ran a headline: "HAYES—Wanted for Travel." They found me just in time. Here I am posed with my high school football coach, Earl Kitchings, on the corner where my parents lived.

Charles Sutton, one of my best friends during my first year at Florida A & M University; Jake Gaither, a great coach; and me.

Driving to the wire and winning at the 1964 Olympics in Tokyo.

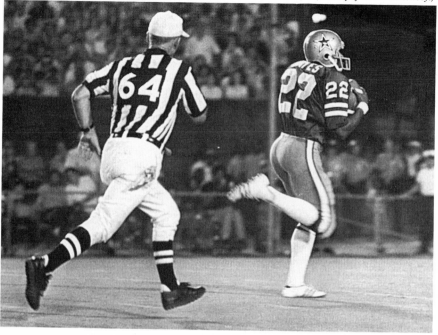

A preseason game against the Saints, and only the official has a chance of catching me.

My first wife, Altamease, inspected my badly sprained ankle after a Cleveland Brown stepped on it in 1965.

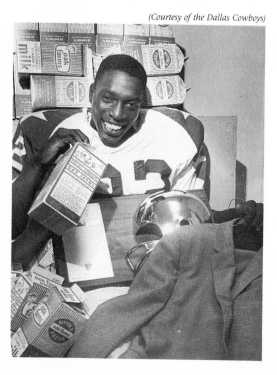

Displaying my "trophies"—a month's supply of free milk—after being named Cowboy player of the week during my rookie season.

"Run, Bobby, Run!"—one of Coach Landry's few emotional outbursts. Besides Ken Houston trying to get the angle on me, that's Mike Ditka holding the clipboard; to the right, Jim Meyers and Gene Stallings.

Coach Landry sending in a play.

I cradle the ball after catching it over Chicago Bear defensive back Joe Taylor for another of my Cowboy-record 71 touchdown receptions.

I didn't have my most stand-out games in the Super Bowl—but I'm still the only person to own both an Olympic gold medal and a Super Bowl ring. Here I am in Super Bowl VI as we beat the Miami Dolphis.

Testifying at my trial. The flag behind me felt like a whole different flag from the one I raced for at the Olympics.

Released from prison, I hug Roger
Staubach at the reunion of the
greatest Cowboys.

My second wife, Janice (mother
of Bob Hayes, Jr.), and I at a
Cowboys reunion.

9

BACK TO THE
ICE AGE

After two All-Pro seasons with the Cowboys, I was looking forward to even bigger things in 1967. We had acquired Lance Rentzel in an off-season trade with Minnesota, and for the first time we would have a third outstanding receiver (Frank Clarke was the second one) to take some of the pressure off me.

I got off to a good start in the regular-season opener in Cleveland, which we approached as probably the biggest game on our schedule. The New Orleans Saints had entered the league as an expansion team, and the Eastern Conference had been split into two divisions, with us, the Redskins, the Eagles, and the Saints in the Capitol Division, and the Browns, the Giants, the Cardinals, and the Pittsburgh Steelers in the Century Division. We didn't figure to have much competition in our division, and the experts were predicting that we would be facing the Browns again in December for the Eastern Division championship.

With three seconds left in the first quarter of our opening game, I made sure I would be back on the scoreboard this season. On first and 10 from the Cleveland 25, John Brewer, the Cleveland linebacker on the left side where I was, lined up to the inside of Bill Glass, the defensive end, which indicated a blitz was coming. Don Meredith called an audible, a quick screen to me, and it worked like a charm—easy catch, good blocking, no problem going all the way for a touchdown. That tied the game, 7 to 7.

I almost scored again on our next play from scrimmage. We had stopped Cleveland on downs early in the second period, and on first and 10 from our 30, Meredith aimed a bomb my way. Mike Howell had a good shot at intercepting it for the Browns, but all he did was tip it, and it came down in my hands for a 50-yard gain to their 20. But Meredith's pass for Reeves in the end zone two plays later was intercepted by Ross Fichtner. We took the lead for good on our next series, when Meredith connected with Reeves for a 17-yard touchdown, and we went on to win, 21 to 14. I got off humming, with 5 catches for 125 yards (our total passing attack was 205 yards) and the touchdown.

Our home opener was against our favorite patsies, the Giants, and they didn't disappoint us. This year they arrived with a rookie cornerback, Scott Eaton, and a rookie linebacker, Freeman White, for us to feast on. Though the Giants got off to a 10 to 0 lead, I came up with some late first-quarter magic for the second week in a row. After I made a fair catch of Ernie Koy's short punt at the Giants' 43, Don Meredith called a bomb to me on the first play. We used play action to freeze Spider Lockhart at free safety, and I ran right by Spider and caught the ball in stride for a 43-yard touchdown, this time with four seconds left in the quarter.

It was still a fairly close game, with us ahead 28 to 17, as we entered the fourth quarter. But our favorite little swing pass from Meredith to me worked for a 20-yard touchdown to ice the game at 35 to 17 with nine and a half minutes to play. We went on to win 38 to 24, and my totals were 4 catches for 118 yards and 2 touchdowns. My old track rival, Homer Jones, matched me with 2 touchdowns for the Giants, but the Giants didn't have anyone else. Homer scored on a 52-yard pass from Fran Tarkenton and on a 46-yard end around. I'll never forget that run: Homer went by our guys like they were standing still. What a big, fast athlete he was—the fastest for his size I had ever seen. After the game, though, Homer made a comment that would come back to haunt me at the end of the season: "If we [meaning he and I] were to run a race on a football field in uniform for a hundred yards and Hayes were to cross the goal line, I'd at least be right there patting him on the back."

I caught a touchdown pass for the third straight week, a 4-yarder late in the third quarter against George Allen's Rams, but it didn't help much. Los Angeles beat us, 35 to 13, and we made it easy for them with 4 turnovers. My only other catch was for 14 yards, and my 18 yards total was one of my lowest ever.

The game was kind of an anticlimax after what had happened the previous week. Every day while we practiced, we noticed a yellow Chevrolet parked near our practice field. Someone in the Cowboys organization finally checked the license plate, and it turned out to belong to Hertz, which had rented it to Johnny Sanders, the chief scout for the Rams. George Allen—Richard Nixon with a whistle around his neck, as he was known in the NFL—was at it again. We complained to the NFL that George was spying on our practices, which was a no-no, but the league couldn't prevent George from using anything he had learned from Sanders when he put together his game plan. About the same time, they built a high-rise hotel behind our practice field, and after the Johnny Sanders incident, the Cowboys rented all the rooms facing our practice field to keep rival scouts from snooping on us.

That wasn't the only car trouble we had that week. One night, Don Meredith went to Casa Dominguez, a Mexican restaurant in downtown Dallas, and left the keys in the ignition of his brand-new Camaro. Someone stole the car, along with his playbook, which cost him a fine of $500. Tom Landry had a hard-and-fast rule: Every day when you came to our team meeting, you had to have your playbook. If you didn't have your playbook, no matter how good your story was, you could say good-bye to $500.

Even though we were 4 and 1 and in first place, Tom Landry got on my case before we played Pittsburgh. He pointed out that I had caught a total of 5 passes for 63 yards in our three previous games—the loss to the Rams and close wins over the Redskins and Saints—and we had averaged only 2 touchdowns a game. One of my nicknames was "Bullet Bob," and the newspaper headlines called me "The Missing Bullet." Landry said he expected more production out of me; for that matter, so did I.

As was usually the case, criticism lit a fire under me. Late in the first quarter, with first and 10 at the Dallas 45, I ran a deep turn-in, faked out Brady Keys, and caught a bomb from Craig Morton on the Pittsburgh 18. I ran in for a 55-yard touchdown, the first score of the game.

Brady tried to play me tough after that. Toward the end of the half, on third and 4 from the Steelers' 35, he knocked me down as I started my pass route. But I got up, kept running, and Craig found me for another touchdown, which put us ahead, 14 to 0.

The Steelers made a comeback, but we held on to win, 24 to 21, and I had 170 of our 297 yards passing on 7 receptions. This was the fifth out of six games in which either Lance or I had over 100 yards receiving, and our offense was going on all cylinders, no matter who the quarterback was.

Our game in Philadelphia was the closest thing we had to a "crucial" game all year. Going into the game, we were 5 and 1 and the Eagles were in second place, two games behind us at 3 and 3. If we won, we would have just about clinched the division crown, halfway through the season; a loss by the Cowboys would let the Eagles back into the race.

I had another good day, accounting for 131 yards, nearly half our total offense, on 6 catches, but it wasn't enough. Philadelphia jumped out to a 21 to 0 lead midway through the second period, and we couldn't catch up. I helped get us back in the game with a couple of catches for 22 yards on a drive that ended with a 15-yard touchdown pass from Craig Morton to Lance Rentzel right before halftime, and Craig and I connected for a 64-yard touchdown in the third quarter. Craig threw me a short toss along the sideline, and Aaron Martin, Joe Scarpati, and an Eagle linebacker were waiting for me when I caught the ball. Martin grabbed me around the waist as I made the catch, but I knocked his hand off, juked around Scarpati and the third Eagle, and was gone.

My touchdown made it 21 to 14 Philadelphia with twenty-two minutes still to play, but there was no more scoring after that—in part, because Morton threw two of his three interceptions with the game on the line. He had also fumbled on our 24-yard line in the second period to set up an Eagles touchdown. So Philadelphia was still alive, one game behind us.

I should have been feasting on the expansion clubs, but the Saints had my number for the second straight time. I had a grand total of 1 catch for 15 yards, plus 31 yards on 3 punt returns. One reason the Saints closed me down was that they kept getting penalized for pass interference against me, and one of those penalties, on my former teammate Obert Logan, kept our drive alive for the go-ahead touchdown in the second quarter. Even without me contributing much to our offense, we won, 27 to 10, to make our record 7 and 2. The Eagles lost again, so we were now three games up on them with five to play.

Glad as I was that we won, the New Orleans fans overshadowed the game for me. They were a crazy bunch to begin with, and Al Hirt, a part-owner of the team, stirred them up even worse with blasts on that horn of his. At one point, their fans got upset over a call and started booing so loud they held the game up for ten minutes. To get onto the field at Tulane Stadium, we had to make our way past some concession stands and through a bunch of fans, and the rowdiest group of people always seemed to be sitting where we had to go. We had been the hometown team before the Saints joined the NFL, and now we were the villains. Coach Landry told us to be sure to wear our helmets instead of carrying them in our hands as we came on and off the field so the fans couldn't hurt us if they threw anything at our heads.

New Orleans, of course, was in the heart of the racist South, and two incidents that occurred during our visit reminded me that Louisiana hadn't yet joined the twentieth century. After our plane landed, I went to the airport gift shop to buy some magazines to read in my room. A nice-looking blond boy, about ten or eleven years old, was standing next to me, and I said to him, "Do you see a *Sports Illustrated?*" He looked up at me and answered, "I don't talk to your kind." I thought to myself, "Wow, in this day and age!"

Then, during pregame warmups, I noticed a homemade sign at the top of the stadium. Dandy Don Meredith and I were tossing a ball back and forth, and I pointed out the poster to him. Some of the locals apparently objected to the fact that Don and I, a white man and a black man, were close friends; the sign showed a white guy wearing jersey number 17 (Don's) and a black player with jersey number 22 (mine) with nooses around their necks. This was only three years after James Earl Chaney, Andrew Goodman, and Michael Schwerner—the three civil rights workers, two whites and one black—were lynched in Mississippi, the next state, and I didn't appreciate that poster at all. If the Saints' organization had had any class, they would have had their security people destroy it, but they did not.

I had gone without a touchdown for three games in a row, but that Thanksgiving, I got back on the scoreboard on national television against St. Louis. Nine minutes into the game, we were tied, 7 to 7, when Chuck Latourette of St. Louis got off a 50-yard punt that I fielded at our 39. I broke through the first wave of St. Louis tacklers around the 40, but then I saw a huge Cardinal coming after me. I ducked my head, and he barely hit me on the top of my helmet with his forearm, which spun me around. That actually got me free from several Cardinals who had me all lined up, and I broke loose, with nobody but Latourette between me and the goal line. I cut toward the sideline to use more of the field and outran him easily for a 69-yard touchdown. That was my first punt return for a touchdown as a Cowboy; it tied the club record for longest punt return and was the first time a Cowboy had gone all the way with a punt in three years.

St. Louis hung tough for a while, and we were ahead by only 17 to 14 with four minutes to play in the half. That's when Cornell Green intercepted a pass from Jim Hart at our 13 and ran it back 28 yards to the 41. As Cornell came off the field, I went up to him and said, "You know we could have beaten a lot of teams worse than we did if you and Mike Gaechter could just catch the ball. Your hands are so bad, you ought to carry a pistol." I wonder how the hell he could have been a basketball player with those hands. Cornell told me to get my ass on the field and see if I couldn't catch one myself, and I did, on the next play. Don Meredith threw me a quick pop on the left, the Cardinals cornerback slipped down, and I took off. Fifty-nine yards later, we were ahead 23 to 14 (Danny Villaneuva's kick was too low).

I caught another touchdown pass from Don, this one for 34 yards, to put us up by 37 to 14 late in the third quarter, and we went on to win in a rout, 46 to 21. I had a great day, with three touchdowns and 220 total yards gained—110 on 4 catches, 93 on 4 punt returns, and 17 on 1 kickoff—and my teammates made my day by awarding me a game ball.

For the first time in my career with the Cowboys, we played a regular-season game against Baltimore and John Unitas. We had faced them in our final exhibition game that year and Unitas had looked great, leading the Colts to a 33–7 rout, but this time was for keeps. A Unitas-to-Raymond Berry pass gave the Colts a 10 to 0 lead five minutes into the second period, but a little while later, we went to work. We backed the Colts up near their goal line, forced them to punt, and took over at the Baltimore 47. Don Perkins carried twice for 12 yards, and then Meredith called for me to run a deep pattern. Rick Volk was the safety, and I could see by the way he was set that he was expecting me to go deep. But I had the option of running a corner or a post route. Lenny Lyles was also covering me, and I knew that if I ran a corner, he would drop back and possibly make an interception, so I headed for the right post. Volk saw it coming and leaped as high as he could. But Don Meredith's pass was just over his fingers. I caught it on the 2, went into the end zone for a 35-yard touchdown, and then ran out of the end zone into some ice that sent me skidding into the bleachers in the open end of the horseshoe in Baltimore's Memorial

Stadium. That made it 10 to 7 Baltimore, with five minutes left in the half, and on Baltimore's first play from scrimmage, Dave Edwards batted a Unitas pass into the air, intercepted it, and returned it all the way, 26 yards, to give us the lead, 14 to 10.

We extended our lead by three points in the third quarter, but we should have had four more. The Colts had a second and 6 at their 46 when Tony Lorick took a handoff from Unitas and Bob Lilly took Lorick. Lorick fumbled, and Willie Townes recovered and started making like a running-back. A very slow runningback. Willie got 17 yards to the Colts' 29 before he was pulled down—and guess who made the tackle? John Unitas. Willie had four blockers in front of him, so he got pulled down by a quarterback who weighed a hundred pounds less than him. He never lived it down. Willie was one of those guys who harrassed everybody, all in fun, and after Unitas tackled him, he didn't want to come back to our bench. He wanted to head straight for the dressing room, take his shower, and get out of there before we could hit on him. We got to the 10 after Willie's return, and Danny Villaneuva kicked a 17-yard field goal, so we were ahead, 17 to 10.

We were still leading, 17 to 16, after two fourth-quarter field goals by Lou Michaels, but Unitas led the Colts on one of their famous two-minute drills, and they went ahead, 23 to 17, with a minute and a half left, on a 2-yard run by Lenny Moore. After catching just 2 passes for 42 yards all day, I had a chance to match my old hero Lenny, fourth-quarter touchdown for fourth-quarter touchdown, when Meredith threw me a Hail Mary pass on fourth and 18 from our 27, but Alvin Haymond batted it away deep in Colts territory, and we lost.

In spite of the defeat, we clinched the division championship. The Redskins had won two of their last three games to get back in the race, and they and the Eagles each went into that week one game under .500 and three games behind us. One of them would have been eliminated even if we lost, but the amazing thing was that they eliminated each other, playing to a 35–35 tie. The best either of them could finish now, with two games left, was one game over .500, and even after losing to Baltimore to make our record 8 and 4, the worst we could finish was 8 and 6.

We finished out the regular season with a 24–16 loss to the 49ers in San Francisco. Gil Brandt spent the whole day lying low. We had beaten the 49ers in an exhibition game four months earlier in San Francisco, and the game had ended in a brawl. Gary Lewis, a 49er runningback, had been elbowing Bob Lilly in the face all day, and on the last play of the game, Bob punched Lewis. Then George Andrie, Walt Garrison, and Dan Reeves got going with Ed Beard, a 49er linebacker, and some of the other 49ers. Gil was on the sidelines as the game ended, and he ran out on the field and kicked and kneed Beard, just like Gil was a football player. There was Gil, a lot smaller than Beard, not half as mean, with no uniform, attacking Beard. Beard went out of his mind, and players on both squads had to hold him away from Gil. (I was looking for one of the 49ers kickers or George Mira or someone like that.) After things settled down, I found myself walking off the field next to Beard, and he said to me, "Bobby, if I ever see that Gil Brandt again and catch up to him, I'm going to kick his ass."

I had been looking forward to our return trip to San Francisco because I was walking through Haight-Ashbury on my way to Kezar Stadium before our game in August and I saw hippies making love on the floor of several of the shops. I was just a country boy from Florida; I had never seen anything like that before.

Christmas came a day early for me in 1967. The playoff game against Cleveland in the Cotton Bowl on Christmas Eve was probably my best game as a Cowboy, or at least my best game with money on the line. I handled the ball 8 times and gained 285 yards—over 35 yards each time. When folks think of me as a superstar in the NFL, this game has a lot to do with it. My performance wasn't wasted, either; the final score was Dallas 52, Cleveland 14, the most one-sided conference playoff game in NFL history. Tom Landry said it was "our greatest game ever, considering the strength of the opponents and how much depended on the game."

We scored on an 80-yard march off the opening kickoff on a short pass to Craig Baynham from Don Meredith. The game developed into a punting duel after that; Cleveland punted, we punted, they punted. On their second punt, Gary Collins kicked it 47 yards to me at our 23. I got into the clear and almost went all the way, but Gary had the angle on me and pulled me down at the Browns' 13 after a 64-yard return. We scored four plays later on a 4-yard plunge off right tackle by Don Perkins to go ahead 14 to 0 late in the first quarter.

Then we blocked a field goal from Lou Groza early in the second quarter and took over at our 10. Baynham ran up the middle for 4, and the Browns showed blitz on second and 6 at our 14. Meredith saw a blitz coming, called an audible for me to go deep, and hit me in stride right in front of the Cowboys' bench. Mike Howell of the Browns was a mile or so behind me as I coasted the rest of the way for an 86-yard touchdown that made the score 21 to 0.

The score was 24 to 7 in our favor early in the third period, when I beat Ross Fichtner for 46 yards to the Cleveland 5. One of the Browns got a little frustrated over what I was doing to his team and piled on while they were making the tackle, which cost the Browns another 3 yards to their 2. It took us four plays to go the two yards, but on fourth and goal from the 1, Baynham went over left guard to make it 31 to 7.

That was still the score a few series later, when we held the Browns at their 24 and Collins had to kick to me again. This time, his punt went 46 yards downfield in the air and 68 yards back upfield in my arms. Gary kept me out of the end zone again, downing me at the Cleveland 2 when I ran out of gas. I tried to leap over him, but he got me for the second time. While we were lying on the ground, Gary teased me: "Bobby Hayes, you're supposed to be the world's fastest human, and I've caught you twice." Getting tackled by Gary wasn't so embarrassing because he wasn't just a punter; he was a fine receiver and a hell of an athlete. We turned my runback into another touchdown, a 1-yard run by Perkins, to make it 38 to 7 with three and a half minutes left in the third quarter. I took the rest of the day off—no sense risking another injury with Green Bay just ahead.

My output for the day was 144 yards on 5 receptions and 141 more yards on 3 punt returns. Dave Brady of the *Washington Post* observed that I "turned the Dallas-Cleveland Eastern Conference playoff into maybe the worst mismatch since Moshe Dayan promised the Israelis he would keep an eye out for the Arabs [in the Six-Day War the previous June]. Hayes spread panic among the Browns. He even did a dance that humiliated a Cleveland defender [linebacker John Brewer], who could not even close a tackling gap a yard away on what looked like TV 'stop-action.' "

Amen!!

I'll tell you how cold it was on the last day of 1967 in Green Bay when we played the Packers for the NFL championship, in the game that came to be known as "The Ice Bowl." After the Packers scored a last-minute touchdown, I ran onto the field for the extra-point attempt. Not only was I not on our kick-blocking team, but I ran toward the Green Bay huddle—and I certainly wasn't on the Packers' kicking team. I was so cold that I literally could not think any longer, and a couple of my teammates had to help me off the field. I almost passed out from the cold three or four times.

None of us was too thrilled to begin with about having to play in Green Bay. When you get off the plane and ride through the Wisconsin countryside in late December, everything is so cold and dark that it's like the end of the world. After the big city, here we were in this little nothing town. On the way from the airport to our hotel, the Holiday Inn in Appleton, Wisconsin, the busdriver insisted on giving us a tour of downtown Appleton. Mike Gaechter yelled, "Get us to the hotel!" We don't want to take a sightseeing tour in Appleton! If you want to give us a tour, take us to Hawaii! Take us to Europe!"

The weather was chilly, but still bearable, when we worked out at Lambeau Field the day before the game. Vince Lombardi had had some heat pipes installed under the grass, and he assured everyone that the field would be playable, no matter how cold it got. And when we practiced that Saturday, the field did seem okay, the temperature was about 20 degrees, and I even worked up a little sweat.

Sunday was entirely different. I woke up about 7 A.M. when I heard a dog barking and someone walking downstairs and asked, "What's the temperature out there?" A woman answered, "Ten below zero." I jumped straight out of bed and tried to look out the window, but it was covered with ice. I could just see well enough to spot Mike Gaechter in the middle of the pool standing on the ice. I thought, "I'm from Florida, and here it is ten below. What the hell am I doing here?"

The first time I actually got to feel how cold it was was when we walked out of the motel to get on our bus. As we were riding to the stadium, I said to no one in particular, "I'm freezing to death on this bus, so what am I going to feel like on the field? How are we going to play football in this mess?" On top of everything else, I had had problems with my tonsils all season, which made it harder for me to breathe in weather like that. My tonsils were removed a few weeks later.

When we reached the stadium, the team owners, the family members, and the rest of our entourage were in the locker room putting on sweats under their clothes. Tom Landry took the field wearing a fur-lined hunter's cap over the hood of his sweater and an overcoat. I can't blame Tom, but those of us who had to go out there and play couldn't dress like that. And this was before wide receivers wore gloves anytime the temperature fell below 80 degrees. Do you remember that Monday-night game between the Rams and the Redskins in Washington in 1987 with the temperature in the fifties? Art Monk of the Redskins was wearing gloves, and he proved what I have always believed—that gloves aren't worth a damn for a wide receiver, except under conditions like those we played in Green Bay. Monk dropped two passes in the end zone that would have won that game for the Redskins as time ran out; I think those gloves cost the Redskins the game. But in 1967 nobody except linemen who didn't handle the ball wore gloves. Some of the guys who played the skills positions, the running-backs and receivers, asked Landry if we could wear gloves that day. He said the runningbacks could as long as they didn't fumble the ball, but the receivers couldn't because he didn't think we'd be able to catch passes with gloves on. We didn't have hoods to wear over our heads, either, like the ones sprinters first wore in the 1988 Olympics in Seoul to cut down wind resistance—the kind the players wore in the 1988 NFC championship in Chicago between the Bears and the 49ers. Well, the wind-chill factor in Chicago for that game was minus 26, but in Green Bay in 1967, it was about minus 40, with a temperature of minus 20 and wind speed of 15 miles an hour.

There was almost dead silence in the locker room as we got dressed for the game. There's enough pressure on players for a championship game, but we could hardly think about the game because of the weather. It was just, "Let's get this over with as fast as we can, let us survive, I hope we win." It was so cold when we took the field that our noses ran and the mucus stuck to the mustaches of those players who had them. Vince Lombardi had said the ground would be heated to 52 degrees, so Cornell Green said, "If that's the case, I'm going to lay down on the ground; it'll be warmer than standing up." In the stands all the fans looked like Vikings, with their hoods and ski masks. But they couldn't even drink coffee to keep warm because the coffee froze as soon as it was poured into the cups.

The field was like a sheet of ice. It was so slippery that I could hardly get off the line of scrimmage, let alone make a cut. Sometimes, as we broke the huddle, we would slip down before we could even get up to the line. This was the coldest it had ever been for a championship game, and Coach Landry said he thought they should have postponed it. He was right, and I don't say that because we lost. It wasn't a fair test of the two teams. But the truth is that it was worse for us, not only because we were from the South and the Packers were used to it, but because we had a more diver-sified offense. We relied on the pass more than they did, but that day we just about had to abandon our passing attack and rely mostly on our ground game.

Ironically, the Packers jumped us early with their passing. To repeat, Bart Starr and his receivers had played and practiced in cold weather a lot more than we had. Starr threw two touchdown passes to Boyd Dowler, and the Packers led 14 to 0 three minutes into the second quarter. We got on the scoreboard with four minutes left in the half, when Willie Townes knocked the ball out of Starr's hands and George Andrie picked it up and went 7 yards for a touchdown. Then Phil Clark recovered a fumbled punt and Danny Villaneuva kicked a 21-yard field goal with 32 seconds left in the half, to bring us to within 14 to 10.

Danny Reeves hit Lance Rentzel on an option pass for 50 yards and a touchdown on the first play of the fourth quarter, which gave us the lead, 17 to 14, and set the stage for one of the most famous finishes of all time. Neither team could score until Green Bay made us punt and took over at their 32 with four minutes, fifty seconds to play. They went down the field, using flat passes and runs by Chuck Mercein and Donny Anderson, until they had a first and goal at our 1 with thirty seconds left. We stopped them twice, which left them on our 1 with sixteen seconds to play and no time-outs remaining. They could have kicked a field goal, and then, God help us, we would have gone to sudden-death overtime, but the Packers elected to go for the win. Starr surprised the hell out of us by sneaking it in over right guard, and that was that—21 to 17 Green Bay. For the second year in a row, they were on their way to the Super Bowl, and we were on our way to the bars and the golf courses. Ernie Stautner, one of our assistant coaches, said the quarterback sneak was a dumb play because if the Packers had failed, the clock would have run out before they could have gotten their field-goal team in on fourth down. But, as Landry said, "It was a dumb call, but now it's a great play."

I was limited to 16 yards on 3 catches, all in the first half, and none of them led to any points for us. But I still tied Reeves for the team lead in receptions; we gained only 109 yards total through the air, and 50 of those yards came on the option pass from Reeves to Rentzel. Meredith was only 10 of 25 for 59 yards, no touchdowns, and 1 interception—but who could blame him?

In the dressing room afterwards, we had to get people with warm hands to unbutton our uniforms because we had no feeling in our hands. I had to run water on my hands for fifteen minutes to get the feeling back. George Andrie, Jethro Pugh, and Mel Renfro were treated for frostbite, and our team physicians said they were afraid that some of us might have suffered exposure or lung damage, but at least we had no permanent injuries. We did have to take showers in cold water because our bodies were so cold that hot water would have peeled our skin off. Our legs were stiff and the blood had stopped circulating properly; it was just the coldest I have ever been.

Some of the experts said those two championship games we played with the Packers in 1966 and 1967 were two of the best games ever. Maybe so, but not if you were on the losing side.

I went to the Pro Bowl in Los Angeles for the third year in a row, and this time I accomplished something during the game. But I also got involved in a big controversy with Glenn Davis, the 1946 Heisman Trophy winner from Army who was director of the Pro Bowl, and I never got invited to the Pro Bowl again. Even though I know that the players and coaches vote on who makes the Pro Bowl, I have wondered ever since if there was a connection between my argument with Davis and my failure to make the Pro Bowl, because I had several outstanding seasons after 1967.

Glenn Davis called me a week or so before the game and asked me if I would race Homer Jones of the Giants at halftime. His proposal was that we would run in full uniforms and carry footballs. Any of the other Pro Bowl players could enter the race, and Davis was offering $500 for first place, $300 for second place, $200 for third place, and $100 for fourth place. The Pro Bowl had drawn a crowd of only 15,000 the year before, largely because of terrible weather, and Davis wanted to make this year's game a big attraction. Davis certainly had a good idea, I give him credit for that. It was just three years after the Tokyo Olympics and at the start of another Olympic year. I was the defending gold medalist in the 100-meters, and a race with me in it would have gotten plenty of attention.

I told Davis I would think about it. A few days later, I decided not to run. Homer had been a world-class sprinter in college and he had had several shots at me in the 100 then, but he had never beaten me. No disrespect to Homer Jones, but I knew who the fastest runner in the world was, and so did Homer. I had earned the title of world's fastest human by beating him and every other challenger, culminating in Tokyo. And I didn't want to risk losing my title for $500. If I had run that day and Homer or anyone else had beaten me—and the race would have been on national television at halftime—a lot of folks might remember that to this day. Instead, everywhere I go, I'm still the world's fastest human. Would I have raced Homer and the rest of them for more money? Yes, but it would have had to be for a lot more than $500. Davis would have had to add a zero or two to his offer.

Anyway, after deciding I wouldn't run, I called Davis to tell him. He wasn't there, so I left a message that I had called, but he never returned my call. Meanwhile, he went ahead and announced to the press that I had agreed to race Homer and all comers from the Pro Bowl squads at halftime. Davis also told the press that Homer had beaten me once in the 100-yard dash when we were in college, which wasn't true, although he had beaten me in the 220 at the 1962 NAIA meet in Sioux Falls.

I caught up with Glenn Davis when I arrived in Los Angeles a few days before the game. I told him I had tried to reach him, and he apologized for not calling me back; he said he had been too busy making arrangements for the game, which was understandable. Then I told him I had decided not to run, and he went crazy. "You told me you would do it!" he shouted at me. "No, I didn't!" I yelled back. "I told you I would think about it." "You're a liar!" he screamed, and then he threw down the notebook he was carrying and tried to hit me, but there were other people there and they got between us.

Then Davis made his second mistake. He went to the East head coach and asked him to try to talk me into running. The coach came to me and said, "Glenn said you told him you would run, and I think you ought to do it." The trouble was, the head coach was Otto Graham, and anything he had to say didn't mean much to me. I told him, "Otto Graham, you and Glenn Davis can both go to hell. I came out here to play in the Pro Bowl, not to run in a track meet, and that's what I'm going to do."

At least the whole trip wasn't that grim. Redd Foxx invited the players from both Pro Bowl squads to his nightclub on Sunset Boulevard. I had met Redd several times before, and we were buddies. When he came out on the stage he looked out into the audience and yelled, "Bob Hayes, you and all the Dallas Cowboys, you all get in back, I want the world champion Green Bay Packers to sit up front." Everybody enjoyed it.

The way the Pro Bowl turned out, I had to do a lot more than my share anyhow. Ernie Koy of the Giants was supposed to do the punting for us, but he hurt his ankle in practice a day or two before the game. He played runningback in the Pro Bowl in spite of his injury and had a good game, in fact, but his ankle was too sore for him to punt. So at our last practice, Charley Taylor, Chuck Howley, and I had a tryout to see who would have the opportunity to embarrass himself on Sunday. I won, or, to be more accurate, I lost. Anyway, I outkicked Taylor and Howley, which meant I would be doing the punting on Sunday.

When we got to the coliseum on Sunday, the wind was blowing up a storm. I was punting during warmups, but the ball wasn't going anywhere, so I told Howley, "Okay, Chuck, I'm turning it over to you." He wouldn't go for it, though; he said I already won the punting job fair and square.

When I dropped back for my first punt in the opening period, I looked up toward the line of scrimmage, and there was Deacon Jones staring at me from the West side of the line and licking his chops. And Lem Barney, the cornerback from the Lions, was yelling, "We know what Hayes is going to do. He's going to run. We're going to kill you, Bob!"

Punters like to get the ball way high so that the guys covering the kick have lots of time to get downfield under the ball. My first punt was plenty high—high and straight up. It landed only 6 yards past the line of scrimmage, giving the West the ball at our 28-yard line. The West scored its first touchdown a few plays later on a 4-yard run by Les Josephson of the Rams. My next punt, in the second quarter, was a lot better. More than twice as good, in fact. It went 14 yards, and pretty soon the West scored again, on a 39-yard pass from Roman Gabriel to Mel Farr of Detroit. And there wasn't much of a rush on me on either of those punts. My story was that my line did *too good* a job of blocking, so I had too much time to think about my kicks and shanked both of them.

After that I got it going a little bit. My next two punts went 34 and 47 yards, and then I really got off a boomer. From midfield I kicked the ball way into the end zone, but we were penalized for having too many men on the field—see what I mean about my teammates letting me down?—and I only got 38 yards on the rekick. I wound up with a 25.2 average on 5 punts.

I was also the game's leading receiver, with 6 catches for 84 yards, one of them a 45-yarder that set up one of our two touchdowns. We lost, 38 to 20, but we drew over fifty-three thousand fans, and I think everyone, fans and players, had fun. The crowd gave me a huge ovation every time I punted, especially on my longer punts. Afterwards, one of the sportswriters who voted for "Back of the Game" named me on his ballot. His theory was that "Hayes starred for both teams." So who beat me out for the Back of the Game award? Gale Sayers. I just could not shake that dude.

When I got back to Dallas after the Pro Bowl, I found myself in the middle of some more controversy. After the championship game, some of the Packers had said that they could tell when we were running the ball because I had my hands inside my waistband to try to keep them warm.

Sounds great, but the three times I caught a pass, my hands were in my pants when I started out and I still caught the ball.

The Packers' claim that I was tipping off our plays drew a lot of attention in the Dallas press, but I hadn't heard about it in Los Angeles. Clint Murchison called me into his office when I got back from the Pro Bowl and told me not to worry about the criticism and just try to do my best. He said, "Next time, try not to put your hands in your pants," and I finally had to tell him, "Mr. Murchison, I'm sorry, but I don't know what you're talking about." He explained the situation to me and told me to ignore what people were saying because some folks would look for any excuse to make you look bad. Mr. Murchison was a prince of a guy, and he looked out for me from the day I signed with the Cowboys in 1964 until the day he died in 1987.

I wound up the 1967 season almost dead even with Lance Rentzel for the team lead in pass catching. Lance had 58 catches for 996 yards, a 17.2 average, and 8 touchdowns. I caught 49 balls for 998 yards, a 20.4 average, and 10 touchdowns. If Lance and I had gained just 6 more yards between us, we both would have hit the 1,000-yard mark. I finished fourteenth in the league in receptions, fourth in yardage, fourth in average per catch, and fourth in touchdowns receiving. I was also among the league's leaders in punt returns, with the most yardage, 276 on 24 returns, and the second-best average, 11.5. My 69-yard punt return for a touchdown against St. Louis was also the second-longest punt return in the league that year and one of only four that went all the way for a touchdown. The *Sporting News* named me to its All-Pro team for the third year in a row.

It had been another good year for me—Tom Landry said after reviewing the season that I was still the Cowboys' game breaker—and for the team as well. We hadn't made it to the Super Bowl, but we had come close. And there was always next year.

10

A "FAT MAN" WHO STILL COULD FLY

Ever since college, when I became the World's Fastest Human, the banquet circuit had been a big part of my life. Sports fans, business leaders, black people—a lot of folks wanted to meet me and hear what I had to say about athletics and life. After I became a star in the NFL, as well in the track world, the invitations poured in faster than ever. I generally made several dozen appearances a year, most of them in the off-season, while I was with the Cowboys, going to awards banquets sponsored by groups like the Touchdown Club in Washington, D.C., high schools, boys' clubs, and many others. The food definitely wasn't the attraction; it was often half-cooked roast beef or something equally unappetizing. I got paid for some of my appearances, but I went to a lot of them just to be a good citizen.

When I went to small cities and towns throughout Texas—places like Greenville, Commerce, Athens, and Waco—the most interesting thing about these banquets as far as I was concerned was that they would roll out the red carpet for me because I was Bob Hayes, Cowboys star and Olympic champion. But if I had passed through some of those towns back in the mid- to late sixties as just an ordinary black man, I would have been in trouble. The police officers who escorted me around those towns and guarded my hotel rooms would have run me out of town or tried to put me in jail if I had not been a sports hero.

. . .

I was ten pounds overweight, after a busy off-season on the banquet circuit, when I reported to Thousand Oaks for our 1968 training camp, and I was assigned to sit at the Fat Man's Table in the dining hall. My dining partners were Don Meredith and Ralph Neely; Tom Landry had decided to make examples of three of the biggest stars on the team (and I don't mean big as in overweight). It only took me a few days to get down to my playing weight, 185, what with two-a-day workouts in the hot sun and our diet, which was pretty much limited to fruits, vegetables, orange juice, and water. My gut wasn't hanging over my belt to begin with, but Willie Townes, who had done a much longer sentence at the Fat Man's Table the year before, gave me the most grief. Every time he saw me, he piped up, "There's Fat Bob Hayes." Willie was feeling real cocky because he had reported at his prescribed weight for once.

Right away I found that the Cowboys had made a change that was to my liking. Raymond Berry had retired from the Colts a few months earlier, and we signed him as an assistant coach in charge of the wide receivers. When the team announced that it was hiring Berry, Tom Landry used the opportunity for his annual put-Bob Hayes-down speech to the press: "Bob Hayes hasn't even started to fake. He uses his speed alone to do almost everything. If Berry gives Hayes two or three moves, there's no way you can cover him with one man." I guess Tom had spent the whole off-season looking at our game films without noticing that the opposition already was double covering me on nearly every play. And I always felt that my moves were a lot better than I had been given credit for, but people usually focused on my speed and assumed I didn't have the moves, or the hands, for that matter. A lot of sprinters before me had proved by failing in the NFL that it took more than plain speed to succeed in professional football. With thirty-five touchdown catches in three seasons, I had caught more touchdowns in three years than any receiver in the history of the NFL other than the legendary Don Hutson of Green Bay, who caught thirty-eight touchdown passes from 1941 to 1943. So I must have been doing something right.

But I was glad to have Berry to learn from. I knew that there was always room for improvement, and if anyone was the direct opposite of me, it was probably Raymond. He was one of the slowest wide receivers who ever lived, but one of the best, because of his moves and his hands. Give him my speed or me his moves and hands, and you would have had the perfect wide receiver. Raymond talked to me about concentrating on the ball at all times and finding the gap in the zone defense. It wasn't as if no one had ever told me those things before, but hearing that kind of talk from someone who had been as great as Raymond reinforced things for me. And Raymond was easy to relate to. He was still like a player when he was with us, running routes with the other receivers, and, believe me, his routes were perfect. Raymond was a stickler for detail, and he impressed the hell out of me when he discovered right after he arrived at Thousand Oaks that our practice field was five yards too narrow. Raymond gave rubber balls to all the receivers, and made us carry them around all the time and squeeze them to strengthen our fingers. It was boring, but effective. I spent all the time I could working with Berry, and I felt good when he said, after a few weeks of observing both me and Lance Rentzel, who was known for having great hands, that I caught the ball just as well as Lance.

We opened the regular season at home against the Lions, who had finished 5–7–2 in 1967 and weren't highly regarded in 1968 either. We had a little trouble getting started; the Lions scored first on a 45-yard pass from Greg Landry, Detroit's rookie quarterback (no relation to Tom), to Mel Farr. We were behind by only 6 to 0 (Detroit missed the point after), still in the first quarter of our opening game, and our fans were already booing Meredith, who had had four passes intercepted in our final exhibition game against Baltimore.

Don and I shut up the boobirds fast. We had noticed on the films that the Lions usually blitzed on third and long. On third and 10 at midfield, sure enough, one of the Detroit linebackers, Mike Lucci, blitzed Meredith, but Don Perkins wiped out Lucci. Lance and I had lined up on the same side in our new "flip formation," and I ran a deep turn-in route and beat Tom Vaughn, the Lion safety, by a mile; Meredith's pass hit me in stride at the Lion 20. Just like that, we had a 50-yard touchdown and the lead at 7 to 6.

My total production for the day was 4 catches for 70 yards and the 1 touchdown. But my proudest moment, aside from scoring the "winning touchdown" (if there is such a thing in a game we won, 59 to 13), occurred on a 6-yard run around left end by Don Perkins, when I blindsided Vaughn and hit him so hard he had to be helped off the field. I went upfield to draw the cornerback toward me, but I was watching Vaughn all the way, and when Vaughn started to go for Perk, I nailed him. I never had much of a reputation as a blocker, but I thought I was a pretty good one, and I always prided myself on my really great hits, the way a baseball pitcher talks forever about the base hits he gets. I was especially proud to make a block like that on one of Perkins's carries because his blocks helped me get open so many times. In fact, his hit on Lucci on Meredith's touchdown pass to me knocked Lucci out of the game. Perk and I were really terrorizing Detroit that day.

By the end of our third win in a row, in Philadelphia, I was glad that football is played for sixty minutes instead of thirty. It gave me a chance to go from goat to hero. In the first half, I dropped a sure touchdown pass at the Eagles' 5 on a halfback option from Dan Reeves, and I turned the ball over when Dave Recher of the Eagles stripped it away from me on a punt return. We were ahead by only 14 to 13 at the half, against an Eagles team that had lost its first two games to the Packers and the Giants by big scores.

Raymond Berry took me aside during halftime and told me to forget the pass I had dropped and concentrate on the next one. I got my chance early in the third period. We had first and 10 at the Eagles' 44, and I ran a short slant-in from right to left, cut in front of my man, Al Nelson, at full speed, and split Nelson and the weak safety, Joe Scarpati, who hadn't learned from the past and was still playing too deep. The result was a touchdown that broke the game open, and we went on to win, 45 to 13. I was our leading receiver, with 4 catches for 98 yards and the one score.

Although I wasn't involved in any more of the scoring, I did make a contribution—decide for yourself whether it was major or minor—toward the touchdown that iced the game for us. On our next drive after my touchdown catch, we had the ball second and 13 at the Philadelphia 43, and Meredith passed to Lance around the Eagles' 20. One of the Eagles hit Lance at the moment the pass arrived, and the ball popped up in the air, allowing Nate Ramsey to intercept it. Malcolm Walker, our center, went for Ramsey, and Nate fumbled the ball, left it lying on the field. Walker got knocked to the ground and kicked in the ribs, and as he rolled around in pain, he accidentally kicked the ball toward the Philadelphia goal line. I tried to scoop the ball up, but Alvin Haymond hit me in the back just as I got my hands on it, and all I did was knock it farther toward the Eagles' goal. John Niland had come in to block for me, and he finally dove over my shoulder and fell on the ball at the Philadelphia 8. We scored a couple of plays later on a pass from Don Meredith to Don Perkins. That made it 28 to 13, and the rout was on.

. . .

I was involved in a play almost as weird as the "fumblerooski" when we won our fourth straight game in St. Louis. With the Cowboys leading, 10 to 3 in the second period, I was split out wide right, all set to run a deep turn-in. One of the outlaws on the Cardinals' defensive unit decided to help out on our snap count, and he was yelling, "Hut, hut!" along with Meredith. I went on the third "hut," but it turned out that only two of the huts were called by Meredith and the third was called by the Cardinal. About two seconds after I took off, I found myself 20 yards downfield, without a player from either team in sight. That was because the other twenty-one players were still in their set positions at the line of scrimmage, staring at me. It was embarrassing enough to be out there practically naked, but my move cost us 10 yards. The officials didn't hear the St. Louis baddy who was illegally imitating our snap count, so they called me for going offside and let the play continue. Don thought the whistle had blown to stop the play, but it hadn't, and the Cardinals sacked him for a 10-yard loss. "You ran a beautiful pattern, Bob," Dandy Don told me when I got back to the huddle. "Too bad it was before the snap."

I caught 6 passes for 62 yards on the day, as we won, 27 to 10. Although I didn't score, I did account for 29 yards on 2 catches during our opening drive, which went 70 yards and ended with Don Perkins catching a touchdown pass for the second week in a row. Perk was supposed to have bad hands, and here he had caught twice as many touchdown passes as I had in the last two games.

The NFL decided to see if there was a market for "Monday Night Football," and the first nationally televised Monday-night game in the league's history was on October 28, 1968. That game matched the teams who had played in the last two NFL championship games: The Packers and the Cowboys. Vince Lombardi had retired, and the Packers were only 2–3–1, and they looked ripe for a beating by a group like the Cowboys; our record was 6 and 0. So much for looks.

I finally broke out of a minislump late in the first quarter. We had a first and 10 at our 32 and I ran a turn-in and go against Herb Adderley. I beat him good, Don laid the ball in, and I went fifty yards before Tom Brown tackled me at the Green Bay 18. Meredith's pass over the middle for Rentzel on first down was incomplete, but Lance and I lined up in the flip formation on second down, and I got free on a deep out pattern for the touchdown that broke a scoreless tie. That touchdown meant a lot to me because it was my first one in a month. When you're paid to score touchdowns and you either fumble or don't make touchdowns, it doesn't take long before you start getting down on yourself.

We were ahead 10 to 7 at halftime, but the second half was all the Packers'. Starr threw 3 touchdown passes to go with one he had made in the second quarter, and they beat us again, 28 to 17. This game hurt a lot less than the two championship games did; we were now 6 and 1 and still a game ahead of the second-place Giants, who had beaten the Redskins the day before. I wound up with 68 yards on 2 catches and 16 on 1 punt return.

The game might have turned out differently, but Willie Davis leveled Don Meredith and broke his nose at the start of the second half. Willie was called for a personal foul and a 15-yard penalty, although I wouldn't say it was a particularly dirty play. Willie wasn't that type of player, but Ralph Neely turned him loose too fast, so Willie had a real head of steam when he got to Don, and that big beak of Don's got in Willie's way. Don came back after missing a few plays, but he wasn't the same and he threw a couple of second-half interceptions that killed any chance we had of winning.

I stayed hot when we went to New Orleans, breaking a scoreless tie for the second straight week with a 54-yard touchdown catch early in the second quarter. It was raining off and on, the ball was wet, and Dave Whitsell, who was covering me on the play, helped out by tipping the ball right before it got to me. That meant the ball wasn't traveling as fast and made it a little easier to catch.

I had another touchdown catch, a 75-yarder, in the third quarter, but it was one of those Ralph Neely touchdowns—called back for holding. A few minutes later, though, early in the fourth quarter, I beat Gene Howard, a Saints' defensive back, over the middle for a 13-yard touchdown that did count, to make the final score 17 to 3 Dallas. I could feel a lot better about this day's work: 6 catches for 108 yards and our only 2 touchdowns, 1 kickoff return for 19 yards, and 1 punt return for 7.

I had a touchdown for the fifth consecutive game on the Sunday before Thanksgiving, and we crushed the Bears at Wrigley Field, 34 to 3. We were ahead 7 to 0 late in the first quarter when I returned a punt 26 yards to the Bears' 44. A few plays later, on third and ten from the Bears' 15, Craig Morton threw a beautiful pass to me, open in the end zone, to make it 14 to 0. Craig played the whole game at quarterback while Meredith rested a sore knee, but Don's absence obviously didn't hurt us any.

I finished with 3 catches for 50 yards and the touchdown. On my touchdown catch, the Bears blew their coverage, which left Dick Butkus the closest man to me. I still have a photograph of Butkus lying flat on his face, with me 5 yards or so behind him in the end zone as the ball drops into my hands. The best thing about my touchdown was that it came over Butkus, who had speared me in the back a few minutes earlier. Butkus hit me after I lost my footing on some loose turf, slipped down, and was lying on the field, minding my own business. Butkus and I had been friends since we were teammates on the College All-Stars three years earlier, but he was so crazy on the field that he would try to kill anyone in an opponent's jersey. Butkus's hit on me really pissed me off, and after it, I played angry all day. I was jogging past the Bears' bench after one play, and Gale Sayers, who missed the game because of an injury, yelled, "Bob, don't be so mean out there!" "You better tell Butkus to cool it," I answered, "because I'll tell you, man, I'm not going to give up. The more he comes after me, the more I'm going to come after you guys. And my team's better than yours today, Gale."

Not only did the Bears have to play without Sayers, but his replacement, Brian Piccolo, had to leave the game after he hurt his right leg in the third quarter. Of course, the world would hear a lot more about Sayers and Piccolo in a few years, a story that did not have a happy ending. Brian was a Florida boy from Fort Lauderdale, and he and I had become friendly when we played together in the North-South All-Star game in the Orange Bowl on Christmas Day of our senior year in college. He was a real character, but every bit as nice as you may have heard, and his death from cancer at an early age was truly a tragedy. Brian gained 74 yards running and receiving that day in Wrigley Field, exactly one yard more than half the Bears' total offense, 147 yards. Chicago's other main threat was my former Florida A & M teammate, Clarence Childs, who returned a kickoff 53 yards in the second period to set up their only score.

The game lasted only fifty-nine minutes and fifteen seconds, but I think forty-seven thousand fans got their money's worth. We had just scored our final touchdown on a 14-yard run by Walt Garrison, and while we were kicking the extra point, Butkus started fighting with John Wilbur, our guard. Ed O'Bradovich, a defensive end who was from the Butkus-Ditka school of fair play, had also started a brawl with some of our linemen, and the officials called the game with forty-five seconds to play.

The handwriting was on the wall for Otto Graham, when he brought his Redskins into Dallas on Thanksgiving night. After going 7–7 and 5–6–3 his first two seasons as the Redskins' coach, Otto had guided his team to a 4 and 7 record before we played them for the second time in eleven days. They had also lost their last two games and five of their last six, and the word was that Redskins' president Edward Bennett Williams wasn't going to invite Otto back for a fourth season. I hoped that this would be my last game against Otto, and I wanted to do everything I could to contribute to his departure.

This game against the Redskins broke my five-game scoring streak, but I gained 53 yards on 3 catches and 32 more on 2 kick returns and helped get us moving toward two touchdowns, as we won, 29 to 20. In the second quarter, with us leading, 3–0, I went 18 yards with a pass from Meredith before Brig Owens tackled me at the Washington 31. Three plays later, with a third and 7 at the Redskins' 28, Meredith aimed a probable touchdown pass my way, but Jim Smith ran up my back to keep me from catching the ball, and we got a 27-yard penalty and a first down at the Redskins' 1 out of it. Craig Baynham went over right guard on the next play to put us ahead, 10 to 0. We stopped the Redskins at their 33 on the next series, forcing a punt from Mike Bragg, which I returned 12 yards to our 38. From there, we went 62 yards on seven plays, and Don Perkins's 9-yard run up the middle gave us a 17 to 0 lead just before halftime.

The Redskins actually came back and went ahead, 20 to 19, on a pass from Jim Ninowski to Pat Richter early in the fourth quarter, but Mike Clark kicked a field goal and Larry Cole clinched the win by intercepting a pass by Ninowski and returning it 5 yards for a late touchdown. I think every defensive lineman and linebacker who ever played much for the Cowboys during my ten years scored a touchdown except for my best friend, Jethro Pugh. Buzz just couldn't run. Sometimes we'd give those big guys the silent treatment after they scored. They'd come running off the field, so excited, and I'd turn my back and get a drink of water and then look at the guy and say, "What happened? I didn't see it, man. You mean you scored a touchdown? That's great!" And then everyone would laugh. The guy would say, "I'm going to tell Coach Landry that all you guys are watching women up in the stands and not paying attention to the game." But Landry used to give 'em the cold shoulder, too. We had a lot of fun, so many good times.

The Redskins, by the way, finished 5 to 9, and the rumors about Otto Graham turned out to be true. I'm not sorry to say I haven't seen the man since Thanksgiving Night, 1968. Of course, we wouldn't have been so eager for Otto go get fired if we had known his replacement was going to be Vince Lombardi, but there you have it. Otto blamed his final loss to us (we were 4 and 2 against the Redskins while he was their coach) on the referees: "I thought the officials stole the game from us. When the kids play their hearts out like this and the officials steal the game from them, it's a crime." Gale Sayers was with the Bears (and hurt), I was with Dallas, and Otto couldn't very well have blamed the loss on Charley Taylor, who played for his Redskins and caught a touchdown pass that night. So it had to be somebody else, and this time it was the referees. Being Otto Graham meant never having to admit that anything was your own fault.

Our victory over the Redskins left the Giants with a slim mathematical possibility of catching us, but they couldn't stand the pressure. Playing like the dogs they generally were in those days, they lost to Cleveland 45 to 10 the Sunday after Thanksgiving, which clinched the division title for us; our record was 10 and 2, and the Giants were 7 and 5 with two games to play. Although the last two games were now meaningless, I still wanted to do my best, both to put the finishing touches on another good season and to get ready for the playoffs.

If only I could have played every week the way I did those last two games of the 1968 regular season! Our next-to-last game was at home against Pittsburgh, and the Steelers helped get me going by making a bad decision for a good reason. The wind was blowing about ten miles an hour that day, and Jethro sacked Dick Shiner, the Pittsburgh quarterback, for a loss of 5 yards at the end of the first quarter. That left the Steelers, who were moving into the wind, with fourth down and 23 at their own 35, and they elected to let time run out in the quarter before they punted, so that Bobby Walden could punt with the wind at his back. Walden got off a great kick, a 55-yarder that I fielded at our 10. The only trouble was that he had outkicked his coverage. Lance Rentzel threw the first block for me and then Malcolm Walker took out two more Steelers. D. D. Lewis was also trying to block for me, but he was more in my way than anything else, and I kept pushing him from behind and yelling, "Get out of my way, D. D.!" One of the Steelers had a shot at me 15 yards or so upfield, but I sidestepped him and I was gone—90 yards for a touchdown that put us ahead, 14 to 0. That punt return stood as the longest in Dallas history until Dennis Morgan (a runningback out of Western Illinois who was a one-season flash) carried a punt back 98 yards in 1974.

The Steelers didn't go anywhere on their next drive, and this time Walden had the good sense to punt to Lance, who called for a fair catch at our 38. Meredith rolled around right end for 9 yards on first down, and then on second and 1 at our 47, Don hit me on a play-action pass over the middle, and I went 53 yards for another touchdown and a 21 to 0 lead. On that play the guy I beat was Lou Harris, a rookie safety for Pittsburgh, and he tried to make up for it by tackling me after I was already in the end zone, which I didn't like at all.

I should have rested on my laurels and sat out the second half. On the second play of the half, Meredith threw me a screen pass and I went 15 yards with it, but then fumbled the ball and Clendon Thomas of Pittsburgh recovered at our 45. On the last play of the third period, I took another flat pass from Don and got nailed for a 1-yard loss by Andy Russell, who was one of the best linebackers I ever played against.

And then came one of the most unusual episodes of my entire career. With about four minutes left in the game, and the Cowboys leading 28 to 7, which would be the final score, a lot of the sportswriters came down from the pressbox to the sidelines. Steve Perkins of the *Dallas Times Herald* pointed out to me that I had returned 13 punts so far that season, one less than was required to qualify for the NFL punt-return title, so I went back in the game, took a Walden punt at our 34 with one of the Steelers right on top of me, and gained just 3 yards before I was tackled. That move later came back to burn me.

My record for the day showed four receptions for 74 yards and 1 touchdown, 3 punt returns for 122 yards and 1 touchdown, and 1 carry, late in the first half, for a loss of 4. So I had a net gain of 192 yards, my best day of the year.

Our "showdown" in New York turned out to be not such an important game after all. After beating us five weeks earlier, the Giants were only one game behind us, but since then we had won four in a row and the Giants had lost three out of four, including their last three. We arrived in

New York for the final game of the regular season with a record of 11 and 2, four games ahead of the Giants, who were 7 and 6, and it didn't look like the Giants had much chance of catching us.

That was fine with us, but the Giants fans weren't too crazy about the situation. Allie Sherman was in his eighth year as New York's coach, and the crowd in Yankee Stadium was chanting, "Good-bye, Allie" all day. Some fans threw a big red smoke bomb onto the field during the game, but the police dumped it into a snow drift and extinguished it. The "Good-bye Allie" folks got their wish—he was fired after the season. This was the second time that year that we had run into the same thing. When we had stomped the 0 and 2 Eagles in Philadelphia in September, the fans in Franklin Field were chanting at Joe Kuharich, "Joe's gotta go!" all day. Kuharich spent most of the game drinking water. He had a bucket of water next to him on the sidelines, and he must have drunk thirty cups of water during the game. I don't know if he was nervous or what. The Eagles fans also got their wish right after the season was over. Those Northeast crowds could really be tough. And, of course, the Redskins fired Otto Graham at the end of the 1968 season, so all three of our division rivals dumped their coaches at the end of the year. Maybe the fact that we beat New York, Washington, and Philadelphia five out of six times that year and won almost as many games (12) as the three of them combined (14) had something to do with it.

I had some extra incentive in this game because it was cold—20 degrees at game time and about 10 degrees when the game ended, with winds of up to 30 miles an hour. It wasn't quite as cold as it had been for the championship game in Green Bay, but it was bad enough, and I wanted to prove that I could play in cold weather.

I got us going in the second quarter in New York, with the Cowboys trailing 3 to 0 on a field goal by Pete Gogolak. After Gogolak missed his next field goal attempt, we went 80 yards in 11 plays, and Craig Morton threw me a 13-yard touchdown pass that put us ahead for good. Don Meredith had said to me at the start of the game, "This is your town, Bobby. You like it so much, let's see what you can do." But Don was having an off day and after he went 1 for 9 for 6 yards and had one pass intercepted, he suggested that he take the rest of the day off and they let Craig Morton play. I caught Craig's pass near the back of the end zone, and my momentum carried me into a snowbank. I was trying to dig myself out of the snow when some of my teammates came up and started throwing snowballs at me.

I caught only three passes for 30 yards all day, but I did the rest of my damage on a punt return about two minutes into the second half. We were leading 7 to 3 at the time, and Ernie Koy was forced to punt to me. I fielded the ball at the Dallas 37 and headed for the right sideline as fast as I could, to try to get around the corner ahead of the Giants' lead tackler, a linebacker named Rich Buzin. I made it to the corner just in time; at that instant, Chuck Howley wiped out Buzin, but if I had been a split-second later, Chuck probably would have smeared me instead of Buzin. Chuck's block was really vicious; one of the great things about the Cowboys was that we took special teams just as seriously as we did offense and defense, so you had first-stringers like Chuck, Lee Roy Jordan, Mel Renfro, and me playing on them. As soon as Chuck nailed Buzin, I cut upfield; saw an opening; cut back across field, behind blocks by Phil Clark and Ron East; and went all the way for a 63-yard touchdown to make the score 14 to 3. The final score was 28 to 10, and Tom Landry said my runback with the punt was the turning point of the day. Until my punt return, it had been a real close game, and Landry kept telling me, "Bobby, you have to make a big play to fire the guys up. If you make a play, the guys will want to play football."

We had made the playoffs for the third straight year, and this time, the Green Bay packers, who had beaten us in the NFL championship game the previous two years, were out of the running. The Packers, without Vince Lombardi, had gone 6–7–1 and finished third out of four teams in the Central Division. Dallas was the heir apparent to the NFL title and the chance to play in Super Bowl III. Before we could play in the Super Bowl, we probably would have to face Baltimore, which had won 13 of 14 games and would play Minnesota for the Western Conference championship. To play Baltimore, we had to visit Cleveland first, but that was just a formality required by the NFL playoff system. At 12 and 2, we had finished 2 games better than the Browns; we had easily beaten them earlier in the year, 27 to 7; and we had that rout of them in the 1967 playoffs, 52 to 14.

I figured in the first scoring drive of the game, although not the way I wanted to. We had third down and 14 at our 23 the first time we had the ball, and Meredith threw a pass for me at our 39, just past the first-down marker. I had run a turn-in, but the Browns were in the right defense, with their linebackers flowing to the strong side of our offense, and Mike Howell, their free safety, cut in front of me, intercepted the pass and returned it to our 19. Our defense drove the Browns back 12 yards, but

Don Cockroft kicked a 38-yard field goal to give Cleveland the lead, 3 to 0, ten minutes into the game.

We went ahead late in the first period, when Chuck Howley forced Bill Nelsen to fumble and picked up the ball and ran 44 yards for a touchdown. Then Cleveland scored on a 45-yard pass from Nelsen to Leroy Kelly to tie the game 10–10 with less than a minute left in the half, but after that Don Meredith and I started making connections. After the Cleveland kickoff, we took over at our 32 with only forty-three seconds to go before halftime. Dandy hit me three straight times, for gains of 12, 16, and 14, to move the ball to the Cleveland 31 with fourteen seconds left. His pass into the end zone for Dennis Homan was incomplete, and on the final play of the half, Mike Clark's 37-yard field-goal attempt was off to the right.

Clark's miss was a preview of the second half, which was a disaster for the good guys. We received the second-half kickoff, and on our first play, from our 30, Don Meredith aimed a pass for me in the left flat. Dale Lindsey was the Cleveland linebacker on my side, and he was supposed to look for Don Perkins coming out of the backfield for a pass. But Perk stayed back to block, and Lindsey came running toward me as soon as he saw the play start to develop. I was open, but Meredith's pass was a little underthrown, and it hit that lucky bastard Lindsay right in the hands. "I was just standing there," he said after the game. "Then I looked up and saw the ball." He batted the ball with both hands and then caught it for a real fluky interception. My momentum had already carried me past him, and he had an easy time running 27 yards for a touchdown. Don Meredith was our only guy with a shot at him, but two of the Browns got in Don's way and he never had a chance.

Things went from bad to worse after the Cleveland kickoff. Carries by Craig Baynham and Don Perkins left us with third and 4 at our 35, and then Don tried to hit Lance. The ball bounced off Lance's hands and Ben Davis, the Cleveland cornerback, intercepted it at our 39 and returned it 3 yards. Jim Kanicki, a 270-pound defensive tackle for the Browns, buried Lance with a block during the interception return, and Lance was so angry over causing the interception and then getting creamed on the block that he picked a fight with Kanicki. I was rooting for Lance, but I have to admit that I didn't exactly go after Kanicki myself. My mommy didn't raise any dummies. Ben Davis, who made that interception and who covered me for much of the day, was the brother of the famous black militant, Angela Davis. We all knew about Ben's relationship to Angela, but it didn't matter at all on the football field, to the black players or the whites. We respected him as a man and as a football player, and whatever his sister was doing was her business.

On the first day after Ben Davis's interception, Jethro stopped Leroy Kelly for a gain of 1 yard, but on second down, Kelly took a pitchout and went 35 yards for a touchdown to put us behind, 24 to 10.

Meredith had completed just 3 of 9 passes for 42 yards, no touchdowns, and three interceptions, and Landry sent Craig Morton in to replace him after the kickoff. We were two touchdowns behind, but there were still twenty-seven and a half minutes left to play, and we had plenty of time to catch up. I'm sorry to say it, but we could have played for twenty-seven days and we wouldn't have caught up to Cleveland, not with Craig Morton at quarterback. Craig had a great arm, but he never studied the game plan well enough; he wasn't willing to pay the price a winning quarterback has to pay. Craig also would panic under a pass rush, and then he would start throwing interceptions. After we traded Morton a few years later and we had to play against him, Tom Landry would always tell our defenders that all they had to do was put a heavy rush on Craig, and he would start throwing the ball over the middle and high and we could intercept it.

There was one more thing I didn't like about Craig: He played favorites, and I wasn't one of them. Craig and I were generally on good terms, but he and Lance were best friends. They hung around together all the time off the field, and on the field Lance was the first receiver that Craig would look for—and usually the last one, too. This game against Cleveland, with our championship hopes on the line, was the perfect example. Craig played the rest of the way and threw twenty-three times. Ten of those times were for Lance, but he only completed three to Lance. He threw toward me just four times the rest of the game, and three of those four passes were on our last drive when it didn't make any difference; we took over the ball with two minutes, nine seconds to play and we were behind, 31 to 13. I caught a 39-yard pass from Morton down to the Cleveland 10 and another pass of 2 yards to the Browns' 2, and Walt Garrison scored on the next play, but all that accomplished was to make the final score a little closer. Craig's first drive of that game, which lasted for nine plays and ended up with Clark missing another field goal, was another example of his play selection. He threw to Lance four times, completing two of them, and didn't throw a single ball my way.

Craig cost us any chance to get back into the game by going to Lance once too often and throwing an interception. We were trailing just 24 to

13 with almost the whole fourth quarter to play, and we were driving for a score that would have pulled us to within four points of the Browns. We had a third and 8 at the Browns' 30, Craig aimed a pass for Lance at the Browns' 20, and Erich Barnes was waiting for it. Barnes stepped in front of Lance and intercepted the ball at the 21, returned it 2 yards, and that was the old ball game. The Browns went 77 yards, and Ernie Green scored on a 2-yard sweep around right end to drive the final nail into our coffin.

I was so furious after the game that I couldn't even look at Craig. The game actually ended with forty seconds left to play when the Cleveland crowd stormed the field after the touchdown. I was saying to myself, "Why couldn't it be us? Why couldn't it be our fans rejoicing over the victory?" It hurt me to my heart to see the championship at stake and have our quarterback take an individual stance instead of putting the football team first and doing whatever was necessary to win the game.

I was the leading receiver in the ballgame with 5 catches for 83 yards— big deal!! Lance caught only 3 passes for 75 yards, in spite of all the times Morton threw it his way. I also fielded 2 punts and had to call fair catches on both of them, and Lance called a fair catch four times. Lance and I were the most dangerous punt-return pair in the league, and Don Cockroft kept punting the ball so high all day that we couldn't return it. Cockroft punted seven times; we had to call fair catches on six of them, and the other one rolled dead at our 11 near the end of the game. Cockroft averaged 36 yards a punt, and we averaged 0.00 on returns. I had to take my hat off to him.

To make it an all-around perfect day, our plane had to circle Dallas for an hour and a half because of fog. We didn't land until 8 P.M. It was just one of those bad days.

Cleveland got our date with Baltimore, and maybe it was just as well for us. The Colts annihilated them, 34 to 0, and then went on to lose to the Jets and Joe Namath in the Super Bowl. If we had beaten the Browns, maybe the Colts would have embarrassed us the way they did the Browns, or if we had gotten past Baltimore, perhaps Namath and the Jets would have upset us instead of Baltimore in the Super Bowl.

Lance and I finished in almost a dead heat for the regular season. He caught 54 passes; I caught 53. His average yardage per catch was 18.7; mine was 17.2. I did catch 10 touchdown passes to his 6. The only other real difference between us, and this is pretty significant, is that he finished with 1,009 yards to my 909. When we went into New York for our final regular-season game against the Giants, I was leading Lance in catches, 50 to 47, and we were dead even in yardage, each with 879. With Morton going most of the way at quarterback, Lance wound up with one more reception for the season than I did and he broke the 1,000-yard mark, which was an important goal for players, the media, and the fans. I finally got so disgusted that I went up to Morton in the fourth quarter and said, "Look, if you want Rentzel to have his 1,000 yards so bad, just throw the ball to him." I figured if I wasn't going to get it, at least Lance should. Lance came over to me after the game and told me, "You're a hell of a man as well as a hell of a football player, and I respect you for it."

I finished fifth in the NFL in receptions (Lance tied Danny Abramowicz of New Orleans for third). I was sixth in yards gained receiving and third in touchdowns receiving, behind Paul Warfield and Roy Jefferson. I was also among the league's leaders in average gain per catch, and I had a total of 12 touchdowns from all sources, to tie Warfield and Jefferson for third, behind Leroy Kelly, who had 20, and Bill Brown of Minnesota, who had 14. I also led the league in punt returns, with a 20.8 average on 15 returns for 312 yards. There were only 8 punts returned for touchdowns all year, and I was the only player with 2 of them. One thing that has amused me ever since is that the only guy in the league who gained more total yards on punt returns in 1968 than I did was Chuck Latourette of St. Louis, who had 345 yards on 28 returns. The thing about Chuck is that he was also the Cardinals' punter, and he finished third in the league in punting, as well as being one of the leaders in returning punts—and in returning kickoffs, too.

I mentioned before that the advice Steve Perkins of the *Dallas Times Herald* gave me, to go back into the next-to-last game against the Steelers and return a punt so I could qualify for the league lead in punt returns, backfired on me. Here's what happened: As it turned out, I would have qualified anyway with my 63-yard punt return the final week against the Giants. The only reason I returned that last one against the Steelers was to qualify for the title; we had clinched the division championship before that game and we had iced that game before my runback, so there was no need, from the team's standpoint, for me to do it. And I only got 3 yards on that return. Without that return, my average would have been 22.1, on 14 returns for 309 yards. And that would have broken the all-time NFL record of 21.5 yards per punt return, set by Jack Christiansen of Detroit in 1952. So Steve's advice cost me the record. I know Steve meant well, and he was a super guy, but this is one time I wish a sportswriter had followed the old rule in journalism of staying out of the story and just reporting what happened.

One more curious thing about the 1968 season: Although I was all-Pro for the fourth consecutive season, I failed to make the Pro Bowl for the first time. Even though I was one of the outstanding pass receivers in the league and was the top punt returner that year, I wasn't good enough to play in the Pro Bowl. Well, so many Cowboys had played in the Pro Bowl in past years that the NFL placed a limit of eight players per team. And eight Cowboys made it in 1968: Don Meredith, Don Perkins, and John Niland from the offensive unit and Bob Lilly, George Andrie, Lee Roy Jordan, Chuck Howley, and Mel Renfro on defense. I always suspected that I got elected to the team, but somebody from the Cowboys had to go, and Glenn Davis decided to kick me off. After all, Glenn had said I embarrassed him the previous year when I refused to run against Homer Jones at halftime; Glenn had called me a liar; Glenn had tried to fight me. Glenn wouldn't do a thing like that, would he? Would he?

Along about 3 P.M. on the rainy afternoon of January 5, 1969, in the NFL Playoff Bowl in Miami against Minnesota, Don Meredith threw me a pass for an 11-yard gain to the Dallas 47 and a first down. Karl Kassulke of the Vikings tackled me, and I got up, ran back to the huddle, and got ready for the next play. At the time that pass meant nothing to me; it was just a routine play in an insignificant game, which we won, 17 to 13.

Six months later to the day, that play started looking a lot bigger. On July 5, 1969, Don Meredith shocked the Cowboys, the city of Dallas, and the entire NFL by announcing his retirement at age thirty-one.

I didn't even know Don was contemplating retirement, and it really hit me. I was coming out of an office building in downtown Dallas, on my way to a parking lot to get my car, when someone told me Meredith had retired. I turned right around, went back upstairs, and had a couple of drinks.

Nineteen sixty-eight had been Don's best year. He came within an eyelash of leading the NFL in passing, losing the title in our last game of the season when he went 1 for 9 for just 6 yards against the Giants. I knew that Don had quit because of the way the Cowboys treated him. Landry had benched him in the playoff game against Cleveland—blaming Don even though Don's last pass had hit Rentzel in the hands before Ben Davis intercepted it, so it certainly wasn't Don's fault. The Cowboys had refused to pay Don what he was worth, and people within the organization had talked about him behind his back, which got back to Don. During our game against the Packers in 1965, Landry had let Craig Morton, a rookie, call his own plays—something that Meredith, a six-year veteran, had never been allowed to do before then. Don was real loose on the outside, but he was actually a very sensitive man, and all these things ate him up.

By letting Don retire so young, the Cowboys made a tremendous mistake. They should have done whatever it took to get him back. But they had a lot of confidence in Craig Morton at the time, which was their second mistake. The team should have given Don more money, showed more trust in him, and gone the whole nine yards.

The truth is that Tom Landry had a personality conflict with guys like Meredith; Don was just too easygoing for Tom. Tom thought Don wasn't serious enough about the game. What Tom didn't see, or at least refused to acknowledge, was that Don spent a lot more time practicing with us on his own than Morton did and he was willing to work harder and pay the price it took to win. And even though Don was one of those good old boys from East Texas and SMU, he was fair to everyone on the team, not just to the white guys. I would say that the black guys felt more comfortable around Meredith than we did around any of the other white players on the team.

The bottom line was that we won with Meredith, we were happy with Meredith, and we were comfortable with Meredith, and Meredith was a leader on the team. He may not have been the all-out serious leader. But leadership is leadership. Who measures how you do it?

As far as quarterback skills go, Morton had a stronger arm than Meredith or Roger Staubach, for that matter. But Meredith used to get me the ball faster, right on the cut of my routes. Meredith didn't give the cornerback time to react to me or the other wide receivers. We got more bumps and hits playing with Morton than we did with Meredith because Morton's timing was never as good as Meredith's. Craig also liked to throw the ball high to make it a perfect picture. That would make you run faster to get it, which wasn't necessarily good. The faster you're running when you get to the ball, the harder it is to catch it. You have to gather yourself and control your speed. Morton was nowhere as good a quarterback as was Meredith or Staubach.

In spite of all my success in athletics—the world records, the Olympic gold medals, the training, and all the effort I put into sports—if it hadn't been for Don Meredith's ability, his confidence in me, and his sticking with me, I wouldn't have been nearly as successful in pro football as I was. Don Meredith meant a great deal to me—not only as a football player and a teammate, but as a man and a friend. Years later, when I was down and out, he came to my aid and lent me money. He still calls me all the time from his home in Santa Fe. Don has been so much more to me than a friend, so much more than a teammate. I can never thank him enough.

Don's sudden decision to retire was one of the worst things that ever happened to me. My career, my whole life—nothing was ever the same.

11

ANOTHER GOOD YEAR, BUT NOT QUITE GOOD ENOUGH

Tom Landry waited until after our first exhibition game against the Rams in 1969 to voice his annual complaints about me to the press. He announced that he was benching me for lack of hustle on plays when I wasn't the primary receiver. The move was big news, complete with headlines like "Bullet Benched for Shooting Blanks." Landry told the media, "We reached a certain level of play for three years. Apparently it hasn't been enough to get the job done," considering that we had lost in the playoffs all three years. Tom needed to make an example of someone to get his point across, and once again, I was that someone. And once again, I didn't like it. I had some nagging injuries, like slight pulls in my groin muscles, and I had started drinking (not that Landry knew I had a drinking problem), so I couldn't get down the field quite as fast as I used to. But I was still faster than anybody else on the team, still one of the fastest players in the league, still getting open, still catching the ball. I didn't understand why Landry insisted on benching me.

That off-season had been one of the busiest in many years for the Cowboys. A lot of changes took place. The only move on defense was the trade of Willie Townes to New Orleans, and I really missed him. Willie was a character who got on the coaches' nerves regularly, but the players loved him. But most of the moves were on offense. Before Don Meredith took the team by surprise with his retirement, the club traded Jerry Rhome to Cleveland. That meant that Craig Morton was the only one of our three quarterbacks coming back, although Roger Staubach was joining the team after completing his military commitment.

218

Don Perkins also announced his retirement, but it looked like Calvin Hill, our number-one draft choice, would replace Perk. Don was one of the leaders among the black players on the team, but he was also popular with the white guys. I remember the time he "avenged" Dan Reeves because Dan thought Bill Glass was mistreating him. Glass, a Cleveland defensive end, was a religious guy off the field, but on the field he was 100 percent football player, and for a defensive lineman, that spelled mean. In one game against Cleveland, Dan Reeves started bitching about Glass, and he lifted his jersey and showed me this big red spot on his back. I asked him what had happened and he said, "That damn Bill Glass, he pinched me." Perkins overheard the conversation and said, in his heavy voice, "Don't worry about it, Dan, I'll get him back for you." "Thanks, Perk, thanks, Perk, thanks, Perk," Reeves kept repeating.

After the next play, Reeves couldn't get back to the huddle and over to Perkins fast enough. "Did you get him? Did you get him?" Perk answered, "Not yet, but I'll get him." We ran two or three more series and every time Reeves came back to the huddle he would say, "Did you get him yet?" Finally, Reeves said, "You're just teasing me, you're not going to get him." On the next play, Perk went over and told Glass to kind of lie down on the grass so that Reeves could see him. Glass laid down on the field and Perk told Dan, "I got him, Dan, I got him." Reeves started yelling, "Great! Great! We got that sucker back!" He was all excited. Then he asked Perkins, "What did you do to him, anyway?" Perk said, "I goosed him." Reeves was real disappointed, he said, "I thought you done cracked back on him and tore up his knee or something. All you did was goose him. That's not getting him back."

In addition to all the other changes as we entered the 1969 season, the receiving corps was going to be a lot different because we had acquired Bobby Joe Conrad and Mike Ditka, and Pete Gent had been shipped to the Giants. Pete, who was my partner in a printing company at the time, didn't fit the Cowboys image. The coaches and team executives viewed him as a big mouth and a hippie—he was one of the first white players on the team to wear long hair, and the brain trust didn't like it. Another change among the receivers involved Lance Rentzel, who had married Joey Heatherton during the off-season. I had to make a personal appearance, which kept me from attending their wedding in New York in April. Too bad Craig Morton didn't have something to keep him away from the wedding, too. He got into a fight outside a New York nightclub two nights before the wedding, and a couple of guys beat the shit out of him.

I had cut down my banquet dates between seasons and I came to camp in great shape and ready to go, which made what happened to me all the more shocking. I did well in training camp, too, or, to be more accurate, I survived, which was quite an accomplishment. Tom Landry ran the toughest training camp in our history, with a heavy dose of "whoas and goes," in which we would get down in a three-point stance, sprint for fifteen or twenty yards, stop, get down in our stance again, sprint again, and so on. We would do that for one hundred yards at a time, as often as eight times a day, in addition to all other drills, and by the end of the day we all had our tongues hanging out.

Even though I had averaged over 1,000 yards and more than 11 touchdowns a year receiving, Landry benched me. For the first time in my five years with the Cowboys, covering exhibition, regular-season, and play-off games, I would not be starting a game while I was healthy. In our second exhibition game in San Francisco, Bobby Joe Conrad started in my place, and I never got into the game on offense. I played only on special teams, returning 2 punts for 16 yards and fumbling another punt and then recovering it after I had called a fair catch.

After catching a touchdown pass against Green Bay, I was back in the starting lineup, and I was our leading receiver in our 14–11 victory over Houston, with 5 catches for 90 yards. I felt that I was on a roll again, and I was looking forward to facing the defending world champion Jets and my old pal Joe Namath in our next-to-last exhibition game. I was a little disappointed when the Jets announced a few days before the game that they were giving Joe the week off and he wasn't going to be facing us, but I still was excited about seeing him and playing the Jets. Every player in the NFL gets two tickets to the Super Bowl, and Altamease and I had sat near the 40-yard line behind the Jets bench the previous January in Miami when they upset the Colts, 16 to 7, in the Super Bowl. I got goose-bumps all over watching Joe lead the Jets in that game, one of the most famous ever, and that's when it hit me how much I really, really wanted to play in the Super Bowl and to win at least one before my career was over.

When we took the field in the Cotton Bowl that Saturday night, it looked like my kind of evening. It was real hot and clear, there was hardly any wind, we had a full house, and I was in the starting lineup opposite Lance for the second week in a row. In those days, most players didn't wear their pads for pregame practice in real hot weather, and with the thermometer at 95 degrees, I had left most of my pads in the locker room.

I was running a sideline pattern on a quick pop pass from Craig Morton, and I was so busy concentrating on catching the ball and keeping my feet inbounds that I tripped, flipped over in the air, and landed with all of my weight on my left shoulder.

When I got up, the pain was so bad that I almost passed out. The medical staff came over and felt my shoulder and then led me into the training room, where they taped the shoulder. I went back out and sat on our bench during the game until I couldn't stand the pain any longer, and then they X-rayed it and found out that I had separated my shoulder, complete with torn ligaments, a chipped bone, and internal bleeding. It was my first serious injury in twelve years of football, including two in high school, five at Florida A & M (counting my redshirt year), and five with the Cowboys. It was also the most painful injury I ever had. The prognosis was that I would be out of action for about six weeks, all because of a fluke play in warmups before an exhibition game. Nobody even touched me, and here I was, a damn cripple! I had surgery on my shoulder the next morning, and they put a pin in it to keep it in place. On top of my injury, Craig dislocated a finger late in the first half when he banged it on the helmet of John Elliott, a defensive tackle for the Jets, on his follow through on a pass. He was going to be out too, for at least a week.

Craig was able to return to the lineup for our second game of the regular season, but I wasn't. The doctors' forecast for me was right on the money. I was out for six weeks. Maybe I would have been ready to play sooner if some of the rehabilitation techniques that are used now were available then, but about all they did was put me in a hot tub and work on my shoulder with a sound machine. I missed our final exhibition and our first four regular-season games, victories over St. Louis, New Orleans, Philadelphia, and Atlanta. Dennis Homan, who had been our number-one draft choice from Alabama the previous year, started in my place and caught seven passes, none for touchdowns, while I was gone.

I made my debut against the Eagles in the Cotton Bowl, and I started making up for lost time right away. We went 80 yards on 15 plays for a touchdown after the opening kickoff, and I caught two passes for 22 of those yards. My second catch was a 10-yarder over Leroy Keyes on second and 17 from the Philadelphia 18; we scored on the next play on an 8-yarder from Craig to Lance. From there the game quickly turned into a rout. The Eagles fumbled our kickoff, Craig Baynham recovered it, and we went 19 yards for our second touchdown. George Andrie sacked Norman Snead on the Eagles' next possession, and my man Jethro had a chance for what would have been the first touchdown of his life. But the ball went through his hands, and Bob Lilly picked it up and "sprinted" 9 yards for another touchdown, to put us ahead 21 to 0 with less than eleven minutes gone in the game. Lilly didn't look like a football player; he wasn't muscular like a football player and wasn't shaped like an athlete. He also did some weird things; for example, when we wore our Cowboy sweats in practice, he would take scissors and cut holes like polka dots in the back, what he called his air-conditioning. But when he put on his game uniform, he came to play. He didn't look strong, but he was; the opposition would double team him and try tricks on him, and he would still beat them.

Following Bob's touchdown, Snead hit Harold Jackson for a 65-yard touchdown the next time Philadelphia had the ball, but several plays after the Eagles' kickoff, with first and 10 at our 33, I beat Keyes again and took a pass from Craig Morton 67 yards for my first touchdown of the season, making the score 28 to 7.

The final score was 49 to 14, and I caught a total of 4 passes for 92 yards and 1 touchdown. Lance, who had caught 4 touchdown passes while I was injured, caught 3 more in this game; he was our leading receiver with 6 catches for 97 yards and I was runnerup. Even Landry was glad to have me back, commenting that "when Hayes is running through that secondary it changes the complexion of things pretty quickly." At least three players also noticed my return, and two of them weren't so pleased about it. Leroy Keyes said that "Hayes kills you with his speed, and Rentzel with his moves." Irv Cross, who was back with the Eagles after several years with the Rams, commented, "Dallas has terrific balance with Hayes and Rentzel and I tip my hat to a great team. When you concentrate on stopping one individual, someone else comes up and hurts you. Hayes just being on the field hurts you because you have to give him all of your respect." And Lance himself observed, "It's great to have Pepper back. That's Bobby. I'm Salt and he's Pepper. He makes my job a lot simpler."

Lance didn't mind sharing the credit with me himself, but he didn't like for anyone else to point out that part of his success was because the defenses were keying on me. The year 1969 was Bobby Joe Conrad's only one with us, and he used to ride Lance all the time. He would say to him, "You know, Lance, all these passes you're catching, you ought to go over there and thank Bob Hayes." And Lance would say, "Why thank Bob Hayes? Bob Hayes is not my quarterback." Bobby Joe would say, "*Anybody* who plays opposite of Bob Hayes could catch as many passes as you do." Every time Bobby Joe started saying that, it would drive Lance crazy.

The Giants came to town with their usual powerhouse, trying to cover the best one-two receiving punch in the league with such household names in their defensive backfield as Tom Longo, Scott Eaton, Willie Williams, and Bruce Maher. If you remember any of those guys, it certifies you as a bona fide NFL trivia expert. The Giants actually scored first, on a 23-yard field goal by Pete Gogolak in the first period, but after that it was all Dallas. Literally. We scored the remaining 25 points of the game; the final score was 25 to 3. Lance broke open a 9 to 3 game with a 16-yard touchdown catch from Morton in the fourth quarter, George Andrie accounted for a couple of points when he sacked Fran Tarkenton in the end zone for a safety, and I finished off the scoring on a 40-yard catch off an option pass from Calvin Hill with four minutes to play. My touchdown was on what we called a "rooster and go," a play we used to run a lot. Morton tossed the ball to Calvin out of the I-formation, and I ran up to the corner-back who would be the most dangerous potential tackler to Calvin. I roosterblocked him—just got in his face so he couldn't penetrate while Calvin was building up his momentum—and then ran past him when he committed himself.

I was feeling pretty good by then because I had gotten crunched by two of the more giant Giants on a play in the third quarter, and my shoulder held up fine. We had a first and 10 at the New York 30, and I took a pass from Morton for 5 yards before Tommy Crutcher, one of the Giants' line-backers, and Fred Dryer—then a defensive end and now "Hunter" on television—both got me. Defensive linemen didn't usually tackle me, but Dryer was a quick, fast, defensive end—he played almost like a linebacker at times. After the tackle, I told Fred that if he ever hit me like that again, I was going to send Lance after him.

This time I was the leading receiver in the game, with five catches for 96 yards and 1 touchdown. I also returned Gogolak's kick after the Giants' safety for 46 yards and added another 39 yards on 3 punt returns, plus 5 yards on an end around in the second quarter. My total was 186 yards, not a bad day's work.

We were now 6 and 0, and the only team in our division that was close to us was the Redskins, for whom Vince Lombardi had taken over as coach; the Redskins were 4−1−1. New Orleans, which had traded places with the Giants and was back in the Capitol Division, and Philadelphia were way behind.

Our first loss came in Cleveland. And it was a bad one, 42 to 10. At least it didn't hurt us much, since the Redskins also lost big that day, to Baltimore. I caught 2 passes for 40 yards, but none of us did much. Morton threw three interceptions and got sacked five times, and Garrison and Baynham fumbled the ball away three times between them, two by Walt.

Mike Ditka was in a pretty bad mood by the end of the game, and he got into a fight with less than a minute to play, received a 15-yard penalty for a personal foul, and was ejected. Ditka was a madman; he played that way every game. Willie Galimore had told me about Mike when Ditka was a rookie with the Bears. "We have a new tight end who will run over anybody, hit anybody, and fight anybody at any time," Willie told me. And Ditka always lived up to his reputation, as both a player and a coach.

Dirty as he was, Ditka was also a hell of a tight end, and he was a lot faster than people gave him credit for. On the first play of our next game, against New Orleans, he caught a pass from Morton and ran 51 yards to the Saints' 29. I caught one for 16 yards a couple of plays later, and right after that, we had a second and 12 at the New Orleans 14. Morton went back to pass, and I was wide open in the end zone, but he was looking for Lance and didn't see me. Craig's pass bounced off Lance's hands and ricocheted over to me. I was just standing there in the end zone, and all of a sudden, the ball landed in my hands. It didn't count, though; in those days, a pass that was touched by two offensive players without someone on defense touching it in between was incomplete.

Mike Clark kicked a field goal two plays later to put us ahead, 3 to 0, and on our next drive, I scored a touchdown that counted, on a 23-yard pass from Morton, one of my 4 receptions for a total of 48 yards. That gave us a 10 to 0 lead after just six minutes; the Saints came back to tie it at 17 near the end of the third quarter on a pass from Billy Kilmer to Danny Abramowicz, but we pulled it out in the fourth period, 33 to 17.

We faced the Rams in late November in what everyone was calling the NFL's biggest game of the regular season; the Rams were 9 and 0 and we were 8 and 1, and we were expected to play each other again for the

NFL championship. For once my old coliseum magic didn't work for me. We were trailing, 17 to 10, in the third quarter, with third and 10 at our 39, when Los Angeles showed blitz at the line of scrimmage and Morton called an audible for me to run deep over the middle. The play worked to perfection—I was wide open, Craig's pass was right in my hands around the Rams' 30, and I caught it and was off for the tying touchdown. But this time my track background actually *hindered* me on the football field. Jim Nettles, the Rams cornerback, was hot on my heels after I caught the pass, and I was trying for the perfect arm pump to get up a full head of steam. My arm pump was great—so great that I swung my arm with the ball in it too far up; the tip of the ball hit my shoulder pad and bounced out of my hand, with me on my way to a sure touchdown. I reached for the ball as I ran along, but I couldn't control it and it finally hit the ground. Now the ball was behind me, and so was Nettles, but he overran it, and I doubled back for it and got there right before Nettles did. He and I were down on the ground fighting for possession like two roosters in a cockfight while some of the players on both teams watched us, and I finally came up with it at the Los Angeles 18. Morton threw twice to Rentzel, the first time incomplete and the second one for a 3-yard gain. On third and 7 from the Rams' 15, Morton's pass for me was broken up by Maxie Baughan and Eddie Meador, so we had to settle for a field goal by Mike Clark that left us behind, 17 to 13.

The Rams gave me a rough time from there on in. Near the end of the third quarter, Morton threw a long pass for me, but Nettles interfered with me, and we got a 39-yard gain to the Los Angeles 29 on the penalty. I'm not positive I could have scored on that play, but anyway, Los Angeles stopped us again and Clark kicked another field goal to pull us to within one point of Los Angeles.

The Rams came right back with a 67-yard drive that ended with Roman Gabriel sneaking over from the 1 to put them ahead by 8 at 24 to 16 with nine and a half minutes left. After one of Morton's passes for Rentzel was intercepted by Clancy Williams and a Rams punt, we took over again at our own 1 with six minutes, twenty-five seconds to play. We showed our character, going 99 yards to close to within a point of the Rams again. The longest gainer on our 10-play drive was on a pass from Morton to me; I picked up 31 yards to the Los Angeles 23 before Clancy Williams clothes-lined me and knocked me silly. By the time I knew what was happening, Rentzel had scored on an 8-yard pass from Morton, the score was 24 to 23 Los Angeles, and the Rams were punting again. Pat Studstill got off a beautiful 46-yarder and I fielded it at our 36, but Jim Purnell, a linebacker playing special teams for the Rams, stopped me in my tracks for no return.

Now we had less than two minutes to play and sixty-four yards to go, so what did Morton do? He started throwing to Rentzel on every play, and Meador finally intercepted one at midfield. Gabriel fell on the ball twice, and the final gun sounded.

I wasn't the only Cowboy who got worked over by the Rams that day. One of the Rams linebackers kept holding Ditka, and Ditka got crazy and wanted to fight. While they were scuffling, Jack Pardee—another Rams linebacker, but one who always played clean football—was standing next to me. I asked Pardee (now the head coach of the Houston Oilers) if he was going to get into the fight Ditka had started, and he said, "Not me, I'm not going to touch that Ditka."

That was a loss that hurt me both physically and mentally. Forget Morton's fourth-quarter interceptions. I cost us the game by losing the ball when I had Nettles beaten for the touchdown. That fumble cost us four points, since we got a field goal instead of a touchdown out of it, and we lost by one point. Though I caught 2 passes for 74 yards and I gained another 55 on 4 kick returns, I still felt lousy—not to mention that my head was buzzing for several hours from being hit by Williams.

I was sitting in front of my locker after the game, trying to get my bearings, when Buddy Hackett, the comedian, walked up to me. He introduced himself and went on, "You must feel terrible from that pass you fumbled that cost you the game. Look, I know you're down. Why don't you come back to Las Vegas with me tonight on my jet, stay at my place, and enjoy my show?" I told him I couldn't do it that night because we had to fly home and start preparations the next day for our Thanksgiving game against San Francisco, but I would take a raincheck if I could. So Buddy arranged for me to make the trip after the game against the 49ers. While we were talking in the locker room in Los Angeles, Hackett reached in his pocket, pulled out a watch with the numbers in Hebrew, and gave it to me. What a character he was!

The day after our Thanksgiving tie with the 49ers, I took Buddy Hackett up on his offer, and Altamease and I and another couple flew to Las Vegas. Buddy Hackett put us up in his penthouse suite at the Sahara Hotel, of which he was part owner, and gave us the red-carpet treatment for three days. The highlight was a brunch he took us to at Totie Fields's house. Wayne Newton, Sammy Davis, Jr., and many other Las Vegas heavyweights were there, but Totie Fields couldn't take her eyes off me. She had an indoor swimming pool and she kept looking at my butt and my body. She finally said to me, "Would you please dive in that pool naked? You got the most gorgeous ass I have ever seen on a man." I declined. I also passed up the gambling, which never was one of my vices. We spent a total of forty dollars in the casinos the whole time we were in Las Vegas, a world record on the low end, for all I know.

We ended the regular season by beating Washington 20 to 10 in what turned out to be Vince Lombardi's last game. Lombardi learned he had cancer a few months later and died before the 1970 season began. I was the leading receiver in the game with 7 catches for 55 yards, and I figured in the 4 scoring drives that led to our 2 touchdowns and 2 field goals, but the play that sticks in my mind went for a loss of 2 yards. I had gained 6 yards on a carry around right end in the first quarter, and we tried the same play to the same side early in the second half. Brig Owens was waiting for me this time, and he tackled me 2 yards behind the line of scrimmage. Brig had been a quarterback in college, he was a smart ballplayer, and he recognized the play immediately. "Where do you think you're going, buddy?" he asked me as we got up. The turkey had not only tackled me, he had cut my average gain per rush for the day from 6 yards (1 carry for 6 yards) to 2 yards (2 carries for 4 yards)—just when I was starting to think I might be the next Gale Sayers.

We met the Rams in the playoffs, but it didn't turn out exactly the way we—or the Rams—had expected. Before we played each other, the Cowboys had to play Cleveland for the third consecutive year in the Eastern Conference championship and Los Angeles and Minnesota had to fight it out for the Western Conference championship.

In the game against Cleveland in the Cotton Bowl, the Browns scored first (a 2-yard run by Bo Scott), second (a 6-yard pass from Bill Nelsen to Milt Morin), third (a 29-yard field goal by Don Cockroft), and fourth (another 2-yard run by Scott right after the Browns' linebacker Jim Houston intercepted Craig Morton's pass and returned it 35 yards to our 19). By then we were down 24 to 0, and all we could do was to trade touchdowns with the Browns. The final score was 38 to 14.

I was involved in a play that led to Cleveland's first score, although I wasn't to blame. The Browns received the opening kickoff, but didn't get anywhere. Cockroft's punt from the Browns' 32 was high and short. It landed around our 40 and started bouncing, and I decided to get out of the way instead of risking a fumble. But Rayfield Wright was coming back to block for me and he didn't see the ball. It hit him in the leg, Bob Matheson recovered for the Browns at our 34, and the Browns quickly scored their first touchdown.

Cockroft's field goal, on the last play of the half, was more my fault. We had third and 5 at our 35 with a little over a minute left in the half, and Morton threw a quick flip to me. I had crossed the 40 and picked up the first down, but I thought I could gain more, so I danced backwards, looking for more running room, and Dale Lindsey tackled me at the 37, 3 yards short of the first-down marker. That was a bad mistake on my part; as a wide receiver, you never give up the yardage you need for the first down. You never go backward; you always go forward, even if you have to take a hit to get the necessary yards. Jogging back to the sideline after that was not fun. We had to punt, and the Browns went 44 yards in twenty-six seconds to get within field-goal range.

The score was 17 to 0 at halftime, we had gained 39 yards in total offense (I had our longest gain of the first half on a 12-yard pass from Morton), and our home fans—nearly seventy thousand of them—booed us like they never had before when we left the field at the end of the half. We didn't like being booed, but we deserved it. We had played a bad half, and the fans paid our salaries; they felt like they should get more for their money. Hell, they could have paid the SMU football team that day (as some of them did in the 1980s) and gotten a better return on their investment.

Just when it looked like we might get going with the second-half kickoff (Craig Morton hit me for thirteen yards and then for seventeen out to midfield), his pass was intercepted by Jim Houston. The Browns scored, and that pretty much ended our chances.

Once again I was our leading receiver with 4 catches for 44 yards, although it didn't mean much. But Jerry Tubbs, who had retired as a linebacker a couple of years earlier and was now one of our assistant coaches, told me that I was the only guy on the offensive unit who did anything. Craig certainly didn't help our cause. He was 8 for 24 for 92 yards, no touchdowns, and 2 interceptions, the second of which was returned 88 yards by Walt Sumner for Cleveland's last touchdown. He also got sacked 3 times, before Roger Staubach replaced him late in the game with the score 38 to 7 and passed 5 yards to Lance Rentzel for a touchdown that left us only 24 points behind with four minutes to play. Craig apologized for his play that day, and no one tried to tell him, "Oh, no, Craig, it wasn't your fault."

It was after that game that some of the Cowboys started muttering about Craig. If I had known Craig was going to stab me in the back the next year, I might have gone to Tom Landry and told him that Craig was not prepared for the Cleveland game. I knew Craig wasn't mentally ready to play. Even the day before the game, he didn't have his offensive game plan together. He was still studying the game plan; Landry had given us a whole new concept for the game, and Craig hadn't grasped it. Normally Craig was ready, but that day, he could not remember some of the formations we were supposed to run from and some of the audibles even in the huddle. If I had told Landry, he would have gotten Craig and gone over those plays and made sure he understood them precisely before the kickoff.

It was an all-around shitty day—raining and cold—and the field was muddy and in terrible shape. After the game I did my best to be cheerful. I told the press, "We were playing on a wet field and they were playing on a dry field." One thing I had learned from Jake Gaither early in my career was to keep everything in perspective.

As I said, we did get to play the Rams. In the Playoff Bowl in Miami, after they lost to Minnesota, 23 to 20. The best thing I can say about the Playoff Bowl (in which I was again our leading receiver with 3 catches for 50 yards) was that it was over quickly. It lasted just two and a half hours (this was before the typical NFL game started running well over three hours), and the final score was 31 to 0—not in our favor. George Allen, who was awarded the game ball by his team, said afterwards that this was "probably the biggest win for the Rams in four years." In the *Playoff Bowl!* Way to go, Rams. Way to go, George. Anything that turns you on.

Even though I missed our first four games, I came within 3 catches of tying Lance for the team lead. He had 43 to my 40. I gained 746 yards receiving, to Lance's 960, and my average per catch, 18.7 yards, was sixth in the NFL (Lance led the league with a 22.3 average). But after being in double figures in touchdown catches my first four seasons, I had only four touchdowns receiving in 1969; Lance had three times as many.

I did have another good year returning punts, finishing third in the league behind Alvin Haymond of the Rams and Rickie Harris of the Redskins with a 9.9 average on 18 returns for 179 yards. I also rushed 4 times for 17 yards and returned 3 kickoffs for 80.

Not a bad year, but certainly not a great one. And even though we won forty-two regular-season games from 1966 to 1969—more than any other team in the NFL—1969 was another year with an unhappy ending.

12

OFF THE BENCH AND INTO THE SUPER BOWL

By the time we reported to training camp for the 1970 season, we were a team with racial problems, largely because of Craig Morton. I won't say that Craig was an out-and-out racist, but a lot of players—including Cornell Green, Jethro Pugh, Rayfield Wright, Danny Reeves, and Mel Renfro—were angry because Craig wouldn't throw the ball to me and he was always looking for Lance Rentzel. And then Craig went to the coaches and told them he didn't have confidence in me and got me benched, first for Dennis Homan and later for Ron Sellers—both of whom were white, but nowhere near as good as I was.

Roger Staubach and Craig had a quarterbacks' meeting with Landry and some of the offensive coaches. Afterwards Roger came to me and said, "Bob, I didn't do it. I didn't do it." What Roger was referring to was that Craig had complained about me during the meeting, saying I wasn't running my routes right and wasn't getting open and he had lost confidence in me. That's when Landry decided to bench me and put Homan in. The truth is that Craig was lazy. He just didn't have the mental toughness, on or off the field. Off the field he was a playboy with some personal problems (he once got arrested for urinating on a street in Dallas). On the field he liked to take the easy way out, and it was easier for him to throw to someone else since I was double covered a lot than to stand back and risk taking a hit from those big, fearsome defensive linemen while I was getting open. I lost all respect for Craig after he went to the coaches about me, which started my downfall with the Cowboys. Even an outsider like Howard Cosell caught on to what was happening and asked how the Cowboys could have the fastest man in the world sitting on the bench, after all my success.

The Dallas press picked up on the situation, too. "Without Hayes, Dallas has no consistent deep pass threat," Frank Luksa wrote in the *Fort Worth Star-Telegram.* "The enemy can double Lance Rentzel and there is not sufficient speed at either tight end or at the other wide receiver to pose an all-the-way danger." And Bob St. John, a Dallas sportswriter, wrote in the magazine *Pro Quarterback* that "the defense just knows it faces a different job when it is facing a split end who covers 40 yards in 4.4, rather than someone who runs it in 4.8, like Dennis Homan, for whom Landry benched Hayes."

All the black players could see what was going on: White coaches had benched a black player who was the fastest man in the world, in favor of a slower and inferior white player, because a white quarterback had asked them to. And this was a white quarterback who already was favoring his white friend, Lance Rentzel, when Lance and I were on the field at the same time.

The controversy that Craig started over Homan and me finally brought the racial problems on the team out in the open. Race had been an issue at least as long as I was on the team. I know that when I came on the team in 1965, the Cowboys had a rule that black and white players could not room together. When I asked, in a general team meeting, why I, after representing our entire country in the Olympics (where I was free to room with any U.S. athlete, regardless of color), couldn't room with Don Meredith or anyone else I wanted to, the management didn't answer; it would have been too embarrassing for them.

The whole housing situation was a mess. The team trained in North Dallas, and most of the white players lived near the practice field. But blacks couldn't live in North Dallas in those days; most of us lived in Oak Cliff, which is south of downtown, about twenty miles from the Cowboys' headquarters. After practice all the players were eager to get home, and if we wanted to go out at night, the blacks and the whites lived too far apart to go out together. So the team split into black and white cliques.

Also, there were more white players than black players, and the white players outvoted us on everything. When we had parties for the whole team, all the players would vote on what kind of music to have. The blacks would vote for soul music, but the whites would vote for country and western, so we always had country-and-western music. That may not sound like a big deal to an outsider, but it was. The white players could have been gracious and allowed soul music once in a while, but they didn't. And the white majority also decided how the team split up our playoff money—which led to the team's black employees getting short-changed. A black man named Otis Jackson took care of the practice fields. He was the hardest worker in the entire Cowboys organization, out on the field from sunup until sundown, but when it came time to divide the playoff shares, the white majority would give more money to Jack Eskridge, the equipment manager—a white man. Although it seemed to me that Eskridge didn't do a good job (he didn't keep our helmets clean, for instance), he always got a bigger share of the money than Jackson did. We black players didn't like that, and we voted to give Jackson $200 each out of our share.

The truth is that racism ran throughout the whole organization—starting with some of the top Cowboys executives, who used to refer to me behind my back as "Supernigger." Even the little things divided us. Some of the black players started wearing Afros, and some of the whites began making comments about "Nigger hairdos." For the first two-thirds of the 1970 season, we played like a team with serious problems, which is what we were.

Most of the Cowboys opened the season playing against the Eagles in Philadelphia. I opened it standing on the sidelines, drinking Gatorade. We won, 17 to 7, no thanks to Homan, who caught 2 passes for 15 yards. Does that give you some idea of how well he replaced me?

Homan was even worse in our home opener against the Giants. He caught 1 pass for 4 yards, and we were losing 10 to 0 at the half and ahead by only 14 to 10 going into the fourth quarter. By then the coaches had seen enough and sent me onto the field. They also sent in a new play, and with eight and a half minutes to play and second and 11 at our 42, Roger Staubach pitched the ball to Lance Rentzel, and Lance threw it to me for a 58-yard score. Lance's pass was a perfect spiral, in the air about 50 yards. Lance was always telling the coaches he wanted to throw an option pass, just like Dan Reeves and Calvin Hill did regularly, and Tom Landry finally put in a flanker reverse pass. Lance worked his tail off in practice, getting everything down just right, and he told me, "Bobby, if you drop my pass, I will kill you." If I had dropped it, I would have had to keep on running straight through the end zone, out of the Cotton Bowl, and on down the street. Lance was as happy as a man could be; he never stopped talking about that pass. Landry must not have wanted to risk having people think Lance was a potential quarterback because he commented that "Lance certainly throws the ball better in game conditions than he does in practice," but Lance insisted, "I completed a couple in practice."

Everyone was in a good mood, especially me, when I caught another touchdown pass, a 24-yarder from Staubach with 11 seconds to play, which made the final score 28 to 10 Dallas. I was by far the leading receiver in the game, with 5 catches for 112 yards, more than half our 191 yards passing, and our only 2 touchdowns through the air.

After my great day against the Giants, I was more than a little surprised when Landry told the press a few days later that I was still second string and that Homan would start our next game against St. Louis. Landry informed the media that "Hayes has not been a particularly good blocker." Right, and Roger Staubach didn't run a very good pass route and Ralph Neely wasn't much of a ballcarrier. Landry apparently wanted me to go from the world's fastest human to the world's most vicious blocker. Or could it have been just an excuse?

Well, the coaches got their way. Staubach and Morton didn't complete a single pass to a wide receiver, and the Cardinals held us to 269 yards in total offense and beat us 20 to 7. We almost got shut out; our only score was on a 2-yard run by Calvin Hill with three minutes to play, following a drive of just 40 yards (Herb Adderley, whom we had picked up from Green Bay, intercepted one of Jim Hart's passes at our 30 and ran it back 30 yards to give us good field position).

We, or I should say the rest of the team (I didn't get into the game for a single down), played almost as badly the following week, managing to win only because our opponents were the Atlanta Falcons, who were awful. Even so, we won by only 13 to 0 and we didn't score our only touchdown until the last period. And the week after, Minnesota humiliated us, 54 to 13, with Homan again going most of the way and me playing hardly at all.

Praise the Lord! Praise Tom Landry, too; he finally figured out that defensive backs around the league weren't losing much sleep over Dennis Homan. He told me I would make my first start of the year in Week 6 in Kansas City against the defending Super Bowl champions. By then we were struggling with a 3 and 2 record, and the games we had won we had won ugly.

Duane Thomas had just run 47 yards over left guard to give us a fairly comfortable lead over Kansas City, 20 to 10, early in the second half, when our defense held the Chiefs on downs. I returned Jerrell Wilson's punt 13 yards to our 24, and, after a 4-yard carry by Dan Reeves, Craig Morton threw a screen pass to Duane, who went 72 yards for a touchdown. But the play was called back for holding—this time on Dave Manders—and after Willie Lanier nailed Claxton Welch for a loss of 3 yards on a draw play, we were backed to our 11, third and 23. We expected the Chiefs to blitz, and they didn't disappoint us. I ran by an old home boy from Bishop College, Emmitt Thomas, and Morton laid the ball in my hands near midfield, with Emmitt right on my heels. Emmitt was Kansas City's fastest defensive back, and everybody, including Emmitt and me, wanted to see how our race would come out. We ran step for step for about 10 yards and then I just blew him out and went 89 yards for a touchdown.

That iced the game, although Jan Stenerud kicked two fourth-quarter field goals for Kansas City to make the final score 27 to 16. Stenerud was an awesome ballplayer. After his third and final field goal, he kicked off over the goal line, through the end zone, and almost into the stands before the ball hit a wall. And the wind was hardly blowing. That guy had some leg! We should have asked the officials to check it and make sure it wasn't bionic.

We gained 160 yards passing, and I accounted for 100 of them on two receptions. Morton, who went all the way at quarterback, completed only 7 passes all day, 3 to Lance and 2 to Dan Reeves. I hoped I had made my point.

For the first time in my six seasons with Dallas, the Giants had a good team in 1970. The Giants gave us a tough time in September and then beat us 23 to 20 in the November rematch at Yankee Stadium. I went the whole way and Homan didn't get into the game for the second week in a row. As a matter of fact, Reggie Rucker was our backup wide receiver that day.

For the third straight week, I scored; this time I had both of our touchdowns. The first one almost didn't happen, because of me. Late in the first quarter, Bill Johnson of the Giants got off a short punt, only 29 yards, and I fielded the ball at our 35. I fumbled the kick, but Mel Renfro, who was back deep with me, bailed me out by recovering it at our 27. Calvin Hill and Duane Thomas moved the ball to the Giants' 38 and on first down, Craig hit me for a touchdown over Ken Parker that gave us a 10 to 3 lead. We were leading 10 to 6 with six minutes to play in the half when Johnson punted 50 yards into our end zone for a touchback. On first down from our 20, Morton threw a bomb to me. Willie Williams, the Giants cornerback, batted the ball and I caught the deflection at the Giants' 30 and ran the rest of the way untouched for an 80-yard score, putting us ahead 17 to 6.

The Giants started catching up, and Ron Johnson pulled them to within 20 to 16 on a 4-yard run in the third quarter. That was still the score early in the fourth quarter when we tried one of our trick plays, a reverse with me carrying the ball. We had first and 10 at our 20 after Pete Gogolak missed a field goal, and I came tearing around the right side— right into the arms of Spider Lockhart. Spider downed me for a 3-yard loss, and you should have seen the smile on his face. His smile got even bigger when he found out that we had been called for holding, which moved the ball back to our 8. After that, we got into a punting duel with the Giants, until they finally marched 73 yards late in the game to win, 23 to 20, on a 13-yard pass from Fran Tarkenton to Ron Johnson.

Morton had 191 yards through the air that day, and I accounted for 129 of them on 4 receptions. Too bad it was in a losing cause.

Don Meredith was in the Cotton Bowl on November 16, 1970, for our first appearance on ABC's "Monday Night Football," but he was in the wrong spot—up in the broadcast booth along with Howard Cosell and Keith Jackson (Frank Gifford didn't join the ABC team until 1971). The Cardinals, who were in first place with a 6 and 2 record, a half game ahead of the Giants and a full game ahead of us, also showed up. The only guests missing from the party were the Dallas Cowboys. The final score was 38 to 0 St. Louis, and we couldn't do anything right. We ran the wrong way, turned the ball over, you name it. Morton and Staubach completed nearly half as many passes to guys in St. Louis jerseys, 4, as they did to our receivers, 10, and we lost 2 fumbles as well. I didn't catch a single ball all night, so I was as much to blame as anyone else for our poor showing. One of Morton's passes clanked right through my hands and bounced off my chest, incomplete. That was in the second quarter when we were still in the game, down only 14 to 0. My contribution, if you want to call it that, was 3 punt returns for a total of 6 yards.

A lot of the 69,000-plus paying customers spent a good bit of the evening chanting, "We want Meredith!"—a sentiment I shared. At one point I looked up to the booth, waved to him, and said under my breath, "Sure wish you were down here, pal." People in the stands may have thought I was talking to myself or praying, but I was just expressing a wish that wasn't ever going to be fulfilled.

Everyone on the team knew we had our backs to the wall, with a 5 and 4 record that left us two games behind St. Louis, one behind New York, and only one ahead of Washington. As I look back, Tom Landry made one of his most brilliant moves the week after the St. Louis defeat. When we assembled for a light workout the next day, he handed us the plays for our next game, in Washington, and told us, "Here's the game plan. I'm not even going to go over it. You all look at it and go out and play touch football and loosen up and enjoy yourselves." We had an easy week, didn't practice that long, and got our legs back under us. Then we started kicking butt, and Landry started coaching us again. And we started winning again, beating the Redskins on the road, 45 to 21, and the Packers at home, 16 to 3.

None of us knew what to expect when we took the field in the Cotton Bowl to play the Redskins for our first game without Lance Rentzel, whom the team had decided not to use after his arrest for indecent exposure. Many of us had our minds as much on him as we did on football. The furor may have affected Craig Morton, who had an off day. At least Craig's ineffectiveness didn't matter because we won our third straight, routing the Redskins, 34 to 0. Once again, I had more than half our passing yardage, 92 out of 166 total yards, on 4 catches. But my only score of the game didn't count. I broke a 70-yard punt return for a touchdown near the end of the third period; we were flagged for holding and the play was called back. I thought I was going to go all the way on a sideline pass in the fourth quarter, but it didn't happen. I reversed my field and picked up 18 yards to the Washington 47, but just when I was thinking six points, one of the Redskins ran me down. I was also open a couple of times in the first half for what probably would have been touchdowns, but Craig's passes were off target both times. On the bright side, St. Louis lost at Detroit, and we and the Giants, who beat Buffalo, were now only half a game back.

For the third week in a row, I was responsible for more than half our passing yardage, this time against Cleveland, since I caught 3 passes for 43 of our 72 yards passing. One reason why I was accounting for such a large percentage of our passing game was that Morton was horrible—8 of

20 for 100 yards against Washington and just 8 of 17 for the 72 yards in Cleveland. I also scored again, but this time for Cleveland. In fact, I gave the Browns their only points, late in the first quarter. Don Cockroft punted from midfield, and I fielded the ball on our 10, fumbled it, recovered it, and found myself in our end zone, where Chuck Reynolds, Bob Matheson, and Fred Hoaglin smothered me for a safety. We came back with two 3-run home runs, or, I should say, Mike Clark field goals. I did gain 28 of the 54 yards on our second field-goal drive, but neither offense could do much. The final score was 6 to 2, and I felt sorry for the 75,000 fans who sat through such a game on a cold, rainy day.

The best news of the week came from St. Louis, where the Giants beat the Cards, 34 to 17, to leave us tied with New York for first place in the Eastern Division at 9 and 4, with St. Louis half a game back at 8–4–1. We still had a good shot at winning the division, or, depending on what happened to the Rams, who went into the final week of the season with an 8–4–1 record, and Detroit, which was 9 and 4, we could make the playoffs as the NFC's first wild-card team.

I never had another birthday like the one on December 20, 1970, the day I turned twenty-eight. I would have been up for this game anyway, with the division title and a playoff shot on the line. Also, Jake Gaither had made his annual visit to see me play. And the prospect of facing the Houston Oilers excited me, since they played a lot of bump-and-run pass defense, which was still the rage in the AFC. The bump and run was easy for me to beat because once I got past the guy at the line of scrimmage, the Oilers' free safety, Johnny Robinson, would have to cover me, and I didn't think he could. I had already proved he couldn't cover me in our exhibition game that year, scoring three touchdowns against the Oilers.

Adding to the pregame excitement was the mood on our team. We were calling this the "Ralph Neely Bowl" because it was the first regular-season game between the two teams that had signed Ralph right out of college. In fact, Houston signed him before the 1964 Gator Bowl, which made Ralph ineligible to play for Oklahoma in that game. Houston sued the Cowboys when Ralph decided to play for us instead of for the Oilers, but the dispute was settled as part of the merger between the two leagues. Houston let us keep Neely in exchange for several draft choices, including a number one. Whenever the subject came up, Ralph would say, "Bring on one of the Canadian League teams. I'll sign with them, too."

There was also the memory of our exhibition game in Houston, when the Oilers had beaten us badly, 37 to 21, in spite of my three touchdowns. Dave Manders and a few other guys went around all week telling us to "Remember the Astrodome!"

A final element in the hype over this game was that Jerry Rhome was Houston's starting quarterback, and all of us were looking forward to seeing Jerry again and playing against him. He was one of the good guys.

The game was tied 3 to 3 in the first quarter when I helped break it open by doing something I wasn't supposed to be able to do—block. With the ball at our 48, Reggie Rucker and I lined up in a flip formation on the same side, and I ran full speed down the field, taking two Oilers with me. I yelled all the way for Craig Morton to throw the ball to me, but Craig dumped it off to Reggie at the Houston 35. I cut off the last Oiler who had a shot at Reggie, who went 52 yards for his first NFL touchdown, which gave us a 10 to 3 lead.

That's when I really went to work. By the time I was finished, we were ahead 38 to 3. We had the ball in Houston territory, still in the first quarter, when I went deep. The Oilers didn't get any pressure on Morton, who waited for me to break open on a deep-post pattern and hit me behind Leroy Mitchell for a 38-yard touchdown that made the score 17 to 3. Tex Schramm had found out it was my birthday, so after that touchdown "Happy Birthday, Bob," flashed on the scoreboard.

It was going to get a lot happier. We were back on the Houston 38 in the second quarter, when Craig threw a long pass for me that was a little too high. I made a leaping catch, landed on the Oilers' 3 and rolled and crawled into the end zone while Zeke Moore of the Oilers just stood there watching me. He thought the play was dead when I hit the ground, but he was wrong. My second 38-yard touchdown, and the score was 24 to 3.

My next big play came in the third quarter when Morton, fading back from the Oilers' 15, found me at the Oilers' 5. Ken Houston, probably the best strong safety of all time, got his hands on me, but he didn't have a good grip, and I was able to break free. Johnny Peacock of the Oilers was trying to tackle me, too, but he and Ken got in each other's way, and I squirmed free and made it across the goal line for my third touchdown and a 31 to 3 lead.

I wasn't finished yet. Later in the third quarter, I ran a deep slant and was wide open at the Houston 25 when I caught Morton's pass. I went the rest of the way eased up, for a 59-yard touchdown to make it 38 to 3. After that play, I was feeling so good that I sent Jack Eskridge's son into the stands with a game ball for Altamease, who was sitting with Mrs.

Landry. The final score was 52 to 10, and I was named Associated Press Offensive Player of the Week for my performance, which included 187 yards on 6 catches, 4 of them touchdowns. About the only nonbeliever was Johnny Peacock, who said after the game that I was *"one* of the fastest receivers in the game." He must have been in a daze from getting beaten so often. Or maybe my 7 touchdowns in two games against his team didn't impress him. My 6 catches against the Oilers that day also gave me 286 for my career, which made me the leading receiver in the Cowboys' history, ahead of Frank Clarke, who caught 281.

The downside to the game was that Jerry Rhome separated his shoulder on a tackle by Jethro Pugh late in the first quarter. Jerry and Jethro were close friends before Jerry was traded, and Jerry had said to me during pregame warmups, "You tell that goddamned Jethro he better not get close to me and try to nail me today." Jethro put a good clean tackle on Jerry, and when we saw that Jerry was hurt, no one felt worse about it than Jethro.

Jerry's injury was the only bad thing that happened that day, though. We finished the season 10 and 4 and the Rams did a number on the Giants, 31 to 3, to leave the Giants 9 and 5 and make us division champs. Best of all, we had come through, winning our last five games after it looked like we might be out of it, while the Cardinals choked, losing their last three, to finish 8–5–1.

The Houston game was Craig Morton's first good game in three weeks, and he picked a bad time to start playing badly again—in the playoffs. We won our first playoff game over Detroit by one of those baseball scores that were becoming too common for us, 5 to 0. And Craig wasn't exactly the most valuable player. I accounted for over half our passing yardage with *1* catch for *20* yards—not a great day, by any means. But Craig completed just 4 of 18 for 38 yards and 1 interception. The 3 passes he threw toward me in the second quarter were typical of the whole game. The first was underthrown, the second was wide, and the third was overthrown. And these were from the guy who had gone to the coaches and gotten me benched for a while. My only reception was in the third quarter, and it moved us from our 13 to our 33. We started to drive then and got to the Detroit 40. But Craig ended our drive when he got sacked by Paul Naumoff for a 16-yard loss and we had to punt. Roger Staubach never got off the bench. Why, I don't know.

. . .

Craig wasn't much better the next week in the NFC championship game in San Francisco. He was only 7 of 22 for 101 yards, and this time I didn't catch a single pass. The 49ers double- and triple-teamed me all day, but that helped open up the field for our running game. Duane Thomas rushed for 143 yards, Walt Garrison had another 71 yards, and we maintained possession of the ball for 35 minutes to San Francisco's 25.

Even though I was shut out receiving, I contributed in other ways. With the game tied 3–3 in the second quarter, Dan Reeves and I were back to return a punt. Dan was the up man, and Steve Spurrier's kick was short. Dan fielded it but fumbled and I fell on the ball at our 15 to save a probable San Francisco touchdown. On a play like that, I always went up near our other punt returner in case he fumbled, and this time it paid off.

My other big play came late in the third quarter when the score was 10 to 3 Dallas. Following Mel Renfro's interception of a pass from John Brodie that was intended for Gene Washington, we had the ball second and 10 at the San Francisco 29. Craig Morton threw a bomb for me and I was open, but Mel Phillips hit me before the ball got there. The pass-interference penalty gave us the ball on the San Francisco 5, and Craig passed to Walt Garrison on first down for the touchdown that put us ahead 17 to 3. Brodie took the 49ers down the field after the kickoff and passed to Dick Witcher for a touchdown to make the score 17 to 10, but that was the last score of the game.

We were in the Super Bowl. At last!

I came home to Florida, to Miami, to the Orange Bowl as the leading receiver on the best team in football. Winning the gold medals had been the number-one thrill for me, but that was halfway around the world. Now I was going for the ultimate trophy in football on my own turf. My mother and all the rest of my family except for my father were in the stands, along with dozens of friends.

Super Bowl V started off well enough. We took a 3 to 0 lead on a 14-yard field goal by Mike Clark, nine minutes into the game, then started driving again from our 20 after David Lee punted into our end zone for a touchback late in the first quarter. We got out to our 47, first and 10, and I beat Jerry Logan on a bomb. Craig Morton got the ball to me, but Logan tackled me on the Baltimore 12. Logan wasn't that good a defensive back, so he tried to intimidate me. He hit me a little harder than I thought necessary, and then he sat on me and wouldn't let me off the ground. I pushed him away and we came up swinging. Neither of us got penalized, but the Colts did; Fred Miller, the Colts' defensive tackle, was called for roughing Morton after the pass, and the ball was moved half the distance to the goal line, giving us a first down at the 6. For the second straight series, though, Morton couldn't get us into the end zone after we had a first down inside the 10. Clark kicked another field goal, but we had only 6 points instead of the 14 we might have had.

After Johnny Unitas threw to John Mackey for a 75-yard score (Mark Washington blocked the extra point to leave the game tied), Lee Roy Jordan nailed Unitas near the Baltimore 20. Unitas fumbled, Jethro Pugh recovered at the Colts' 28, and we were in business. A 4-yard run by Duane Thomas and a 17-yard pass from Morton to Dan Reeves got us to the 7 and then Craig passed to Duane for a touchdown that gave us a 13 to 6 halftime lead.

But the difference in the game was at quarterback. The Colts changed quarterbacks, sending in Earl Morrall to replace Unitas after our touchdown, but we didn't. Craig Morton had been fair in the first half, 8 of 16 for 100 yards and 1 touchdown, but in the second half, with all the money on the line, he was 4 of 10 for 27 yards, no touchdowns—and 3 interceptions. Our defense kept us ahead, shutting out the Colts for a quarter and a half, but then Craig threw the game away. First, with third and 7 at our 23, his pass was picked off by Rick Volk at our 33 and run back 30 yards to our 3. Baltimore quickly tied the game on a 2-yard run over left tackle by Tom Nowatzke. We exchanged punts, and I caught the second one and went out of bounds immediately at the Baltimore 48. A tie game, with one minute, fifty-two seconds left to play, and we were just 20 yards or so from field-goal range.

It wasn't to be. Bubba Smith tackled Duane Thomas for a loss of 1 on first down, and then Fred Miller sacked Craig Morton for a loss of 9 more. On top of that, we got called for holding, and the ball was moved all the way back to our 27, second and 35. Craig threw for Dan Reeves near our 40, but the ball bounced off Dan's hands and was intercepted by Mike Curtis, who returned it to our 28. With fifty-nine seconds left, Baltimore was in the driver's seat. The Colts ate up the clock with two running plays that left the ball on our 25, and Jim O'Brien broke our hearts with a 32-yard field goal with five seconds left.

We did have one more shot—we took over after the kickoff at our 40 with one second left. Craig Morton's pass to Walt Garrison was (guess what?) intercepted by Jerry Logan at the Colts' 29. I don't know what Craig was thinking on that play because *Walt Garrison* wouldn't have scored from the 29 even if he had caught the ball. After Logan's interception, the final gun sounded, and we had lost, 16 to 13.

My 41-yard catch in the first quarter was my only reception of the day. For that matter, it was the only pass Craig completed to anyone but a running back. Tom Landry summed it up after the game: "We beat ourselves." Tom didn't point the finger at anyone then, but nearly twenty years later, Gerald Strine, a sportswriter, hadn't forgotten whom to blame. Early in 1989, just before the 49ers beat Cincinnati in Super Bowl XXIII, Strine wrote, "Baltimore triumphed, 16–13, when quarterback Craig Morton proved to be too heavy a load for his Cowboy teammates to carry. Morton could bury any team he was on in pressure situations, as Denver discovered seven years later, losing to Dallas in Super Bowl XII, 27 to 10." Too bad Craig wasn't playing for Baltimore that day in Miami. By the time the Cowboys beat Denver, I was retired.

Because of the Lance Rentzel situation and the ineffectiveness of our other receivers, I was our leading receiver that year, even though I was benched for several games. I caught 34 passes for 889 yards, and my 26.1 average was the best in the league. I finished third in the NFC in touchdowns receiving with 10; our whole team only had 18 touchdown passes. (Dennis Homan, the guy they benched me for, caught a total of 7 passes for 105 yards and no touchdowns.) I was also seventh in the NFC in punt returns, with 15 for 116 yards, a 7.7 average. And I carried the ball 4 times for 34 yards and 1 touchdown; my 11 total touchdowns also placed me among the league's leaders.

13

THIS YEAR'S CHAMPIONS

I played out my option in 1970, which I think had a lot to do with the Cowboys benching me for part of the year. I was the first Cowboy who had ever played out his option, and a lot of people in the organization resented that, plus the fact that I was black and outspoken. At the end of the 1970 season, I became a free agent—"free,"at least in theory, to negotiate with any team in the NFL. Several clubs were very interested in signing me, particularly the Redskins, the Jets, the Dolphins, the Rams, and the Chiefs. The idea of playing for the Jets really excited me—teaming with Joe Namath and being in New York where the major media and the opportunity for endorsements were. But none of the other teams actually offered me a contract. The situation in the NFL was pretty much the same then as it is now: A true star didn't really have much opportunity to change teams because the team he signed with would have had to pay too much to his old team. If a player changed teams, NFL Commissioner Pete Rozelle had the right to decide what compensation was due the player's old team. I know that the Redskins, for instance, were afraid that if they signed me, Rozelle would award Charley Taylor to the Cowboys. It made sense—one outstanding receiver for another, we were about the same age, and Charley is from Dallas. And the same thing happened with the Dolphins. They wanted to sign me, but they were worried that Rozelle would award Paul Warfield to Dallas. The "Rozelle rule," as it was known, left me without much hope of actually signing with another team.

The reason I had played out my option was that the Cowboys weren't paying me enough, and a lot of talk back and forth between the team and me was reported in the Dallas newspapers during the 1970 season. I didn't reveal it until we got to training camp in 1971, but I received anonymous calls in October 1970 from people who said they didn't like the way the Cowboys were treating me and that they were going to bomb the houses of Tom Landry and Tex Schramm unless the club gave me a fair shake. I told the callers that was ridiculous, and then they said, "You're either with us or you're against us," and threatened to kidnap my daughter Rori, who was eighteen months old at the time. I asked them, "How about if I pay you two hundred dollars, will you leave me and the team officials alone?" They said they would, and I dropped off two hundred dollars in cash at a school playground and never heard from them again. I guess that giving money to people like that was a stupid thing to do, but I was afraid for my family. If they had called back, I would have contacted the police and the FBI, which I know is what I should have done in the first place.

My negotiations with the Cowboys kept dragging on and getting more and more bitter. After six seasons in the league, I was only making about $40,000 a year, and I thought I was worth a lot more. Even Tom Landry, who didn't participate in salary negotiations, told me he was very disappointed by my salary when I showed him what I was making. Toward the end of May 1971, when the Cowboys and my agent, Steve Falk, a Miami lawyer, were in the middle of their talks, the Cowboys pulled two blockbuster trades that were triggered by Lance Rentzel's situation. Dallas sent Lance to the Rams in exchange for Billy Truax, a tight end, and Wendell Tucker, a wide receiver, and traded Pettis Norman, Tony Liscio, and Ron East to San Diego for Lance Alworth. That was a low point for me for two reasons.

First, I heard that Alworth was making about twice as much money as I was. Here I had been with the team for over six years, since they started winning, and they didn't want to pay me that kind of money. Don't get me wrong. I respect Lance Alworth. He was an outstanding wide receiver and a nice guy. But he was more than happy playing on the other side from me, knowing he wouldn't get as much attention from the defenses as I did. I was still number one, and the other teams feared my speed.

Second, I hated to see Pettis go. I'm the godfather to his oldest daughter, we had been neighbors and close friends when blacks couldn't live in

North Dallas, and he had been one of the black players that younger blacks like me looked up to from the moment we joined the Cowboys.

Steve Falk and I were negotiating with Al Ward, an assistant to Gil Brandt. Al was one of the nicest guys I ever met, but at one point during our contract talks, he looked at me and said, "Who the hell is Bob Hayes? Bob Hayes ain't nothing." That really pissed me off. I know that pro football is a business, but I was the all-time leading receiver for the Dallas Cowboys and the guy tells me I'm not worth a damn.

Gil Brandt took over the negotiations after that, but it didn't help. I asked for $100,000, and Gil didn't want to pay me more than a base salary of $55,000. We finally agreed on a five-year contract that paid me the $55,000 base plus $15,000 just for reporting to training camp and another $10,000 at the end of the season. With other incentives, it came to about $85,000 a year, making me one of the highest-paid wide receivers in the league at the time. And I got a no-trade clause in my contract, something I really wanted.

I wasn't the only Cowboy who was unhappy with what he was making; in fact, most of the players felt the same way. Craig Morton, Mel Renfro, Blaine Nye, and Jethro Pugh reported to training camp without contract agreements because the team hadn't offered them enough money, and Chuck Howley felt the team was treating him so badly that he announced his retirement. (Chuck eventually changed his mind and played until 1973.) Here we were, the most winning team in pro football, but far from the best paid. Things soured so much between Duane Thomas and the Cowboys—and money was one of the big factors—that they couldn't be patched up, and the team had to trade him the following year.

The players' dissatisfaction with how much we were making had a long history. In my third or fourth year with the team, when we were going through a period when we couldn't quite get over the hump and win the big game, Tex Schramm gave a speech to the team in training camp—something he had never done before. He said, "I want this team to do better, and whatever it takes for us to do better, we're going to do it. If you guys have any questions or suggestions, I want to hear them and I want to have a good relationship between management and the players so that we can all work toward our common goal, winning the championship."

George Andrie held his hand up and called out, "Why don't you pay the players what we deserve? I make the Pro Bowl every year, and there are guys out there playing my position on other teams making more money than I do." Everybody else joined in with George, and old Tex got real red in the face the way he did when he was angry and left the meeting as fast as he could.

With a record of 3 and 2, we were two games behind George Allen's Redskins, who opened with five straight wins, including a 20 to 16 victory over us in Dallas, when we made our Texas Stadium debut against the New England Patriots on October 24, 1971. Lyndon B. Johnson—whom I had met once before when he invited the gold medal winners to the White House after the 1964 Olympics—Lady Bird, and Mamie Eisenhower were guests in Clint Murchison's box for the opening of the new stadium.

I was psyched for the game and I got us started with a 20-yard catch out to our 44 on the third play of the game. Duane Thomas ran 56 yards around right end on the next play to put us up, 7 to 0. We had extended our lead to 20 to 7 near the end of the half, and then I made it a day to remember. Lee Roy Jordan recovered a fumble by Jim Nance on the Patriots' 35, and on first down, Roger Staubach came my way with a pass at the Patriots' 15. The ball was thrown a little low, but I scooped it up, stayed on my feet, juked one cornerback, and was gone for a touchdown. Our defense went right to work, and between four tackles behind the line of scrimmage and a 15-yard holding call, the Patriots had fourth and 61, if you can believe that, at their own 9. Charlie Waters called for a fair catch of Tom Janik's punt at the Patriots' 48, Roger passed to Lance Alworth for 20, and on first and 10 at their 28, he found me open across the middle again for another touchdown, with twenty-nine seconds left in the half. That made the score 34 to 7, and the only question after that was what the final score would be—it was 44 to 21. Jim Plunkett, the second great rookie quarterback we had faced in two weeks (we had played against Archie Manning and the Saints a week earlier), looked good, and so did his Stanford teammate, Randy Vataha, that little wide receiver, but the Patriots' defense couldn't stop us. I was our leading receiver with 3 catches for 83 yards and the 2 touchdowns.

Lyndon Johnson visited the locker room after the game and talked about the time he called Jake Gaither when I was at Florida A & M and asked Jake to keep me off the football field until the Olympics were over, to prevent me from getting hurt. Johnson said Jake's answer was, "Mr. President, Bob Hayes is a football player. He just happens to be the world's fastest human. He came here on a football scholarship, and I'm going to let him do what he wants to do, play football."

Some of our players didn't like our new stadium. Pat Toomay, for one, used to say there was no breeze and the air was too heavy because it was built in the swamps, but it's a beautiful stadium, and I always liked it. I missed the Cotton Bowl, with all its memories, and many low-income people couldn't afford the higher prices at Texas Stadium, but other than that it didn't make much difference to me where we played. It may be surprising that it didn't matter too much to me, even though I was a sprinter, whether we played on natural grass as in the Cotton Bowl, or on artificial turf as in Texas Stadium. I just figured I was faster than anyone else on any kind of surface.

Lance Rentzel spent Thanksgiving Day 1971 where he had the previous four years—in Dallas. But this time he was a member of the Los Angeles Rams. We were all glad to see him, but that didn't mean we were going to miss our one chance to welcome him home with a hard time. We goosed him, we pinched him, and we teased him; when he would run back to the huddle after going out for a pass, our defensive players would push him out of the way. Lance knew that we were trying to help him out of what might have been a very uncomfortable situation, and he didn't stop smiling the whole day. He and I were held to one catch each, but mine was a 51-yard touchdown just before halftime that tied the game 14–14. I ran a simple turn-in and go, and Roger Staubach laid it in. Tom Landry called it the key play of the game, and we went on to win our fourth straight, 28 to 21, making our record 8 and 3.

When I think about that game, it reminds me again of how hard it is to get to the top and how easy it is to fall off. Not only did Lance and I run into problems, but so did Travis Williams, the ex-Packer, who was one of the Rams' stars that day and kept burning us with long kickoff returns. I was reminded of that game several years ago when I heard that Travis was a homeless person, living on the streets of Los Angeles.

The Giants gave us a much tougher game than the Jets did. After running up a 52 to 10 score against the Jets, we beat the Giants by only 42 to 14—our sixth win in a row. I opened the scoring when I ran a deep post, Roger Staubach found me at the Giants' 5, and I breezed in for a 46-yard touchdown. That touchdown more than made up for a clipping call I had gotten a few plays earlier for a hit on one of the Giants' linebackers that nullified a long gain by Calvin Hill on a screen pass. After seven years in the NFL, I still got a kick out of making a vicious hit, even an illegal one, as long as it didn't cost us the game.

The next time we had the ball, I went 29 yards to the New York 29 on a pass from Roger. A few plays later, on first and 10 at the 14, I took a pitchout around left end and had visions of one of my rare touchdowns running. One of the Giants got me at the 3, but Duane Thomas scored on the next play to make the score 14 to 0. We added another touchdown and then with second and 2 at our 15 late in the half, Roger sent me on a deep route. I didn't find out about it until after the play, but Roger had to duck a Giants defender and then stiff-arm him on the helmet to get the pass off. I was sandwiched between two former Cowboys, Otto Brown and Richmond Flowers, and damned if they didn't collide, just as if they were still working for us. I caught the pass at the New York 35 and trotted the rest of the way for an 85-yard touchdown. That touchdown increased our lead to 28 to 0, and we coasted from there. I had one of my last great games, with 4 catches for 154 yards and the 2 touchdowns and 1 carry for 11 yards.

As we went into our last game against St. Louis, our record was 10 and 3. But the Redskins had won three straight since we beat them, and their record was 9–3–1. If they beat Cleveland and we lost, Washington would win the division championship, although we were guaranteed of at least making the playoffs as the wild-card team.

Our game with St. Louis was on Saturday, and we made the next day's game between Washington and Cleveland meaningless by whipping the Cardinals, 31 to 12. I caught 3 passes for 46 yards, and, like the rest of the Cowboys, I took a back seat that day to Duane Thomas, who scored all four of our touchdowns. That was Duane's last regular season game as a Cowboy, and that's the way I'll remember him: totally unstoppable.

Our playoff opener on Christmas Day in Minnesota matched the teams with the best records in the NFL. We had both finished 11 and 3, and the Vikings had allowed the fewest points in the league with that powerhouse defense of theirs—Carl Eller, Alan Page, Jim Marshall, Paul Krause, and the gang. We got a break on the weather, which wasn't too bad, and from the Vikings' offense, which turned the ball over five times (we didn't give up the ball once). The Vikings' defense shut us down with just 183 yards of total offense all day, but they couldn't overcome their own offensive unit. I was held to 3 catches for 31 yards, but the last one was the biggest play of the game. I beat Ed Sharockman and was all alone at the rear corner of the end zone when Roger found me for a 9-yard touchdown that put us ahead 20 to 3 with less than two minutes to go in the third quarter. Page tackled Roger for a fourth-quarter safety, and Gary Cuozzo connected with Stu Voight for a late touchdown, but we still came out with a pretty comfortable win, 20 to 12, and a berth in the NFC championship.

The 49ers beat Washington in the first round, setting up a Dallas–San Francisco match in the playoffs for the second straight year. This game turned out to be a defensive struggle, which we won, 14 to 3. Roger completed only 9 of 18 for 103 yards; I caught 2 for 22 yards. I also returned punts after returning only one the whole year, but I couldn't get loose there either. I fielded 3 punts altogether, but had to call fair catches on 2 and returned the third for just 3 yards. I didn't figure in our only scoring drive, an 80-yard drive that led to a 2-yard run by Duane Thomas in the fourth period. (Our first touchdown, a 1-yard run by Calvin Hill in the second quarter, came after George Andrie intercepted one of John Brodie's passes at the San Francisco 9 and returned it to the 2.) This one certainly wasn't a pretty victory, but it was all we needed to make it to New Orleans and a date with the Miami Dolphins in Super Bowl VI.

January 16, 1972, was probably the second biggest date in my athletic career after the Olympics in Tokyo. We were favored to beat the Dolphins, and on my way to Tulane Stadium, I thought, "Man, if we can win this, I'll be the first guy to win both an Olympic gold medal and a Super Bowl ring."

The Dolphins did us a big favor by playing Larry Csonka and Jim Kiick at running back the whole game. We stacked our defense from tackle to tackle because Csonka and Kiick were too slow to run outside. If Don Shula had used Mercury Morris some, the Dolphins might have caused us trouble, but Morris never got to carry the ball. Bob Griese threw the ball short all day for the Dolphins, which I thought was also a mistake. The Dolphins' game plan was just bad, and their offense never really got going. The final score was 24 to 3, and now I had made history in two sports and the Cowboys were no longer "Next Year's Champions," as the cynics called us.

We really only had three scoring drives (Chuck Howley set up our final touchdown by intercepting a pass and returning it 41 yards to the Miami 9 in the fourth quarter), and I figured in two of them. Roger got sacked for a 13-yard loss, leaving us with second and 23 at the Miami 36 late in the first quarter, and on the next play he hit me over the middle for 18 yards to the Dolphin 18, where Jake Scott tackled me. We got a field goal from Mike Clark out of that to break a scoreless tie. My big moment, the one that let me believe that I really had had something important to do with beating the Dolphins, came early in the third period with the Cowboys ahead 10 to 3. On first and 10 at the Dolphins' 22, Roger faked the ball on a sweep left to Duane and then handed it to me on a sweep right. Duane had been tearing up the Dolphins all day, and most of them fell for the fake and started chasing him. I had plenty of room to run and I gained 16 yards to the 6 before Bob Heinz, a defensive tackle, got me. Walt Garrison picked up 3 yards and then Duane ran the final 3 around left end to give us a 17 to 3 lead that we all felt was safe, the way our defense was holding down the Dolphins.

This was another of those games where we didn't do that much passing—12 completions for 119 yards—and I had 2 catches for 23 yards, as well as the 16-yard gain rushing. My numbers weren't that great, but my feelings were when I picked up the Super Bowl trophy and later when I put the ring on my finger. I got another thrill when Lyndon Johnson visited our locker room after the game and singled me out for praise. It was really nice to have at least one president on our side, because Richard Nixon had called Don Shula before the game and suggested that the Dolphins throw a down-and-in route to Paul Warfield. The Dolphins did try Nixon's play, but Mel Renfro broke up the pass.

All things considered, 1971 was a pretty good year for me individually. I had 35 catches for 840 yards (the second most yards receiving in the NFC) and my 24.0 average was the best in the league. My 8 touchdowns receiving were the most in the NFC, and I was disappointed at not making the Pro Bowl. I thought that I played *at least* as well as the four wide receivers who were named to the NFC team—Dick Gordon of Chicago, Bob Grim of Minnesota, Roy Jefferson of the Redskins, and Gene Washington of San Francisco. The four of them *averaged* only 5 touchdowns a man, and I gained more yardage than all of them except Gene Washington, who had 44 more yards than I did. It's true that my 35 receptions ranked only seventeenth in the NFC, but I was getting so much double and triple coverage that other guys were open. Roger led the league in passing that year because, unlike Craig, he was willing to spread the ball around. We had four receivers with 30 or more catches; Walt Garrison with 40, me with 35, Lance Alworth with 34, and Mike Ditka with 30.

Still, what I had to show for 1971—a Super Bowl ring at last—was all I really wanted.

14

A COWBOY'S
LAST RIDE

As the 1972 season began, sportswriters were comparing me to "Willie Mays and Hank Aaron, chasing the ghost of Babe Ruth." I was in hot pursuit of Don Hutson's all-time record of 99 career touchdown receptions, with 67 in my first seven seasons, which worked out to 9.6 a year. That average was higher than Hutson's 9.0 a year, Lance Alworth's 8.3 a year, Don Maynard's 7.2 a year, or anyone else's. Frank Luksa of the *Dallas Times Herald*, the one who said I was like Mays and Aaron, also wrote while we were in training camp that I was "the greatest climax receiver active in the game today, perhaps of all time." But by the end of 1972, which was my worst season, the talk was that I was washed up.

Even though I had pulled my hamstring during our final exhibition game against Oakland, I started our regular-season opener against the Eagles. And I ran into disaster on the first play of the game. We started at our own 19 and Craig Morton, playing in place of Roger Staubach, who had separated a shoulder in the preseason, faded back and aimed a bomb toward me. I was running a deep slant-in and I had Leroy Keyes beaten, but when the ball came down out of the hole in the top of Texas Stadium, the sun was shining right in my eyes, and I never saw the pass. Instead of being an 81-yard touchdown, the ball hit me in the back of my hands and fell to the ground. Bill Bradley started to chase me after I beat Keyes and yelled, "Hey, Bobby, don't catch that ball!" After I dropped the ball,

Bill told me he must have scared me. My muff didn't keep us from winning easily, 28 to 6, but my only catch of the day was for 5 yards. And now Craig had something else to blame me for.

My hamstring injury kept me out of our 23 to 14 win over New York. It had to be hurting bad for me to miss a game against the Giants; I had played twelve games against them and scored a touchdown in every one. In those twelve games, of which we had won ten, I had caught 53 passes for 1,292 yards and 18 touchdowns, an average of 4.4 catches, 108 yards, and 1.5 touchdowns a game.

Although I was healthy again after a week off, Ron Sellers and Billy Parks were getting most of the time at wide receiver, and I was spending a lot of time on the bench. Sellers and Parks started again when we went to San Diego midway through the 1972 season, but I did play some—my bad luck. On one play, Deacon Jones, who was then with the Chargers, hit me while I was in the air and knocked me backwards about five yards. After that hit, I had to make sure all my parts were still where they were supposed to be. Herb Adderley and I didn't get along while he was with the Packers, ever since he speared me one time while I was on the ground, but we became friends after the Packers traded him to us in 1970. During the game against the Chargers, Herb and I were standing on the sidelines looking at Deacon, and Herb said to me, "Speedo, is he ugly?" "He's ugly, all right," I answered. Deacon and I were friends, but he was still ugly. Bubba Smith used to say that Deacon was the ugliest player in the league. Of course, Bubba was even bigger than Deacon, and he played defense, so he never had to play against Deacon. For that matter, neither did Herb. But Deacon saw Herb and me talking about him, and when I got in the game I had to pay the price.

Craig complained about me after we faced San Francisco in the opening round of the 1972 playoffs, and this time I did screw up. Not that I complained about him when he made a mistake. The 49ers had beaten us badly a month earlier, 31 to 10, and it looked like they were going to repeat. They had us down, 28 to 13, late in the third quarter, when I finally entered the game. We had third and 10 at midfield, and Craig sent me out on a deep route. I beat Jimmy Johnson and was wide open at the goal line, but the pass bounced off my hands incomplete. We had to punt and when we got the ball back, Tom Landry benched Craig (which seemed strange; Craig was not having a good day, but I could have turned it around and pulled us to within 8 points by catching that perfect pass), and went to Roger.

I guess you could say my miss had a lot to do with the course of the Cowboys' history. Craig's star faded from then on, and Roger came in and led us to one of those miracle finishes he became so famous for. Roger's pass to Billy Parks got us to 28 to 23 with a minute and a half to play, and then Mel Renfro recovered an onsides kickoff at midfield. Roger scrambled for 21 yards and hit Parks for 19 to give us a first down at the San Francisco 10 with 56 seconds left. Then came the play of plays: Roger to Sellers for the touchdown that won the game for us, 30 to 28. Actually, I was in the same part of the end zone as Sellers and I thought the ball was coming to me, but Sellers ran right in front of me and caught it. Happy as I was that we won, I couldn't help wishing I had been the one to make the catch, which would have helped make up for a lousy year. I guess that only happens in Hollywood.

Washington beat Green Bay 16 to 3 in the first round, so we went to Washington for the NFC final. I was back in limbo. I hardly played, although most of the Cowboys who got onto the field didn't play either, because the Redskins totally dominated us, 26 to 3. We had 169 yards of total offense and only 73 passing, and I couldn't help wondering if things might have been different if I had played. I wasn't alone; Mike Bass, the Redskins cornerback who often covered me, expressed his thanks to the Cowboys organization after the game for making his day a lot easier by not using me.

The 1972 season was a forgettable one for me: 15 catches for 200 yards, a 13.3 average, and *not 1 touchdown!* Without me as a deep threat, the Cowboys scored only 16 touchdowns passing, and our longest pass of the year, which was only 55 yards, was thrown by Calvin Hill! Tom Landry said he thought I had lost my confidence, between my injuries (I had two pulled hamstrings and a sore hip that left me limping for much of the regular season) and dropping a few passes like the one on the opening play of our opening game against Philadelphia. But to me, his excuse was just bullshit. My injuries weren't that serious, and I could have made up for the balls I dropped if he had played me. By now I was wishing that the team would trade me to a team that understood what all the defensive backs who didn't have to play against me meant when they expressed their thanks to the Cowboys: Speed kills!

Partly to prove I wasn't over the hill, but mostly to help give track athletes a chance to earn money as professionals, I joined the new International Track Association (ITA) after the 1972 football season. Jim Ryun, Bob Seagren, and Randy Matson were some of the other track stars who signed on with the ITA. My role over the next few months was to run the 40-yard dash against other NFL stars in towns where they were stars. That meant that I ran against Willie Buchanon of the Packers in San Diego, where he had gone to college; Greg Pruitt of the Browns in Oklahoma (he had starred at the University of Oklahoma); and so forth. The winner of each race earned $500, and the loser earned $400, plus expenses. The money wasn't great, but, like I say, it was a chance to redeem my reputation and help the professional track circuit get going. And it was fun, too.

I did great in those track meets. I won fifteen out of sixteen races, all of them against guys several years younger than I was. The only race I lost was to Cliff Branch of the Raiders on a night when I had just finished going through a new weight-lifting program with the Cowboys and was sore all over. I wanted a rematch with Branch, but he declined. The night he beat me, I ran only a 4.8, but when I beat Mel Gray of the Cardinals in St. Louis, I ran a 4.3, which was an unofficial world record. (St. Louis was still a good track town for me, ten years after I had set my 100-yard record there.) "Is it possible that at 30 [and more than two Olympics cycles after the Tokyo Olympics] he is still the world's fastest human?" asked Kenny Moore, a former world-class distance runner who covered track for *Sports Illustrated*, in a story about me. To ask that question, I think, was to answer it. And don't forget, I ran that 4.3 race indoors, without any heavy training for track, practicing starts, or anything like that. We all wanted to win, but nobody was out there getting in track shape, and we weren't even in top-notch football shape because this was during our off-season.

As usual, there were changes in our wide-receiver corps between the 1972 and 1973 seasons. Players kept coming and going, and I kept staying. It was like the Cowboys wanted me, but didn't want me. The new challengers were Otto Stowe, who had been acquired from Miami in a trade for one of the old challengers—Ron Sellers—and a number-2 draft choice, and Golden Richards, our second-round choice in 1973 out of Hawaii. I finally got to the point where I met with Tom Landry and told him I didn't know why the team kept on bringing in all these deceivers when I had played such a big part in his offense over the years. I told him I thought I should still be playing, and he agreed.

We opened the regular season at Soldier Field with a 20 to 17 victory over the Chicago Bears, and I scored my first touchdown except for exhibition games since our 1971 playoff against Minnesota. It came with 19 seconds left in the half on an 18-yard pass from Roger Staubach; I ran a quick post and beat Joe Taylor to the end zone. That catch, my only one of the game, gave us a 17 to 3 lead and was a big play in a game that tight. It was nice—a lot more than nice—to be back on the scoreboard. Those out-of-town sports fans who didn't read anything except the box score would at least know that Bob Hayes hadn't died or been put out to pasture.

I had another good game, 3 catches for 50 yards, when we beat the Saints the next week, 40 to 3. And the following week, when we ran up another big number on the Cardinals, 45 to 10, I caught only 2 passes, but they were both big gainers—47 yards and 20 yards—and led to our first 2 touchdowns. But in our first loss, a big Monday night game in Washington, with Roger playing the first half and Craig playing the second, not a single pass was thrown to me. This was the famous game in which the Redskins beat us 14 to 7 when Ken Houston stopped Walt Garrison, who must have outweighed Kenny by at least 10 pounds, just short of the goal line at the end of the game. The Redskins had played in the Super Bowl the year before, and Kenny, who was in his first season with the Redskins after several years with the Oilers, told me after the game that this was everything he had dreamed about in football. National television; a big rivalry involving everyone, from national political figures to local disc jockeys; a capacity crowd; a beautiful night, outdoors; natural grass; and a big game—and he had saved it for his team. I knew what Kenny meant, and I felt lucky to have been a part of that game and that rivalry. I just wished I had played as big a role as he had and won the game for us.

* * *

Otto Stowe broke his ankle in a game in Philadelphia halfway through the 1973 season, putting him out for the year. With him gone, I was starting at one wide receiver spot, and Drew Pearson, a free agent from Tulsa, and Mike Montgomery, a converted runningback, were sharing the other one. I got back in the scoring column on a 39-yard pass from Roger and had a total of 5 catches for 74 yards as we beat Cincinnati, 38 to 10. I felt I had proved that I was still the same old Bob Hayes: Get me the ball and I would score and we would win. But what I remember best about this game is old Buzz, Jethro Pugh. We were ahead 31 to 10 in the fourth quarter and having a good time when Ken Anderson of the Bengals completed a pass to Essex Johnson, who fumbled the ball near midfield when Mel Renfro tackled him. Jethro picked up the ball at the Cincinnati 42 and started steaming down the field. This was the closest he ever came to going all the way, but the Bengals caught up to him at their 7. All I could do was shake my head and tell him, "I don't know what's wrong with you. Everybody but you scored a touchdown. Even Baby Cakes [Willie Townes] scored once." Landry's analysis was that Jethro had shown great open-field ability, but might have to work a little bit on his speed.

Our passing game was ineffective, and I caught just 2 for 21 yards in a 23 to 10 win over New York. On one of my catches, a screen pass that gained 7 yards in the third period, the Giants really buried me. Richmond Flowers and Otto Brown were Giants defensive backs who had played for us, and they knew our audible signals. When the weakside linebacker moved inside the defensive end and over our tackle, that was a tipoff that the opposition was getting ready to blitz, so our quarterback would audible a quick screen to me. The quarterback would fake the ball inside and throw it out to me 2 yards or so up the field, with our tackle coming out to lead the screen. That was one of our most successful plays. So on this particular Sunday in Yankee Stadium, Staubach saw the blitz coming and called "54," the quick screen to me on the right. By the time I caught the ball, the whole Giants team was running after me, laughing like hell and yelling, "We know your audible system." Flowers and Brown were laughing the hardest. Even the linebacker, who was supposed to be blitzing, was one of the first guys after me. I don't know how I got 7 yards before they swarmed over me, but I think I was under about a ton of Giants by the time they all finished getting in on the tackle.

I scored another touchdown when we beat the Eagles 31 to 10 the Sunday before Thanksgiving. We had noticed a play Atlanta had run against the Eagles a week earlier and it worked real well, so we decided to use it ourselves. Early in the third quarter, with us leading by only 14 to 10, we had second and 9 at the Eagles' 28 and I ran a delay, hiding behind our big offensive linemen. There was no way the Eagles linebackers and defensive backs could see me, and all of a sudden I burst out of the backfield, Roger tossed the ball over the head of Marlin McKeever, the Eagles middle linebacker, and into my hands at the Philadelphia 24, and I ran the rest of the way for the score that put us in command. As I got near the goal line, Bill Bradley was waiting for me, and I tried to run right over him, but he ducked under me and didn't make much of an effort to stop me. He and Roger had gotten into a fight earlier in the game when Bradley was lying on the ground in Roger's way as Roger scored on a 1-yard run and Roger stepped on Bradley's head on purpose—we were always out to get Bradley. My touchdown was my only catch of the game, but it did the job.

I pulled a muscle early in our final game in St. Louis and missed almost the entire game, but we routed the Cardinals, 30 to 3, to clinch first place even though the Redskins beat Philadelphia. So now for the eighth year in a row (ninth, if you count the runnerup game we played against Baltimore in my rookie year), we were in the playoffs. And we were in a good position because winning the division meant we got to play at home in the playoffs, while the Redskins, as the wild card, had to go on the road.

My only catch in the playoff opener against the Rams was near the end of the game. We had third and 7 at the Los Angeles 41 and Roger found me free at the 15; I gained 3 more yards before Steve Preece downed me at the 12. Toni Fritsch kicked a 12-yard field goal several plays later for the final score in our 27 to 16 win.

■　■　■

And then it was time for the final playoff game of my career, on December 30, 1973. I was our leading receiver, but, unfortunately, that was with just 2 catches for 25 yards as the Vikings held us to 153 yards of total offense and beat us easily, 27 to 10. The Vikings defense was just too good for us that day, especially without Calvin Hill, who hurt his elbow near the end of the game against the Rams and had to sit out this game.

The year 1973 was so-so for me. I caught 22 passes for 360 yards, a 16.4 average, and 3 touchdowns. Calvin Hill was our leading receiver with only 32 catches, and we had three wide receivers finish with virtually identical statistics—Otto Stowe with 23 catches and Drew Pearson and I with 22 apiece. We hadn't quite made the Super Bowl, but we had come close, and I hadn't quite had a great season, but it wasn't a terrible one either.

I'd love to say that I ended my career with the Cowboys in a blaze of glory, but that's not the way it happened. My career pretty much just petered out.

I got off on the wrong foot in 1974 when I was an outspoken leader of our players' union and the Associated Press quoted me while I was in Miami in March as saying that players like Bob Lilly, Pat Toomay, and Lee Roy Jordan would be "marked men" if the NFL Players Association called a strike and they didn't support it. I had been trying to get all the players on the team to pay their union dues; everyone benefited from the union, and the dues were completely tax deductible. But some of the older guys didn't want to pay. "If they're not going to back us, to hell with them," I told the Associated Press. "They can feed them to the fish as far as I'm concerned. [If they don't support the strike] they'd better be looking out the corner of their eye [on the playing field]."

Naturally, my comments caused a lot of controversy when they were reported in the Dallas press. Tom Landry called me to his office when I got back to town and told me, "Bobby, you cut your teammates up and I don't like it." I responded, "Coach Landry, what I'm saying is the truth, it benefits them as much as it benefits me, but I'm spending my money and they're not. Now if you're going to call me in here about something that I believe in, that's honest and true and can help this ball club on the whole, then something is wrong here." Tom repeated that he didn't like me cutting up his players, and we didn't end the meeting on the best of terms. The thing is, I was right; it didn't matter whether we were in favor of the strike or opposed to it, just as long as the whole team stuck together. The Redskins proved that in the two most recent strike seasons—1982 and 1987—they were the most unified team and they won the Super Bowl each year. It's no coincidence, in my opinon, that the Cowboys were divided over the strike in 1974 and failed to make the playoffs for the first time in nine seasons.

By the time we opened the regular season with a 24 to 0 win in Atlanta, I was benched for good. I had been out picketing when Golden Richards reported to training camp. On the sidelines, Golden Richards always hung around Mike Ditka, the assistant coach in charge of receivers, and puckered up to him so he could get to play. Ditka told Landry that I was a troublemaker and that I was a distraction on the team. Ditka wasn't fair to me during my last season with the Cowboys, although we have made up since then. I cannot go around hating people because of my immaturity or theirs, their bad judgments or mine. I can be putting my energy into something else.

Golden Richards, meanwhile, was always saying that my era was over and that he had beaten me out. I went to practice one day early in the season on a light workout day and said to him, "Golden, you think my era is over? You think I can't run any more? Right now, in the forty-yard dash, in front of all our teammates, I'm going to give you two yards, meaning you only have to run thirty-eight yards, and I'm going to beat you." The entire team got excited, they were lined up on both sides, and we ran between them at the Cowboys' practice field on Forest Lane, and I beat him. He couldn't believe it. He said, "You've got to do it again." I said, "Okay, if you want to do it again, I'm going to bet ten dollars." He said, "Fine." I beat him again. After that, he hung around me and puckered around me all day like a puppy.

The coaches still wouldn't let me play. But they had a lot of guilt, knowing that they weren't honest and fair with me. Tom Landry tried to rationalize it to the reporters who covered the team by telling them that I had the flu when I reported to training camp and that I had never gotten in shape as a result. Well, I did have the flu at the beginning of training camp. But that was more than a month before the regular season began, and the flu just doesn't last that long. Landry may not have wanted to admit that he and his coaches thought Golden Richards was a better player than I was, but that was the truth—not the flimsy excuse he gave to the press. I was in shape by the time the season opened, and Landry knew it.

By now I was playing so little that it was an occasion when I caught a pass, the way it used to be when I scored a touchdown. After our opening-game win over Atlanta, we lost four straight for the first time in my career with the Cowboys. I got 1 pass for 16 yards in our second game, a 13 to 10 loss to Philadelphia. Then I achieved a milestone of sorts in our next game: With eleven seconds to play, I caught what would be the last touchdown pass of my NFL career—a 35-yarder from Roger. Fittingly, it was against the Giants, and also fittingly, considering what had happened to my career, Mac Percival's point-after attempt hit the goal post and was no good—not that it made any difference, since we lost, 14 to 6. Another thing that showed where we stood that day was that only 46,000 fans showed up, our smallest crowd for a regular-season game at home since my rookie year. The fans knew that we didn't have the best team and that without me in the lineup, we weren't exciting.

I caught my fifth pass of the season (for six yards, oh, boy!) in our seventh game of the year against the Giants, who were now playing in the Yale Bowl. But what was significant about that game was that New York's first-string quarterback, Jim Del Gaizo, got off to a bad start and the Giants went to their backup quarterback in the second quarter. The backup was Craig Morton. Yes, Craig had been traded to the Giants a few days earlier, and he was now their second-string quarterback behind Jim Del Gaizo. You don't remember Jim Del Gaizo?

During the pregame warmups, I was the first guy Craig came over to greet and hug. After all, we went back a long way, didn't we—all the way back to the College All-Star camp. I guess I should have snubbed him for what he had done to me, but I just couldn't. I hugged him and said, "Hi, Craig, how you doing?" Some of the black Cowboys like Jean Fugett were upset with me over my friendliness to Craig. "This guy tried to ruin your career here and you're hugging him? Screw him!" Jean told me with a lot of heat. All I could say was, "Jean, I just don't stay mad."

At least Craig was still in form, which meant we won the game. We were ahead by only 7 to 0 when he entered the game, but he threw 3 interceptions, which helped make our day easy. We won, 21 to 7, our third victory in seven games.

My last impact play for the Cowboys came in another one of our famous games, the Thanksgiving 1974 thriller with the Redskins. We were down 16 to 3 after Duane Thomas—whom the Redskins had acquired from San Diego as one of George Allen's reclamation projects—caught a 9-yard touchdown pass from Billy Kilmer early in the third quarter. On our next drive, Roger Staubach was knocked out by Dave Robinson after Roger scrambled for 9 yards, and Clint Longley had to come in to replace him. Diron Talbert had said before the game that the Redskins were going to put Roger out, and now they had done it and left us in a hole and with an unknown rookie quarterback to try to dig us out of it.

When Longley replaced Roger, Landry turned to me and said, "Bobby, now we have to depend on you because you are our most experienced wide receiver." I was so hurt because I was playing behind the great Golden Richards—not because he earned the job but because the job was given to him—that I said to Landry, right there on the sideline, "I can't believe that. I've been on the bench all year." Landry turned real red and yelled, "Get out there!" I went in as an offensive back, a running back in the slot, and Brig Owens had to cover me.

We started making things happen right away. Longley took us 47 yards down the field, completing an 80-yard drive that Roger had begun, and we scored on a 35-yard touchdown pass from Longley to Billy Joe DuPree to cut the Redskins' lead to 16 to 10. The next time we got the ball, Longley marched us 70 yards, with Walt Garrison scoring from the 1 to put us ahead, 17 to 16. But Kilmer brought the Redskins back, and they scored on Duane Thomas's 19-yard sprint around left end early in the fourth quarter, to retake the lead 23 to 17.

All that play did was set the stage for one of our great finishes. We got the ball back at our 40, trailing by six points with one minute, forty-five seconds to play. We were facing a fourth and 6 at our 44 when Longley hit me for a first down at the 50, with one minute on the clock. It was only a 6-yard gain, but afterwards even Landry said it was one of the biggest plays of the game. After throwing one pass incomplete, Longley found Drew Pearson open at the Redskins' 5, and Drew ran into the end zone to complete a 50-yard play and win the game for us, 24 to 23.

While George Allen called it "the toughest loss I ever had," we were going crazy in our dressing room after the game, which was our sixth win in our last seven starts. Our record was still only 7 and 5, and we weren't going to make the playoffs, but as it turned out, our miracle win cost the Redskins the division title. St. Louis and Washington both finished 10 and 4, but St. Louis beat Washington twice, which made the Redskins the wild-card team. Washington would have won the division if they had beaten us that day. I felt better than anyone, although I might not have felt so good if I had known that my key play was the last catch I would ever make in Dallas. We had one more home game, the next week against Cleveland. But I didn't get to play in that one. All those years, all those great plays, all those memories, all those wonderful fans. And now it was over.

My last game as a Cowboy was on December 14, 1974, in Oakland. And that was fitting, too, because I would wind up my career the following year across the bay in Candlestick Park. I always loved the Bay Area, but if I had to play there, I sure wish it could have been for Al Davis and the Raiders. Al didn't just pay his players or treat them as gladiators; he treated them as men. That's why he has had such a successful franchise. I've never heard a ballplayer who played for the Raiders say anything bad about Al Davis, and players usually gripe about the owners and coaches. Also, I've always admired Al because he brought a lot of his former players back and gave them jobs, unlike the Cowboys and most other teams. And he found a place for shit-disturbers like Kenny Stabler and gave a chance to rejects like John Matuszak, the Tooz. Al doesn't care that much about image. He knows that you play to win, so you ought to have the best football players on the field. In the standings, all there is is a "W" for wins, an "L" for losses, and a "T" for ties—no "I" for image. One more reason I would have loved playing for Al is that his teams always threw the bomb.

Before the game it was just like old times. I was exchanging insults with some of the Raiders like Phil Villapiano. I told Villapiano, "You give me any cheap shots, I'm going to kick you in the ankle and you won't play any more." He said, "Bobby, I don't want you. I just want those manhunters who come after me and I know you don't come after no linebackers."

George Atkinson, the Raiders' strong safety, always had a big mouth. During warmups he told me, "I'm going to kill you, Hayes. And I'm going to get Jack Tatum to kill you, too." I answered, "You always have to rely on someone else. Why don't you do it by yourself? You let Tatum take care of his job and you take care of yours. I know for sure that *you* can't cover me one on one, Atkinson."

Drew Pearson and Jean Fugett started that day at wide receiver. Jean was really a tight end, but they let him open at my position instead of me. The team called on me for one last stab at the old magic, with Oakland ahead 27 to 23 and less than a minute to play. On fourth and 10 at our 14, Roger completed a pass down the right side to me, hoping I could turn on the afterburners and go all the way, but Atkinson pulled me down at our 45 after I gained 31 yards. After that catch, my last as a Dallas Cowboy, I said to Atkinson, "I *told* you I was going to beat you." And he came back with, "I'm going to get you yet."

But it was all over after one more play, leaving us with an 8 and 6 record and third in the NFC East. Used hardly at all that year, I finished with 7 catches for 118 yards, a 16.9 average and 1 touchdown. I would never again put on jersey number 22 in royal blue, metallic silver-blue, and white.

During the off-season, when we were preparing for the 1975 season, my friend and then lawyer, Sonny Margolis, was talking to Gil Brandt, Tom Landry, and Tex Schramm about rumors that I was going to be traded. Gil Brandt told Sonny I was definitely going to be traded and Golden Richards was there to stay. Most of the black guys on the team—Jethro Pugh, Jean Fugett, Rayfield Wright—were disappointed. They knew that Golden Richards wasn't as good a football player as I was, nor were any of the other receivers the Cowboys kept bringing in to replace me before they found out that none of them could and got rid of them. Some of these players were:

- Golden Richards, who played five seasons for Dallas and caught a total of 90 passes for 1,650 yards and 16 touchdowns.

- Ron Sellers, who was brought in from the Patriots in 1972, supposedly to make everyone forget me, and was gone the next year, traded to Miami, and who totaled 31 catches for 653 yards and 5 touchdowns for the Cowboys.

- Otto Stowe, who came to the Cowboys in the Ron Sellers deal, and caught 23 passes for 389 yards and 6 touchdowns in his one year with Dallas.

- Dennis Homan, on whom the Cowboys wasted a number-one draft choice in 1968, totaled 23 catches for 437 yards and *1 touchdown* (that's correct, 1 touchdown!) in three years with Dallas, before he was traded to Kansas City.

- Margene Adkins, the Cowboys' second-round selection in 1970, who lasted two years and caught 4 passes for 53 yards and no touchdowns.

Not long before our 1975 training camp, Gil Brandt called Sonny Margolis and said they wanted to bring me to camp to see what I could do. Sonny relayed the message to me, and I told him to tell Gil to go fuck himself. I had been there for ten years, and they knew what I could do. Why the hell should I go to training camp and prove what I could do in 1975? They had seen me outrun the White Lightning, as they called Richards, whom they welcomed to training camp, with open arms and the red carpet.

If it had not been for Ray Renfro, the receivers' coach, I probably would have quit or demanded to be traded a couple of years earlier. Ray, who was a coach with the Cowboys from 1968 to 1972, told me, "Bobby, don't quit, you're too valuable to this team." He talked to me just like a brother. I'll never forget his kindness to me. He was really good to me. He kept me motivated. But he was the only one. I used to play and work out with Ray's son Mike when Mike was a teenager and Ray was my coach. Mike wound up with the Cowboys from 1984 to 1987. I hope I helped Mike some, and that just as I was part of Ray's legacy to the Cowboys, Mike was part of mine. That's what I mean when I say I have learned that what goes around in this life comes around.

Even after all that had happened, I was still dedicated to the Dallas Cowboys. Calvin Hill was jumping to the World Football League and I had offers from the WFL, too, but I didn't want to leave the Cowboys or Dallas. Landry was the only coach I had played under in professional football, and I still wanted to play for him. He was a damn good coach, and I knew I couldn't find a better one. But I just wasn't in their plans any more.

So they finally traded me. I had been expecting it, but it still hurt when it actually happened on July 17, 1975, right before we reported to training camp. After Gil Brandt informed me of the trade, Dick Nolan, the former Cowboys assistant coach who had been head coach of the 49ers since 1968, called me and told me it was wonderful to have me. I said,

"It's a wonderful city. I love Frisco." "First mistake you made," Dick told me. "Don't call it 'Frisco.' "

You could say the Cowboys made a mistake, too. All they got in return for me was a number-3 draft choice in 1976. Commenting on the trade, Bob St. John of the *Dallas News* wrote that it was "surprising that the club did not get more for [me] considering what he has done and the fact that he still has excellent speed." The Cowboys got even less for me than folks suspected at the time; they used the draft choice they got from San Francisco to pick up a wide receiver from San Diego State named Duke Fergerson. If you haven't heard of Duke Fergerson, welcome to the club; not many other people have. Fergerson never made the Cowboys squad, although he did play for the expansion Seattle Seahawks in 1977 and 1978.

And I hate to say it, but the 49ers made a mistake in trading for me. After winning the NFC West in 1970, 1971, and 1972—and losing to the Cowboys in the playoffs each year—San Francisco had been under .500 in 1973 and 1974. The 49ers were clearly on a downward trend (they had another bad year, 5 and 9, in my one season with them), and they should have been conserving their draft choices and going with young players instead of older guys like me. I would have been better off with a contending team that liked to throw the bomb, like Oakland, Pittsburgh, or St. Louis.

As it was, I didn't fit in with the 49ers. One of the leaders on their team was Cedrick Hardman, a defensive end, who was a cocky, arrogant ballplayer, the Dexter Manley of his day. I never was one of Cedrick's favorites and he did his best to make me feel unwelcome after I joined the team.

And I had a lot of trouble adjusting to a rinky-dink organization like San Francisco. We beat New Orleans, 35 to 21, in mid-October to run our record to 2 and 3, and from the way some of our players were acting, you would have thought we had just won the Super Bowl. The Saints won just 2 of 14 games that year, but some of the 49er players had a big party and celebrated. I said, "I don't celebrate beating a noncontending football team like the Saints," but some of my teammates didn't understand. In Dallas you didn't do that; you'd beat some lousy team and then go home and get ready for the next game, instead of having a big party.

I caught just 6 passes for 119 yards and no touchdowns for the 49ers, and late in the season I hurt my leg and couldn't play. I walked into the dressing room one day before practice and found out they had released me. I found out that I had been released when all my stuff was taken from my locker and put in boxes in the storage room and my locker was given to someone else. Saying goodbye was not a class act, at least in the 49ers organization.

Compared to the Cowboys, the 49ers didn't have good coaches, the trend of pro football had bypassed them, they didn't have the personnel. Tom Landry always tried his best to keep his athletes prepared, but San Francisco was more of a country club. Discipline was very loose, and one of their defensive backs used cocaine in the bathroom before games. During my eleven years in the NFL, this man was the only player I saw using drugs on the team's premises. When I retired in 1975, drugs like cocaine and marijuana were still not that much of a problem in the league. A lot of players drank too much, but not in the dressing room or anywhere around the team. We didn't meet as long with the 49ers and didn't go over specific plays, as we had done with the Cowboys. In Dallas, we had first down and 10 passing and running plays, second down and 5-plus passing and running plays, and third down and 15-plus and third down and 20-plus. In San Francisco, Nolan just called the plays he thought would go. It was like playing sandlot football after having been with a true professional organization like the Cowboys.

Nolan wasn't that bad a football coach, and he had a lot of success with the 49ers in the early seventies. We had some great playoff games between the two teams.

Dick Nolan and I had gotten along real well when we were both with the Cowboys. I had looked forward to playing for him after he called to tell me he had made a deal for me, but it didn't work out. He got fired after my one season with the 49ers, later was head coach of the Saints for several years, and then returned to the Cowboys as an assistant coach in 1982.

But I still have to say that ending my NFL career with the 49ers was a shitty way to go out. Though I received a call from the Chargers saying they would like to sign me, I wanted to go home to Dallas and I knew my best days as a football player were behind me, so I turned them down.

Now I had to get on with the rest of my life. I had had several different jobs in the off-season, mostly doing public relations for R.C. Cola and Braniff Airlines, but the truth was that I had never believed my football career would actually end, and I wasn't really prepared for life after football.

No one, least of all me, would argue that my old pal Gale Sayers does not belong in the Pro Football Hall of Fame in Canton, Ohio. But compare my lifetime statistics to Gale's: I caught 371 passes for 7,414 yards and 71 touchdowns; gained another 68 yards rushing on 28 carries and scored 2 touchdowns rushing; returned 104 punts for 1,158 yards and 3 touchdowns; and returned 23 kickoffs for 581 yards. I gained a total of 9,221 yards and scored 76 touchdowns and 456 points. Gale had 9,435 combined yards and 336 points. Whenever I wonder why I have never been admitted to the Hall of Fame, the records of six players in particular make me angry. Consider these:

• Dante Lavelli, an end with the Browns in the 1940s and 1950s, caught 386 passes for 6,488 yards and 62 touchdowns.

• Elroy (Crazylegs) Hirsch, who also played in the 1940s and 1950s for the Chicago Rockets of the old All America Football Conference and the Rams, had lifetime records of 387 catches for 7,209 yards and 60 touchdowns.

• Tom Fears, who played on the Rams with Hirsch, caught 400 passes for 5,397 yards and 38 touchdowns.

• Pete Pihos, who played for the Eagles in the same era as Lavelli, Hirsch, and Fears, caught 373 passes for 5,619 yards and 378 points.

• Mike Ditka, my old friend, enemy, teammate, and coach, caught 427 passes for 5,812 yards and 43 touchdowns.

• And get this: Wayne Millner, who played for the Redskins in the 1930s and 1940s, was an offensive end who caught a total of 124 passes.

I'm not saying that any of these players *don't* belong in the Hall of Fame, just that I should be in it, too. My career records were better than some, not as good as a few, but comparable to all of them.

Also, coaches like Tom Landry and Don Shula and many others say that I revolutionized the passing game in pro football. Looking back over my career in 1989, Landry called me "a great catalyst for us when we turned the corner in 1966. That's when we started to win and win big for many years. Bobby with his speed was something that no other team in professional football had. Most teams were playing man to man coverage and that was right down Bobby's alley, because nobody could cover him. Bobby pretty well changed the game. He caused the teams to go more into zone defense so they could cover him short and long. When somebody's that fast you can't cover them with one man. That's what you're looking for in offensive football, to be able to force the defense to adjust to what you're doing.''

It hurts me that although they named me the fastest runner in history a couple of years ago in England, I've never even been named to the Cowboys' Ring of Honor in Dallas. When I signed with the Cowboys, I carried their name around the world, because I was the only world-famous athlete in professional football. I was asked to organize several American football games in Japan a few years ago, and I wore my Dallas Cowboys' uniform there with pride and respect. I was an outstanding player for the Cowboys for many years, and I helped turn that franchise around. And I helped make professional football at least challenge, maybe even surpass, baseball as the national pastime.

But then that final gun fired, and I became a nonperson.

15

A STAR BEHIND BARS

The prison gates really do swing shut with a heavy metallic clang. They sound just like they do in the movies or on television. And from the inside, when those gates swing shut behind you and you're cut off from the real world, that clang sounds like the gates of hell. I know. I've been there.

How do you lose your freedom, your reputation, your money, even your right to vote? In my case it involved a person (me) who just couldn't say no to someone I thought was a friend, some guys who smoked marijuana (I wasn't one of them), a business that involved shipping chickens to South America (sounds ridiculous, but it's true); and a dispute over a seat on an airplane. It also involved an undercover cop who added all these elements together and saw a chance to get even for a grudge he'd been carrying against me for a long time and maybe to make a drug bust that would have folks compare him to Sherlock Holmes, Eliot Ness, and James Bond.

A lot of people who know me well have said that I'm my own worst enemy, that I'm too nice a guy to say no, which gets me in trouble. It's true that I have always tried to please people, and sometimes I have paid for it. I tried to be Mr. Nice Guy once too often, and it cost me everything. But the strange thing is, my fall from glory was triggered by one of the few incidents in which I treated someone badly.

It all began in the early 1970s, when I was traveling around the world, doing promotional work for Braniff Airlines, which was based in Dallas. I had been in South America on Braniff business for about ten days, and

I was tired and ready to head home from São Paulo, Brazil. I checked out of my hotel, which was about an hour and a half from the airport, drove to the Braniff terminal, and registered for a flight to New York. A few minutes before the plane took off, one of the employees behind the Braniff ticket counter told me I was being bumped off the flight, which meant I would have to wait two days for another flight. He explained to me that paying customers were occupying every seat but one on the flight, that they had had to choose between me and a Braniff pilot who was dead-heading back to the States, and that they had given the final seat to the off-duty pilot. I showed the guy my Braniff pass, which gave me top priority for seating and was signed by Harding Lawrence, the head of the airline. Braniff's regional manager was called to the scene, but he wouldn't budge. I admit that because of fatigue and disappointment, I got hot under the collar and said a few things to this guy that Tom Landry and the Fellowship of Christian Athletes wouldn't have approved of. I was wrong and I should have apologized. But by then the damage had already been done, although I wouldn't find out about it until years later.

Skip ahead a few years to 1978. I was vice president of a Dallas-based company called Dycon International, a computer company owned by two brothers, Bobby and Michael Adler, who were friends of mine. We were selling a voice-activated computer that is connected to a telephone system to sell products over the phone. We had Arthur Godfrey selling term life insurance, Tony Dorsett selling Dallas Cowboys season tickets, and other products. The computer was sophisticated enough to call people, ask them a question, and wait for an answer. We transcribed the tapes and got the names, addresses, and telephone numbers of interested people off the tape and then sold leads to companies that could use them.

Our office was in Campbell Center, the beautiful golden, twin towers you see at the start of the "Dallas" television series. Bob and Mike Adler's mother was an interior decorator, and she fixed up our office so it looked like Hugh Hefner's den—mirrors, chandeliers, glass tables, expensive paintings, and lush plants. We had at least one gorgeous woman working for us, too: Barbara Clancy, our secretary. We were doing well and living high; the Adler brothers drove Mercedeses, and I had a Cadillac.

Another element: Mike Adler had a close friend who owned a pharmacy, and when we needed medicine for a cold or something minor like that, Mike's friend would give us medicine without making us go to a doctor for a prescription. That's illegal, but it didn't seem like such a big thing to us. Oh, something else: the father of the Adler brothers was in the chicken hatchery business, shipping chickens and eggs from Miami to Rio de Janeiro.

Barbara Clancy and I became good friends (we were not involved romantically). By then I had remarried. Toward the end of my career with the Cowboys, while I was at my usual hangout one night, Buddy's oyster bar in downtown Dallas, I met a gorgeous lady named Janice McDuff. Janice, who was in her mid-twenties, had a great job as a secretary for an industrial oil company in Dallas. When I was traded to San Francisco in 1975, she gave up her job and moved out there with me. We got married a few months later, and we were still very happy together at the time I was working for Dycon, so I wasn't looking for a romance with Barbara. But she used to confide all her troubles to me. Barbara's husband had had a heart attack and dropped dead not long before she went to work for us, and Barbara herself had cancer, and she was depressed.

The next thing I knew, Barbara Clancy was in an automobile accident in which she ran into a Corvette driven by a guy named Denny Kelly. Not only did their cars collide, but Barbara and Kelly hit it off and started dating.

Denny Kelly, as it happened, was an airline pilot and on the side worked as an undercover cop for the police force in Addison, a suburb of Dallas. Needless to say, the Adlers and I didn't know that Kelly was a cop. One Friday afternoon, while Bob Adler and I were in Philadelphia on business, Mike Adler and some salesmen from California celebrated the end of another workweek by smoking a few joints in our offices. Barbara had been bringing Kelly to our offices all the time. Kelly saw the whole picture, including the plush offices, our lifestyles, and the marijuana, and he got the idea that we were part of some major-league drug ring, shipping chickens to South America and smuggling dope from there to Miami. What a feather in Denny's cap if he, almost all by himself, could break up this drug operation.

Kelly started getting friendlier and friendlier with me. He invited me to lunch and said, "I know this very wealthy man from Florida. He wants to come to Dallas and open up a restaurant in Addison [which had just started to boom as restaurant row]. We could use your name and give you thirty or forty percent of the business. You wouldn't have to put up any money. Would you be interested in something like that?" My answer was, "Damn right." Kelly set up a meeting with a real estate agent, at which we talked about sites, even went to look at a few.

Meanwhile, for ten years or so, I had been using methaqualone every once in a while. Methaqualone pills, also known as Quaaludes or "Ludes," are sold on the street as downers. They'll cure a headache and they'll give you a great feeling—an "I don't give a damn" feeling—so relaxed and so goooood! I got my first Lude from Ralph Neely one day in 1968 or 1969 when I had a headache. I went home and took it, and it made me so high that when I tried to get up from bed, I fell and bumped my head. Another time Tody Smith, Bubba's younger brother, was in the hospital. I went to see him on my way home from practice, and he gave me half of a Lude. After I took it, I couldn't move and I had to sit in Tody's hospital room for a couple of hours before I could get going. Ludes were easy enough to get, either from friends or from one of the Cowboys' physicians. I used to take one at night before I went out partying, and I usually had at least one on hand for the woman of my choice. Nothing would make a woman give it up quicker than a Lude. You give a female a Lude, and all she knows how to say to you is yes. I don't care if she's the most reserved woman in the world, give her a Lude and she'll do anything you want.

Kelly had seen me take Ludes, and while he and I were looking at one possible location for the restaurant, he said he had a headache and asked me for one. I gave it to him, then he asked for another one and tried to give me ten dollars for the two of them while we were riding in the elevator. I refused the money, but I was out of gas and I didn't have any cash on me, so I asked him to lend me ten dollars for gas, which I said I'd pay back the next day after I cashed a check. Right across from the real estate agency was the police department, which was filming the whole episode. Now it looked like I sold Kelly two Ludes, when all I was doing was borrowing money for gas from a buddy. And don't forget, we're talking here about a ten-dollar "drug deal." A real major-league drug operation!

The next thing Kelly did was to come to me and say, "I'm hurting, man. I wish I had a gram of cocaine. Do you know where I can get a gram of cocaine?" Of course, every time Kelly called me, he made a point of asking, "Is this my pal Bullet Bob Hayes, the world's fastest human?" and I would answer, "Yes, that's me." Of course, he was taping all our conversations, both over the telephone and in person.

I knew that my neighbor, Ben Kimmell, was using cocaine. I told Ben that one of my buddies wanted a gram of cocaine, and he said, "I use it, but I don't sell it. But for you I'll take care of him." So I introduced Ben to Kelly over the telephone and they agreed to get together and have Ben sell a gram of cocaine to Kelly.

Kelly kept asking about cocaine, but Ben Kimmell only sold it to him twice. One transaction occurred in my office (cocaine from Ben to Kelly and money from Kelly to Ben), and one took place in Ben's car outside my office, with a police photographer taking pictures. I just happened to be sitting there. And Kelly still was wired during the sales.

Then Kelly asked if I could get a key of cocaine. I didn't even know what a key was. I called a friend Alfred Terry and asked him, and he said, "Man that's a kilogram of cocaine. That's forty or fifty thousand dollars worth of cocaine." Alfred said, "You know anybody who wants that, put me in touch with him. Because I know where to get it." I told him I would put him in touch with the guy who wanted the cocaine but that I didn't want to be involved. Alfred was lying when he said he could get a kilogram, but I had no way of knowing it. I introduced Alfred to Kelly in the parking lot of a Holiday Inn, but Alfred didn't have any cocaine, and we all left after I told them I didn't want anything to do with their business.

Denny Kelly's unsuccessful meeting with Alfred Terry occurred on the evening of April 15, 1978. I went home to bed afterwards, and about 3 A.M., I heard a knock on the door. I got out of bed without any clothes on, went to the door, and asked, "Who's there?" Kelly answered, "It's Denny, Bob, I need to talk to you." So I opened the door, and there were about a dozen police officers. I was standing there naked, and someone put a gun to my head. Kelly played the bigtime cop: "You fucking nigger, where's that coke?" I answered, "If you want a Coke, Denny, look in the refrigerator. If you don't find a Coke in there, you'll find a Dr. Pepper." Janice finally brought my robe and put it around me. The police told me I was under arrest on two counts of delivering a total of five grams of cocaine for five hundred dollars and one count of delivering Quaaludes. Then they let me get dressed, handcuffed me, and took me away. Of course, no big-time drug bust would be complete without the press, and Kelly had arranged for a reporter from a radio station to be with him and get the scoop when the police arrested me.

Now here's the real kicker: After they handcuffed me, Kelly said to me, "You don't remember me do you? From down in São Paulo?" I told him I didn't. "The first time I met you, you got bumped off a Braniff flight in São Paulo. I'm the one they bumped you for. It was you or me, and I got the seat because I'm a pilot. I'll never forget the way you talked to those white people down there, and I've hated you for it ever since, nigger. What do you think of that?"

I felt sick to my stomach. That's what I thought of that.

After the police arrested me, they took me to Bob Adler's house. Bobby was asleep in his apartment, his mother was there, and they kicked the side window out, broke into his apartment, and arrested him too. Then they went for Benny Kimmell, who lived in the same apartment complex I did. He wasn't home, so they kicked in his windows and left.

They drove Bobby Adler and me directly to the North Dallas home of Justice of the Peace Robert Cole. When Judge Cole came to the door, the first thing the police said was, "We finally got this asshole." The judge laughed and said, "Great." He went and got dressed and took us into one of the bedrooms that he was using as an office. Then he signed papers placing my bond at $30,000, $10,000 for each count, and Adler's at $10,000.

Then they drove us downtown, with our hands handcuffed behind us. It hurt like hell, but none of the cops cared; we were big-time criminals. When we got to the jailhouse, the first things I saw were the bars, the drunk tank, and all the employees looking at me—some laughing at me and a few looking sad, just like when I had gone there with Lance Rentzel after he got arrested for exposing himself to a little girl in 1970. That time Lance had had a friend—me—and his lawyer with him, but here I was, going through exactly the same thing, all by myself. The only person who kept me from feeling all alone was one of the clerks at the jail who was a neighbor of mine. He said, "Bob, I'm sure sorry this happened to you, man."

As I was being processed, Denny Kelly kept saying, "I know you're going to get your ass out of here, and you better go back and tell your teammates about this because I'm going to bust some of their butts, too." Meanwhile, they fingerprinted me and took mugshots—the whole bit.

I spent several hours in a holding cell, with all kinds of jail employees, police, and other people coming by to look at me like I was an animal in the zoo. And about fifty lawyers stopped by and asked if they could represent me. This was obviously a case that was going to attract a lot of publicity. I decided to have Sonny Margolis call Phil Burleson, who was one of the best criminal lawyers in Dallas. Phil had been Lance's lawyer in 1970 and had done a good job for Lance. Phil sent someone to bail me out a few hours later, and, of course, when I left the jail, there were dozens of reporters outside waiting to shout questions at me. I had hoped to avoid the press, but this, after all, was Dallas. If they couldn't get Lee Harvey Oswald out of the jail alive, I guess they couldn't get me out without having the press there.

There seemed little question that Kelly had entrapped me. The cocaine Kelly bought wasn't mine, and I didn't get any money for it. Every time he wanted to talk about drugs, he called me. In fact, he testified in court that I couldn't call him because I never had his phone number. He didn't want me calling him at home, and the only other phone number he had was at the Addison police department, and obviously he couldn't have me calling him there. The main fallacy in the prosecution's theory was that if I was sellings drugs, the first people I would have gone to would have been my ex-teammates because I knew they had money. Instead, my former teammates all testified for me because they knew I never sold drugs.

I passed a lie-detector test proving that my version of what had happened was true, but there was another problem: I had gotten in trouble in college with James Vickers, pleading guilty to what was literally a nickel-and-dime robbery. Texas law specified that if I went to trial and a jury found me guilty, I would definitely have to go to prison for many years because of my previous offense.

As a result, my lawyers; my wife, Janice; my college football coach, Jake Gaither, who was still like a father to me; Tom Landry; Tex Schramm; and a number of my close friends—Pettis Norman, Willie Townes, Jethro Pugh, Harvey Martin, Drew Pearson—as well as Roger Staubach, my mother, and everyone else who had influence in my life, advised me to plead guilty in the drug case. The crimes I had been charged with carried a possible maximum sentence of life in prison, but under Texas law, if I pleaded guilty, the judge could immediately place me on probation without ordering me to serve time in prison. My lawyers also pointed out that if I demanded a jury trial, the prosecution would try to pack the jury with white, middle-aged rednecks from East Texas who hated blacks, especially famous blacks who had done better in life than the jurors had, and would be likely to find me guilty of a crime that would result in a long prison term.

March 14, 1979, was the worst day of my life. On that day, I stood before Judge Richard Mays of Texas District Court and pleaded guilty to the three charges against me. The way the Texas judicial system works, you then have what amounts to another trial, called the punishment phase, in which witnesses testify for the prosecution and defense and then the judge imposes the sentence. Judge Mays set the punishment phase for a week later, and my attorneys started rounding up character witnesses.

The prosecutors went to Tom Landry, Tex Schramm, and Roger Staubach before the trial and told each of them not to show up, that I was going to jail and that they didn't need to be seen protecting a drug dealer. I went to the Cowboys' offices and talked to Tex, Tom, and Roger. I told them, "Look, guys, I didn't do it, this is what happened, I didn't use any cocaine, I didn't buy any cocaine, it just crossed my desk. I did set it up, but I didn't get anything for it and I need you to support me." I have to say one thing for Tex Schramm: He and I had some differences over the years, but he immediately said, "Bob, I'll be there." Tom Landry and Roger Staubach both said they would have to think it over. They both eventually agreed to testify for me, but neither of them came out and said they would do it the way Tex did as soon as my lawyers asked him. Tex told the judge that although I was "easily led," I "was never a bad person." Roger conducted his own investigation of my case and concluded that I really was innocent before he decided to speak up for me. He testified in court that he was completely against drugs, but he said he had known me for a long time and knew I was a good person.

When I got to the courtroom, several dozen of my former Cowboys teammates were there to show support for me. Even Ulis Williams, my old friend from the track circuit and the 1964 Olympic team, was there. When I saw all my old friends, I broke down and started crying.

In addition to Tex Schramm, Tom Landry, and Roger Staubach, Drew Pearson, Cornell Green, Pettis Norman, and several other of my old Cowboy teammates testified for me. So did Jake Gaither, who told Judge Mays that he and his wife never had any children of their own, but "if there's ever been a kid I wanted to adopt, it was Bob Hayes." And Jake said that no matter what I had done, he would stand behind me "until hell freezes over." I testified in my own defense that I had been stupid, but that I wasn't a criminal: "I'm not the smartest guy in the world. If I was, I wouldn't be up here. I just have a weakness. I like to make everybody happy and that's just a mistake that I made."

After hearing the prosecutor point out that a former SMU track star had recently received a fifteen-year prison sentence on similar charges and argue for jail time, Judge Mays decided not to let me off on probation. He gave me five years in prison on the two cocaine counts and seven years' probation on the Quaalude charge. The two five-year sentences were to run concurrently, which meant that the maximum time I would spend in prison was five years, not ten.

After Judge Mays sentenced me, I was taken to a cell in the Dallas jail and ordered to take off my three-piece suit and put on a prison uniform. The guards gave me the most ragged uniform they could find, all full of holes; handcuffed me again; marched me through a crowd of people, including a number of women; and put me in the backseat of a car for the drive to the Ferguson unit of the Texas Department of Corrections, outside Huntsville, about two hundred miles from Dallas.

The guard who was riding shotgun in the front seat was an older man who had a son-in-law who owned a service station near Huntsville. When we pulled up to that station to get gas, the guard jumped out of the car and ran in, and I heard him say real loud, "We got that son of a bitch! We got him! There he is in the car out there!" And everyone came outside and stared at me like I was a fucking toy.

When I got to prison, all the guards were waiting for me. One guard told me, "We hate you, nigger. Mike Ditka came down here and told us about you; you don't like whites." Ditka, who was still an assistant coach with the Cowboys then, had made a personal appearance in the city of Huntsville and all the rednecks attended and asked him about me. I know it's a cliché, but over the years, especially since I retired from football in 1975, a number of my close friends were white. If Ditka told the guards I didn't like white people, he was lying.

Before I went to prison, the prison officials told me to be sure to bring a coat and tie because I would be doing a lot of interviews. When I got to prison, the redneck guards took my clothes off; sprayed me for lice; made me take a shower; cut my hair till I was nearly bald; gave me a uniform; and rumpled up my suit and all my other expensive clothes, threw them into a bag, and sent them back to Dallas.

As of April 18, 1979, I was no longer number 22 of the Dallas Cowboys; I was inmate number 290973 of the Texas prison system. Instead of having my name in big letters on the back of my Cowboys jersey, I had my name stenciled on a nameplate that I wore on the top half of my white prison uniform. About 2,000 inmates, mostly young blacks who were first-time offenders, were incarcerated at Ferguson, which was classified as a maximum security prison, but didn't have any of the real hard cases. Even so, Ferguson was a real prison, surrounded by a chain-link fence topped by barbed wire. There were guard towers manned by officers carrying shotguns, the whole bit.

After living the good life—a nice house, and the best hotels when I traveled—I found myself in an eight-by-ten-foot cell for several weeks of orientation and then in a dormitory with about a hundred other inmates, most of whom were fifteen or so years younger than me, using a public shower like I had with the Cowboys and eating in a mess hall. We had to be counted four times a day to make sure that none of us was missing, and a count could take as long as an hour if someone was unaccounted for.

Every inmate had a job, and mine was "assistant gym director." The job amounted to being an assistant coach, helping to supervise the athletic activities of the other inmates.

I would get up about 5 A.M., have breakfast, and go to the gym. We broke for lunch at noon and then went back to the gym for the afternoon, until my day ended at 5 P.M. After that I had dinner in the mess hall and then had free time until the lights out at 10 P.M. I spent my evenings watching the news on television, reading; and answering my mail, which used to come in by the sack from all over the world, a lot addressed simply to "Bob Hayes, Huntsville, Texas, U.S.A." The most unusual letter I got was one wishing me well—from the Washington Redskins Alumni Association. Yes, the Redskins were our bitter rivals on the field, but I had so many friends on that team—Brig Owens, A. D. Whitfield, Roy Jefferson, Charley Taylor, Billy Kilmer, Diron Talbert, Mike Bass, and Allen George— that Washington was the only NFL club that remembered me while I was in prison.

I spent a lot of my time exercising and playing sports. I pitched and played first base for the prison softball team, the Ferguson Falcons. Actually, we lost most of our games, and we were so bad that I started calling us the Bad News Falcons. We played many of the other state prison units. To get to away games, we rode on schoolbuses with bars on the windows and two guards riding shotgun, one in front and one in back.

My only break from prison life came in October 1979, after I had been at Huntsville for six months. Although I was swamped with requests from the media—all three TV networks, the wire services, and the major newspapers and magazines—the only interview I gave while I was in prison was to Tex Schramm for the *Dallas Cowboys Weekly* newspaper and television show. At that time, the Texas prison system had a furlough program under which inmates could be released for five days, and Tex arranged quite a surprise for me, a furlough to attend the fifth annual Cowboys reunion for the game against St. Louis on October 21, 1979. I was free from Thursday until the following Monday, and when the other old Cowboys and I were introduced at halftime at Texas Stadium, I got a tremendous ovation, which made me feel like the fans didn't hold my troubles against me.

. . .

When I was furloughed for the Cowboys reunion, the other inmates cried when I left and were happy when I got back. They caught so much hell when I wasn't there, but when I was there the guards tried to hide things from me because they knew eventually I would get out and talk or write about what I had seen.

There was a volatile mix in prison—mostly black inmates, a lot of them looking for trouble, and mostly white guards who came from the lowest elements of society and were hardcore racists. Some of the guards used to say that they had been out hunting but couldn't find any animals, so they shot at niggers instead. But the problem wasn't just with the gaurds; it was on both sides. Some of the inmates were so bad that if we were playing softball and a guy hit a grounder to shortstop and got thrown out at first, the batter would run out to shortstop and want to beat up the guy who had thrown him out. I saw a fight in which one prisoner stuck a broomhandle up a guy's rectum and hurt him so badly that the guards had to tie four or five towels around him like a baby's diaper and rush him to the hospital. I saw homosexuals come down into the gym and bring their grease and lotion with them and screw other inmates. And I saw inmates cut each other with homemade knives.

But I have to say that most of the trouble was caused by the guards. They beat inmates and screwed them. The guards would accept money, watches, and anything else of value from the inmates and then sneak in drugs or alcohol for them or let the homosexual prisoners come in late at night and take showers, steam up the room, then all go into the corners and make out. To get something of value to trade to the guards, inmates would go to another unit, steal a watch from another inmate, and then give it to a guard in exchange for a joint or two, some cocaine, some liquor, or a favor. I saw guards make the worst inmate get in a fight with another guy so they could enjoy watching the fight. Then they would punish the guy they had told to start the fight.

The worst abuse by the guards was over food. Food for the prison was delivered to the guards' dining area, and the guards would steal most of the meat and take it home to their families. Then they would give us the scrubs of the food. I had steak one time in my ten months there and chicken twice. They fed us soup made from a hog, which they called swine soup, and in weather of 100 degrees or more, they'd give us hot tea instead of cold tea. The only prisoners who got to eat well were the basketball players. The guards used to take the best basketball players out of their cells and play basketball all night with them and then sneak the inmates into the officers' dining room and give them decent food. That's how we found out that the guards were keeping the best food for themselves.

My only problem with a guard occurred a few months after I got to Huntsville, when one of the guards came into my dorm and pushed me for no reason and knocked me against a window. I slapped the shit out of him, and they handcuffed me and put me against a wall, but they didn't do anything else to me. That guard was so dumb and so illiterate that he couldn't even write his name correctly or fill out a report about the incident. Later, he tried to make friends with me and even asked me to help him with his income tax forms.

Texas Governor William Clements described me as a "deserving, model prisoner" and approved me for release after I served ten months in prison, the earliest possible date I could have been paroled. I was set free on February 27, 1980, but the police did their best to ruin that day, too. Janice and a friend of ours picked me up, and about forty minutes later, as we were driving near a town called Centerville on I-45 between Huntsville and Dallas, Janice was behind the wheel when a state trooper pulled us over, even though other cars were speeding faster, passing us. The trooper did a strange thing: Instead of just giving Janice a ticket, he stuck his head through the window of her side of the car, looked right over her to the passenger's seat, and said, "Hi, Bob, how are you? You all are speeding." Then he wrote Janice a ticket for going 61 miles in a 55-mile-an-hour zone. I honestly believe the cop was waiting for us, had our license plate number, and gave Janice the ticket just to harass us. But at least I was a free man.

Being in prison taught me a little more about the values of life. I saw the things I was missing and how I always took things for granted. You don't really miss freedom until you don't have any choice. Just being able to get a glass of milk or a Pepsi whenever I wanted one meant so much more to me after I got out.

Unfortunately, being in prison ruined my second marriage. All the pressure I was under after my arrest, plus the separation while I was in jail, destroyed our relationship, and we split up several years later. This marriage produced my second child, Bob Hayes, Jr., who was born August 4, 1977. I may be a little bit prejudiced, but I think Bob Jr. has the makings of a better athlete than his old man was. I know he has at least one advantage I never had: a father who adores him.

My whole prison experience turned out to be a waste, a nightmare that never should have happened. After I went to prison, my lawyers filed a fairly routine appeal, arguing that the indictment against me was improper because it used the word "cocaine," which was not specifically mentioned in the Texas criminal law at the time of my arrest. It may sound like a Mickey Mouse technicality to reverse my case, but the whole thing was Mickey Mouse to begin with. More than a year after I was released from prison, in June 1981, the Texas Court of Criminal Appeals overturned my conviction on the cocaine charges that had sent me to prison. Today I am no longer guilty of the cocaine charges, although the Quaalude charge—selling two pills for ten dollars—never was overturned. As a result, I had to report to a parole officer every week for three years and to this day, I cannot vote in the country I once represented so proudly in the Olympics.

16

THE WORLD'S
FASTEST DRUNK

Picture this: You're a guy and you know this gorgeous lady. You and she are friends, and you wish you were a lot more than friends, but she never lets you get anywhere with her. Maybe she has a steady guy, maybe you've got a steady woman, maybe you work together and she just doesn't think it's a good idea to mix business with pleasure. You know she's right, too. But you still want her so bad you can taste it. Then one night you have dinner and everything changes; you know she's yours for the taking. You bring her back to your place and you start going at it hot and heavy. The same reason for not doing it is still in place— she's married, you're married, the job, whatever. But you've never wanted anything like you want this lady, and here's your chance. You start undressing her, you're almost ready, and then—then the words "Just Say No" flash through your mind. Does anybody think those three words are going to stop you?

Of course not. Those words are not going to keep you from finishing what you started with that beautiful lady. Nancy Reagan's intentions may have been good, but "Just Say No" is an incredibly naive slogan. Drugs— and liquor—are every bit as seductive as that sexy lady I was talking about. If you're an addict, your drug of choice, whatever it is, makes you feel so good inside that just saying no isn't going to come close to making you stop.

The idea of legalizing drugs is just as ineffective as Nancy Reagan's "Just Say No" campaign; drugs will send you to one of three places: prison, a mental institution, or the graveyard. The NFL's present drug policy is just as stupid. It lets most players with drug and alcohol problems slip by and stay eligible to play, which is all the NFL really wants. Take away all the star players with drug problems like Lawrence Taylor and what do you have left? More on that later.

When I talk about drugs, I speak from experience. I'm an addict myself. My drug is liquor, and I can't help myself once I start drinking. Fortunately, I haven't had a drink since July 1985, but every day I have to wake up and live with the fear that today could be the day I lose it—that I stop being sober. When you're recovering from addiction to drugs or alcohol— and there are 20 million admitted addicts in the United States today— that's the most terrifying thought you can have.

I broke a half dozen world records in the sprints when I was still a teenager, but that was the good side of my early years. The bad side was that I grew up without a father to look up to. I knew that George Sanders was my dad, even though he denied it for a long time, but he wasn't the best role model anyway. The first time I got drunk was when I was twelve years old. My father and I and a friend of his and his son went to the beach one day at a place called Fernandina Beach, about forty miles north of Jacksonville. George and the other man had brought some liquor along, and they started arguing about whose son could drink the most ("My kid can drink more than yours can"). So they passed the bottle to us in the backseat, and we started drinking. Pretty soon the backseat was all covered with you know what. The next day I was working at my father's shoeshine parlor when his friend showed up. George asked him where his son was and he said, "Home, sick in bed." That gave my dad bragging rights, which was all he really cared about.

I didn't know how bad my father's drinking problem was until about five years ago, when I finally started admitting to myself that I had a drinking problem. I went to my mother and told her I wanted to see my adoption papers. "What are you talking about?" she asked me. I said, "Mom, I have to be adopted. I drink a lot and you don't even drink. So I'm not a part of you. Where are the papers?" She started laughing and said, "Get out of here, son. You're not adopted. You're my kid." She told me that her side of the family didn't have any drinking problems, but that I was the fifth generation of males on my father's side, going all the way back to my great great grandfather, to be an alcoholic.

Joseph Hayes, the man my mother was married to when I was born, was an alcoholic, too. He and my mother have been divorced for almost thirty years, although he and I are still very close, and I'll tell you what alcohol does to you. Before Joseph Hayes started drinking, he was a developer. He built homes on his own, and now he's just a security guard. But he was powerless, he was unmanageable, just like all of us alcoholics.

The main drug of choice when I played for the Cowboys was alcohol. We were not a marijuana team or a cocaine team, we were a drinking team. With the exception of Roger Staubach, Calvin Hill, and several others, almost everybody on the team drank beer by the case and liquor by the bottle. Some of the more notable drinkers were Bob Lilly, Ralph Neely, Walt Garrison, Craig Morton, Cornell Green, Pete Gent, a defensive lineman named Don Talbert, Willie Townes, Dave Edwards, and, of course, Mike Ditka. Mike was pretty picky about what he drank—he insisted that it be fermented or distilled.

Wanting to be one of the guys, I started drinking heavily my third or fourth year with the Cowboys. Cornell Green and I used to drive to practice together and on the way home, we would stop by a store and get us some beer or whiskey and drink while we drove home. The rush hour traffic was very heavy and we had to go all the way from North Dallas, where the Cowboys practiced, through downtown, and out to Oak Cliff. We would get a good buzz going and then we would have the patience to fight traffic after being so exhausted from practice. We would get a fifth of bourbon or gin, mix the bourbon with Coke or the gin with tonic, or buy half a case of beer. We did that three or four times a week, and what we didn't drink in the car we would finish off that night at home. Then on Friday nights before a Sunday game, Cornell and his wife, Frank Clarke and his wife, and Altamease and I would get together and have dinner at each other's homes. We would eat, talk, watch TV, dance, listen to music, and drink—anything to relax us and take our minds off the upcoming game. I always had a low tolerance for alcohol and I got drunk from one or two drinks every time. Even though I was already drunk, I would usually continue to drink. I would have as many as ten drinks, which would leave me stumbling around and unable to function properly, although I never passed out. I often got drunk at team parties, and once I got drunk, I would be a completely different person, cursing a lot, hugging white girls who went around with the players, and kissing other players' wives. A lot of guys got drunk, not just players but coaches like Mike Ditka, Dick Nolan, and Ernie Stautner, but I'm sure my behavior offended people in the Cowboys' organization.

Cornell Green had been drinking for as long as I had known him. Whiskey affects everyone differently, and it never hurt his play. But I think it did hurt my play because it was taking a toll on my body. Drinking may have slowed me down some, although it was hard to tell because I was the fastest man in the NFL from the day I entered the league until the day I was released by the 49ers. It wasn't just my speed, though; toward the end of my football career I found out that I was anemic, my liver was affected, I had high blood pressure; in short, I was a sick person, even though I looked fit on the outside.

With all the drinking going on in our team, you'd see a number of the players brushing their teeth and using mouthwash all the time, so the coaches couldn't smell the liquor on our breath. We weren't allowed to drink on team flights, but most of the players carried flat little bottles that fit into their briefcase, and by the time the plane landed in Dallas, there would be bottles all over the floor. That was our way of taking the edge off the pain, of getting rid of the hurt from the game.

Before I went to prison, I had used cocaine about three times in my whole life, and although I did have a drinking problem, it didn't keep me from playing football or from showing up for work every day after I retired. As long as you don't miss work and keep your appointments, it's hard for people to see that you have a problem and try to make you get help. Going to prison destroyed my life, and I really got on drugs and alcohol in 1980 after I got out of jail. I couldn't find a good job, I was frustrated and depressed, my self-esteem was low, and a lot of people had turned their backs on me. I'd go to restaurants and people would say, "Bob Hayes, can I get an ounce from you?" All my accomplishments were forgotten, everyone thought of me as a drug dealer. I was just a vegetable at the time, walking around in a daze.

Tex Schramm, who had helped me while I was in jail, helped me get a job with the Murchison family in their real estate business and I went to real estate school, but I couldn't get my license because of my guilty plea to a felony. Then I went to Roger Staubach, who hired me to help manage some of the real estate he owns in the Dallas area. I was doing well in that business, but I was still drinking and I would use cocaine sometimes on weekends when people gave it to me. I never bought any and I never freebased it or shot it up. I don't think I used cocaine more than twenty-five times in my life, but when I did, it increased my reflexes and stimulated me. It gave me an incredible high, just like liquor, but cocaine works faster than alcohol and gives you a better high.

But my real devil came from a bottle, a bottle of Tanqueray gin mixed with tonic. During my worst binges, I would spend money; the next day, I would have a hangover and not know where the money had gone. I had blacked out and didn't remember the night before. I wasn't the kind of drinker who woke up and wondered where I was; I could always drive home and go to bed. To myself I was in control, but to other folks, I was crazy. That's the way it is: You don't tell yourself you're crazy; someone else has to tell you that. People don't just walk into a rehabilitation center and say, "I'm a drug addict." Someone else has to recognize your problem and take you or make you go for help. For me, that person was Roger Staubach.

I finally faced my problem and admitted that I was an alcoholic in spring 1985. Admitting that you're an addict and that you're powerless over your own life is the first step toward recovery, but it's a long journey with many chances to fail, and I did fail, more than once. In May 1985 I entered the rehabilitation unit at Baylor-Parkside Lodge outside Dallas for a twenty-eight-day stay. It wasn't nearly long enough. A couple of weeks after I got out, I was drinking and using drugs again.

My relapse began one day when I was walking on the patio around the pool and the hot tub at the Town Creek Apartments, which Roger owns and where I was living, and I found some cocaine that someone had left. It was only about half a gram in a clear plastic bag, worth maybe fifty dollars. Even so, I was delighted. "Bingo!" I said to myself. I knew I should throw it away, but I couldn't. Cocaine dissolves in water, so I stirred it up in some hot tea and drank it fast. That got me high that night. I stayed up watching television all night because I couldn't sleep. Roger was upset, really bent out of shape, when he found out that I was using again. But he was determined to get me straight, and he saved my life.

First he sent me back to Baylor-Parkside for ten days to get detoxified. Dr. Michael Healy, the director there, recommended the Alina Lodge in the Pocono Mountains near Blairstown, New Jersey, and Roger arranged for me to go there. He paid the fee, about $25,000 out of his own pocket; the money came from Roger's personal bank accounts, not from his corporate accounts.

I will pay him back one day. I admire Roger totally. He is not only a teammate, a friend, and a neighbor, but one of the best men that I've ever met. Before Roger became famous and wealthy, he was the same person he is today. He cares for people, and I'm just lucky to have a man like him care about me. I would do anything for him, although he seldom asks anyone for a favor. He finds a way to get things done for himself. The only thing I can do for him is to stay straight, and, like I say, I've been straight since July 1985. Not one drop of alcohol, not one gram of cocaine, not one joint of marijuana since then. And I feel better about myself than I ever did, even better than when I was the world champion in track or a star in pro football.

When the time came for me to leave Baylor-Parkside and go to Alina Lodge, Roger had one of his employees, Tom Anderson, pick me up at Baylor-Parkside, drive me to the airport, and stay with me until my flight took off for Newark. When I landed at Newark, a driver from Alina was waiting to pick me up and take me to the lodge, about an hour away. He was a recovering alcoholic who had once been a champion sailor from South America, and he said he had seen me on television during the 1984 Olympics in Los Angeles, complaining that no one had invited me to the Olympics because of my conviction and jail term. "I could just tell that you were using then," he said. I said, "You could not tell if I was using or not," but he knew. A person who's using doesn't know that everybody can see through him, and I didn't want to believe he was right.

Addiction to drugs or alcohol is all about ego gratification. An addict is like a child who wants what he wants when he wants it. In rehabilitation, they break down your ego by treating you like a child who has to be told what to do. At Alina Lodge the first thing they do is take away your driver's license and all other identification, your cash, your jewelry and other personal belongings, and your luggage, which is locked away in a room that only the director and top staff have a key to. There's no fence, but you're two or three miles from anywhere. Some people tried to leave on their own and the neighbors would call the lodge right away, because they knew that's where the people were from. If the police stopped you, they would take you and put you in jail for vagrancy because you had no identification and couldn't prove who you were. Then Geraldine O. Delaney (she signed her initials G.O.D.), a widow who is about eighty years old and is director of the lodge, would come down to the jail and get you out. I did not walk off the property once in five months except for Thanksgiving, when I was invited to her house for dinner.

When I was at the lodge, there were ninety-five of us—one black besides me, one Oriental, and all the rest whites. More than half of us were addicted to alcohol, the rest to drugs. One fellow student was a state senator from Illinois, and the rest were lawyers, employees of major airlines and AT&T, people from the movie industry, and stockbrokers.

During our whole time at the lodge, the staff referred to us as students. They don't call you patients because they don't want you to think of yourself as being in a hospital; instead, you're a student, at the lodge for a minimum of ninety days and usually longer. The idea is that you're relearning your life. They deflate your ego by denying you the right to get whatever you want whenever you want it. At several individual and group counseling sessions a day, we talked about ourselves and our character defects—why we were so self-centered that we had gotten ourselves into the trouble that we were in.

It was a very regimented existence, with rules for everything. Among the rules were these:

- We couldn't use the telephone and could communicate with our families and friends only by mail. A friend and fellow "student" who was an attorney used to sneak out at night and walk a couple of miles to the nearest telephone to call his wife. He had been to four or five rehabilitation programs, but none had worked, and it was easy to see why.

- We got up at 7 A.M. and went to sleep at 10:30 P.M. No exceptions. And during the day, we couldn't go back to our rooms for a nap.

- The "students" were divided about evenly by sex, and no dating, fraternizing between the sexes, or talking was allowed outside of the classes and group therapy sessions. We weren't even allowed to stare at a member of the opposite sex, and since most students were there for four or five months, believe me, it got very lonely. Violation of this or any other major rule was punished by expulsion from the lodge, and several people got kicked out while I was there.

- Everyone had a job, like cleaning the dormitories, the kitchen, the dining hall, the bathrooms, the showers, or the main living room; distributing the clean laundry and the mail; even serving as host in the dining hall, which meant deciding the order in which the tables would be served, escorting the people at a table to the serving line, and telling them, "Enjoy your dinner."

- Everyone ate together, men on one side of the dining hall and women on the other. We got our food from a serving line, and nobody could eat until everyone at the table had been served.

- Men had to wear a coat and tie to dinner, and women were not allowed to wear pants. No tennis shoes were permitted; women had to wear panty hose instead of socks. If you weren't dressed right, you had to go back and change and you would get a penalty, like extra-duty work.

- We were allowed only four showers a week, each about four minutes long. The lodge got its water from wells, and there wasn't enough water for long, daily showers. This was a real change in lifestyle for most of the students, including me.

Before the staff at the lodge would say you were ready to go home, they had to see a big change in you. They watched you every minute. You had to be honest and serious and show that you had matured while you were there.

One day in early December, Mrs. Delaney asked me to get up in front of the class and read "How It Works," the bible of Alcoholics Anonymous. Ordinarily it takes about two minutes to read it, but it took me about five minutes that day. I was so nervous; I felt so humiliated. Before, if someone had told me to get up and read something out loud, it would have been a piece of cake for me with my ego, but there I was shaking so hard I couldn't read the words on the page in front of me. Also, I had a pencil in my hand and I kept banging it on the podium next to the microphone. I kept seeing everybody in the audience laughing every time I hit the pencil, and I didn't know why. When I finished, Mrs. Delaney said, "You're ready to go home." My ego had finally been broken to the point that I was ready to take my place in society again.

Mrs. Delaney made me wait until after the Christmas holidays, which are the worst time of the year for someone as vulnerable as me, with parties and liquor everywhere. But in January 1986 I went home, a free man again after what amounted to my second term in jail.

I joined Alcoholics Anonymous, and I haven't had a drink or used drugs since I left Alina Lodge. Like I say, I feel a lot better about myself. Not long after I got home from New Jersey, a girl I was with offered me some cocaine and I turned it down. She couldn't believe it. She'd never seen a person who had used coke before say no because everyone who uses it likes it so much. And most of the people I knew who were drinking were using cocaine, too. Being able to turn it down lets you know that you're not so powerless any more.

I earn a living now by serving as a consultant to corporations and organizations that have me talk to their employees about substance abuse. And I give speeches by the hundreds urging people to avoid alcohol and drugs, mostly at high schools and in front of other youth groups. But I don't accept money for helping young people. Nothing gives me more pleasure than to slap drugs out of the hands of young athletes or take drinks away from them. They get angry at me for a while, but later they thank me.

Speaking from my own experience, I don't think drugs should be legalized. The idea of making drugs legal is stupid, it's insane. We don't need any more addicts than we already have. Drugs are so seductive— and they will kill you. They stop your brain from growing. It's just like Muhammad Ali taking thousands of punches to his head. It comes out the same. After you stop using, your brain works better and you can remember more. When I was drinking, I lost a lot of my memory; many times, I couldn't even remember the names of my friends.

Drugs (including alcohol) not only destroy your mind, they hurt you in many other ways. For one thing, they make you egocentric. Lord knows, I was plenty egocentric before I started drinking too much and using drugs, but most athletes are egomaniacs; maybe their concern with themselves and their need for self-gratification make them more prone to abusing substances. Drugs give you the attitude that they're the only important thing in your life. When you're doing drugs, drugs take away everything else that you want out of life. You're dishonest, lazy, impatient, intolerant, and self-pitying; you have no gratitude; you think negatively; you blame other people for your own mistakes; and you're jealous, insecure, and filled with false pride, arrogance, resentment, and greed. That's what drugs and drinking do to you—everything bad. You're a Dr. Jekyll and a Mr. Hyde. When you're straight, you may be a nice person, but when you're using, you're a different person with all these character defects.

And you don't get off drugs or liquor until you look at yourself in a mirror, which I have done, and take an inventory of your character defects. You have to clean house and start all over again. You have to change yourself totally. You have to believe that there is a power higher than you; in my case, I choose to call that higher power God. You have to understand that you're powerless and cannot manage your life.

■   ■   ■

One member of the Cowboys tested positive for cocaine use four times during the 1988 season, but the team couldn't do anything about it because of the NFL's drug policy, which is a joke. The policy has been worked out between the league and the NFL Players Association.

At the beginning of the NFL drug manual, it says that one of the league's main concerns about drug abuse is "adverse fan reaction." Believe it! With drugs, just like everything else, the NFL isn't concerned about anything except covering its own ass. Former commissioner Pete Rozelle; the team owners; and, for that matter, Gene Upshaw, the former Raiders star who heads the Players Association, just wanted to maintain a good public image for the league and keep players eligible to play. Maybe things will change under the new commissioner, Paul Tagliabue.

The NFL management doesn't know what it is to be addicted to alcohol and drugs. They have a program, give players drug tests, and hire people to talk to the players about the dangers of drugs, but that's not going to help. The players don't pay attention to talks about the dangers of drugs. If the Giants had a drug counselor who was around every day, just like a regular coach, going over the drug situation and keeping after the suspicious or marginal guys, Lawrence Taylor might never have had the problems he did.

The NFL makes a lot of noise about being against drug and alcohol abuse, but that's all it is—noise. Look at what happened to Lawrence Taylor in 1988 after he tested positive for drug use for at least the second time in his career. The league suspended him for thirty days, or four games, but he still got paid about a quarter of a million dollars while he was suspended. Taylor has bragged that he doesn't need to enter a rehabilitation program, that he got off cocaine by playing golf for a month. He's kidding himself; that's not how you get off drugs. I'm afraid that drugs are going to sack Taylor a lot worse than he ever sacked any quarterback, including Joe Theismann, whose career was ended when Taylor broke his leg during a game in 1985.

The first thing you have to do to beat a problem with drugs or alcohol is admit you have a problem, which Taylor has never done. One of these days, they may find him in really bad shape, maybe even dead. That's what happened during the 1988 season to a player who wasn't nearly as well known as Taylor, David Croudip of the Atlanta Falcons. Unlike Taylor, no one knew that Croudip, a defensive back and special teams player, even had a drug problem. Then, on October 10, 1988, he turned up dead of a cocaine overdose. The same thing happened to Len Bias, the University of Maryland basketball star; Don Rogers of the Browns; and too many other athletes.

I honestly don't believe the NFL wants to face its drug problem. From what I've heard, there are a dozen or more players on almost every team who abuse drugs or liquor or both and are still allowed to play. The NFL is entertainment, and if you take Lawrence Taylor, Dexter Manley, Mark Duper, Mark Clayton, and stars like that out of the league, who's going to pay to see the games? If you went to a movie expecting to see Jack Nicholson, Bill Cosby, Jane Fonda, and Kathleen Turner and you found out they couldn't be in the movie because of drug problems and were replaced by unknown actors and actresses, you wouldn't pay to see that movie. Likewise, the fans and the television networks aren't going to pay to see NFL games without the best players in them.

The two main things that are wrong with the NFL's drug policy are:

- A player can be tested for drug use only three times: during training camp; at scouting combine sessions, where most of the teams get together and work out college seniors every January or February; and when there is "reasonable cause," which means when a player is intoxicated repeatedly, gets arrested for drug use or drug dealing, gets a ticket for driving under the influence, or tests positive during training camp or at the scouting combine.

The fallacy is that if a player drinks or takes drugs privately and doesn't get into any trouble, he doesn't fall in the reasonable-cause category. So for the rest of his career, once he has finished with the scouting combine when he's a college senior, the only time he has to be tested is during training camp. If a guy knows when he's going to be tested—and only once a year, at that—it's easy for him to beat the system. All he has to do is stop using drugs for a few weeks before training camp. Once he passes his test, he can start using again, and as long as he does it discreetly, the team and the league can't do anything about it.

The Cowboys player whose test came out positive four times in 1988 couldn't be disciplined because he beat the system. He passed his test during training camp and hadn't gotten in any trouble, so the four tests he failed during the season didn't come under the reasonable-cause category and the Cowboys couldn't use them to suspend him, force him to go into rehabilitation, or take any other disciplinary action.

- Counting the players on injured reserve, each of the 28 NFL teams has about 60 players under contract, a total of about 1,700 players. But the NFL has just one "drug adviser," and he's not even full time. Until recently that drug adviser was Dr. Forest S. Tennant, who was also a professor at UCLA, a consultant to the Los Angeles Dodgers, the California State Department of Justice, and the National Association for Stock Car Auto Racing. *And* he was responsible for all 1,700 NFL players, if you can believe that.

I've offered my help to the league and to the Cowboys, based on what I've lived through, but they don't seem to want it. I wrote a letter to Gene Upshaw, and he never answered me. I've told Tom Landry and other Cowboys officials many times that I would like to help, but they never asked me. One low-level Cowboys employee asked me to talk to the guy who was caught using cocaine in 1988, but that request was unofficial and on the qt; it didn't come from anyone in command. The funny thing is that top executives of both the Dallas Mavericks of the National Basketball Association and the Texas Rangers baseball team have asked me to help players with drug and alcohol problems. The only major league team in the Dallas area that hasn't asked for my help is my old team, the Cowboys.

If the NFL and the Cowboys were to ask my advice, I would give them a five-point program:

1. Each team must hire its own full-time, year-round drug adviser. All together, the adviser's salary, office space, equipment, and anything else might cost $200,000 a year. Each NFL team grosses tens of millions of dollars from the television networks, ticket sales, sale of radio rights, and other sources of income. You would think the teams might be able to afford $200,000 a year to fight alcohol and drug abuse.

2. Players must be tested for drug abuse several times a year, and the times of the tests must be unannounced. Any player who is under contract should be tested year-round, not just once during training camp, and the test has to be a surprise. You call the player in and say, "Give me a urine sample. Now. And if you can't produce one now, stay here until you can." No ifs, ands, or buts.

3. Any player who tests positive should be suspended immediately and sent to a treatment center. I'll leave the length of the stay up to the doctors, but it would probably be for much longer than a month. The

player might miss all or most of the season, but he would have a much greater chance of living to a ripe old age.

4. If a player tests positive during the season and gets suspended, his pay should be limited to either the NFL minimum, or, at most, to about $10,000 a week. If Lawrence Taylor knows he's going to make something like $62,500 a week while he's suspended, he doesn't have much incentive to stop using drugs on his own. I do *not* advocate cutting the players off with no pay because that might create serious financial hardship for them. They have enough problems if they're on drugs, so give them enough money to live comfortably, but not their million-dollar-a-year salaries.

5. The league's drug program has to be implemented as soon as the players are drafted. On draft day, when the teams fly the players to their headquarters, the first thing the clubs should do is test the players for drugs and have the drug adviser explain the drug policy to the new players. You need to reach the players right out of college, before they spend all their money on big cars, diamonds, jewelry, furs, women, and drugs. Drug dealers are all around the professional teams—the players have the money and they pay cash immediately. It's just fast money for the dealers. They contact the players at bars and nightclubs and through women or friends, or maybe they live in the same apartment complex.

The bottom-line message to players who abuse drugs has to be: You can't do it your way. You weren't successful doing it your way before, so you've got to do it somebody else's way now.

I know that people like Geraldine Delaney can cure anyone who honestly wants to get off drugs. Believe me—if they got me straight, they can get anybody straight.

17

A COWBOY TILL I DIE

I'm 47 now and my life certainly has had its ups and downs. And some of the downs have been pretty low:

- I pleaded guilty to a crime I don't honestly believe I committed, lost ten months out of my life while I was in prison, and had my reputation and finances ruined—all without cause.

- My arrest and my guilty plea, which is the same legally as being convicted of a crime, cost me hundreds of thousands of dollars in endorsements. I had just signed contracts to promote Hershey Foods and American Express and taped a Miller Lite Beer commercial that I really enjoyed. The Miller people had me standing beside a chair at the start of the ad. They introduced me, and I immediately disappeared from the screen. Then all of a sudden, I showed up on the *other* side of the chair, and the announcer declared, "That's the world's fastest human!" But all that ended. Also, at the time of my arrest, Hershey Foods had just mailed me a large check to do commercials, but they voided the check and canceled their contract with me.

- I was born ten or fifteen years too soon. If I had played in the 1980s, I probably would have earned a million dollars a year or more for playing football, at least that much for running track in the football off-season, and at least a couple of million a year in endorsements.

- All those years of football ruined my health. The ligaments in my

297

left knee are shot, and I have arthritis in several different places in that knee. I never got hit solidly on my knee; it just wore out over the years. The Cowboys knew when they traded me to San Francisco that my legs were almost gone, but I didn't know it myself. I knew my knees swelled up a lot, but a lot of the players had that problem. When I got to San Francisco and my knee was bothering me, a friend had his doctor check me over, and that's when I found out that my days as a sprinter were numbered. Today I can only partially run. I doubt if I could run a hundred yards in twenty seconds. Once I was the fastest man in the world, now I'm as slow as a blimp, and I'm going to have this ailment for the rest of my life. And calcium deposits grow over and over in my left shoulder. Nothing can be done for my knee, and nothing can be done for my shoulder except to scrape out the calcium from time to time.

NFL team physicians treated the players pretty well overall, although to some extent we were like pieces of meat that had to get on the field to fulfill the team's obligations to the fans who bought tickets and to the television networks. We were just a bunch of interchangeable parts. The doctors did the best they could in the short time they had to treat each of us, but they were paid by the team, not the players, and their loyalty had to be to the team, not the players. I wish now that I had gotten more than one medical opinion so I could have made more intelligent decisions. I'm still not sorry; I loved football and all I wanted to do was play, and I was dumb enough not to ask for a second opinion. During my last five years in football, I got my knee drained at least once a week. I probably shouldn't have been playing those last five years. But nobody ever told me that I would be a semicripple the rest of my life.

I've done a lot to mess up my own life, too. I didn't have much of a sense of judgment for most of my life, and being pampered the way a star athlete is can keep you from developing a sense of judgment. I've made a lot of mistakes along the way—and made everything worse by blaming other people for my own fuckups. If I had my life to live over, I wouldn't have been stupid enough to put myself in a position to get arrested and sent to jail for selling drugs; I would have admitted I had a drinking problem and gotten help years earlier; and I would have been a better husband to my two wives and a better father, especially to my daughter Rori. At least I finally know what I did wrong, and I've learned from my mistakes and improved myself as a human being. Maybe I'm not the world's best human being—I don't need to call myself the world's *best* anything any more—but I'm a pretty darned good one. Unfortunately, I had to learn life's lessons the hard way.

Those are the minuses. Then there are the pluses:

- God gave me the gift of speed, and I think I made the most of it. I experienced triumphs that very few other men ever have—setting all those records in track and becoming the world's fastest human, winning my two Olympics gold medals, becoming the only athlete in history to earn both Olympics gold medals and a ring for being on the team that won the Super Bowl, and playing in the NFL for eleven years and being a superstar in the league for five or six seasons.

- I lived the good life from the time I signed with the Cowboys in 1964 until my arrest in 1978. I had the best homes, clothes, cars, food, and hotel rooms when I traveled—everything a person could ask for.

- I had the opportunity to play for two incomparable coaches, Jake Gaither and Tom Landry, and I started friendships during my track and football careers that have lasted a lifetime. Guys like Curtis Miranda and Jesse Jackson from my college football days and Ralph Boston, Ulis Williams, Don Meredith, Jethro Pugh, Cornell Green, Roger Staubach, Drew Pearson, Don Perkins, Frank Clarke, Pettis Norman, Brig Owens, Spider Lockhart, Gale Sayers, and so many more.

- I was lucky enough to play for a team owner like Clint Murchison, who treated me not only as one of his players, but as a friend and a fellow human being. Clint looked out for me until the day he died. When I got out of jail, instead of turning his back on me the way many other people did, Clint invited me to his home and gave me a job. He paid my way through real estate school and he gave me a share of real estate investments he had in Washington, D.C., and Palm Springs without asking me to put up a dime. He told me I gave a lot to the Dallas Cowboys and he wanted to give something back to me. He was one of the finest men I ever met, a real man in every sense of the word, and I will never forget him and his kindness to me.

- I got to meet presidents of the United States, leaders of other nations, Henry Kissinger and many other top officials of our country, movie stars, media giants, and too many other celebrities to shake a stick at.

I was the only kid who came out of Hell's Hole in Jacksonville, Florida, when I did who had all those opportunities. The chances are that if God hadn't given me my athletic abilities, I would have died at an early age, spent most of my life in prison, or wound up on welfare. That's what happened to the guys I grew up with in Hell's Hole who weren't good enough at sports to get college scholarships. Athletics were the only way out of Hell's Hole, and I was lucky. If I couldn't have been an athlete, I would have wanted to be a teacher and work with young people, but I never could have gone to college to become a teacher without an athletic scholarship.

So, taking everything into account, I think the Bob Hayes story is a happy one. If you go to the hospital, the way I do, and see all the kids with cancer who lose their coordination, go blind, suffer incredible pain, and die young, you know what suffering is. When I compare myself to other people, I think the ups in my life have definitely outweighed the downs.

Even though I missed out by a few years on making really big money, I certainly don't begrudge football players, track stars like Carl Lewis, and other athletes what they earn now. The more, the merrier! Athletes have short careers, they have to plan for a second career after they retire, and they run the risk of being injured seriously. Don't forget, the owners can increase the ticket prices, the prices of concessions, and the television revenues all the time, and that covers the increased salaries. The owners make plenty of money and nobody complains, but when people find out how much money the players make, everyone says they make too much.

A lot of the owners act like little boys. I was in a meeting once at which one owner told Gene Klein, who owned the San Diego Chargers at the time, that he was a loser because his team had been predicted to go to the Super Bowl that year and they didn't make it. Gene Klein made hundreds of millions of dollars in business, but because his team failed to go to the Super Bowl, some other owner called him a loser. A man who makes hundreds of millions of dollars in his business, I don't consider a loser.

I certainly think players in all major sports should have free agency. The owners are free agents; someone like Robert Irsay can pick up and move the Colts at 4 A.M., so why shouldn't the players be able to move, too? Let's have free agency across the board or let's stop it across the board.

One specific improvement that should be made is to eliminate incentive clauses, which generally are a bad idea. Incentives can hurt a team because the players just do what they get paid to do. On defense, for instance, guys get paid for quarterback sacks and interceptions. But, look at it this way: Each team runs sixty plays or so in an NFL game, or about a thousand over the course of a sixteen-game regular season. A guy who has twenty sacks—equal to 2 percent of all the plays in the season—or 10 interceptions—equal to 1 percent of all the plays—will be among the league's leaders. That's the basis of how much money you make and who gets elected to the Pro Bowl and All-Pro teams. But what were these guys doing on the 98 or 99 percent of the plays when they weren't making sacks or intercepting passes? Were the defensive linemen ignoring the run in hopes of getting a sack, and were the defensive backs taking unnecessary risks so they might make an interception? The same is true for the offensive players. Don't get me wrong—sacks, interceptions, passes caught, yards gained, and touchdowns scored are all important, but they're not the whole story.

Incentive clauses can hurt not only the team, but the individual player, too. The management never tells you, "Good going, man, you took two defenders with you and made it easy for the other receiver to catch a pass." On every play, all I had to do was run out for a pass, and two guys would chase me. That's better than one block, but they said, "Get aggressive. We want you to block." And when I was negotiating a new contract, the team executives mentioned how many passes I caught, how many yards I gained, and how many touchdowns I scored, but they didn't have any statistics, and neither did I, that showed how many points the team scored because I was double and triple covered and someone else caught the ball or ran for a long gain.

As for the Olympics, the United States has lost its dominance in international competitions because other countries put more money into their facilities, their training, and their research. They support their athletes better. From the U.S. Olympic Committee on down, the United States doesn't put as much effort into track as do many other nations. We have plenty of excuses for losing, and I don't mean excuses like the ones Mary Decker Slaney gives when she gets beaten, which is every time she runs in an important race. Mary Decker Slaney is a crybaby, but I think we can point out that other countries have advantages over us now in the Olympic competitions without being crybabies.

In the United States, the top athletes in track and field and swimming face too much competition from other sports like football, baseball, basketball, tennis, and even golf. Except for the Carl Lewises and the Flo-Jos, athletes can make a lot more money in the other sports than they can in track and field and swimming, so the chances are that a young athlete will go where the money is.

We can make a start by paying decent salaries to our track athletes so they can afford to train year-round. Most of these kids are poor and can't afford to train without pay. The money for training ought to come from the federal government, as well as from the major corporations. Other countries' governments give money to their athletes. American athletes are representing their country, but the government hasn't given them a dime. That's pathetic! If we paid our most promising athletes to stay in training, we would have a competitive edge because we would have a bigger pool of athletes to choose from.

It's about time that professionals are finally being allowed to compete in the Olympics in sports like basketball. There's no doubt in my mind that pros should be allowed to compete in all the Olympics sports. We should have Magic Johnson, Larry Bird, and Michael Jordan playing basketball on our Olympic team. The trouble is that we were under the influence of Avery Brundage, the American who was president of the International Olympic Committee, when I ran in the Olympics. Avery Brundage wanted all the athletes to be simon-pure amateurs, which was fine for him because he was wealthy. Even then, of course, none of the athletes from the Eastern block nations was a pure amateur. Let's send our best athletes, just like everyone else does.

One place where I know we're weak is training, but that's because of a basic weakness in our national character. It takes discipline to be number one in anything. We can't compete with the Japanese in making cars and electronics, and we can't compete with other nations in track because we have basically gotten lazy. We're spoiled brats, we want what we want when we want it. We don't have the desire any more to go to any length, no matter what it takes, to be champions. That's depressing. I felt so embarrassed when I saw what happened to our Olympic team in 1988.

I suggest that all high school graduates—regardless of color or wealth or anything else—should have to take at least six weeks of basic military training before they go on with their lives, whether they go on to college, the work world, sports, or anything else. High school dropouts should start their military training on their eighteenth birthday. I know that I gained a lot of self-discipline when I spent six months in the U.S. Army Reserve between my 1966 and 1967 seasons with the Cowboys, and discipline is something that's lacking throughout our society. That lack of self-discipline shows itself in so many ways: drug abuse, crime, and our inability to compete with the Japanese and other nations. We need to get ourselves under control and get back a sense of national purpose.

We still have plenty to do to eliminate racism from this society and from sports. Since I know sports the best, I want to address that. When I played, and it's still true today, the attitude throughout the coaching and executive hierarchy was that if a black player didn't produce every day, he was wasting his God-given talent, but if a white player didn't produce every day, he was just having an off day. Coaches still say that the black player has natural talent, but the white athlete hustles and he gives everything he has to win. Whites also waste great athletic talent, but you don't hear about it the way you do with blacks.

That same attitude laps over into drug and alcohol abuse. White players who drink too much are regarded as good old boys having a great time; blacks are drug addicts, problem drinkers, and alcoholics. Unfortunately, blacks are more likely than are whites to become involved with illegal drugs like cocaine. There are exceptions—white athletes like Steve Howe, the former pitcher for the Dodgers and the Rangers who was addicted to cocaine—but for the most part, black athletes do drugs and white athletes do alcohol. My own theory is that it's because the drug rings generally are minority controlled. The distributors of drugs are minorities, so they have more access to other minorities, especially in sports. And blacks still have such a bad time throughout our society that often the only alternative for them is to turn to drugs to forget the lives they have to lead. Drugs and alcohol both will kill you, but people who use drugs, and most of them are black, suffer more because drugs are illegal, which means they cost more than liquor and carry a potential prison sentence. We need to get drugs out of our society, but someone smarter than me will have to tell us how to do that.

We have made a lot of progress in race relations in the past twenty-five years or so, but we still have a long way to go, not just in sports, but across the board in this country. The best time to start is today, and the best place to start is in the schools and in the business world, ensuring that blacks and other minorities have the same opportunities to get a decent education and find a good job that whites do.

I've talked a lot about how Jake Gaither and Tom Landry influenced me. Two other men had a tremendous influence over me, one perhaps a bad influence and the other a good one. The philosophy of my father, George Sanders, was, "Every day's a holiday." George, who was straight out of *Guys and Dolls*, taught me to enjoy every day to the fullest because yesterday's gone and tomorrow isn't promised to you. I still use "Every day's a holiday" as a greeting to people, but I have paid a heavy price to learn that there's a lot more to life than that. I try to make every day not only a holiday, but a productive day as well. Have fun, but do something good.

The other person who influenced me greatly had the same effect on millions of other blacks. I signed to do promotional work for R.C. Cola a few months after the Olympics. Not long after that, R.C. Cola hosted a banquet in Cleveland for top executives from major corporations and black leaders from around the country. R.C. Cola wanted to use the black leaders and celebrities to help sell its products in the black community. It was at that banquet that I met Martin Luther King. Dr. King knew all about me, and he took me aside for a private talk and told me, "Make sure you don't trust anybody but yourself. Nobody! A lot of people are trying to do favors for you now because you're the world's fastest human, but one day they all will have forgotten you and you'll be on your own. Be ready for that day!"

And he asked me, "Do you continue to have God in your life? It's something you may not ever see, smell, or hear, but I guarantee you there's a higher power." All I could say was, "Thank you very much. I'll try my best to live by those principles." I hope that if Dr. King could review my entire life, mistakes and all, he would be proud of me.

Two final things about me:

I have always been a patriot, and I always will be. Hearing the national anthem played during the Olympics meant so much to me, and even after all the years I played in the NFL, when I was on the sidelines and they played the national anthem, I still got goosebumps. I've been to dozens of countries around the world, and in spite of our problems, the United States is still number one.

And I still bleed Cowboy silver and blue. Regardless of some of the things that happened between the Cowboys and me, I will always cherish my ten years with the Cowboys, and if I had it to do over, I'd be a Cowboy again. I was a Dallas Cowboy yesterday, I'm one today, and I will be one tomorrow.